THE STRUCTURE OF THE JAPANESE ECONOMY

STUDIES IN THE MODERN JAPANESE ECONOMY

General Editors: Malcolm Falkus, *University of New England, Armidale, New South Wales, Australia*; and Kojiro Niino, *Kobe University, Japan*

An understanding of the modern Japanese economy remains both important and elusive. Its importance needs little stressing. Since the 1950s Japan's economy has grown at a rate unparalleled elsewhere and, despite predictions that such success could not last, the economy remains strong, dynamic and sustains full employment. Yet an understanding of the many unique features of Japan's economic and social life is essential if we are to appreciate the Japanese achievement, but on the other hand this very uniqueness makes communication difficult. Straightforward translations of Japanese works frequently mean little to Western readers because the underlying attitudes and assumptions are so unfamiliar.

This series has been planned in the belief that there is an urgent need for scholarly studies on the modern Japanese economy which are written by experts (both Japanese and Western) and aimed at Western readers. Accordingly, we have planned a series of books which will explore all the major areas of Japanese economic life. The books will present up-to-date material, and, where necessary, they will place Japan in its wider international context.

Published titles include:

Yujiro Hayami
JAPANESE AGRICULTURE UNDER SIEGE

Kazuo Koike
UNDERSTANDING INDUSTRIAL RELATIONS IN
  MODERN JAPAN

Ryōshin Minami
THE ECONOMIC DEVELOPMENT OF JAPAN

Mitsuaki Okabe
THE STRUCTURE OF THE JAPANESE ECONOMY

Yoshitaka Suzuki
JAPANESE MANAGEMENT STRUCTURES, 1920–80

Seiichiro Yonekura
THE JAPANESE IRON AND STEEL INDUSTRY, 1850–1990

The Structure of the Japanese Economy

Changes on the Domestic and International Fronts

Edited by

Mitsuaki Okabe
Professor, Faculty of Policy Management
Keio University
Japan

St. Martin's Press　　New York

First published in the United States of America in 1995

Printed in Great Britain

ISBN 0-312-12219-5

Library of Congress Cataloging-in-Publication Data
The Structure of the Japanese economy : changes on the domestic and
international fronts / edited by Mitsuaki Okabe.
p. cm. — (Studies in the modern Japanese economy)
Includes bibliographical references and index.
ISBN 0-312-12219-5
1. Japan—Economic conditions—1945–1989. 2. Japan—Economic
conditions—1989– 3. Japan—Economic policy—1945–1989. 4. Japan–
–Economic policy—1989– 5. Japan—Foreign economic relations.
I. Okabe, Mitsuaki. II. Series.
HC462.9.S69 1995
330.952—dc20   94-17219
                                                        CIP

Contents

PART III

THE FINANCIAL MARKETS, MONETARY POLICY AND THE POLICY INSTITUTIONS

PART IV

INTERNATIONAL ECONOMIC RELATIONS

Preface

The outstanding performance of the Japanese economy over recent decades has invariably attracted the attention of economists and policy-makers around the world. No other economy has so often been cited as such a typical example of an achiever of high growth and overall stability, or as a model to be emulated by developing countries and former centrally-controlled economies. And, in recent years, the Japanese economy seems to have been associated increasingly with the image of an incongruous member in the international economy because of the largest trade surplus of all nations.

Despite the fact that the performance of the Japanese economy has often been described in detail and the social and economic structure has been increasingly subject to scrutiny by various academic disciplines, there still appear to be many commonly-held stereotypes or exotic perceptions about the way in which the entire economic system is made up and how it functions. Moreover, it needs to be noted that the Japanese economic system, as with any other system, cannot be excluded from undergoing its own evolution as a result of domestic circumstances and policies as well as through external forces.

When one looks for a deep understanding, however, there does not seem to be a readily accessible scholarly book providing both rigorous analyses based on the mainstream of economics and a good coverage of all the major aspects of the economy. This book, consisting of fifteen research papers, intends to fill that gap. It aims to illuminate and analyze the basic structure of, and the changes in, the contemporary Japanese economy, both broadly and from the viewpoint of modern economic analysis. The editor hopes that the book as a whole will provide new insights and perspectives on the key issues in understanding the nature of that economy.

This publication is the outcome of a research project at the Centre for Japanese Economic Studies at Macquarie University, Sydney. In this endeavour, the editor, as Director of the Centre, has benefited enormously from the co-operation of many individuals. I am most grateful to the contributors of this volume, all of whom are leading researchers in their respective areas, for initiating their research for this book, bringing their draft papers to the conferences and seminars in Sydney, and finally jointly producing this volume. My heartfelt appreciation is extended to Vice-Chancellor Professor Di Yerbury of Macquarie University for her continuous encouragement of this project. Also, I must mention my indebtedness for the support and advice of my colleagues at Macquarie University, including Eddie Oliver, the late Victor Argy, Leslie Stein, John Purcal, Richard Braddock, Misuzu Chow and Bill Norton; to many senior members of the Bank of Japan, including Governor Yasushi Mieno, Kazuho Sawamoto, Kagehide Kaku; to my mentors Yoshio Suzuki (Nomura Research Institute) and Kumiharu Shigehara (OECD); and academic friends, including Peter Drysdale (Australian National University) and Malcolm Falkus (University of New England); and to Setsuya Tabuchi of Nomura Securities for proving the initial funds to establish the Centre. Helen Smith assisted me enormously in the editorial work, as did Glennis Yee in organizing seminars and conferences. Tim Farmiloe of Macmillan has energetically encouraged me and assisted with the publication. Without the support of these individuals, this book would not have been produced.

March 1994   MITSUAKI OKABE
Sydney

Notes on the Contributors

Kenn Ariga
Professor, Institute for Economic Research, Kyōto University, Japan
Professor Ariga, a holder of a PhD from Yale University, specializes in macroeconomics, labour economics and microstructure of markets and transactions. He has served as Special Research Adviser to the Institute of Monetary and Fiscal Policy, Ministry of Finance, Japan, and has recently published a book entitled *Japanese Distribution Systems as a Barrier against Entry* (1993).

Giorgio Brunello
Associate Professor of Economics, University of Venice, Italy
Professor Brunello, a specialist in labour markets and industrial relations, has carried out research in a number of universities in Japan, including the University of Ōsaka and Kyōto University. He has published a number of papers in these fields, the most recent being 'Promotion, Corporate Hierarchy and Firm Growth: Japanese Internal Labour Market in Transition' in *Journal of the Japanese and International Economies*.

Thomas F. Cargill
Professor of Economics, University of Nevada at Reno, USA
Dr Cargill specializes in financial markets, regulation and monetary policy, and financial developments in Pacific Basin countries. He has published many research papers on the Japanese economy as well as a co-authoring a book with S. Royama called *The Transition of Finance in Japan and the United States: A Comparative Perspective* (1988). He has been a visiting scholar at several institutions in Japan.

Robert Dekle
Assistant Professor of International Relations and Economics, Boston University, USA
After completing his PhD at Yale University, Professor Dekle went on to do further research at Harvard University and the Bank of Japan as its visiting scholar. His research of the Japanese economy includes household behaviour, land prices and financial markets. One of his most recent papers, 'Japanese Defence Spending and its Impact on

Economic Growth', is about to be published in Jeffrey Frankel and
Miles Kahler (eds), *Regionalism and Rivalry: Japan and the US in
Pacific Asia*.

Jeffrey A. Frankel

*Professor of Economics and Director, Centre for International and
Development Economics Research, University of California at Berkeley,
USA*
Professor Frankel is a specialist in international economics, finance
and macroeconomics. His research interests relating to the Japanese
economy cover a wide range of issues such as the cost of capital in
Japan, trade issues in Pacific Asia, and trade and currency blocs. His
monographs include *The Yen/Dollar Agreement: Liberalising Japanese
Capital Markets*, and in 1991 he won first prize in the AMEX Bank
Review Awards for his essay 'Is a Yen Block forming in Pacific Asia?'
He received his PhD from Massachusetts Institute of Technology.

Koichi Hamada

Professor of Economics, Yale University, USA
After obtaining his PhD from Yale University, Professor Hamada held
the chair of Economics at the University of Tōkyō. He has taught at
many universities worldwide, including Massachusetts Institute of Technology, the London School of Economics and the University of Chicago. He has written numerous books and papers on international
economics and on the Japanese economy in both English and Japanese. *The Political Economy of International Monetary Interdependence* (1985), which is a translation of his work from the Japanese,
has triggered a new, growing area of research in international policy
co-ordination.

Akiyoshi Horiuchi

Professor of Economics, University of Tōkyō, Japan
Professor Horiuchi, a holder of a PhD from the University of
Tōkyō, has been an active researcher in the field of financial markets
and monetary policy, and has also served as chairman of various research committees of the Japanese Government. He has published many
papers, in both Japanese and English, with his most recent paper 'Financial Liberalisation: The Case of Japan' being published in *Financial Regulation: Changing the Rules of the Game* (1992).

Takeo Hoshi
Assistant Professor, Graduate School of International Relations and Pacific Studies, University of California at San Diego, USA
Professor Hoshi's research interests are in the Japanese financial system and monetary policy. He has conducted a number of ground-breaking empirical studies on the Japanese main banking system. His most recent research is 'The Economic Role of Corporate Grouping and the Main Bank System' in the forthcoming book by M. Aoki and R. Dore (eds), *The Japanese Firm: The Sources of Competitive Strength.* He received his PhD from Massachusetts Institute of Technology.

Yukinobu Kitamura
Economist, Institute for Monetary and Economic Studies, Bank of Japan, Tōkyō, Japan, and Visiting Lecturer, Hitotsubashi University, Japan
Mr Kitamura obtained his PhD in Economics at Oxford University and worked for the Organisation for Economic Cooperation and Development (OECD) in Paris for several years before he took up his current position. He specializes in macroeconomics, public finance and applied econometrics, and one of his most recent papers is forthcoming as 'Public Policies and Household Savings in Japan' (with T. Ito) in J. Poterba (ed.), *International Comparisons of Household Savings*, vol. 1.

Fumiko Kon-ya
Senior Fellow and Director of Public Policy Research, Japan Securities Research Institute, Tōkyō, Japan
Ms Kon-ya, an expert in the Japanese capital markets, has published many papers in both Japanese and English, including a research paper of 1991 entitled 'Speculative Behaviour in the Stock Markets: Evidence from the United States and Japan (co-authored with R. Shiller and Y. Tsutsui), NBER Working Paper No. 3613. She has also taught at several universities in Japan.

Mitsuaki Okabe
Professor, Faculty of Policy Management, Keio University, Japan; and former Professor and Director, Centre for Japanese Economic Studies, Macquarie University, Sydney, Australia
Before taking up his current position, Professor Okabe carried out research on the Japanese economy for more than twenty years at the Bank of Japan and taught at the University of Pennsylvania and Princeton University, as well as at Macquarie University. He has written many

papers on the Japanese economy and monetary policy, co-edited books including *Towards a World of Economic Stability: Optimal Monetary Framework and Policy* (1998). In April 1994, he was appointed as a professor at Keio University in Japan.

Paul Sheard
Associate Professor, Faculty of Economics, University of Ōsaka, Japan and Senior Lecturer, Department of Economics, Australian National University, Australia
Dr Sheard specializes in the structure and behaviour of the Japanese firm and Japanese financial institutions. He has been invited as a visiting scholar by Stanford University, University of Ōsaka and the Bank of Japan. The most recent book of his is *International Adjustment and the Japanese Firm* (1993). He obtained his PhD in Economics from the Australian National University.

Toshiaki Tachibanaki
Professor of Economics, Institute for Economic Research, Kyōto University, Japan
Professor Tachibanaki's research interests cover a wide area including labour economics, public and financial economics, and applied econometrics. He has published numerous papers, a recent one being 'Labour Supply and Unemployment in Japan', in *European Economic Review* in 1991. He has served on the editorial board of many leading economics journals, and has been invited as a visiting scholar to prominent institutions in Europe, the USA and Australia. He has a PhD from Johns Hopkins University.

Wataru Takahashi
Senior Economist, Institute for Monetary and Economic Studies, Bank of Japan, Tōkyō, Japan
Mr Takahashi, a holder of degrees from the University of Tokyo and Oxford University, has been working for the Bank of Japan, mainly in the area of economic research. He is a specialist in monetary economics and monetary policy. His paper, 'Rational Expectations and Money Supply Policy: An Empirical Examination of the Macroeconomic Rational Expectations Hypothesis in Japan', which was published in *Bank of Japan Research Papers* in 1982, has been deemed a seminal empirical work in the field in Japan.

Shinji Takagi
Associate Professor of Economics, University of Ōsaka, Japan
After receiving his PhD from the University of Rochester, USA, Professor Takagi worked as an economist at the International Monetary Fund for many years and was once invited as a visiting scholar by the Bank of Japan. Along with his appointment at Ōsaka University, he is currently serving as a senior economist with the Japanese Ministry of Finance. He has an extensive publications list, especially in the field of monetary economics and international finance, and has recently edited a book called *Handbook of Japanese Capital Markets* (1992).

Atsuhiro Taki
Associate Professor of Economics, Toyama University, Japan
After doing his undergraduate and postgraduate work at Kyōto University, Professor Taki continued to conduct his research at Nagoya University before he was appointed to his current position. His research interests cover labour and financial economics. While many of his papers have been published in Japanese, some others have been contributed to books in English, examples being 'Wage Determination in Japan: A Theoretical and Empirical Investigation' (with T. Tachibanaki) in H. König (ed.), *Economics of Wage Determination* (1990).

Mahito Uchida
Senior Economist, International Department, Bank of Japan, Tōkyō, Japan
Mr Uchida, who holds degrees from the University of Tōkyō and the Paris School of Political Science, has had many years of research experience at the Bank of Japan. He has published a number of papers on inflation and international finance. A jointly authored paper, 'Development of the Eurocurrency Markets and its Effects', appeared in 1988 in *Monetary and Economic Studies* published by the Institute of Monetary and Economic Studies of the Bank of Japan.

Takashi Ui
Economist, Research and Statistics Department, Bank of Japan, Tōkyō, Japan
Since obtaining his undergraduate and postgraduate degrees, both in engineering, from the University of Tōkyō, Mr Ui has been working for the Bank of Japan. He specializes in research into the Japanese economy, especially its monetary and international aspects. He has written several papers, including 'Puzzling Movements of M2 in Japan since

mid-1980s: Is it still a Useful Indicator of Monetary Policy?', a Working Paper of the Centre for Japanese Economic Studies of Macquarie University, 1992. He is currently conducting research at Stanford University, USA.

Hiroshi Yoshikawa
Professor of Economics, University of Tōkyō, Japan
Professor Yoshikawa has widely researched macroeconomics, especially in investment, growth, business cycles and financial markets, and has been awarded a number of prizes for his books on the Japanese economy. A comprehensive book called *Macroeconomics and the Japanese Economy* is forthcoming from Oxford University Press. He holds a PhD from Yale University.

1 The Japanese Economy in Transition: Introduction and Overview

Mitsuaki Okabe

The performance of the Japanese economy, especially its strong international competitiveness in export markets resulting in a huge trade surplus, has led foreign observers to perceive that Japan's economy works differently from those of Western industrial countries. If that perception is correct, in what way does the whole Japanese economic system differ from those of other industrial economies? Should the distinctive features of the system be regarded over recent years as changing because of various forces: for example, by experiencing in the early 1990s the deepest depression in post-war history and facing increased internationalization in transactions? These are the general themes that run through much of the book. In this overview chapter, Section 1.1 reviews major developments in the Japanese economy since 1980, providing a general background to the understanding of the structure of the economy; Section 1.2 explains the aims and methodology used in this book; and Section 1.3 provides summaries of the papers together with some general conclusions emerging from them.

1.1 MAJOR DEVELOPMENTS IN THE JAPANESE ECONOMY SINCE 1980

When we look at Japanese economic developments since 1980, we can point out some noticeable characteristics which clearly distinguish recent developments from previous ones.

1.1.1 Changes in the Japanese economy

First, although the nation's economic activity has shown ups and downs and experienced three recession periods since 1980, as is particularly evident in industrial production (see Table 1.1), the mechanism for

1

TABLE 1.1 Major economic indexes of Japan, 1980–93

Year	Economic growth rate (% change)	Industrial production (% change)	Unemployment rate (%)	Public construction expenditures (% change)	Official discount rate (%, at year-end)	Money supply (% change)	Inflation rate (% change)	Share price (Nikkei Index) (at year-end)	Land price (% change)	Current account balance (US$ billion)	Long-term capital account (US$ billion)	Yen exchange rate (yen/dollar, year-end)	Net external assets (US$ billion)
1980	3.5	4.8	2.0	6.4	7.25	9.2	7.7	7 116	12.3	−10.7	2.3	204	12
1981	3.4	1.0	2.2	2.9	5.50	8.9	4.9	7 682	11.4	4.8	−9.7	220	11
1982	3.4	0.3	2.4	−3.5	5.50	9.2	2.8	8 017	8.3	6.9	−15.0	235	25
1983	2.8	2.9	2.6	−2.0	5.00	7.4	1.9	9 894	5.1	20.8	−17.7	232	37
1984	4.3	9.5	2.7	−2.8	5.00	7.8	2.3	11 543	3.0	35.0	−49.7	252	74
1985	5.2	3.7	2.6	−1.5	5.00	8.4	2.0	13 113	2.2	49.2	−64.5	201	130
1986	2.6	−0.2	2.8	8.2	3.00	8.7	0.6	18 701	2.2	85.8	−131.5	160	180
1987	4.3	3.4	2.8	7.4	2.50	10.4	0.1	21 564	7.6	87.0	−136.5	122	241
1988	6.2	9.7	2.5	3.9	2.50	11.2	0.7	30 159	25.0	79.6	−130.9	126	292
1989	4.8	5.8	2.3	2.6	4.25	9.9	2.3	38 916	7.9	57.2	−89.2	143	293
1990	4.8	4.1	2.1	7.6	6.00	11.7	3.1	23 849	17.0	35.8	−43.6	135	328
1991	4.3	1.7	2.1	18.6	4.50	3.6	3.3	22 984	10.7	72.9	37.1	125	383
1992	1.4	−6.1	2.2	8.7	3.25	0.6	1.6	16 925	−5.6	117.6	−28.5	125	514
1993	0.1	−4.5	2.5	3.6	1.75	1.1	1.3	17 417	−8.7	131.4	−78.1	112	611

Source: Bank of Japan, *Economic Statistics Annual 1993*.

starting each recession has changed. The years 1980–82 are characterized as the 'oil recession' following the second oil crisis, which reduced domestic aggregate demand by transferring Japanese income to oil-producing countries. The 1985–6 recession may be termed the 'yen appreciation recession', which was brought about by a significant decline in external demand, because of the sharp appreciation of the yen triggered by the Plaza Accord of the Group of Seven countries agreeing to depreciate the US dollar and appreciate other major currencies including the yen. In contrast to these recessions, which were triggered by various external forces, the recession observed after 1991, which may be called the 'asset deflation recession', was triggered by a domestic factor: the large-scale decline of domestic asset prices which adversely affected the activities of households, firms and financial institutions. This first experience of a domestically generated recession, as we see below, can be viewed as reflecting the many structural changes in the Japanese economy.

Second, in terms of both the depth and length of the recession and of the unusual movements of key economic variables, the recession after 1991 seems to be unprecedented in Japan's post-war economic history. In 1992 the economic growth rate declined to just 1.5 per cent, and only 0.1 per cent growth was recorded in 1993, a substantial change compared with the previous twelve years, when the growth rate was stable at around 3–5 per cent (for the growth rates during 1980–91, the average was 4.1 per cent and the standard deviation 1.0; see Table 1.1). A similar drastic decline and instability can be observed in other important macroeconomic variables, such as money supply and land prices. The most recent recession has caused the external current account surplus to increase and the yen to appreciate to unprecedented levels, while somewhat surprisingly, the amount of long-term capital outflow has become smaller during the current recession than it was when Japan's current account surplus was even smaller (in fact, in 1991 there was a net inflow rather than a net outflow of long-term capital). The sharp downturn of the economy has been brought about as part of an unavoidable reverse adjustment process to the preceding longest boom in Japan's post-war economic history (1987–90), in which the average economic growth rate recorded was 5.0 per cent. But the fact that both the nature of the boom (in its duration and level) and the subsequent drastic and unprecedented changes in key economic variables have never previously occurred in the Japanese economy suggests that some kind of structural changes have been taking place.

Third, the conduct of macroeconomic policies appears to have changed after the mid-1980s, being closely related to the extended boom and the subsequent economic downturn. Although a series of large fiscal measures have been applied in the current recession which started in 1991, fiscal policy generally tended to be less flexible in the 1980s, especially before 1985 when fiscal reconstruction to reduce the budget deficit was maintained as a medium-term goal. Monetary policy was eased successively by lowering the official discount rate, eventually to as low as 2.5 per cent, and this level was kept for more than two years, 1987–88. The latter action seems to be one of the main reasons for a surge in money supply (an increase at an average rate of 10.8 per cent for the four years 1987–90) as well as for a large-scale rise in share and land prices in the midst of a relatively low level of inflation, as measured by the consumer price index. The subsequent tightening of monetary policy seems to correspond very well to the crush of the 'bubble' in asset prices and the subsequent recession. Some of these policy responses, especially the easing of monetary policy in 1987 in the middle of an upward swing in the economy, seem to be related to changes in the philosophy of the policy. The changes, if any, should be assessed against the broad context of structural changes in the economy, especially, in this case, internationalization.

Fourth, contrary to the above-mentioned large changes, the unemployment rate, one of the most visible and most important economic variables in any industrialized economy, has stayed surprisingly stable in Japan over the entire period, including during the recession after 1991.[1] This implies on the one hand that the Japanese economy and society have succeeded in maintaining their stability, but on the other hand that some kind of adjustment pressure, especially since 1991, must be permeating somewhere else in the economy thus necessitating structural changes in traditional Japanese labour relations and corporate organizations.

Fifth, the presence of the Japanese economy in the world arena has continued to increase and the role expected of it has become very important. After having become the nation, in the mid-1980s, that possessed the largest net external assets in the world, Japan has been accumulating external assets continuously (see Table 1.1). This trend has naturally been changing the role of Japan in the world economy, both economically and politically, and it has inevitably influenced Japan's own economic policies.

1.1.2 Factors behind the changes

These changes in macroeconomic aspects are a reflection of changes in sociocultural, economic and international aspects of the Japanese economy and society affecting the behaviour of Japanese firms, households and governments, as well as, in some instances, the interaction between the Japanese and overseas economic agents. Since 1980 the trend of liberalization (deregulation) has been one of the most important, if not *the* most important, changes that have been taking place in many spheres of the Japanese economy, particularly in financial markets. The accumulation of financial and other assets, as a result of continuous economic growth, is another important aspect of structural changes in the economy. The gradual ageing of the population has begun to influence the consumption and saving patterns of society, the external trade imbalances, and fiscal policy as a means to allocate resources intertemporally. The internationalization or global integration of financial and other markets has been another notable stimulus for change during this period, influencing the role of the Japanese economy and the way that Japan's economic policies are conducted. These are some of the important underlying factors, certainly not exhaustive, that have brought about changes in the performance of the macroeconomy as well as economic policy. In any case, it should be noted that structural changes have been taking place for inherently complex reasons and have often been interacting each other, so that their effects are being felt in many areas of, and in many different forms within, the economy.

1.2 AIMS OF THIS VOLUME

The intention of this volume is both to illustrate the various distinctive traditional structural features of the Japanese economy and to examine their changes in recent years, brought about by forces such as deregulation; accumulation of assets; the ageing of the population; and internationalization. To that end, the book has tried to cover major aspects of the entire economy. The areas examined by the authors include: microeconomic units such as the firm and the household; various markets including labour and financial markets; macroeconomic relationship of consumption, saving, investment and growth; monetary and financial policies and the policy-implementing institutions; and international economic relations.

The approach utilized in this book is primarily economic analysis, rather than a cultural, sociological or political approach. This method, whose basic explanatory presumption is rationality, provides many interesting insights into the 'uniqueness' of the Japanese economy and its workings in an easily comprehensible way (Okabe, 1992). The way the papers in this volume address issues is generally not by conducting a survey on the relevant issues of a given area,[2] but by investigating in depth a narrowly specified, and important, issue in the given area. This means that the analytical methods used in each paper vary substantially: while all the papers intend to be as empirical as possible, some papers are more theoretical (for instance, Chapters 2 and 8); others conduct historical analysis (Chapter 11) or institutional analysis (Chapter 13); a comparative approach is utilized by several papers (Chapters 5, 10 and 13); highlighting the issue from a fresh perspective is the aim of some papers (Chapter 2); and in some instances an analysis of political economy is included (Chapters 7, 10, 13). In utilizing these methods, the editor believes that each paper has become a genuine addition to research in respective areas. It is to be emphasized that this kind of in-depth research inevitably unearths fundamental issues relating to the basic structure of the Japanese economy or its changes. It is in this way that the volume as a whole intends to provide new insights into Japan's economic structure.

The book takes up the most important areas of the economy. Part I covers the fundamental microeconomic unit, the Japanese firm, and the closely related labour market. This is followed in Part II by analyses of key macroeconomic variables, such as consumption, saving, investment and economic growth. Then the financial markets are looked at in Part III, where financial and monetary policies are analyzed, together with the policy institutions. While the earlier analyses are primarily of domestic economic aspects, the international aspects of the economy are taken up in Part IV.

1.3   BRIEF SUMMARIES OF THE CHAPTERS

Although readers are strongly urged to read each chapter for a detailed discussion, a brief, and somewhat courageous, summary of each chapter is provided below for the convenience of the reader.

1.3.1 Part I: The Japanese firm and the labour market

The Japanese firm has often been alleged to display characteristic behaviour, such as an unusual preference for growth, long-term orientation in making decisions, and forming groups. It has been argued recently that these behavioural features are closely related to, and in fact are the result of, the organizational features of the Japanese firm, including its distinctive labour relations. In Part I, some of the important aspects relating to these issues, such as corporate organization, governance and finance, are addressed (in the first two chapters), and employment and the labour market are taken up in the following two chapters.

Chapter 2, 'Long-termism and the Japanese firm' by Paul Sheard, closely examines one of the most commonly encountered views about the Japanese firm: that Japanese management has a long-term orientation (longer horizon), in contrast to the short-term decision-making of US managers, in the sense of being able to plan for and implement long-term investment strategies. This aspect is often argued as providing a competitive edge in the international scene by avoiding the short-termism that many believe plagues US business. The author reviews this argument critically, from both empirical and theoretical viewpoints, and finds that the empirical basis for this view is rather weak and that the theoretical arguments are more complicated than popular opinion suggests. Arguing from an economics viewpoint, he first points out several common misconceptions in the horizon debate, and then explores the implications of asymmetric information between the capital market (investors) and the firm (managers), and the effects of managerial incentives. By utilizing recently developed ideas in the literature, the author explores what it might mean when it is said that Japanese management is long-term orientated. His interpretation is that various features of corporate practices or corporate governance in Japan, such as the main bank system, a system of stable interlocking shareholding and long-time employment practice of managers, make the degree of information asymmetry less salient and managerial incentives different from the US case. The author concludes that full consideration of information asymmetry and managerial incentives is essential in order to make the discussion of long-termism economically meaningful, and that more careful studies are needed to conclude how the above-mentioned features in Japan translate into a long-term orientation.

Chapter 3, 'Financial structure and managerial discretion in the Japanese firm: an implication of the surge of equity-related bonds' by Akiyoshi Horiuchi, asks a fundamental question of how the Japanese firm is governed, to what extent the incumbent managers have discretionary powers and why, and then conducts an empirical analysis of this question by looking into the financial structure of the Japanese firm. In the Anglo-American system, the corporation is generally understood to be governed ultimately by the shareholders, by way of open capital markets which play a role in disciplining corporate managers. In Japan, however, substantially different institutional arrangements, such as the mutual shareholding and stable shareholding by main banks, are thought to have effectively prevented the open capital market from exerting substantial influence on the behaviour of incumbent managers. The author, drawing on the experience of the surge in the so-called 'equity-related bonds' during financial liberal-ization in the 1980s, econometrically examines whether this kind of Japanese corporate financial structure contributes to expanding the discretionary power of incumbent managers. He finds that (i) the discretionary power of incumbent managers rests on mutual shareholding between corporations, since they may be presumed to mutually refrain from interfering in the discretionary power of their partners; (ii) the main-bank relationship, that is, the stable bank–firm relationship, does not, contrary to many other previous studies, seem to suppress the discretionary powers of managers of client corporations, implying that the main bank does not always monitor the client firm in all the activities of the firm; and (iii) in some contingencies, as in financial distress of the firm, the monitoring role of the main bank may be valuable, and it is important to clarify when main bank monitoring works and when it does not. The paper thus provides an empirical answer to the question of the source of the discretionary power of Japanese management and suggests a subject for future research.

Many distinctive features of the Japanese firm have been associated with characteristic labour relations in Japan, which in turn have several distinctive features when compared with Western counterparts. The Japanese labour market has often been described and summarized most conveniently by the 'three pillars', namely the life-time employment system, the seniority-based pay and promotion system, and the enterprise union system. Whether and to what extent this characterization is accurate has been a debatable issue. But a proper understanding of labour mobility, training and the compensation scheme is essential in assessing these alleged features. Some aspects of these fundamental issues are examined empirically in the following two papers.

Chapter 4, 'An analysis of labour mobility in Japan' by Toshiaki Tachibanaki and Atsuhiro Taki, analyzes the mobility in the Japanese labour market by examining the pattern and reasons for the changes in the job category and in the workplace for various groups of Japanese workers. Authors systematically estimate the tendency (the transition probabilities) of workers to move between various labour force statuses, such as employed, unemployed, and not-in-labour-force, and investigate reasons for these tendency. They also estimate, for employed labour, the pattern and reasons for changing the workplace (turnover functions).

Their findings are many, but some of the interesting ones include: (i) the tendency of self-employed workers to become unemployed or to leave the labour market is very low, and this, combined with the fact that the percentage of self-employed workers in Japan is high when compared internationally, explains the low unemployment rate in Japan; (ii) for workers in smaller firms or for female workers, the tendency to change their status (especially to become unemployed) is considerably greater than for workers in larger firms or for male workers, implying that the former categories are the main sources of labour mobility in Japan; (iii) middle-aged workers show far more stability in their status (especially relating to staying in employment) than the younger or older generations (older generations tend to change status even in larger firms); and (iv) the longer the duration of employment (job tenure), the greater the tendency to remain in employment, regardless of a worker's age, sex or type of job. These findings shed new light on the nature of the Japanese labour market. For example, finding (iii) implies that the well-known 'long-time employment system' prevails in Japan but that, when combined with (ii), it is understood to be a practice applicable primarily to large firms and male workers. Also, (iv) can be interpreted as a result of another celebrated Japanese practice, the seniority-based pay and promotion system.

Chapter 5, 'Is the tenure-earning curve really steeper in Japan? A re-examination based on UK–Japan comparison' by Giorgio Brunello and Kenn Ariga, examines the profiles of workers' earnings in relation to age or length of service (job tenure). For many countries, it has been extensively confirmed that age (or tenure) and wages of workers are positively correlated, or that the relationship (age–wage profile) is upward-sloping. Many interpretations have been offered to explain this phenomenon. In particular, in the case of Japan, it has commonly been argued that the slope is not only positive but also generally steeper than in other countries and that it provides both evidence for the so-called 'seniority-based' wage system and a foundation for 'long-time (life-time) employment', both of which are celebrated features of Japanese labour relations. The authors re-examine this reputedly positive relationship in the UK and Japan by considering explicitly one additional element, that is, rank (the position filled by an employee in the firm hierarchy), along with other traditionally cited elements such as the skill of a worker (human capital), which usually increases over time. After discussing many theoretical and econometric issues regarding the estimation of the earning function, they find that, if rank is taken into account, (i) in Japan the importance of rank is relatively greater than in the UK; and (ii) although age and tenure remain important factors in both countries they lose their importance when examining the relatively steeper slope of the Japanese age–wage profile. The authors interpret these results as being consistent with some notable practices in the Japanese firm. For instance, in Japan each job within a firm is relatively less independent than in the UK, so that more emphasis is placed on promotion as a work incentive device, as is implied by (i) above. This pattern, they argue, is also consistent with the fact that Japanese firms provide more on-the-job training across jobs within a firm, which is an important element in career ladders. This research provides not only a new insight in the understanding of Japanese labour relations but also a different perspective on debates about Japan's 'uniqueness'.

1.3.2 Part II: Consumption, saving, investment and growth

Many key features of a national economy, including importantly the growth path of the economy, are determined by the macroeconomic pattern of household consumption, private saving and investment. Naturally, this pattern is an outcome of a variety of institutional, historical, policy-related and international factors. Each of the chapters in this section deals with this macroeconomic aspect of the Japanese economy from a specific and unique viewpoint.

Chapter 6, 'Consumer behaviour in Japan under financial liberalization and demographic change' by Wataru Takahashi and Yukinobu Kitamura, is motivated by the unusually widely fluctuating, and somewhat puzzling, movements of consumption and saving of Japanese households, especially since about 1980. The chapter aims to present a new analysis of Japanese consumer behaviour, behaviour that has an important implication for Japan's external current account balances. By introducing a theoretical model in which durable consumption, non-durable consumption and saving are simultaneously determined and incorporating therein some important structural changes, such as financial liberalization and demographic change, they have shown by a careful econometric analysis that (i) durable consumption is determined quite differently from non-durable consumption; (ii) consumer credit expansion has had a significant influence on durable consumption; (iii) inflation has negative effects on consumption; (iv) contrary to popular arguments, the ageing of the population in itself has not had a clear effect on reducing saving; and (v) the wealth effect has not been significant. The authors also discuss policy implications of these results. They argue that, since the ageing of the population is not expected to result in decreased saving, which would rectify the domestic saving–investment imbalance and thus eliminate the Japanese current account surplus, some active policy actions are called for to reduce the surplus. In this regard they assert that far-reaching deregulation of various economic activities be considered which, they argue, would lower the domestic price level and thus increase household consumption. Since the huge Japanese trade surplus has commonly been debated as being a result of domestic under-consumption or excess saving rather than the 'closed' Japanese markets (see Chapter 15), this study sheds a new light on the policy debate.

Chapter 7, 'Saving, investment, and capital mobility: lessons from Japanese inter-regional capital flows' by Robert Dekle, conducts an empirical analysis of two key macroeconomics variables. In an early study, covering many countries, of the relationship between saving and investment it was found that national saving rates correlate very closely to national investment rates for the period before 1975 (the Feldstein–Horioka proposition). This has been interpreted to mean that a country was required to supply the source of its investment domestically since the international capital mobility of that period was relatively limited, and accordingly it was presumed that an increase in international capital mobility would make the relationship increasingly loose. Surprisingly, however, all the later studies covering recent years have shown that the close saving–investment correlation is still observed. The author tries to give an answer to this intriguing puzzle by examining the Japanese inter-regional case where capital may be deemed to be perfectly mobile. By breaking down the saving and investment of each region into private and government components, he finds that (i) high capital mobility between domestic regions shows that regional *private* saving and investment rates differ; (ii) regional *public* saving and investment do not affect regional private saving and investment; and, accordingly, (iii) fiscal transfers by the government between regions have made regional *total* saving and investment correlate and this correlation is a negative one, meaning that economic assistance flows from richer to poorer regions. The author interprets these results as suggesting that (i) in the international scene there still remain factors that restrict free capital mobility; (ii) various arguments about the effect of public investment on private investment, whether the relationship is positive or negative, need to be re-examined; and (iii) a programme of economic assistance within a highly integrated group of countries, such as within the European Community (EC), is effective even in an environment of high capital mobility.

Chapter 8, 'High economic growth and its end in Japan: an explanation by a model of demand-led growth' by Hiroshi Yoshikawa, re-examines the fundamental mechanism of one of the most fascinating periods of the Japanese economy. This period of high-speed growth, which recorded an average 10 per cent real growth rate for more than ten years, has been studied widely, and the termination of this high growth has commonly been attributed to a supply-side factor, namely the outbreak of the first oil crisis in 1973. The author maintains the importance of the supply-side issues for economic growth, such as technological progress and capital accumulation, but argues that in understanding the growth process these issues must be analyzed in conjunction with real demand constraints in a different way from which this has ordinarily been done. He argues that (i) particularly instrumental in the Japanese high-growth process was the high household formation due to population flows from rural, agricultural to urban areas, and diffusion of consumer durables; and (ii) the decline of the growth rate was caused by these changes in domestic elements which crucially affected the demand side of the economy. As evidence, he refers to the different outcomes of the first and the second (1978–9) oil crises: although the two crises had roughly the same impact in terms of transfer of payments from Japan to oil-producing countries, a lower economic growth rate followed the first crisis but the trend growth rate did not change after the second crisis, thus implying the importance of domestic demand on economic growth. The author also offers a theoretical model in which growth is led by demand. This chapter adds an important perspective to Japanese high growth, and more generally, the nature of the economic growth process.

1.3.3   Part III: The financial markets, monetary policy and the policy institutions

The basic role of financial markets is to channel a nation's saving into various investment activities, so that the macroeconomic performance of an economy depends heavily on the way the financial market is organized and how it functions, and on the characteristics of both policies and the policy-implementing body, the central bank. The five chapters in this section focus on these issues. The first two review the big swings of the stock market and their effects, either by focusing on the developments after the mid-1980s (Chapter 9) or by comparing that experience with similar ones in the past (Chapter 10). In contrast to these chapters, which deal mainly with the stock market or the market for 'direct finance', Chapter 11 deals with bank finance or the market of 'indirect finance' and traces the historical roots of the distinctive nature of the Japanese bank–firm relationship. Chapters 12 and 13 deal with monetary policy and the central bank.

Chapter 9, 'The rise and fall of the bubble economy: an analysis of the performance and structure of the Japanese stock market' by Fumiko Kon-ya, focuses on the market in Japan that over the past several years has exhibited a most dramatic rise and fall, namely the stock market. After reviewing the trend increase of the Japanese stock price in the late 1980s and the subsequent crash and slump after 1989, the author points out the major reasons for these wild movements and assesses macroeconomic effects of stock price fluctuations. Then the structure and workings of the Japanese stock market are analyzed in detail and a number of improvements are suggested. The author's main conclusions are that (i) the greater part of the stock price fluctuation of this period can be explained by the movements of fundamental factors such as interest rates, risk tolerance or aversion of investors, and the level of expected corporate profits, although in some instances the stock price overshot the boundaries of fundamental reasoning; (ii) stock price fluctuations were magnified by the structure of the Japanese stock market, which is characterized by the dominance of institutional investors with the power to influence each other's decisions greatly; and, accordingly, (iii) the market needs to remove the sources of destabilization by introducing a host of measures, including increased public disclosure of market information, further liberalization of the activity of institutional investors, the introduction of counter-measures against stock-index-futures trading and other large-volume trading, and easier access to the market for individual investors. It is expected that, by implementing these measures, in future the stock market will function more efficiently and in a manner conducive to achieve stable economic growth.

Koichi Hamada in Chapter 10 'Bubbles, bursts and bail-outs: a comparison of three episodes of financial crises in Japan' conducts an analysis of three historical episodes of financial crises in Japan triggered by stock market crashes, and examines public policies relating to these crises. The three crises are (i) stock market crashes and bank runs that culminated in the financial crisis in 1927; (ii) the bail-out of Yamaichi Securities Company in 1965 after the stock market decline; and (iii) the ongoing recession triggered in 1990 by the burst of the stock-market and real-estate-market bubbles. After comparing the magnitude of the shock to the macroeconomy and discussing the transmission mechanism of the financial collapses as well as the political economy associated with the shocks, the author concludes that the following aspects are common to the three episodes. First, when an emergency develops there is a dilemma between the incentive mechanism and the security of the financial and economic systems: fail-safe mechanisms are indispensable to keep the national economy from chaos, but the expectation of too much protection impairs incentives for financial discipline. Second, the maintenance of public confidence is critically important: if rumours create rumours, if a panic psychology becomes contagious, then the financial system collapses as a process of a self-fulfilling prophecy. Third, institutions, such as the bureaucratic powers that control markets, develop as political and economic responses to impasses, and they influence the economic outcome of succeeding years and, in particular, the next phase of financial difficulty. These points are very suggestive in designing public policies to maintain and enhance the stability of financial systems, which is a basis for a stable macroeconomy.

Chapter 11, 'Evolution of the main bank system in Japan' by Takeo Hoshi, describes the nature and function of one of the most important features of the modern Japanese financial system and analyses historically the origin and development of this system. The main bank system is an institutional arrangement between a firm and a bank (sometimes a few banks), in which the bank typically becomes the largest lender to the firm, a holder of equity claims in the firm and a provider of its personnel for managers of the client firm. This bank–firm relationship, as the chapter shows, has been instrumental in Japan not only in rescuing a firm when it becomes financially troubled but also in alleviating the financial constraint of investment activities and thus avoiding under-investment. Therefore, the main bank system has relevance not only to the financial system but also to corporate governance (see Chapters 2 and 3) and to the wider issue of the strength or competitiveness of the Japanese firm. The author argues that the elements of this system can be found in the developments of Japanese corporate finance during the Second World War, which is characterized by (i) an increased concentration within the banking industry; (ii) corporation's higher dependence on bank borrowings; (iii) the development and affirmation of close bank–firm ties; and (iv) the decline of shareholders' power. Many of these aspects of wartime corporate finance, he argues, were carried over to the post-war period because the Japanese government and the allied forces were not sufficiently committed to breaking up the close bank–firm ties and, during the late 1940s and early 1950s, the banks gained substantial power to monitor firms, thus starting the development of the main bank system. Although the development of capital markets in Japan in recent years has naturally changed the character and importance of the main banks, this detailed account of the historical development of the main bank system offers some interesting lessons for developing economies and former centrally-controlled economies.

Monetary policy, as one of the two most important macroeconomic policies, has had a decisive influence on the stability of not only economic activity but also the economic and financial systems. In the next two chapters in Part III, the policy conduct and institutional arrangement of the Bank of Japan are discussed.

Chapter 12, 'Monetary policy in Japan: a perspective on tools, transmission channels and outcomes' by Mitsuaki Okabe, provides an overview of various aspects of monetary policy in Japan, including the tools, transmission channels and outcomes of the policy. Its particular focus is on the transmission channels of the policy and its evolution necessitated by the changes in the economic structure, the regulatory framework, and the international environment. By surveying the literature extensively, the chapter classifies the major policy effects on the economy as working through four channels: namely lending effect; direct expenditure effect; exchange rate effect; and wealth effect. It argues that the relative importance of these effects has changed over the years, because of deregulation and internationalization of financial markets, and accumulation of various domestic assets. Also it argues that the policy effects permeating into the economy with have generally been strengthened, the more diversified channels and with market forces playing a more important role while direct quantitative controls ending. Also reviewed are the policy actions of the Bank of Japan since 1975. The author concludes by pointing out general lessons from the Japanese experience, that (i) the accumulation of financial and other assets requires the central bank to monitor the movement of asset prices more carefully than before because it is deeply related to financial system stability; and (ii) monetary policy should always ultimately aim at stabilizing domestic prices and at achieving the stability of the financial system, even when the external economic situation may sometimes seem to warrant the consideration of other factors, such as the exchange rate. These lessons are expected to be taken into account in developing future policies to achieve a stable macroeconomy.

Chapter 13, 'The Bank of Japan and the Federal Reserve: financial liberalization, independence, and regulatory responsibility' by Thomas Cargill, addresses the questions of how the central bank should be organized and operated, and what the role should be for providing a stable financial and monetary environment, a pre-condition for achieving long-run stability of the macroeconomy. The author considers these issues with the comparative perspective between the Bank of Japan and the Federal Reserve Bank (FRB) system of the United States. He has chosen these two central banks because they not only represent the two largest national economies in the world but also offer meaningful insights in the issues because of their differing institutional structure and performance. The author reviews these two central banks and their performance in terms of institutional arrangement, including independence from the government, the roles played in financial liberalization, and financial regulatory responsibilities over the financial system. He concludes that (i) the role of the central bank to achieve price stability is critically important as a precondition for a smooth transition in the financial liberalization process; (ii) formal independence, in contrast to substantive independence, of the central bank is no guarantee of price stability, and the relationship should be viewed in terms of the proper set of incentives provided to the central bank irrespective of the degree of formal independence that will insure price stabilization; and (iii) although implications for proper regulatory structures gained in this study are limited, conflicts often arise, according to the US experience, between the ultimate price stabilization goal of monetary policy and the formal regulatory responsibilities, if a formal regulatory role is given to the central bank.

1.3.4   Part IV: International economic relations

Japan's increased profile in the world economy has inevitably raised the question as to the possible role it should play in the regional and world economy, and the pattern of trade and capital flows it should show. The three chapters in this section deal directly with these issues in turn, that is, the alleged Japanese trade bloc, the huge current account surplus and the structure of long-term capital flows.

Jeffrey Frankel's Chapter 14, 'Is Japan establishing a trade bloc in

East Asia and the Pacific?', tries to provide an answer empirically to
the question addressed as the title of the chapter. The author utilizes a
systematic framework for measuring what patterns of bilateral trade
are normal around the world (the so-called 'gravity' model) and then
examines Japan's influence by assessing the financial flows and direct investment in the region. He finds that (i) the *level* of trade in
East Asia is biased intraregionally, as it is within the EC and within
the Western Hemisphere, to a greater extent than can be explained
naturally by distance; (ii) there is no evidence of a special 'Japan effect'; (iii) once the rapid economic growth in Asia is properly accounted for, the statistics do not bear out a *trend* toward intraregional
bias of trade flows; (iv) the world's strongest grouping, whether judged
by the rate of change of intragroup bias or (as of 1990) by the level of
bias, is the one that includes the USA and Canada with the Asia–
Pacific countries, that is, the APEC (Asia–Pacific Economic Cooperation) group; and (v) Japan's direct investment in Pacific Asia has grown,
but at most in proportion to its trade in the region. In short, this study
shows there is no evidence that Japan is concentrating on its trade
with other Asian countries in any special way, nor that they are collectively moving towards a trade bloc in the way that Western Europe
(centred on the EC) and the Western Hemisphere (centred on the USA)
appear to be. In understanding the East Asia bloc in comparison with
the other two blocs, these findings provide new understandings and a
basis for the future policy of the region.

Chapter 15, 'Recent balance of payments developments in Japan: is
the current account surplus structural or temporary?' by Mahito Uchida
and Takashi Ui, explores the nature of Japanese surpluses in trade and
current account balances, possibly the most frequently debated international aspect of the Japanese economy. The authors examine the
magnitude and fluctuation of the current account balances, particularly after 1980, first by looking into the components of current accounts and then by conducting econometric analyses viewing the issue
as a macroeconomic phenomenon of domestic investment-saving balance (or imbalance). In order to remove short-term fluctuations in the
surplus, they estimate the size of the underlying or structural elements
in the surplus by calculating the size of the surplus if the economy
utilized all its capital and labour (full-employment-based current account surplus). After estimating this structural surplus by a number of
methods, they conclude that both the level of Japan's underlying surplus and its fluctuation have been quite substantial since the 1980s
and that the fluctuation has primarily reflected autonomous changes

in domestic investment patterns or public expenditures. These results imply that the size of the surplus would not easily decrease even with boom conditions of the Japanese economy in which export pressure was expected to decline and imports to surge. They argue that Japan's continuing current account surplus is likely to intensify trade friction with some other industrialized countries, thereby threatening the free trade system, so that they stress the need to reduce the surplus by making efforts to proceed with further deregulation for increased domestic investment and to liberalize Japan's markets further.

In the last chapter of this volume, Chapter 16, 'Structural changes in Japanese long-term capital flows', Shinji Takagi questions the extent to which Japan will remain a net exporter of long-term capital in the coming years. The author first reviews historically the structure of Japan's balance of payments, capital controls, and qualitative and quantitative developments of major components of the long-term capital account, and then conducts causality tests of current account transactions and long-term capital transactions. He finds that (i) long-term capital outflows from Japan expanded rapidly after 1981, mainly as a result of Japan's liberalization of international financial transactions (in particular, deregulations of the acquisition of foreign securities by resident institutional investors); and (ii) since the trend of this portfolio diversification to increase foreign securities progressed over more than ten years and then gradually abated there have been major structural changes in Japan's long-term capital outflows in recent years. He asserts that this structural change can be confirmed by the causality tests which show that the long-term capital transactions are largely exogenous to the current transactions, and also by judging not only the level of Japan's long-term foreign assets internationally but also the levelling-off of the share of foreign securities in the portfolios of Japanese institutional investors. This structural change, he argues, was statistically apparent in 1991 (Japan became a net *importer* of long-term capital) and in 1992 (while the long-term capital returned to a net outflow, the size of outflow fell far short of the size of the current account surplus). Given these analyses, the author finds it difficult to foresee a major increase in private long-term capital outflow, even though continuation of current account surplus is generally projected, and he predicts that the role of official capital outflows, including official development assistance to the developing countries, will become a significant means of recycling Japanese current account surpluses.

1.3.5 Some overall conclusions

Drawing overall conclusions from the chapters in this volume might be too bold an attempt, but the following points seem to emerge regarding the structure of the contemporary Japanese economy and its changes.

First, the Japanese economy does have many distinctive structural features in various areas which are the sources of the characteristic economic performance. These features are evident particularly in such areas as the corporate organization (the stable shareholding); firm-to-firm relationship (corporate grouping and the subcontracting system); firm-to-bank relationships (main bank system); long-term employment practices; and a high savings rate. These features, many of which are based on long-term relationships, have been understood as generally having efficiency advantages in coping with incomplete information, which characterizes various transactions.

Second, various forces have been at work, especially in the last ten years or so, to change the structure or the character of the Japanese economy. They include liberalization, internationalization (both especially in financial markets); the accumulation of financial and other assets; demographic changes (ageing of the population); international orientation of public policies (especially monetary policy); and the unprecedented large economic fluctuations since the mid-1980s (the longest post-war boom in the late 1980s followed by the deepest post-war recession in the early 1990s). Some of these changes have affected the market and the behaviour of market participants more quickly and more drastically (for example, the wide fluctuations in land and share prices have had an immediate and enormous impact on the behaviour of households and firms), while other changes seem to be relatively slow in affecting the system (for example, the effects of ageing on the saving rate). The changes taking place seem to be making the Japanese economic system less distinctive, by diluting the traditional character of economic transactions that are generally based on long-term relationships and by increasing the elements of arm's length market transactions typically found in the Western system, although the speed of the change is generally slow.

Third, public policies, including macroeconomic policies, have played an important role in fostering various characteristic institutions (such as the main bank system and cross-shareholdings) and in steering the macroeconomic performance (such as the role played by monetary policy in asset price inflation and deflation since the mid-1980s), and thus in influencing the efficiency, stability and growth of the economy. Accordingly, it should be said that, since there remain many areas for improvement, in both the domestic and international arenas, public policies can act effectively and *should* act on these areas (such as in establishing more transparent public policy rules, and maintaining macroeconomic stability) so that the Japanese economy may become a more efficient, stable and equitable one. Internationally, efforts to make the economy a more open and less regulated system with a transparent character (where transactions can readily take place according to easily recognizable rules) should be on the policy agenda, in order to establish amicable economic relations with other economies in the world.

Fourth, there are some areas not explicitly treated in this volume which are nevertheless important for a deeper understanding of the Japanese economy. They include such areas as technology and industrial policy, public finance, the industrial structure, distribution systems, and a fuller treatment of foreign direct investment. Also, the recent change in government is expected to have a substantive change in the future path of Japanese economic policy and the economy. After having been in power for thirty eight years, the Liberal Democratic Party, which achieved the super-high growth from the mid-1950s to the early 1970s and led Japan to be one of the economic giants of the world, was replaced by a seven-party coalition government in July 1993. The new government has been pursuing a more consumer-orientated policy compared with the basically pro-business policies of the previous government. Under the new government, the movement towards deregulation in all the spheres of economic activity, which was already an irreversible move, appears to have been accelerated. Although the outcome of various policies depends on the stability and the political aptitude of the government, there is undoubtedly a possibility that the economy may make a voyage into uncharted seas. Analyses of these issues would certainly add to a more comprehensive picture of the entire economic system and its future, but addressing these issues remains a future agenda for our research.

NOTES

1. Part of the reason for the low and stable unemployment rate in Japan is the relatively strict definition of the unemployment rate (for instance, temporary layoffs are not deemed to be unemployment, while the self-defence force is deemed to be part of the labour force). However, even allowing for this, the Japanese unemployment rate can still be regarded as

relatively low. (The unemployment rate in 1992 in Japan was 2.2 per cent, while in the USA it was 7.4 per cent, the UK 9.2 per cent, Germany 6.6 per cent and France 10.2 per cent.)

2. For surveying purposes there already have been published many books covering the entire Japanese economy. A classic, though voluminous, book providing a comprehensive survey of the economy is by Patrick and Rosovsky (1976). A more handy one is by Allen (1982). Recent publications of this kind include Ito (1992) and the three volumes of *The Political Economy of Japan* edited by Yamamura and Yasuba (1987), Inoguchi and Okimoto (1988), Kumon and Rosovsky (1992).

REFERENCES

Allen, G. C. 1982. *The Japanese Economy*, London: Weidenfeld and Nicholson.

Inoguchi, T., and D. I. Okimoto (eds) 1988. *The Political Economy of Japan: Vol. 2. The Changing International Context*, Palo Alto, Calif.: Stanford University Press.

Ito, T. 1992. *The Japanese Economy*, Cambridge, Mass.: MIT Press.

Kumon, S., and H. Rosovsky (eds) 1992. *The Political Economy of Japan: Vol. 3. Cultural and Social Dynamics*, Palo Alto, Calif.: Stanford University Press.

Okabe, M. 1992. 'An Introduction to the Japanese Economy: What Distinguishes It from Other Economies?', Working Paper 92–2, Centre for Japanese Economic Studies, Macquarie University, Sydney.

Patrick, H., and H. Rosovsky (eds) 1976. *Asia's New Giant: How the Japanese Economy Works*, Washington, D.C.: Brookings Institution.

Yamamura, K., and Y. Yasuba (eds) 1987. *The Political Economy of Japan: Vol. 1. The Domestic Transformation*, Palo Alto, Calif.: Stanford University Press.

Part I

The Japanese Firm and the Labour Market

2 Long-termism and the Japanese Firm

Paul Sheard*

2.1 INTRODUCTION

One of the most commonly encountered views about the Japanese economic system is that management in Japan is 'long-term orientated' in the sense of being able to plan for and implement long-term investment strategies. Abegglen and Stalk (1985, p. 188) argue that 'managements of the kaisha [Japanese business corporation] are freed from the tyranny of accountants, and from the terrible pressures throughout the U.S. organizations for steady improvement in earnings per share . . . The Japanese manager is able to look further into the future and is freer to do what is necessary to ensure a successful future'.

Japanese long-termism is contrasted with the excessive short-term bias alleged to characterize management in the USA. A common claim is that US managers behave 'myopically', passing up potentially profitable long-term projects because of pressures from the stock market to bolster short-term performance. As Okimoto (1987, pp. 93, 100) notes, 'unlike their kaisha competitors, the management of American firms are under constant pressure to deliver the best possible quarterly dividends to their stockholders'. Japanese managers, on the other hand, freed from the tyranny of the stock market by virtue of close bank and intercorporate shareholding ties, and enjoying secure tenure of employment, do not have this handicap, and 'can freely pursue their own objectives, i.e., growth and development' (Matsumoto, 1991, p. 65),

* This chapter is based on work undertaken as a Visiting Scholar at the Institute of Social and Economic Research, Ōsaka University, the Foundation for Advanced Information Research, Japan, and the Institute for Monetary and Economic Studies, Bank of Japan. The research was supported by a grant from the Daiwa Bank Foundation for Asia and Oceania and by the International Cooperation (Ōsaka Gas) research fund at Ōsaka University. An earlier version of the chapter was presented as a paper to the First International Federation of Scholarly Associations of Management Conference, Tōkyō in September 1992. I benefited from discussions with Richard Beason, Mark Fruin, Colin McKenzie, Paul Milgrom, Dan Okimoto and Tom Roehl at various stages in the preparation of this paper. Any deficiencies, however, are my sole responsibility.

and therefore out-invest and out-compete their foreign, particularly US, rivals.[1] Increasingly, policy and academic interest is focusing on this perceived difference in managerial orientation as a key contributor to Japan's corporate competitive success and the perceived US decline in competitiveness.[2]

Interpretation of the causes and consequences of Japanese long-term managerial horizons differs. Some observers emphasize the advantages of the Japanese system of corporate governance and managerial employment in coping with informational and agency problems associated with the separation of ownership and control, and identify these as contributing to the competitive strength of Japanese firms.[3] In this analysis, Japanese corporate organization becomes a potential model for improving corporate competitiveness, if not in the advanced industrial economies then at least in the newly industrializing and transforming socialist economies (Bardhan and Roemer, 1992). Other observers see a darker side to long-termism, viewing it as a manifestation of certain structural features of Japanese capitalism that give Japanese firms an unfair advantage in international competition.[4] In this analysis, long-termism is associated with a pattern of predatory corporate behaviour that needs to be changed in the interests of preserving economic stability in the international trading system. Despite these differences in interpretation, there seems to be little disagreement with the basic proposition that Japanese firms are long-term orientated.

That this view of Japanese managerial behaviour should have become so widely accepted is surprising for two reasons: one relating to the empirical evidence, the second to the conceptual basis of long-termism. First, there is little, if any, rigorous quantitative evidence to support the long-termism view; indeed, there is some evidence that would cast doubt on it.[5] Authoritative quantitative testing of the proposition is, in fact, extremely difficult, as attempts to settle the US short-termism debate have shown.[6] One problem is that it is difficult to design a direct test of the theory, given that key variables of interest, such as missed investment opportunities and decision-makers' information sets, are unobservable. Tests tend to be indirect ones, but the results often permit competing explanations.[7]

Evidence used to support the notion of Japanese long-termism has been of two kinds. One is survey evidence, such as rankings of corporate objectives: an often-cited piece of evidence is the finding that US managers give a high ranking to return on investment and share price increases, whereas their Japanese counterparts give a high rank to market share and a low rank to share price.[8] However, cross-cultural comparisons of survey evidence are fraught with difficulties of interpretation and bias, and economists, for better or worse, are typically sceptical of accepting explanations of the behaviour of economic agents based on those agents' own explanations of the phenomena: to economists 'actions speak louder than words'.

Many argue that the actions of Japanese corporates *do* provide support for the long-termism thesis. This second kind of evidence derives from observation of particular industries and firms. The Japanese semi-conductor industry, and leading firm NEC in particular, are commonly cited as exemplifying long-termism.[9] A problem with this kind of evidence is that it is selective, permitting multiple interpretations. While there are industries and firms in Japan that make what appear to be large-scale, long-term investments, at a time when their US counterparts do not, it is not clear whether this reflects differential time horizons or, also consistent with the evidence, shifting comparative advantage. There is also a problem with selection bias. It may be that the industries focused on are at the top end of a distribution which may have a large variance. This suggests looking at aggregate investment, but at an aggregate level it may be better to rely on macroeconomic models to explain differential investment levels than on theories of short- or long-term horizons. Moreover, even the casual empirical evidence about Japanese corporate behaviour has become mixed: in recent years numerous firms have expanded their investments in short-term financial and speculative assets.[10] None of the above is to argue *against* the view that Japanese management is long-term orientated and US management is short-term, but rather to suggest that clear empirical evidence in support of that characterization is yet to be assembled. At this stage, the proposition is better viewed as an interesting hypothesis deserving further careful testing rather than as a clearly established proposition.

The lack of solid empirical support, of the rigorous econometric kind employed in financial economics, for the long-termism view would not be such a problem were the arguments surrounding the horizon issue straightforward at a conceptual level and it was clear on *a priori* grounds from the nature of the respective institutional environments that long-termism would be expected in Japan and short-termism in the USA. But this is not the case. Although the popular arguments appear straightforward and to many, persuasive, the economic analysis of the issues is not cut-and-dried, and involves a number of puzzles. The notion of long-termism or managerial myopia does not readily fit into the traditional frameworks that economists have relied upon. Sorting out what is meant by short-termism and long-termism, and whether and why the arguments made about Japanese firms have validity challenges economics to develop different frameworks and models than those commonly employed. To make sense of the issue, economists have developed models of corporate governance and managerial incentives under conditions of asymmetric information, strategic behaviour and imperfect contracting, thus relaxing the assumptions of traditional models.[11] Rather than being 'self-explanatory', analysis of these issues takes place close to the research frontier in industrial organization and financial economics (Holmstrom and Tirole, 1989; Milgrom and Roberts, 1992).

The purpose of this chapter is to survey from an economics perspective the arguments surrounding the long-term orientation of Japanese management. Careful empirical work on the issue is needed but it is also important to clarify the conceptual basis of the conventional wisdom.[12] Much of the popular discussion of Japanese long-termism tends to be simplistic and often begs more questions than are answered. Can we take the conventional view at face value? What does it mean in conceptual terms to say that Japanese management is 'long-term orientated'? What mechanisms in the Japanese environment support such behaviour? The paper attempts to address this set of questions by drawing on recent developments in economics, particularly new theories of the firm and economic organization, and on the literature on the Japanese firm and management.

2.2 PUZZLES RELATING TO LONG-TERMISM

The first task is to clarify what is meant by 'long-termism' and 'short-termism', or a long- or short-term orientation or horizon. In a multi-period framework, the horizon of investment projects can be associated with the timing of the associated expected cash flows: a short-term project is one whose expected cash flows occur in the next period(s) or near future, and a long-term project one whose cash flows occur in later period(s). In this framework, 'long-termism' would denote a tendency to invest in long-term projects. One perception of Japanese firms is that they invest heavily in physical assets with long pay-off horizons, and relatively little (traditionally at least) in short-term financial assets.[13]

Contrary to the impression created by popular discussion, there is nothing inherently superior about a long-term as compared to a short-term investment. In the conventional net-present-value (NPV) framework employed in financial economics, there is no presumption that projects that pay off far in the future are superior to short-term projects: use of the NPV rule – implement projects whose present discounted value of cash flows, net of investment costs, is positive – is supposed to guide managers to select the right projects, regardless of the time structure of returns. Quite the reverse is true: monetary payoffs are always preferred the sooner they occur in time; with any discounting of the future, 'short-term' is better than 'long-term', other things being equal (in particular the monetary amount).

The NPV framework is one that essentially suppresses horizon issues, just as the famous Fisher separation theorem allows considerations of the timing of consumption to be separated from investment decisions, and the celebrated Modigliani–Miller theorem allows considerations of how projects are financed to be divorced from ones deciding what projects are selected (Milgrom and Roberts, 1992, ch. 14). Decision-makers need only worry about whether a project is a 'good' one (positive NPV) or a 'bad' one (negative NPV), and this has nothing to do with the horizon of the project *per se*.

There are two ways to consider the short/long-termism issue in the net present value framework. One is to define horizon in terms of the number of periods that the decision-maker considers in calculating NPV. A decision-maker prone to short-termism would be one who truncated the calculation (for example, someone who used a 'payback' rule), and a long-term decision-maker one who included all the relevant periods. On this yardstick of capital budgeting management technique, it is not clear at all that Japanese decision-makers are long-term, and US short-term (Hodder, 1986). An interpretation more consistent with the conventional wisdom is that – regardless of the particular capital budgeting technique used – Japanese managers are more prone to consider periods far into the future because of the lower expected managerial mobility, or have better information because of the nature and quality of information flows between relevant parts of the firm.

A second is to relate the horizon issue to the discount factor that the decision-maker ('cost of capital' for firms) uses to convert future cash flows into a net present value. Higher discount rates will lead decision-makers to pass up long-term projects. Hence much of the discussion of the long-term orientation of Japanese firms has focused on the issue of whether Japanese firms face a lower cost of capital than their US counterparts (Frankel, 1991; Hodder, 1991; Malkiel, 1994).

Two points should be noted, however. First, there is nothing 'wrong' with firms avoiding long-term investments or being 'short-term orientated' when they face a high cost of capital. Long-term projects are not 'good' given the opportunity cost of funds, whereas by definition of the NPV framework, the shorter-term projects that they accept are the right ones to undertake. The problem is the higher cost of capital, not short-termism, which is just a natural, and desirable, consequence of the former. If the reason that Japanese managers are orientated to the long term is because they face a lower cost of capital, the focus of attention should be on *why* they have a lower cost of capital – the cause – rather than on the pattern of investment this induces – an effect. The key issue is not a horizon one *per se*. Proponents of the long-term thesis appear to have something different in mind, which is not captured in the simple NPV framework.

Second, while it is true that a lower cost of capital enables long-term projects to be implemented, it is also the case that it enables short-term projects to be implemented that previously were not. Consider any marginal project, that is, a project with any horizon structure, say, t_1, t_2, t_3, . . ., that has zero NPV. Define an epsilon-worse project as one with the same payoff structure, but having t_i - ε in place of t_i. Then a marginal decrease in the discount rate will always make the epsilon-worse project (weakly) profitable for a small enough ε. This argument holds regardless of the time structure of payoffs.

A reduction in the discount rate expands the set of profitable projects but this says nothing about whether those projects are long- or short-term ones. Suppose that the distribution of projects is such that there are many marginally unprofitable short-term projects, whereas the next long-term project is comparatively infra-marginal; then a decrease in the discount rate will see (profit-maximizing) firms appearing to be 'short-term orientated' in the sense that they will be observed to be implementing many short-term projects. This, of course, is a contrived case, but it helps to make the point that long-termism is not quite synonymous with a low discount rate.

A common argument associates the short-term orientation of managers in the USA with their supposed pursuit of short-term share price maximization as a goal. This is contrasted to Japanese managers who, according to various survey evidence, profess not to place a high priority on share prices (Abegglen and Stalk, 1985, p. 177). This difference in behaviour is traced to differences in the capital market environment and in the nature of the firm as a nexus of contracts, Japanese managers being 'life-time' employees.

A particular version runs as follows: investors are concerned with short-term returns; long-term investments require costs, leading to a reduction in current earnings; by passing up such long-term investments current earnings can be kept high, leading to higher share prices. This is a description of myopic behaviour, because the failure to make long-term investments eventually undermines the competitiveness of the firm. Even if managers would 'like' to make long-term investments, they cannot do so for fear that the fall in current earnings will depress the stock price and invite a take-over.

The fact that managers might focus on short-term share price maximization, however – that is, take actions that maximize the current share price – does not obviously imply that short-term projects will be favoured at the expense of long-term ones. Indeed, much of economic analysis has proceeded on the assumption that maximizing current share price is precisely what managers should do, and, if the 'market for corporate control' operates well, *would* do. Similarly, it is not obvious why a reduction in current earnings should translate into a lower share price if the stock market can recognize the former for what it is: an investment. Financing investments or intertemporal transformations of resources is what capital markets do. To make sense, the argument must hinge on the inability of the capital market to separate an earnings signal into its various components, particularly the part reflecting the payoffs from past investments and the part reflecting costs associated with forward-looking investments.

A distinction needs to be made between when cash flows are expected to occur and when the present value of those cash flows is reflected in stock prices. The fact that payoffs may come far in the future does not prevent them from being appropriately reflected in *current* stock prices. Share prices are established by trading among investors, given current information and expectations. In an 'efficient' market, long-term projects are evaluated in the same way as short-term ones by the stock market.[14] There is no distinction between short-term and long-term maximization as all cash flows, appropriately discounted, are compounded into a single figure, net present value or the share price. It is fallacious, in such a setting, to argue that because managers act to maximize current share price they must be sacrificing long-run benefits. Evidently, a number of crucial links in the argument need to be established.

2.3 INFORMATIONAL PROBLEMS

Two things are missing from the traditional work-horse models of economics, which go to the heart of the horizon debate, namely a consideration of the informational and agency problems that exist between the capital market (investors) and the firm (managers). These stem from the fact that managers – by virtue of what they do – are bound to be better-informed than shareholders, both about the state of the firm and about their own actions and abilities; they can also be assumed to be self-interested in the pursuit of their own goals, which in general will not be aligned with those of investors.

2.3.1 Asymmetric information and horizons

The fact that managers are better-informed than shareholders has a key implication for the horizon debate. The rule 'maximize current share price' is unambiguously defined under symmetric information. When managers have better information than shareholders, however, the situation changes. Suppose that the manager is choosing between two projects, *A* and *B*, both of which will yield cash flows for several periods, and there is asymmetric information: the manager knows that *B* is better than *A* (at least in an expected sense) but, having poorer information, investors initially believe *A* to be superior to *B*. Suppose further that this informational asymmetry will disappear next period, for example, managers 'know' that investors will receive bad news about *A* next period and good news about *B*. The share price will be higher instantaneously when *A* is selected, reflecting investor beliefs, but will be higher next period if *B* happens to have been chosen. Managers now have a choice – to take the action that maximizes current share price or the one that maximizes the eventual share price. The informational asymmetry introduces a distinction not present in the symmetric information context.

This is a contrived example but it suggests a key point, namely that the horizon issue is closely related to the nature and extent of information asymmetries between the capital market and management. The problem is that share prices are determined based on the information held by investors, whereas the optimal decisions of the firm depend on the information held by managers. When these two coincide (symmetric information), maximizing current or short-term share prices is appropriate, but when they differ (asymmetric information) it may be neither appropriate nor meaningful.

The statement 'maximizing current share price' is, upon reflection, misleading. Managers do not 'maximize current share prices' – share prices are determined by trading in the stock market and, unless insider trading is allowed, managers do not participate in that trading. Share prices respond to managerial actions. The statement should be interpreted as meaning that managers take the actions that they believe will be evaluated most highly by the stock market. Putting the matter in this more accurate way makes it clear that the link between managerial decisions and stock prices depends critically on the information that those agents whose actions determine stock prices have about the actions that managers take. Only in the limiting and rather special case of symmetric information does it make sense to talk in shorthand terms of 'managers maximizing current share prices'.

How does the above relate to long-termism? The argument must be that long-term decisions are not reflected as well in stock prices as short-term ones (Shleifer and Vishny, 1990). To see the point starkly, suppose that long-term decisions were reflected in stock prices more efficiently than shorter-term ones. Then a concern with current stock prices would lead managers to have a long-term bias.

One argument would be that informational asymmetries are more acute when decisions relate to long-term investment decisions and that focusing on short-term stock prices induces a systematic bias against long-term projects. But why are current stock prices biased against incorporating long-term factors? One answer suggests itself: long-term payoffs have more uncertainty attached to them, hence the capital market may be biased against them. However, higher uncertainty attaching to more distant cash flows does not imply a capital market bias if it is assumed that well-diversified investors are risk-neutral. Perhaps the effect of uncertainty is to bias the capital market's estimate of the mean (as well as increase the variance). But this does not imply the existence of a *systematic* deviation in the valuation of long-term projects. Uncertainty could lead the market to overestimate just as much as underestimate the mean of future returns.

A different informational factor may be at play: it may not be so much that the capital market has difficulty in evaluating the likely outcome of long-term investments as that it finds it difficult to discern whether or not certain kinds of investments were taken at all. That is, many long-term decisions may be of an intangible kind: making investments in intangible organizational and human capital, for example. The information problem may relate to the input rather than the output side of investment.[15]

This interpretation is consistent with some key empirical evidence. Event studies show that stock prices tend to react positively to announcements regarding long-term investments such as increased research and development (R&D) expenditures, and this kind of evidence is used to refute the proposition that the US stock market is biased against long-term projects.[16] But the sample of long-run events considered in these studies is a biased one of events that readily come to the notice of the stock market. The real problem may be those long-term investments which are intangible and therefore harder for the stock market to evaluate and translate into adjustments to current stock prices.

The issue of take-overs and the market for corporate control plays a key role in the horizon debate. Traditionally, economists have thought of take-overs as a means by which the capital market could discipline management, that is, to minimize or suppress the agency costs that are liable to arise in a world of separation of ownership and control. More recent game-theoretic analyses have questioned the efficacy of take-overs, and suggest that the link between corporate governance and managerial incentives is more subtle and more complicated than economists have traditionally been prone to believe (Holmstrom and Tirole, 1989).

Take-over pressure is frequently held to be the most direct cause of short-termism. One argument is that the constant threat of take-over forces managers to be on their guard and diverts valuable managerial attention and effort into largely unproductive activities. A second argument draws on the earlier logic: takeovers 'force' managers to maximize short-term share prices but do so at the expense of projects that, in the longer term, would prove to be more valuable (but note that these projects need not be 'long-term' as such; the issue is the timing of information, not cash flows). A third argument focuses on takeovers as providing a means for shareholders to opportunistically renege on implicit contracts with managers and employees.[17] Of course, the latter is not an issue in traditional models in finance which, being complete contracting ones, leave no leeway for opportunistic surprises.

The earlier example provides an insight into this issue. A manager who acted in the interests of shareholders in that setting would refrain from the action that maximized short-term share price as this would not be in the long-run interests of shareholders. Would this be a feasible action for managers, however? If a competitive take-over market existed, managers might be 'forced' to take the action that maximized short-term share price, in that any failure to do so would lead to arbitrage in the market for corporate control, the arbitrage opportunity being the difference between the market's valuation of the manager's action and its (higher) valuation of the alternative. The result is that decisions would be made that were suboptimal from the viewpoint of shareholders. If managers are shielded from stock-market (and particularly take-over) pressures, however, it is not clear that this will necessarily lead them to focus on long-term projects, or the 'right' long-term projects. At the very least, a trade-off may be involved: insulation from take-over pressure allows more long-term projects to be implemented (a good effect) but also gives managers more leeway to pursue their own goals (a bad effect); they may choose more long-term projects but be more prone to choose bad ones.

The following simple example illustrates the point. Suppose there are four projects: P_1, P_2, P_3, and P_4, which under symmetric information would be ranked in that order by shareholders, and suppose that only the first three are worth undertaking. Assume that P_1 is a short-term project and the other three long-term, although the argument does not depend on this. Managers have the same ranking but, because of associated non-contractible private benefits (for example, utility from 'empire-building'), regard all projects as acceptable. With take-overs, there is 'short-termism': only P_1 and P_2 are chosen, and P_3 is not. The cost of having take-overs is that some good projects are passed over; the benefit is that bad projects are deterred. Suppose that some protection from take-overs is provided. Then managers may become more long-term orientated, choosing P_1, P_2, P_3 and P_4. The benefit of giving take-over protection is that more good projects are chosen; but the cost is that some bad projects are chosen too. Which scheme is better for shareholders depends on which is bigger, the profit from P_3 or the loss from P_4.

Notice that the information asymmetry analysis is not an analysis of horizon issues *per se*. It may be, for example, that the information managers have is that long-term projects are actually worse than investors believe. Current stock price maximization would have managers behaving more 'long-term' than they 'should'. On the other hand, it may be that the information advantage of managers is systematically related in some way to the horizon characteristics of different projects. For example, it is plausible that managers have systematically better information than outside investors about investments in intangible organization-specific assets, and that these investments are long-term in nature.

2.3.2 Information and Japanese corporate governance

The above discussion provides a framework for interpreting some of the arguments made about Japan. In general, the extent and nature of asymmetric information between the capital market and firms is a function of the systems of monitoring and corporate governance operating in the capital market. The Japanese system of monitoring and corporate governance is an 'insider-based' one, in contrast to the more decentralized arms-length Anglo-American system (Aoki, 1990; Aoki, Patrick, and Sheard, 1994; Horiuchi, 1989; Sheard, 1989, 1991a, 1994b).

Corporate governance in Japan, broadly speaking, is characterized by two features. One is the existence of close bank–firm ties through the so-called 'main bank system', the other a high level of intercorporate shareholdings based on so-called 'stable shareholding arrangements'. The two are closely related because main banks, as well as having the largest loan shares in client firms, play a central role in stable shareholding arrangements (Sheard, 1994b).

Economic theory suggests the existence of an interesting relationship between liquidity and information-gathering in the stock market (Coffee, 1991; Holmstrom and Tirole, 1993). When an investor has a small stockholding, it is likely to be a price-taker in the market and therefore enjoys the liquidity services of the capital market. The investor will trade on its information but, being small relative to the firm, is unlikely to have incentives to invest significant resources in monitoring the firm (and it could be argued that it would be undesirable for it to do so because of the market-wide duplication in monitoring costs that this would imply). On the other hand, an investor that holds a large block of stock forgoes liquidity but has both the means and incentive to expend resources gathering inside (publicly unavailable) information. In fact, there is an even closer relationship between liquidity and incentives for information gathering: the very fact that a large block-holder can be expected to be better informed than smaller investors creates a situation of (at least short-term) illiquidity. This follows from the fact that, if the market knows that the investor has inside information, attempts to sell a large portion of a holding will generally be interpreted as 'bad news' and will result in a large fall in price.

At the risk of oversimplification, the Japanese stock market can be characterized as having a dualistic kind of structure. The majority of a given firm's stock is held by a relatively small number of banks and firms that are usually in some form of ongoing business or transactional relationship with the firm; these stocks are not actively traded (although they may be sold under unusual circumstances, usually by cash-strapped firms to generate cash flow) (Sheard, 1991a, 1994b), and are at the core of the system of corporate governance.[18] The remainder, albeit usually a minority, of the firm's stocks is held by arms-length investors, including individuals, and is traded more actively. The latter stockholders play a limited and indirect role in corporate governance, as proxy battles and take-overs through the market are of negligible importance in Japan (Kester, 1991; Sheard, 1989, 1991a).

Some aggregate figures on stockholding can be cited in support of the above. About two-thirds of total listed stocks are held by financial institutions and non-financial corporations, while individuals (including owner figures) hold about a quarter (see Table 2.1). By normalizing stock trades with respect to size of stock holdings, it is possible to get a crude measure of the extent to which stock portfolios are traded (Table 2.1). Restricting attention to the 75 per cent of total stock trading carried out on customers' behalf, it is seen that investment trusts, securities companies, foreign investors, and domestic individuals are the most active traders (in that order), while financial institutions and non-financial corporations trade much less relative to their holdings.[19]

Most shareholders in a typical listed firm are individuals, and most have minuscule holdings in percentage terms (see Table 2.2), consistent with the notion of price-taking behaviour and well-diversified portfolios from economics and finance theory. However, a majority of the firm's shares is held in blocks of 1000 or more trading units (one unit usually equals 1000 shares), 1000 units being equivalent on average to half a percentage shareholding. Thus, while there is extensive diversification and liquidity among small holders, a relatively small number of investors, who generally are banks and transaction partners themselves interlocked with the firm, form a latent corporate control coalition. To see this starkly, the typical 'average' listed firm in 1992 had 12 941 shareholders, of whom 12 350 were individuals, 394 were non-financial corporations, and 59 were financial institutions, while 64 per cent of its shares were held by the twenty-one largest blockholders (Tōkyō Shōken Torihikisho Chōsabu, 1993, pp. 306–9).[20] The significance of these figures is that, as long as these twenty or so shareholders remain loyal, 'stable' shareholders, the potential for hostile take-over is virtually eliminated.

Although the market-orientated take-over mechanism is muted, as argued in the literature on the Japanese firm (Aoki, Patrick and Sheard, 1994; Sheard, 1989, 1994b), the main bank performs an analogous monitoring and control role, particularly in times of financial distress (Sheard, 1994c). Most large listed firms in Japan have an identifiable main bank relationship with a leading city or long-term credit bank (similar relations are often maintained with a small number of core main or 'sub-main' banks). In about two-thirds of cases a main bank was identified for the 507 listed firms in three major industrial sectors in 1991 using an operational definition based on the bank having the

TABLE 2.1 Share ownership and share trades of listed Japanese firms by type of shareholder, 1991

	Financial institutions	Investment trusts	Securities companies[a]	Non-financial corporations	Sub-total	Government bodies	Japanese individuals	Foreign corporations/ individuals	Total (millions)
Number of shareholders (%)	0.5	0.0	0.3	3.0	3.8	0.0	95.4	0.7	27.254
Number of shares owned (%) (A)	41.5	3.2	1.5	24.5	70.7	0.6	23.2	5.4	405 770.88
Number of shares sold (%) (B)	20.1	14.1	4.4	12.4	51.0	0.0	34.8	14.2	70 301.47
Number of shares bought (%) (C)	22.0	12.0	4.1	10.6	48.7	0.0	31.3	19.9	71 150.75
(B)/(A)	0.48	4.41	2.93	0.51	0.72	0.0	1.50	2.63	0.17
(C)/(A)	0.53	3.75	2.73	0.43	0.69	0.0	1.35	3.69	0.18

Note:
[a] Not including trading on securities' companies own account as stock exchange members.

Source: Tōkyō Shōken Torihikisho Chōsabu, 1993: Shōken tōkei nenpō [heisei 4nen] (Annual Securities Statistics, 1992).

TABLE 2.2 Distribution of listed firm share ownership by size of shareholdings, 1991

	Shares held in blocks of:							
	1–4	5–9	10–49	50–99	100–499	500–999	1000 or more trading units[a]	Total[b]
Number of shareholders (%)	82.2	9.2	7.2	0.6	0.6	0.1	0.2	27 254,407
Number of shares (%)	8.6	3.7	8.1	2.7	7.8	5.0	64.0	405 770,779

Notes:
[a] A trading unit is usually 1000 shares.
[b] Number of shareholders and number of trading units respectively.

Source: Tōkyō Shōken Torihikisho Chōsabu, 1993: *Shōken tōkei nenpō [heisei 4nen] (Annual Securities Statistics, 1992),* pp. 308–9.

largest loan shares and a prominent shareholding (see Table 2.3). The main bank usually has a shareholding of 3–5 per cent, but an interesting fact that emerges from the analysis in Table 2.3 is that in many cases there is also a dominant corporate shareholder: in 43 per cent of the cases where a main bank relationship was identified, the largest shareholder of the firm was a non-financial firm with a 10 per cent or more shareholding.

A key point is that the main bank is usually both a lender and shareholder, as is true in Japan for financial institutions more generally. Table 2.4 presents evidence of this by analyzing the shareholding rank that nineteen leading banks had to the firms in which they had the largest loan shares in 1992. The banks concerned had largest loan shares in 1622 firms, equivalent to 82 per cent of the listed firms in Japan.[21] In 7 per cent of all cases, the largest lending bank also occupied the top shareholding position, and in 74 per cent of cases the bank was one of the top five shareholders.

Two points are suggested by the above discussion that are germane to the asymmetric information issue. One relates to monitoring and the quality of information. First, because main banks, as large debt and equity holders, have the means and incentive to monitor management closely, the degree of information asymmetry may be less than in a well-diversified market setting (Coffee, 1991).[22] Jacobson and Aaker (1993) present some empirical evidence to this effect using comparative US–Japan data, as do Hoshi, Kashyap and Scharfstein (1990a, 1990b, 1991) using data for different kinds of Japanese firms. Also, because of the reduced informational gap, the managerial incentive problem (see section 2.4) may be correspondingly reduced.

Second, interlocking shareholdings provide insulation from hostile take-overs (with the main bank providing a kind of take-over function when the firm is in financial trouble), so the nexus between the share price and managerial decision-making is not as direct as supposed in the stock-market-centric view of capital allocation and corporate control. Arguments about short-termism of US managers focus on two things: the short-trading horizons of investors (who may not be holding the stock when its price eventually falls), and the high mobility of managers between firms (who may not be employed at the firm in the future to bear the consequences (costs) of current actions, or to reap the rewards). Both aspects can be contrasted with the Japanese case, where much of the stock (and other securities such as bank debt) is held more-or-less permanently under 'stable shareholding arrangements', and managers are permanent employees of firms.

TABLE 2.3 Numbers of firms for which main bank identified by type of largest shareholder for listed firms in selected industries, 1991[a]

Industry	Main bank identified: largest shareholder							Main bank not identified			Total
	Financial institution	Non-financial firm with: less than 10% share	less than 50% (10% or more)	50% or more	Family-related[b]	Other	Sub-total	No borrowings 1991	Other[c]	Sub-total	
Construction	34	16	38	7	20	2	118	14	14	28	145
Chemicals[d]	41	8	37	8	8	1	103	23	55	78	181
Machinery	30	11	47	6	12	5	111	25	45	70	181
Total	105	35	122	21	40	8	331	62	114	176	507
Percentage	(20.7)	(6.9)	(24.1)	(4.1)	(7.9)	(1.6)	(65.3)	(12.2)	(22.5)	(34.7)	(100.0)

Notes:
[a] Main bank identified if bank has largest loan share in 1991 and previous two years (or one of these years if it was number two lender to trust or long-term credit bank in other) and has largest shareholding among banks in 1991 (excluding trust banks unless main bank identified as trust bank).
[b] Cases where largest shareholder was individual or corporations clearly identifiable as associated with founder/founding family.
[c] Including cases where zero borrowings in 1989 and/or 1990.
[d] Including pharmaceuticals.

Source: Compiled from Tōyō Keizai Shinpōsha, 1991: *Kigyō keiretsu sōran 1992 nenban* (Directory of Corporate Affiliations, 1992 edn), Tōkyō, Tōyō Keizai Shinpōsha.

TABLE 2.4 Relationship between largest loan shares and rank as shareholder for leading Japanese banks, 1992

Name of bank	No. of firms in which bank has largest loan share	Breakdown of firms according to bank's rank as shareholder (percentages)					
		1	1–3	1–5	1–10	1–20	Not among top 20 shareholders
Dai-Ichi Kangyo	191	5.8	51.3	74.3	88.0	93.2	6.8
Sakura	189	7.4	39.2	71.4	88.4	91.5	8.5
Industrial Bank of Japan	189	8.2	45.6	68.4	84.8	93.0	7.0
Fuji	158	7.0	56.3	84.2	90.5	94.3	5.7
Mitsubishi	154	8.4	48.7	77.9	89.6	93.5	6.5
Sumitomo	148	4.1	41.2	74.3	87.2	89.2	10.8
Sanwa	136	8.1	51.5	75.0	90.4	94.1	5.9
Tokai	92	13.0	57.6	85.9	94.6	95.7	4.3
Asahi	61	3.3	42.6	78.7	93.4	96.7	3.3
Long-Term Credit Bank of Japan	53	9.4	34.0	54.7	81.1	94.3	5.7
Daiwa	52	11.5	51.9	73.1	86.5	90.4	9.6
Sumitomo Trust	38	2.6	65.8	78.9	86.8	94.7	5.3
Mitsui Trust	36	13.9	38.9	63.7	83.3	86.1	13.9
Mitsubishi Trust	27	11.1	48.1	77.8	92.6	92.6	7.4
Yokohama	27	7.4	66.7	88.9	100.0	100.0	0.0
Yasuda Trust	20	5.0	35.0	60.0	90.0	100.0	0.0
Hokkaido Takushoku	19	5.3	52.6	89.5	94.7	94.7	5.3
Nippon Credit	17	0.0	17.6	29.4	88.2	88.2	11.8
Tōkyō	15	0.0	26.7	60.0	60.0	80.0	20.0
Total/weighted average	1,622	7.4	47.5	74.4	88.5	93.0	7.0

Source: Compiled from Tōyō Keizai Shinpōsha, 1992: *Kigyō keiretsu sōran 1993 nenban* (Directory of Corporate Affiliations, 1993 edn), Tōkyō, Tōyō Keizai Shinpōsha.

2.4 MANAGERIAL INCENTIVE ISSUES

When managerial incentives are considered, the horizon issue becomes even more complicated. Principal-agent (agency) theory provides the basic paradigm for incentive issues. Principal-agent theory starts from the premise that managers are self-interested and respond to the incentives that they face, in the form of implicit or explicit compensation packages, concern for reputation, business ethics, and legal and social (including peer group) sanctions.

The principal-agent problem between investors and managers can be stated simply, as follows. Investors, who provide the funds for, in particular, the long-term productive fixed assets of the firm, are concerned about the long-term aspects of the firm; in particular, that the right decisions are made about what assets to put in place and that the assets are managed well to yield the maximum possible flow of profits. Investors can, of course, sell their claims on the firm – and convert their own relationship with the firm into an arbitrarily short one – but even if they do so their interests are long-term, because this is what determines what they take out or capitalize, as present value, when they sell their claims.[23] Investors thus want to give managers incentives to have the same long-term interest in the firm.

There are two solutions to the problem of aligning managers' incentives with those of investors. One is to tie managerial compensation to the share price of the firm; that is, loosely speaking, to encourage managers to care about the same thing that shareholders do. As long as share prices capitalize future profits, managers will tend to make the right decisions from the viewpoint of shareholders. Another, the Japanese solution, is to give managers a long-term employment contract, thereby inducing the manager to be concerned about the future prospects of the firm. This can be viewed as an alternative method of (imperfectly) aligning manager and investor interests.

There are trade-offs between the two systems. One concerns risk. Linking compensation to share prices imposes considerable risks on managers, who, being individuals, can be assumed to be risk-averse; consequently shareholders, in order to meet participation constraints, will have to pay managers higher average compensation than would be the case if they bore more of the risk themselves.[24] In the latter system, managers are largely shielded from short-term risks associated with stock price fluctuations, but two kinds of long-term risk exist: given the lock-in effect, there is a danger of opportunistic reneging on long-term contracts by shareholders (if, as is plausibly the case, the contracts are incomplete state-contingent ones);[25] there is also risk attached to the firm-specific human capital: conditional on the firm remaining viable, shareholders may insure this risk but, if the firm fails prematurely, owners of human capital may suffer unanticipated losses.[26] In the former system, long-term risk may be lower, given that the external managerial labour market serves a kind of insurance function. A manager's long-term income prospects are not tied to the fate of any particular firm, and potential opportunism from the capital market is not such a problem because of the manager's (credible) threat to move to another firm.

A second trade-off concerns flexibility in the use of, and the nature of investments in, human capital. With short-term employment contracts and share-price-linked managerial compensation, managerial human capital can be deployed rather flexibly between firms via the managerial labour market; with long-term managerial employment, firms are to a greater extent 'stuck' with the executives they initially hired.[27] On the other hand, with long-term employment there is greater scope and incentive to accumulate firm (team)-specific human capital, which may be advantageous to the firm as a bundle of specific resources competing in, and against, markets.[28]

A third issue concerns trade-offs in the kinds of managerial moral hazards that the different schemes induce. If managerial rewards are linked to stock prices, managers may reallocate effort and resources away from activities that would be in the long-term interests of the firm and its shareholders and towards activities that inflate current earnings and presumably therefore stock prices also (Stein, 1988, 1989; Bresnahan, Milgrom and Paul, 1990). This seems to be the crux of much of the concern about supposed US short-termism. Since shareholders only observe increased current earnings, but not the underlying source, they may be led to mistake these for a real improvement rather than a cosmetic one, or one that has to be paid for in the future. Thus maximizing current share prices can be problematic for two reasons: (i) differences in the information that investors and managers have; and (ii) the fact that managers may be able to manipulate the current share price strategically for their own ends. Moreover, the two interact as the informational asymmetry between shareholders and managers is partly a function of managers' own actions, including strategic ones.[29] The Japanese system in effect breaks the nexus between stock prices and managerial rewards, at least in the short run. However, the system may induce different forms of moral hazard, for example, managerial slack, over-investment, and aversion to certain kinds of risk-taking.

Recent developments in the literature have fc
a corporate security has two aspects: an income
or decision aspect (Grossman and Hart, 1988). T.
both a market for trading income claims and an arena
rights are traded. Attention has focused on the possi,
may be trade-offs between the two functions (Black, 19%
Milgrom and Paul, 1990; Coffee, 1991; Sheard, 1991a,
suggestion is that the liquidity that the stock market prov
which is valued by investors – may exacerbate the principal-a
lem. If investors trade on changes in information – and in the
is how the necessary impounding of information into stock pric
the market to be efficient occurs – managers may have incentive
produce such short-run information. In such a world, shareholders n.
be able to benefit from credibly committing not to use certain infoi
mation or not to intervene (with 'voice'), or facilitate someone else's
intervention ('exit') (Hirschman, 1970). The system of 'stable
shareholding' arrangements in Japan can be interpreted in this way:
commitment is achieved at the cost of reduced liquidity (Sheard, 1994b).
Whether, and in what way, this commitment translates into a long-term
orientation – and whether this comes at some other cost – needs to be
more carefully studied.

2.5 CONCLUSION

Few propositions about the Japanese economic system appear to have
attracted such widespread acceptance as the idea that Japanese business is long-term orientated. This is surprising given that rigorous
empirical evidence has yet to be presented and given the conceptual
ambiguities and puzzles that surround the notion. Few proponents of
the long-termism view spell out what they mean by this in precise
conceptual terms. This chapter has attempted to clarify the conceptual
basis of the long-termism notion in order to provide a sounder foundation on which to assess the conventional wisdom.

Although attracting widespread acceptance, few of the arguments in
the horizon debate are as self-explanatory as to warrant acceptance at
face value. One problem is that many of the arguments are hard to
understand, or appear fallacious, when judged in terms of the standard
analytical frameworks traditionally employed in economics. This does
not deny the relevance of the notion; rather it has challenged economics
to rethink its own frameworks for thinking about firms and how capital

kets work. In order to talk meaningfully about managerial and investor horizons it is necessary to explicitly take account of the informational asymmetries and agency problems that exist between the capital market and the firm, and the interactions that exist between the valuation mechanisms and the corporate governance mechanisms of the capital market.

The Japanese system of corporate governance incorporates distinctive mechanisms for dealing with the information and agency problems associated with the separation of ownership and control that attends modern business enterprise. Rather than rely on indirect information signalling mechanisms in a diversified liquid market, the Japanese system relies more on direct (and sometimes quite dense) information flows among a smaller set of large blockholders. Rather than rely on trading of control rights in an open market and high managerial mobility as a way of allocating the rights to manage and provide high-powered managerial incentives – the 'market for corporate control' – the Japanese system severs the direct nexus between share prices and managerial compensation and tenure, and relies on direct intervention by existing large blockholders, or 'voice' in Hirschman's (1970) terms, to control managerial failures.

Does the Japanese system give Japanese business a competitive edge by avoiding the short-termism that many believe plagues US business? This chapter has presented some ideas on what the differences in capital allocation and corporate governance might imply for managerial horizons, but to view these differences as translating directly and automatically into a sharp difference in horizons is probably too simplistic. The analysis presented here should be taken as recommending the importance of further serious study of comparative corporate governance and its implications for corporate and national competitiveness, rather than as suggesting that we have answers to the important and complex issues that such a study raises.

NOTES

1. See also Dore (1986, p. 71): 'the fact that the shareholders are dominated by corporate owners more interested in long-term growth and the stability of their trading partners and customers than in dividend revenue, is very much to reduce the pressure from shareholders on corporate managers ... This very much reduces the importance of short-term profits among corporate objectives and permits the development of a managerial culture which makes market shares rather than profits the

index'; and Montgomery (1991, p. 79): 'One of the notable aspects of Japanese corporations is their willingness to take a very long-term view. Freed from the tyranny of accountants by the nature of their financial structure, they are able to pursue strategies which have a long time frame.'

2. See, for example, Black (1992, pp. 862–5), Coffee (1991, pp. 1324–5), Dertouzos *et al.* (1989, ch. 4), Edwards (1992), Gilson and Roe (1993), *New York Times* (1992); and, for a comparison with the United Kingdom, Dore (1987, ch. 6).

3. See, for example, Abegglen and Stalk (1985), Hoshi, Kashyap and Scharfstein (1990a, 1990b, 1991); and, for theoretical analyses, Dewatripont and Maskin (1990), and von Thadden (1990).

4. Writings in this vein include Friedman and Lebard (1991, ch. 14), Morita (1992), and Nakatani (1992).

5. Almost all the quantitative evidence that bears on the issue is for the US and here there is little evidence that supports the notion of US short-termism. See Edwards (1992), Froot, Perold and Stein (1994), Hall (1990), and Jensen (1988, pp. 25–7). For Japan, direct tests are lacking; studies by Kaplan (1994), Kaplan and Minton (1994), and Morck and Nakamura (1992) are consistent with the view that corporate governance in Japan, while operating through different mechanisms, produces similar outcomes as in the U.S., a point also made by Sheard (1989, p. 409).

6. For a discussion of the issues, see Hall (1990, 1994).

7. See, for example, Levin (1990, p. 131).

8. See, for example, Abegglen and Stalk (1985, p. 177), and Milgrom and Roberts (1992, p. 41).

9. See, for example, Dertouzos *et al.* (1989, pp. 248–61), Hatsopoulos *et al.* (1988), Nakatani (1991), Prestowitz (1988, pp. 167–71).

10. Notable cases include the trading company Itoman, the auto parts supplier Ikeda Bussan, the construction company Tobishima Construction, and housing finance companies. Ikeda Bussan had unrealized stock holding losses of 31.2 US billion yen as of March 1992 (Nihon Keizai Shimbun, 1 October 1992, p. 15). See Sheard (1991b, 1992, 1994c) for details of Itoman, Tobishima and other financially distressed firms.

11. Recent analyses include Bresnahan, Milgrom and Paul (1990), Froot, Perold and Stein (1994), Mello-e-Souza (1993), Shleifer and Vishny (1990), Stein (1988, 1989), and Thakor (1990).

12. For an interesting attempt in this direction focusing on the growth orientation of Japanese firms, see Aoki (1988, ch. 5; 1992).

13. Because of the prevalence of interlocking shareholdings, trade credit, and stable deposits with transaction banks, Japanese firms do have relatively high levels of short-term assets in their balance sheets.

14. See also Froot, Perold and Stein (1994) on this point.

15. There are three elements of asymmetric information between investors and managers, relating to: the information upon which managers base their decisions; the actions that managers take; and the (actual or expected) outcome of projects. All these 'interfere' with the current pricing of the firm's projects. The first also poses a particular problem in the reverse direction. If managers do not know what information and expectations investors have – and, in general, how would they? – then

how will they be able to compute (or have rational expectations about) the equilibrium stock price that will result from any given action?

16. See, for example, Jensen (1988, pp. 26–7).

17. For an exposition of this argument, see Ramseyer (1987), Shleifer and Summers (1988), Sheard (1991a, 1994b).

18. In response to a 1993 survey by Fuji Research Institute, 84 per cent of publicly traded corporations reported that 50 per cent or more of their shares were held by stable shareholders; 36.2 per cent of respondents identified the prevention of hostile mergers and acquisitions as the most important benefit of interlocking shareholdings, while 67.8 per cent listed it as a benefit; 90.9 per cent of listed firm respondents stated that in the event that they sold an interlocked shareholding they would seek prior approval from the firm, with a further 7.4 per cent stating that they would give prior notice (Fuji Sogo Kenkyujo, 1993, pp. 98, 106, 127).

19. In 1991, 25 per cent of stock trading volume on the three major exchanges in Japan was by member securities companies on their own account. For more details, see Takagi (1993).

20. Of the remainder, 93 were foreign investors, 39 were securities companies, 5 were investment trusts, and 1 was a government agency.

21. This proportion is slightly inflated due to the existence of a small number of loan share ties.

22. The fact that the main bank becomes well informed, in one sense, just pushes back the asymmetric information problem one stage. However, the structure of lending/shareholding relations and main bank incentives in Japan appears to be such that other major lenders can either become well informed or rest assured that the main bank will not exploit any monopolistic informational advantage that it has at their (undue) expense. See Aoki (1988, pp. 148–9; 1990), Sheard (1994a, 1994c).

23. This point highlights the fallacy in the notion that short-term trading necessarily comes at the expense of long-term value creation.

24. This may partly explain the pattern of US and Japanese managerial compensation: the higher salaries that US managers earn may be compensating them for the higher risks associated with stock-price contingent pay, while the lower salaries of Japanese executives may partly reflect the fact that their pay is not usually tied directly to stock price movements.

25. With short-term contracts there is less firm-specific investment, less lock-in, and less risk of hold-up, but because of share-price-linked compensation there is more short-term income risk.

26. This can also be seen, at one level, as a problem of shareholder opportunism. Shareholders may find it difficult, short of putting the necessary funds in escrow, to commit credibly to compensating employees for human capital investment losses when a firm is being liquidated.

27. This presumably also helps to explain the apparently more rigorous selection procedures of graduate recruits that large Japanese firms engage in. The cost to the firm of making a hiring mistake are larger.

28. One way to distinguish a 'firm' from a 'market' is by the degree of specificity of the assets involved.

29. Of course, it is also partly a function of shareholder actions such as monitoring.

REFERENCES

Abegglen, James C. and George Stalk, Jr 1985. Kaisha, *the Japanese Corporation*, Tōkyō: Charles E. Tuttle.

Aoki, Masahiko 1988. *Information, Incentives, and Bargaining in the Japanese Economy*, Cambridge: Cambridge University Press.

Aoki, Masahiko 1990. 'Towards an Economic Model of the Japanese Firm', *Journal of Economic Literature*, 28, pp. 1–27.

Aoki, Masahiko 1992. 'A Bargaining Game Theoretic Approach to the Japanese Firm', in Paul Sheard (ed.), *International Adjustment and the Japanese Firm*, Sydney: Allen & Unwin; pp. 30–49.

Aoki, Masahiko 1994. 'The Contingent Governance of Team Production: An Analysis of Systematic Effects', *International Economic Review*.

Aoki, Masahiko, Hugh Patrick and Paul Sheard 1994. 'The Japanese Main Bank System: An Introductory Overview', in Masahiko Aoki and Hugh Patrick (eds), *The Japanese Main Bank System: Its Relevancy for Developing and Transforming Economies*, New York: Oxford University Press.

Bardhan, Pranab and John E. Roemer 1992. 'Market Socialism: A Case for Rejuvenation', *Journal of Economic Perspectives*, 6, pp. 101–16.

Black, Bernard S. 1992. 'Agents Watching Agents: The Promise of Institutional Investor Voice', *UCLA Law Review*, 39, pp. 811–93.

Bresnahan, Timothy, Paul Milgrom and Jonathan Paul 1990. *The Real Output of the Stock Exchange*, CEPR Publication No. 215, Stanford, California: Center for Economic Policy Research, Stanford University.

Coffee, John C. Jr 1991. 'Liquidity Versus Control: The Institutional Investor as Corporate Monitor', *Columbia Law Review*, 91, pp. 1277–368.

Dertouzos, Michael L., Richard K. Lester, Robert M. Solow and the MIT Commission on Industrial Productivity 1989. *Made in America: Regaining the Productive Edge*, Cambridge, Mass.: MIT Press.

Dewatripont, M. and E. Maskin 1990. 'Credit and Efficiency in Centralized and Decentralized Economies', Discussion Paper No. 1512, Cambridge, Mass.: Harvard Institute of Economic Research.

Dore, Ronald 1986. *Flexible Rigidities: Industrial Policy and Structural Adjustment in the Japanese Economy 1970–80*, Stanford, California: Stanford University Press.

Dore, Ronald 1987. *Taking Japan Seriously: A Confucian Perspective on Leading Economic Issues*, London: Athlone Press.

Edwards, Franklin R. 1992. 'Managerial Myopia in America: Let Shareholders Make America Competitive', mimeo, New York: Columbia University Press.

Frankel, Jeffrey 1991. 'Japanese Finance in the 1980s: A Survey', in Paul Krugman (ed.), *Trade with Japan: Has the Door Opened Wider?*, Chicago: University of Chicago Press; pp. 225–68.

Friedman, George and Meredith Lebard 1991. *The Coming War with Japan*, New York: St Martin's Press.

Froot, Kenneth A., Andre F. Perold and Jeremy C. Stein 1994. 'Shareholder Trading Practices and Corporate Investment Horizons', in Michael E. Porter (ed.), *Capital Choices*, Boston, Mass.: Harvard Business School Press.

Fuji Sogo Kenkyujo 1993. *Mein Banku Shisutemu Oyobi Kabushiki Mochiai ni Tsuite no Chosa Hokokusho* (Investigative Report on the Main Bank System and Interlocking Shareholdings), Tōkyō: Fuji Research Institute Corporation.

Gilson, Ronald J. and Mark J. Roe 1993. 'Understanding the Japanese Keiretsu: Overlaps between Corporate Governance and Industrial Organization', *Yale Law Journal*, vol. 102, no. 4, pp. 871–906.

Grossman, Sanford J. and Oliver D. Hart 1988. 'One Share–One Vote and the Market for Corporate Control', *Journal of Financial Economics*, 20, pp. 175–202.

Hall, Bronwyn H. 1990. 'The Impact of Corporate Restructuring on Industrial Research and Development', *Brookings Papers on Economic Activity*, 1, pp. 85–135.

Hall, Bronwyn H. 1994. 'Corporate Restructuring and Investment Horizons', in Michael E. Porter (ed.), *Capital Choices*, Boston, Mass.: Harvard Business School Press.

Hatsopoulos, George N., Paul R. Krugman and Lawrence H. Summers 1988. 'U.S. Competitiveness: Beyond the Trade Deficit', *Science*, 241, pp. 299–307.

Hirschman, Albert O. 1970. *Exit, Voice, and Loyalty*, Cambridge, Mass.: Harvard University Press.

Hodder, James E. 1986. 'Evaluation of Manufacturing Investments: A Comparison of U.S. and Japanese Practices', *Financial Management*, Spring, pp. 17–24.

Hodder, James E. 1991. 'Is the Cost of Capital Lower in Japan?', *Journal of the Japanese and International Economies*, 5, pp. 86–100.

Holmstrom, Bengt and Jean Tirole 1989. 'Theory of the Firm', in Richard Schmalensee and Robert D. Willig (eds), *Handbook of Industrial Organization, Vol. I*, Amsterdam: North-Holland, pp. 61–133.

Holmstrom, Bengt and Jean Tirole 1993. 'Market Liquidity and Performance Monitoring', *Journal of Political Economy*, vol. 101, no. 4, pp. 678–709.

Horiuchi, Akiyoshi 1989. 'Informational Properties of the Japanese Financial System', *Japan and the World Economy*, 1, pp. 255–78.

Hoshi, Takeo, Anil Kashyap and David Scharftstein 1990a. 'Bank Monitoring and Investment: Evidence from the Changing Structure of Japanese Corporate Banking Relationships', in R. Glenn Hubbard (ed.), *Asymmetric Information, Corporate Finance, and Investment*, Chicago: University of Chicago Press, pp. 105–26.

Hoshi, Takeo, Anil Kashyap and David Scharfstein 1990b. 'The Role of Banks in Reducing the Costs of Financial Distress in Japan', *Journal of Financial Economics*, vol. 27, no. 1, pp. 67–88.

Hoshi, Takeo, Anil Kashyap and David Scharfstein 1991. 'Corporate Structure, Liquidity, and Investment: Evidence from Japanese Industrial Groups', *Quarterly Journal of Economics*, 106, pp. 33–60.

Jacobson, Robert and David Aaker 1993. 'Myopic Management Behavior with Efficient, but Imperfect, Financial Markets: A Comparison of Information Asymmetries in the U.S. and Japan', *Journal of Accounting and Economics*, 16, pp. 383–405.

Jensen, Michael C. 1988. 'Takeovers: Their Causes and Consequences', *Journal of Economic Perspectives*, 2, pp. 21–48.

Kaplan, Steven N. 1994. 'Top Executive Rewards and Firm Performance: A

Comparison of Japan and the U.S.', *Journal of Political Economy*.

Kaplan, Steven N. and Bernadette Minton A. 1994. 'Appointments of Outsiders to Japanese Boards: Determinants and Implications for Managers', *Journal of Financial Economics*.

Kester, W. Carl 1991. *Japanese Takeovers: The Global Contest for Corporate Control*, Boston, Mass.: Harvard Business School Press.

Levin, Richard C. 1990. Comment on Hall's Paper, *Brookings Papers on Economic Activity*, 1, pp. 129–32.

Malkiel, Burton G. 1994. 'The Influence of Conditions in Financial Markets on the Time Horizons of Business Managers: An International Comparison', in Michael E. Porter (ed.), *Capital Choices*, Boston, Mass.: Harvard Business School Press.

Matsumoto, Koji 1991. *The Rise of the Japanese Corporate System: The Inside View of a MITI Official*, London: Kegan Paul International.

Mello-e-Souza, Carlos A. 1993. 'Mortal Managers and Long-term Goals: An Impossibility Result', *RAND Journal of Economics*, vol. 24, no. 3, pp. 313–27.

Milgrom, Paul and John Roberts 1992. *Economics, Organization and Management*, Englewood Cliffs, N.J.: Prentice Hall.

Montgomery, David B. 1991. 'Understanding the Japanese as Customers, Competitors, and Collaborators', *Japan and the World Economy*, 3, pp. 61–91.

Morck, Randall and Masao Nakamura 1992. 'Banks and Corporate Control in Japan', mimeo, University of Alberta.

Morita, Akio 1992. '"Nihongata Keiei" ga Abunai' ['Japanese-style Management' in Danger], *Bungei Shunju*, February, pp. 94–103.

Nakatani, Iwao 1991. 'The Nature of "Imbalance" between the US and Japan', in *Proceedings of Seventh Biennial Conference of Japanese Studies Association of Australia: Vol. 1, Japan and the World*, Canberra: Australia–Japan Research Centre, pp. 1–7.

Nakatani, Iwao 1992. 'Reforming Japanese Capitalism', *Journal of Japanese Trade and Industry*, 4, pp. 15–17.

New York Times 1992. 'Fixing Corporate America's Short-term Mind-set', 2 September, pp. C1, C5.

Okimoto, Daniel I. 1987. 'Outsider Trading: Coping with Japanese Industrial Organization', in Kenneth B. Pyle (ed.) *The Trade Crisis: How Will Japan Respond?*, Seattle, Wash.: Society for Japanese Studies, pp. 85–116.

Porter, Michael E. 1992. 'Capital Disadvantage: America's Failing Capital Investment System', *Harvard Business Review*, vol. 70, no. 5, pp. 65–82.

Porter, Michael E. 1994. *Capital Choices*, Boston, Mass.: Harvard Business School Press.

Prestowitz, Clyde V. Jr 1988. *Trading Places: How We Allowed Japan to Take the Lead*, New York: Basic Books.

Ramseyer, J. Mark 1987. 'Takeovers in Japan: Opportunism, Ideology and Corporate Control', *UCLA Law Review*, 35, pp. 1–64.

Sheard, Paul 1989. 'The Main Bank System and Corporate Monitoring and Control in Japan', *Journal of Economic Behavior and Organization*, 11, pp. 399–422.

Sheard, Paul 1991a. 'The Economics of Interlocking Shareholding in Japan', *Ricerche Economiche*, 45, pp. 421–48.

Sheard, Paul 1991b. 'Delegated Monitoring among Delegated Monitors: Principal-agent Aspects of the Japanese Main Bank System', CEPR Policy Paper no. 274, Stanford, California: Center for Economic Policy Research, Stanford University.

Sheard, Paul 1992. 'The Role of the Main Bank when Borrowing Firms are in Financial Distress', CEPR Policy Paper no. 330, Stanford, California: Center for Economic Policy Research, Stanford University.

Sheard, Paul 1994a. 'Reciprocal Delegated Monitoring in the Japanese Main Bank System', *Journal of the Japanese and International Economies*, vol. 8, no. 1, pp. 1–21.

Sheard, Paul 1994b. 'Interlocking Shareholdings and Corporate Governance', in Masahiko Aoki and Ronald Dore (eds), *The Japanese Firm: The Sources of Competitive Strength*, New York: Oxford University Press, pp. 310–419.

Sheard, Paul 1994c. 'Main Banks and the Governance of Financial Distress', in Masahiko Aoki and Hugh Patrick (eds), *The Japanese Main Bank System: Its Relevancy for Developing and Transforming Economies*, New York: Oxford University Press.

Shleifer, Andrei and Lawrence H. Summers 1988. 'Breach of Trust in Hostile Takeovers', in Alan J. Auerbach (ed.), *Corporate Takeovers: Causes and Consequences*, Chicago: University of Chicago Press, pp. 33–56.

Shleifer, Andrei and Robert W. Vishny 1990. 'Equilibrium Short Horizons of Investors and Firms', *American Economic Review*, 80, pp. 148–53.

Stein, Jeremy 1988. 'Takeover Threats and Managerial Myopia', *Journal of Political Economy*, 96, pp. 61–80.

Stein, Jeremy 1989. 'Efficient Capital Markets, Inefficient Firms: A Model of Myopic Corporate Behavior', *Quarterly Journal of Economics*, 104, pp. 655–69.

Takagi, Shinji 1993. 'The Organization and Microstructure of the Secondary Stock Market in Japan', in Shinji Takagi (ed.), *Japanese Capital Markets*, Oxford: Basil Blackwell, pp. 302–39.

Thakor, Anjan V. 1990. 'Investment "Myopia" and the Internal Organization of Capital Allocation Decisions', *Journal of Law, Economics, and Organization*, 6, pp. 129–54.

Tōkyō Shōken Torihikisho Chōsabu 1993. *Shōken Tōkei Nenpō [Heisei 4nen]* (Annual Securities Statistics, 1992), Tōkyō: Tōkyō Stock Exchange.

Tōyō Keizai Shinpōsha 1991. *Kigyō Keiretsu Sōran 1992 Nenban* (Directory of Corporate Affiliations, 1992 edn), Tōkyō: Tōyō Keizai Shinpōsha.

Tōyō Keizai Shinpōsha 1991. *Kigyō Keiretsu Sōran 1993 Nenban* (Directory of Corporate Affiliations, 1993 edn), Tōkyō: Tōyō Keizai Shinpōsha.

von Thadden, E.-L. 1990. 'Bank Finance and Long Term Investment', WWZ Discussion Paper 9010, Switzerland: University of Basle.

3 Financial Structure and Managerial Discretion in the Japanese Firm: An Implication of the Surge of Equity-related Bonds

Akiyoshi Horiuchi*

3.1 INTRODUCTION

The mechanisms of corporate governance in Japan are widely believed to be different from Anglo-American mechanisms. Specifically, it is unanimously agreed that the mechanisms of the open capital market to discipline corporate managers, or the contest for corporate control such as the tender-offer, proxy fights, and hostile take-overs have not worked significantly in Japan. In Japan, mutual shareholding, the main bank and other big institutional investors known as 'stabilizing shareholders', and the intimate relationships between managers and employees, are thought to have prevented effectively the open capital market from exerting influence on behaviour of incumbent managers.[1]

However, we have not yet reached a unanimous conclusion regarding the consequences of the Japanese style of corporate governance on the efficiency of corporate management. Some people claim that in place of the Anglo-American mechanisms of disciplining managers, the 'internal capital market' has worked efficiently in the Japanese financial system. Through the 'internal capital market' based on the

* This is a revised version of a paper presented at the Second Conference on the Contemporary Japanese Economy organised by the Centre for Japanese Economic Studies, Macquarie University, Sydney, 19–20 August 1993. The author wishes to thank Thomas Cargill, David Lynch, Mitsuaki Okabe, Marc Ryser, Wataru Takahashi and Hiroshi Yoshikawa for their helpful comments. Quing-yuan Sui provided able research assitance in statistical investigations.

long-term relationship with major banks, companies raised a large amount of funds in the form of loans from the banking sector by face-to-face negotiation. At the same time, the internal capital market has been effective in preventing managers' opportunism and disciplining them to pursue 'efficient' management from the viewpoint of standard economic theory. More specifically, both their long-term relationship with the client firms and their status as major shareholders in firms help the banks to monitor managerial behaviour of firms efficiently and discipline them appropriately when their behaviour is inconsistent with producing profits for shareholders.[2]

Thus, according to this argument, in spite of the absence of competition for managerial control in the open capital market, incumbent managers of Japanese corporations cannot pursue managerial objectives which differ from the maximizing of profits for shareholders. At the same time, the immunity from the pressure of external capital markets gives both managers and employees incentives to accumulate capital specific to the firm, thereby promoting the long-term productivity of the corporation.[3]

On the other hand, some people doubt whether the mechanisms of the internal capital markets are actually pursued in the sense of maximizing the profits of shareholders. According to them, the most important players in the internal capital market are incumbent managers who are not interested in profit-maximization but rather in, for example, expanding the firm's market share, undertaking diversified business not related to their major businesses to preserve job opportunities for employees and so on, at the expense of profits for shareholders. These operations may seem to be a form of 'perks' (perquisites) to shareholders, as pointed out by Jensen and Meckling (1976).

These 'perks' of incumbent managers would decrease the market share prices, thereby intensifying the threat of the hostile take-overs. But mutual shareholding prevents this mechanism from working. Thus managers can extend and preserve their discretionary power under the regime of mutual shareholding between corporations, because they mutually refrain from interfering with the discretionary power of their partners. They utilize their discretionary power to pursue objectives not necessarily consistent with the efficiency criterion of standard economic theory. This argument may lead to the conclusion that Japanese corporations have been successful because the structure of corporate governance makes it possible for managers to pursue the policy of expanding their market shares without honouring shareholders' interests.[4]

These two conflicting views are concerned with the efficiency of the 'internal capital market' in monitoring and disciplining corporate management in Japan. At issue is whether the internal capital market, based on mutual shareholdings or main bank relationships, helps the discretion of incumbent managers to deviate from the objective of maximizing the profits of shareholders. The purpose of this chapter is to investigate this issue statistically.

Before proceeding to the empirical analysis, however, we must be clear about how to measure the degree of deviation of corporate management from the maximization of profits for shareholders. Generally speaking, it is difficult to measure this accurately. In this chapter, we pay attention to the fact that Japanese firms have actively issued so-called equity-related bonds since the mid-1980s. From the viewpoint of the standard theory of corporate finance, it is difficult to understand why they were so active in issuing these bonds, although many business people claimed that the bonds could be issued at very 'low costs'. This chapter proposes the hypothesis that the issuing of equity-related bonds represents the managerial behaviour of seeking 'free cash flow', which is likely to encourage deviation of managers from pursuing the objective of maximizing shareholders' profits.[5] Based on this hypothesis, this chapter examines the relationship between issuing equity-related bonds and some characteristics of the internal capital market of individual firms.[6]

The chapter is laid out as follows: Section 3.2 describes the surge of issuing equity-related bonds during the 1980s based on a simple model of corporate financing. It is emphasized that the neo-classical finance theory, which assumes that corporate managers simply represent the interests of shareholders, cannot explain this surge. In Section 3.2, a tentative assumption is proposed that issuing equity-related bonds indicates the strong discretionary power of incumbent managers. Section 3.3 provides some propositions concerning the relationship between issuing equity-related bonds and the financial background of individual firms, based on the tentative assumption explained in Section 3.2. In Section 3.4, we describe a sample of companies and examine statistically the propositions concerning the bond-issuing behaviour and financial background of individual firms. Section 3.5 gives a summary and the concluding remarks of the investigations of the chapter.

3.2   THE ISSUE OF EQUITY-RELATED BONDS BY JAPANESE FIRMS

During the latter half of the 1980s, a number of Japanese corporations reduced their borrowing from banks and actively issued 'equity-related bonds', that is, both convertible and warrant bonds. Figure 3.1 shows that the firms' reliance on borrowing decreased, and instead the relative importance of equity and bond financing increased. According to Figure 3.2, the majority of corporate bonds consisted of convertible and warrant bonds. In this section, we inquire into why Japanese firms issued equity-related bonds so actively during this period, and propose a hypothesis to answer this question.

First we examine the puzzle of equity-related bonds. Japan experienced sharp increases in stock prices during this period. Many business people explain that the increase in issuing of equity-related bonds was based on the optimistic expectations that the stock prices would continue to rise in the future. According to them, the optimistic expectation substantially lowered the cost of issuing equity-related bonds compared with, for example, borrowing at the long-term prime rate. It was a favourite story among Japanese businessmen that they could enjoy very low levels of coupon rates around the mid-1980s (below 1 per cent) by issuing Swiss Franc convertible bonds.

From the viewpoint of the shareholders, however, it was not obvious that the equity-related bonds were issued at low cost. The equity-related bond is a contract according to which, if the stock price rises in the future, valuable shares will be distributed to the bond holders at low prices. Because of this contract, the company can issue the bonds at a low interest rate, thereby increasing the amount of current cash-flow. Obviously, this financial contract in itself does not imply any benefit to present shareholders, and they therefore have no particular incentive to encourage managers to issue equity-related bonds.

Some observers argue that during the late 1980s corporate managers, shareholders and other investors commonly had over-optimistic expectations that stock prices would continue to go up, and this does seem to be true. The full-scale 'easy-money' policy adopted by the Bank of Japan with a view to reducing a huge surplus of current accounts also stimulated this optimism. It is certain that the atmosphere during the latter half of the 1980s encouraged Japanese firms to raise large amounts of funds and to expand their investments, but this cannot explain why many Japanese firms were particularly active in issuing equity-related bonds: the surge in these still remains a puzzle.[7]

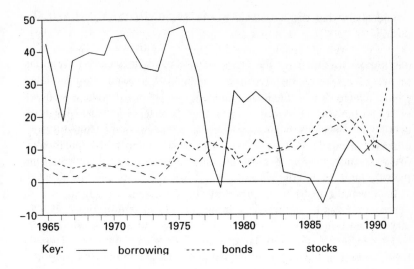

FIGURE 3.1　Composition of fund-raising by major companies,
fiscal years 1965–91 (percentages)

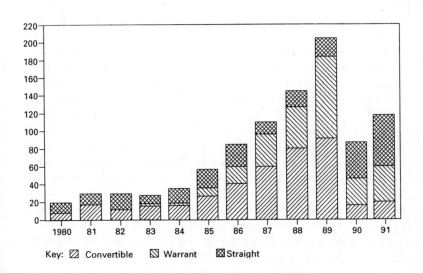

FIGURE 3.2　Corporate bonds issued by Japanese firms,
fiscal years 1980–91 (¥100billions)

The claim that equity-related bonds could be issued at 'low cost' during the 1980s is a nonsense from the viewpoint of the standard theory of corporate finance, based on the assumption that corporations are totally governed by the shareholders. According to the standard theory of corporate finance, it is reasonable for companies to issue equity-related bonds when debt-holders are seriously concerned with the opportunistic behaviour of incumbent managers at the expense of debt-holders' benefits under asymmetric information. In the United States, convertible bonds tend to be issued by smaller and more speculative firms, because they face more difficulties of asymmetric information than do large-scale companies.[8]

In Japan, the restrictive 'eligibility rules' on bond-issuing have prevented small and medium-sized companies from issuing not only equity-related bonds but other types of bond also. In other words, only a small number of relatively large firms could gain access to corporate bond markets in Japan. Therefore, the above reasoning of issuing equity-related bonds does not seem to be applicable to the Japanese case.

One possible reason for the issue of equity-related bonds may be suggested. As was discussed above, the standard theory cannot explain why so many Japanese firms rushed to issue equity-related bonds during the latter half of the 1980s. If we accept the presumption that incumbent managers actually control corporations, and that they could pursue objectives inconsistent with shareholders' profits at their discretion, however, we can understand this phenomenon. From the viewpoint of incumbent managers, the 'cost of issuing equity-related bonds' may have been very low compared with alternative means of fundraising. More specifically, by issuing equity-related bonds, managers can satisfy their preference for 'free cash flow,' as emphasized by Jensen (1986).[9] A simple model may be helpful to make this clear. The following is an extremely simplified version of the model analyzed by Myers and Majluf (1984).

There are two time periods: that is, the 'first' and the 'second' periods. For simplicity, all agents are assumed to be risk-neutral, and the discount rate to be zero. The firm has an investment opportunity with positive net present value in the first period. The firm can finance the required fund by issuing either 'straight bonds' or 'convertible bonds'.[10] The managers can, however, divert a part of the fund ϕ to perquisite consumption of 'free cash flow' Z in the first period. In the second period, the value of the firm will be X_H with probability p and X_L with probability $(1 - p)$, and X_H is definitely greater than X_L.

When the firm issues straight bonds, the face value F must be determined. In the first period, the firm utilizes the raised fund Φ to carry out the investment project I and to enjoy 'free cash flow' Z; that is,

$$\Phi = I + Z.$$

In the second period, the straight bonds must be redeemed at the face value F. Thus the following relationship will hold:

$$\Phi = F \tag{1}$$

The amount of 'free cash flow' in this case is,

$$Z = F - I. \tag{2}$$

Obviously, the value of equity of this firm S is

$$S = p \cdot X_H + (1 - p)X_L - I - Z. \tag{3}$$

In short, the sum of value of equity S and 'free cash flow' Z is equal to the net present value of the investment opportunity.

When the firm issues convertible bonds, it must determine their face value F^* and a call price. We assume that when the firm's value is X_H in the second period, investors exercise the option of converting the bonds into a predetermined proportion θ of the firm's equity value X_H. Consistency requires that $\theta X_H > F^*$. On the other hand, when the value of the firm in the second period is X_L, the convertible bonds are not converted into equity, so the firm is forced to redeem those bonds at their face value F^*. The present value of this convertible bond Φ is determined as follows:

$$\Phi = p \cdot \theta X_H + (1 - p)F^*. \tag{4}$$

As is the case of straight bonds, managers can divert a part of Φ to 'free cash flow' Z. Therefore,

$$\Phi = I + Z.$$

The amount of 'free cash flow' Z is represented by the following equation:

$$Z = p \cdot \theta X_H + (1 - p)F^* - I. \tag{5}$$

The value of equity S^* is

$$S^* = p \cdot X_H + (1 - p)X_L - I - Z, \tag{6}$$

which is the same as the value of equity in the case of a straight bond.

In order to avoid complexity associated with default, it is assumed that if the firm's value in the second period falls short of the face value of the debt F (or F^*), an extremely high cost is imposed on the managers of the firm. Therefore, the face value F (or F^*) of corporate bonds is always determined at a level not higher than X_L (that is, F (or F^*) $\leqq X_L$).[11] If the firm wants to maximize the 'free cash flow' Z in the first period, it must increase the face value of the bond F (or F^*) as much as possible. Therefore, the maximum 'free cash flow' in the case of issuing the straight bonds is attained when $F = X_L$: that is,

$$(Z)_{max} = X_L - I \tag{7}$$

Similarly, in the case of issuing the convertible bonds, the maximum amount of 'free cash flow' can be attained when $F^* = X_L$; that is,

$$(Z^*)_{max} = p \cdot \theta X_H + (1 - p)X_L - I \tag{8}$$

From (7) and (8), we can derive the following equation:

$$(Z^*)_{max} = (Z)_{max} + (\theta X_H - X_L)p. \tag{9}$$

Equation (9) implies that, *ceteris paribus*, the larger the value of converted bond θX_H, and the greater the probability p of conversion of the bonds into equity, the greater amount of 'free cash flow' the manager can enjoy by issuing the 'convertible bonds'. In contrast, both equation (3) and (6) show that the larger the amount of 'free cash flow' Z, the smaller the value of equity will become.

The essence of our argument is obvious. Generally speaking, the higher the face value of bonds (F or F^*.), the larger the amount of 'free cash flow' managers obtain in the first period. But managers cannot increase the face value so high as to incur default associated with extremely high costs. Thus the possibility of default constrains managers' behaviour in seeking 'free cash flow'. The convertible bond is advantageous for incumbent managers in the sense that it mitigates this constraint of default, particularly when the value of the firm is expected to rise substantially. On the other hand, when investors expect that the value of the firm will not go up sufficiently, the convertible bond loses this advantage for managers.

Equity-related bonds and profit rates are connected. The simple model in the above discussion shows that the preference for 'free cash flow' induces managers to issue equity-related bonds when stock prices of their firms are expected to rise sharply. Thus the surge of equity-related bonds implies an increase in the amount of 'free cash flow' likely to lead to managers' decision-making inconsistent with benefits of shareholders. This model can explain why Japanese corporations rushed to issue equity-related bonds, thereby expanding their productive capacities excessively and/or indulging in excessive risk-taking associated with securities investment (so-called '*zaitech*' in Japanese) during the 1980s.

In fact, those firms that actively issued equity-related bonds during the latter half of the 1980s seem to have experienced decreases in their profit rates in the late 1980s and early 1990s. Figure 3.3, based on data about companies that will be explained in detail in the next section, shows that those firms issuing bonds (most of which were equity-related) during the five years 1984–88 inclusive, on average suffered from a decline in profit rates during the three years 1988–90 inclusive, compared

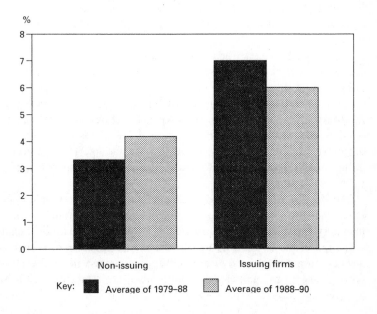

FIGURE 3.3   Profit rates before and after issuing bonds

with the average profit rates during the decade before 1988. By contrast, those that did not issue bonds during the period 1984–88 tended to enjoy mild increases in profit rates during the period 1988–90.

This chapter thus proposes a hypothesis that issuing equity-related bonds represents the preference of incumbent managers for 'free cash flow'. Of course, investors could and should understand the relationship between issuing equity-related bonds and the preference of managers for 'free cash flow'. Then the issuing of these bonds by a company would inform securities markets that the management of the firm deviates from maximization of shareholders' profits, thereby leading to a swift drop in its share price, as equations (6) and (9) suggest. Therefore, managers who are severely disciplined by both open and internal capital markets would refrain from issuing bonds, but other managers enjoying wider discretion by neglecting the profits of shareholders would actively issue equity-related bonds.

To consider the influences of financial liberalization in the 1980s, it is well known that there were restrictive rules concerning the eligibility of bond issues in Japan. Under these eligibility rules, Japanese firms were not allowed freely to issue various kinds of bonds either in domestic or in international markets.[12] As financial globalization and liberalization proceeded during the 1980s in the Japanese financial system, however, the restrictive eligibility rules were gradually but steadily liberalized.

Therefore, financial liberalization surely had something to do with the increase in issuing corporate bonds during the 1980s. Liberalization of itself, however, cannot explain why many Japanese managers considered equity-related bonds as being cheaper than other means of fund-raising. At the same time, some firms actively issued equity-related bonds, while other firms were not so active in issuing bonds despite being in apparently similar circumstances. This difference in attitude of individual firms towards bond-issuing cannot be explained by financial liberalization.

Section 3.4 of this chapter will explain the different behaviour of individual firms with respect to issuing bonds, by introducing the explanatory variables of their financial backgrounds. The empirical analysis will support the hypothesis that financial liberalization provided Japanese corporate managers with opportunities to exert their discretionary power, ensured by mutual shareholdings and other mechanisms to ward off pressure from external capital markets.

3.3 FINANCIAL STRUCTURE AND CORPORATE CONTROL

This chapter proposes a hypothesis that the surge of equity-related bonds during the latter half of the 1980s represented the strong discretionary power of incumbent managers. Starting from this hypothesis, we examine some relationships between financial structure and corporate governance in Japan.

First, we test the role of institutional investors in the mechanisms of corporate governance. Since institutional investors, including banks, are regarded as specialists in monitoring corporate management, they are considered to be able to control the decision-making of incumbent managers and prevent managers from neglecting the profits of shareholders. Predominantly institutional investors are important as both debt-holders and shareholders of corporations. Therefore, if the above hypothesis is true, those firms borrowing heavily from banks and other financial institutions, or whose majority of shares is held by institutional investors, should be forced to refrain from issuing equity-related bonds which will increase 'free cash flow'.

Second, we pay particular attention to the main bank relationships, because the role of main banks seems to be ambivalent in the mechanism of corporate governance in Japan. On the one hand, since the so-called main bank relationship is at the core of this mutual relationship, it can be assumed that the discretionary power of managers has been supported by mutual shareholding between corporations. If so, those firms having stable relationships with their main banks tend to be active in increasing the 'free cash flow' by issuing equity-related bonds.

On the other hand, however, according to some people, Japanese firms have been monitored closely by their main banks, which are often some of the largest shareholders of individual firms, and have disciplined incumbent managers to pursue profits for shareholders. According to this argument, the internal corporate control mechanisms organized by the main banks are effective in limiting the scope of incumbent managers to deviate from the principle of maximizing profits for shareholders. This mechanism can be seen as a substitute for that of the Anglo-American capital market. If this view is true, those firms having a stable relationship with their main banks were not allowed by these banks to issue equity-related bonds during the late 1980s. Even if they were allowed to do so, under the effective monitoring by their main banks, they tended to expand their capacities carefully so as not to incur a decline in profit rates after the late 1980s. We test these hypotheses based on simple statistical methods in Section 3.4.

3.4   STATISTICAL ANALYSES OF CORPORATE GOVERNANCE

This section presents some empirical analyses on the relationship between the financial structure of corporations and their behaviour in issuing bonds. The objective of our investigation is to examine the influence of financial relationships on corporate management. Most big companies, such as those already listed in the first section of the Tōkyō Stock Exchange before the mid-1960s are closely integrated into the traditional *keiretsu* or *zaibatsu* groups. The management of those firms seems to have been significantly influenced not only by financial factors such as main bank relationships but also by non-financial factors such as trading relationships. Therefore, it would be difficult for us to identify any influence of financial structure on their management.

Thus, we chose as a sample a set of manufacturing firms which were listed in the second section of Tōkyō Stock Exchange (TSE) in 1965, and whose financial data does not lose continuity until 1990. The number of these firms in the sample was 345. They seemed to be relatively suitable for our statistical investigations because, as most of them have been fairly independent from the traditional *keiretsu* groups, they are considered to be more sensitive to external influence from financial markets. Some of them have shown good performance since the mid-1960s, and obtained the higher status of being listed in the first section of *TSE*.

To examine bond-issuing firms and non-issuing firms in detail; as has already been explained, Japanese firms rarely issued corporate bonds (including equity-related bonds) before the 1980s. During the 1980s, however, as the restraints on bond issuing were liberalized, the number of bonds issued by Japanese firms, in both domestic and foreign markets, increased sharply. Particularly in the latter half of the 1980s, a dramatic increase was seen in the number of bonds issued by Japanese corporations. The majority of bonds was equity-related. For example, of the sampled 345 firms, 180 of them issued bonds during the five years 1986–90 inclusive. We call those firms 'bond-issuing firms', and the other 165 firms 'non-issuing firms'.

Table 3.1 compares some performance values between 'bond-issuing' and 'non-issuing' firms. As for the total asset (book value) of the fiscal year 1985, the average of 'bond issuing firms' is significantly higher than the average of 'non-issuing firms'. This is because the eligibility rules for bond-issuing tended to favour large-scale companies. The average profit rate of 'bond-issuing firms' was higher, both in

TABLE 3.1 Performance of 'bond-issuing' and 'non-issuing' firms

	'Bond-issuing firms'		*'Non-issuing firms'*	
Number of firms	180		165	
Total assets (¥ millions)				
End of F.Y.1985	40 159	(3 263)	17 374	(1 394)
Investment (%)				
1975–84 average	5.60	(0.22)	4.66	(0.26)
1984–88 average	6.43	(0.26)	4.91	(0.28)
Total borrowing (%)				
1975–84 average	24.10	(1.08)	29.46	(1.26)
1984–88 average	16.74	(1.08)	28.32	(1.39)
The proportion of financial institutions shareholdings (%)				
1975–84 average	24.29	(0.93)	17.25	(0.95)
1984–88 average	29.32	(0.97)	19.46	(0.94)
Current profit rate (%)				
1975–84 average	6.29	(0.39)	3.10	(0.42)
1988–90 average	5.79	(0.31)	3.81	(0.45)
Bond-issuing (%)				
1986–90 average	5.77	(0.33)	–	(–)

Note: Investment, total borrowing, current profit and bond-issuing are all denominated by the total amount of assets (book value) at the end of previous year. The proportion of financial institutions shareholdings is the relative share held by financial institutions of the total number of equities issued by each firm. Figures in parentheses indicate standard errors.

the decade up to the mid-1980s, and in the late 1980s, than that of 'non-issuing firms'. It is noteworthy, however, that the profit rate of 'bond-issuing firms' declined in the late 1980s, whereas the 'non-issuing firms' did not on average experience such a decline in profit rates (see also Figure 3.3 on p. 61).

Comparing the five years after 1984 with the decade up to that year, Japanese firms reduced the amount of their borrowing while the ratio of their equities held by financial institutions went up to some extent. (In this chapter, fund-raising by issuing bonds is not including in 'borrowing'.) During the decade up to 1984, the 'bond-issuing firms' were less dependent on borrowing, and higher ratios of their shares were held by financial institutions than in the 'non-issuing firms'. This suggests that the decrease in reliance of firms on borrowing and the increase in the ratio of shares held by financial institutions encouraged Japanese companies to issue bonds during the 1980s.[13] We investigate this relationship more carefully below.

We divided the sample firms into two groups; one group with stable main bank relationships and the another without such relationships. It is not easy to specify the main bank for individual firms, because the main bank relationship is not an explicit financial contract. Some argue that the main bank for an individual firm can be identified only when the firm gets into serious financial distress.[14] It is widely believed, however, that we can identify the main bank for each individual firm by examining the history of its transactions with various financial institutions, the relationship of shareholding with banks, and its personnel exchanges with banks.[15] The *Keizai Chosa Kai* has compiled detailed time series data of the main bank relationships for most major companies since the early 1960s. This chapter depends on this data to identify the main banks of individual sampled firms.

According to the data compiled by the *Keizai Chosa Kai*, 165 of the sampled firms continued to have a main bank relationship with particular banks between 1965 and 1988.[16] We call them 'the firms with a stable main bank relationship'. The other 180 firms of the sample either had no main bank relationships or changed their main banks at least once during the period 1965–88. Those firms are called 'the other firms'.

Table 3.2 compares some statistics of both 'the firms with a stable main bank relationship' and 'the other firms'. We cannot find remarkable differences between these groups. However, the average profit rate was consistently lower for 'the firms with a stable main bank relationship' than for 'the other firms'. While both groups decreased their long-term borrowing after 1980, 'the firms with a stable main bank relationship' reduced more drastically than 'the other firms'.

As for the total borrowing, each of the two groups continued to decrease their total amount of borrowing. However, the relative importance of the total borrowing was steadily higher for 'the firms with a stable main bank relationship' than for 'the other firms'. On the other hand, the average ratio of shares held by financial institutions has risen slightly since the early 1980s. Generally speaking, while Japanese firms reduced their reliance on borrowing and, in this sense, the influence of banks and other financial institutions on their management seemed to be weakened, the relative shares of equities held by their main banks and other financial institutions continued to rise, suggesting the possibility that those financial institutions strengthened their presence in the corporate governance through their shareholdings.

TABLE 3.2 Firms with stable main bank relationship and other firms

	Firms with stable main bank	*Other firms*
Number of firms	165	180
Total assets (¥ millions) (End of F.Y.1985)	28 237 (2 353)	30 172 (3 001)
Total debts (¥ millions) (End of F.Y.1985)	16 993 (1 205)	17 089 (1 538)
Investment per total asset (%)		
F.Y.1965–74	7.88 (0.30)	8.10 (0.31)
F.Y.1975–84	4.94 (0.23)	5.35 (0.25)
F.Y.1981–90	5.83 (0.22)	6.03 (0.28)
F.Y.1986–90	5.89 (0.26)	5.99 (0.32)
Current profit per total asset (%)		
F.Y.1965–74	5.67 (0.48)	7.67 (0.45)
F.Y.1975–84	4.15 (0.42)	5.34 (0.41)
F.Y.1981–90	4.13 (0.36)	5.13 (0.36)
F.Y.1986–90	3.98 (0.34)	5.00 (0.39)
Long-term borrowing per total asset (%)		
F.Y.1965–74	7.68 (0.31)	7.51 (0.34)
F.Y.1975–84	4.24 (0.24)	4.60 (0.30)
F.Y.1981–90	2.91 (0.23)	3.48 (0.27)
F.Y.1986–90	2.81 (0.30)	3.31 (0.31)
Proportion of shareholdings by financial institutions (%)		
F.Y.1975–84	22.31 (1.00)	19.59 (0.94)
F.Y.1981–90	25.92 (1.02)	23.18 (0.99)
F.Y.1986–90	27.66 (1.05)	25.07 (1.07)
Bonds issued per total asset (%)		
F.Y.1965–74	0.05 (0.01)	0.05 (0.01)
F.Y.1975–84	0.56 (0.09)	0.64 (0.11)
F.Y.1981–90	2.20 (0.21)	2.09 (0.24)
F.Y.1986–90	3.20 (0.32)	2.84 (0.33)
Total borrowing per total asset (%)		
F.Y.1965–74	31.55 (0.94)	28.84 (0.99)
F.Y.1975–84	28.28 (1.12)	25.16 (1.22)
F.Y.1981–90	22.89 (1.20)	21.52 (1.23)
F.Y.1986–90	21.28 (1.28)	20.62 (1.33)

Note: Figures in parentheses indicate standard errors.

Source: NEEDS.TS.COMPANY.

According to Table 3.2, the number of bonds (most of which were equity-related) issued by both groups of sampled firms, have substantially increased since the early 1980s. These increases in bond-issuing accompany the relative decrease in their long-term borrowing. It is notable, however, that 'the firms with a stable main bank relationship' increased the amount of bond-issuing more than did 'the other firms'. Thus, the stable main bank relationship did not appear to restrict expansion of bond-issuing by client firms.

Table 3.3 compares bond-issuing during the five years 1986–90 inclusive for both firm groups in more detail. During these five years, in the case of 'the firms with a stable main bank relationship', 93 of 165 firms issued bonds, while 87 out of 180 firms issued bonds in the case of 'the other firms'. The proportion of firms issuing bonds was a little higher for 'the firms with a stable main bank relationship' than for 'the other firms', although the number of bonds issued was on average slightly larger for 'the other firms' than for 'the firms with a stable main bank relationship'. The essence of both Table 3.2 and Table 3.3 is that 'the firms with a stable main bank relationship' did not tend to refrain from issuing equity-related bonds during the latter half of the 1980s.

Table 3.4 examines the financial structure of 'the firms with a stable main bank relationship' in detail. The relative importance of total borrowing for them decreased steadily after the 1970s. However, the proportion of borrowing from their main banks was around a quarter of the total borrowing during the period before 1974, and the proportion remained at almost the same level after 1980. The proportion of borrowing from financial affiliates (*kinyu keiretsu*), which includes not only the main bank but also insurance and other financial institutions closely linked to the firms, was around 40 per cent before the mid-1970s. After the early 1980s, this proportion did not change greatly.

The proportion of the total shares held by the main bank has increased slightly since the early 1980s. On average, the main bank holds only 3 or 4 per cent of the shares of its client firms. This percentage is, however, large enough to make the main bank one of the largest shareholders of client firms. Needless to say, the shareholdings of financial affiliates were significantly larger than the holdings of the main bank. The proportion of the shares held by financial affiliates has gone up since 1980.[17]

Table 3.4 shows the changes in the average financial structure of 'the firms with a stable main-bank relationship'. There are, however, substantial differences among individual firms with respect to financial

TABLE 3.3   The bond-issuing firms and the amount of bonds issued
(1986–90)

	Firms with stable main bank	*Other firms*
Number of firms	165	180
The number of firms issuing bonds	93	87
The average amount of issued bonds per asset	5.68% (0.41)	5.87% (0.52)
The number of firms issuing convertible bonds	55	57
The average amount of issued convertible bonds per asset	4.99% (0.36)	5.35% (0.61)

Note: Figures in parentheses indicate standard errors.

TABLE 3.4   Statistics of the firms with stable main bank
(average percentages)

	1965–74	*1975–84*	*1984–88*	*1986–90*
Total borrowing[a]	31.55 (0.94)[c]	28.28 (1.12)	23.06 (1.30)	21.28 (1.28)
Borrowing from main banks[a]	10.50 (0.73)	7.66 (0.59)	6.91 (0.61)	6.91[b] (0.61)
Borrowing from financial affiliates[a]	15.37 (0.71)	11.37 (0.65)	9.48 (0.67)	9.49[b] (0.69)
Proportion of shares held by main banks	3.17 (0.23)	4.24 (1.44)	3.88 (0.15)	3.74[b] (0.14)
Proportion of shares held by financial affiliates	15.66 (1.42)	18.95 (1.44)	18.73 (1.40)	18.68[b] (1.39)
Proportion of shares held by financial institutions	n.a.	22.31 (1.00)	25.93 (1.02)	27.66 (1.05)

Notes: [a] Total borrowing, borrowing from main banks, borrowing from financial
affiliates are all percentages denominated by the total assets (book
values), [b] The average over 1986–88. [c] Figures in parentheses indicate standard errors.

Source: NEEDS.TS.COMPANY and Keizai Chosakai, *Keiretsu no Kenkyu.*

TABLE 3.5   Distribution of firms with stable main bank relationships

Ratios of borrowing from main bank	Proportions of shares held by main banks				
	Less than 1.0%	1.0–3.0%	3.0–5.0%	5.0% or greater	Total
Less than 10%	15	1	4	5	25
10–30%	10	20	32	25	87
30–50%	1	4	10	22	37
50% and greater	1	1	8	6	16
Total	27	26	54	58	165

Source: *Keizai Chosa Kai.*

structure. Table 3.5 summarizes these differences. This table shows the distribution of 'the firms with a stable main bank relationship' in terms of two dimensions: the relative share of borrowing from their main bank, and the proportion of shares held by them. For example, the number of firms whose relative shares of borrowing from their main banks are less than 10 per cent and the proportions of main bank shareholding are less than 1.0 per cent is 15. Meanwhile, the number of firms where their main banks both lent more than 50 per cent of the firms' total borrowing and held more than 5 per cent of the total number of shares is 6. This table shows a comparatively wide variation in the financial structure of 'the firms with a stable main bank relationship'. We utilize the information contained in Table 3.5 in the following statistical analyses.

This chapter has provided some hypotheses concerning the relationship between bond-issuing of individual firms and their financial background. In particular, it has been explained that issuing equity-related bonds implies the deviation of corporate management from the maximization of profits for shareholders. If this hypothesis is true, the effective monitoring by institutional investors and/or main banks should have suppressed the active issue of those bonds. However, institutional investors, including main banks, may have helped incumbent managers of their client firms by protecting the managers from the disciplinary pressure of external capital markets. If this is true, institutional investors and main banks could not prevent the active issue of equity-related bonds. In the following, we test statistically which of these hypotheses is true.

We use a 'Probit Model', in which we assign 1 to those firms that issued bonds during the five years 1986–90 inclusive, and assign 0 to those that did not issue bonds at all during the same period. This variable is 'BOND' in the following analysis. We assume that the probability of issuing bonds by a specific firm positively relates to both the total amount of assets of the firm 'ASSET' at the beginning of the time period (1985) and the firm's average profit rate 'PROF' during the decade up to 1984. As has already been explained in this chapter, the eligibility rules for bond-issuing tended to favour those firms with larger amounts of book value assets. At the same time, the higher profit rate of a firm will, *ceteris paribus*, make it easier for the firm to issue bonds.

We then add the average value of borrowing per total asset 'BOR' for individual firms during 1975–84 and the average of the proportion of shares held by financial institutions in individual firms 'FSTOCK' during the same decade. If the discretionary power of incumbent managers of those firms heavily depending on borrowing is constrained by lending institutions, BOR will negatively correlate with the probability of BOND. If financial institutions can restrict the discretionary power of managers through shareholdings, FSTOCK will also be negatively related to BOND.

Table 3.6 presents estimated results of the Probit Model for 345 sampled firms. According to this table, both ASSET and PROF positively (and significantly) influenced BOND, as was expected. BOR, however, had no significant influence on BOND. FSTOCK positively (not negatively) influenced the probability BOND. Thus shareholdings by financial institutions seem to have contributed to strengthening the discretionary power of incumbent managers.

We also estimated the same form of the Probit Model by substituting changes in both BOR and FSTOCK; that is, 'XBOR' and 'XFSTOCK' respectively. Specifically, XBOR is a change in BOR during the ten years 1975–84 inclusive, and XFSTOCK is a change in FSTOCK during the same decade. The estimated result is presented in col. (3) of Table 3.6. According to this result, XBOR negatively and XFSTOCK positively influenced BOND. Thus it was more probable for those firms that reduced their dependence on borrowing to a greater extent during the past decade to issue bonds (including equity-related bonds) during the period 1986–90. Similarly, the greater the increases in the proportion of shareholdings by financial institutions during the past decade for individual firm, the more likely it is for the firm to issue bonds. These results suggest that the rapid decrease in dependence of firms on borrowing since the mid-1970s has led to expansion of the

TABLE 3.6   Estimated probit model

| | All sampled firms (sample size = 345) | | | |
| | Dependent variable BOND | | | |
	(1)	(2)	(3)	(4)
Constant	−0.917	−0.991	−0.754	−0.881
	(−3.55)	(−3.76)	(−5.99)	(−6.01)
ASSET	$0.152*10^{-4}$	$0.150*10^{-4}$	$0.162*10^{-4}$	$0.157*^{-4}$
	(4.06)	(4.06)	(4.52)	(4.44)
PROF	$0.462*10^{-1}$	$0.484*10^{-1}$	$0.390*10^{-1}$	$0.423*10^{-1}$
	(2.75)	(2.86)	(2.77)	(2.97)
BOR	$0.225*10^{-2}$	$0.187*10^{-2}$		
	(0.39)	(0.32)		
FSTOCK	$0.150*10^{-1}$	$0.136*10^{-1}$		
	(2.42)	(2.17)		
XBOR			$-0.791*10^{-2}$	$-0.78*10^{-2}$
			(−1.98)	(−1.94)
XFSTOCK			$0.275*10^{-1}$	$0.274*10^{-1}$
			(2.37)	(2.34)
MAIN		0.220		0.256
		(1.49)		(1.74)
SSR	70.00	69.26	68.54	67.84
R^2	0.188	0.196	0.205	0.213

Notes: ASSET: Total asset as at end of F.Y. 1985 (¥ million); PROF: Average profit rate during F.Y. 1975–84 (per total asset, per cent); BOR: Average of borrowing per total assets during F.Y. 1975–84 (per cent); FSTOCK: Average proportion of shareholdings by financial institutions during F.Y. 1975–84 (per cent); XBOR: Changes in BOR from F.Y. 1976 to F.Y. 1985; XFSTOCK: Changes in FSTOCK from F.Y. 1976 to F.Y. 1985; MAIN: Dummy for the firms with stable main bank relationships. Figures in parentheses indicate *t*-value.

discretionary power of corporate managers, and that the increase in shareholdings by financial institutions promoted this tendency.

We add a dummy variable 'MAIN' to the Probit Model in Table 3.6 in order to examine whether the main bank relationship influenced bond-issuing of individual firms during the period 1986–90. The dummy variable MAIN is 1 for 'the firm with a stable main bank relationship', and 0 for 'the other firms', respectively. The estimated results are presented in cols (2) and (4) of Table 3.6. These equations show that issuing bonds is more probable for 'the firms with a stable main bank relationship' than for 'the other firms', although the relationship was statistically insignificant.

Then, we estimated the same Probit Model by picking up only 'the firms with a stable main bank relationship' to investigate whether the main bank's shareholding or lending have any influence on the bond-issuing behaviour of individual firms. We added the relative importance of the main bank loans 'MLOAN' and the proportion of main bank shareholdings 'MSTOCK' to the explanatory variables of the Probit Model. We also extended the concept of the main bank relationship to the financial affiliates (*kinyu keiretsu*) by adding the relative importance of borrowing from financial affiliates (including main banks) 'KLOAN', and the proportion of shareholdings by financial affiliates 'KSTOCK'.

We cannot find any significant influence of those main bank variables on bond-issuing of individual firms. More specifically, we cannot support the hypothesis that increases in the relative importance of the main bank loan and/or in the proportion of main bank shareholdings tend to suppress bond-issuing by the client firm. The estimated results are summarized in Table 3.7.

TABLE 3.7   Estimated probit model for the firms with stable main bank relationships

| | | *Sample size = 165* | | |
| | | *Dependent variable BOND* | | |
	(1)	*(2)*	*(3)*	*(4)*
Constant	−0.393	−0.419	−0.283	0.052
	(−2.46)	(−1.13)	(−1.11)	(0.16)
ASSET	$0.127*10^{-4}$	$0.113*10^{-4}$	$0.124*10^{-4}$	$0.113*10^{-4}$
	(2.79)	(2.40)	(2.69)	(2.44)
PROF	$0.550*10^{-1}$	$0.488*10^{-1}$	$0.553*10^{-1}$	$0.546*10^{-1}$
	(2.81)	(2.26)	(2.82)	(2.78)
BOR		$-0.443*10^{-2}$		
		(−0.54)		
FSTOCK		$0.977*10^{-2}$		
		(1.18)		
MLOAN			$-0.485*10^{-2}$	
			(−0.83)	
MSTOCK			$0.614*10^{-2}$	
			(0.16)	
KLOAN				$-0.946*10^{-2}$
				(−1.47)
KSTOCK				$-0.249*10^{-2}$
				(−0.45)
SSR	34.49	34.19	34.32	33.95
R^2	0.152	0.159	0.157	0.165

Notes: As notes of Table 3.6.

As has already been explained, the firms that actively issued equity-related bonds during the latter half of 1980s tended to experience decreases in profit rates after 1988. If the main bank or other financial institutions prevent unwise or too risky investment expenditure (including *zaitech*) by incumbent managers, however, issuing bonds would not necessarily lead to a decline in profit rates. We therefore tested the hypothesis that profit rates did not decrease after issuing bonds for the firms that enjoyed stable main bank relationships.

The most simple estimation given in col. (1) in Table 3.8 is to regress the difference of profit rates between the average over the three years 1988–90 inclusive and the average during the decade 1979–88 'XPROF' to the amount of bonds issued during the five years between 1984 and 1988 'QBOND' by the ordinary least square. We find that QBOND is negatively correlated with XPROF. Thus the greater the number of bonds a firm issued during 1984–88, the lower the profit rate in the three years after 1988 than the average rate during the decade up to 1988.

Then, we added a cross term of the dummy variable MAIN by QBOND to test whether the stable main bank relationship in fact reduced the negative influence of the number of bonds issued QBOND. If the main bank relationship disciplines incumbent managers to seek profit-maximization, the coefficient with this cross term MAIN*QBOND is expected to be positive. According to the estimated result presented in col. (2) of Table 3.8, the coefficient is not positive but negative, although statistically insignificant. Thus we cannot find the disciplinary influence of the main bank relationship in this result.

Furthermore, we add two cross terms BOR*QBOND and FSTOCK*QBOND in order to examine whether the characteristics of financial structure represented by dependence of the firm on borrowing BOR and the proportion of shareholding by financial institutions FSTOCK influenced the negative relation between the profit rate and issuing bonds. If incumbent managers of those firms that depended heavily on borrowing, or a majority of whose shares was held by financial institutions, including banks, were strongly constrained in their ability to deviate from the maximization of profits for shareholders, these cross terms were expected to have positive coefficients. According to the estimated result shown in col. (3), the cross term BOR*QBOND has a significantly positive coefficient, while the coefficient of the cross term FSTOCK*QBOND is statistically insignificant. Thus this simple test supports the hypothesis that heavily indebted firms tend to be closely

TABLE 3.8   Profit rates and bond-issuing (OLS)

| | *Sample size = 345* | | |
| | *Dependent variable XPROF* | | |
	(1)	*(2)*	*(3)*
Constant	0.275	0.282	0.281
	(1.02)	(1.04)	(1.04)
QBOND	−0.174	−0.161	−0.384
	(−2.97)	(−2.30)	(−1.83)
MAIN*QBOND		−0.331*10^{-1}	−0.878*10^{-1}
		(−0.33)	(−0.85)
BOR*QBOND			0.133*10^{-1}
			(2.61)
FSTOCK*BONDA			−0.465*10^{-4}
			(−0.01)
SSR	6156.3	6154.4	6027.3
R^2	0.022	0.020	0.034
F	8.840	4.462	4.057

Notes: XPROF is defined by subtracting average profit rate during the decade 1979–88 from the three years average of profit rate during 1988–
90. For the definitions of MAIN, BOR and FSTOCK, see notes to
Table 3.6. Figures in parentheses indicate *t*-value.

monitored by debt-holders including banks, and consequently avoid
the decline in profit rates after issuing bonds.

Tables 3.6, 3.7 and 3.8 suggest the following results concerning the
issuing of equity-related bonds by Japanese firms in the latter half of
the 1980s. There were no significant differences in probability of issuing bonds between the heavily indebted firms and those firms less
dependent on borrowing. Those firms more dependent on borrowing
were, however, more closely monitored by lending financial institutions than those which were less dependent on borrowing and, in consequence, were forced to choose prudent investment outlets for the
funds raised by issuing bonds.

Moreover, the stability of main bank relationships did not significantly influence the behaviour of bond-issuing by corporate managers.
Nor did the presence of financial institutions as shareholders of corporations control bond-issuing decision-making by incumbent managers.
Rather, the increase in shareholdings by financial institutions seems to
have helped corporate managers to use their discretionary powers for
other purposes than the maximization of profits for shareholders during the latter half of the 1980s.

3.5   CONCLUDING REMARKS

The surge of issuing corporate bonds, most of which were equity-related, during the latter half of the 1980s is a puzzle from the viewpoint of the standard theory of corporate finance. This chapter interpreted this phenomenon as representing the deviation of corporate management from neo-classical profit-maximization. Issuing equity-related bonds was not necessarily profitable for shareholders, but it increased the amount of 'free cash flow' for managers. This hypothesis relating the issue of equity-related bonds to 'free cash flow' seems to be supported by the fact that those firms having actively issued corporate equity-related bonds in the latter half of the 1980s tend to have suffered from more a drastic decline in profit rates since around 1990 than those not having issued bonds at all.

Based on this interpretation, we tested the relationship between the scope for incumbent managers to deviate from maximizing profits of shareholders, and financial backgrounds of corporations such as the existence of stable main bank relationships. We obtained the following results from our empirical investigation:

1. The existence of a stable main bank relationship did not suppress issuing bonds by incumbent managers. Specifically, neither dependence of individual firms on borrowing from their main banks nor ratios of shareholdings by financial institutions significantly explain the behaviour of issuing bonds by firms.
2. The decrease in the dependence of firms on borrowing from financial institutions since the mid-1970s contributed to widening the scope for corporate managers to seek 'free cash flow' by issuing equity-related bonds.
3. Financial institutions, including the main banks, gradually increased their shareholdings of client companies. This increase in shareholdings by financial institutions did not, however, narrow the scope for corporate managers to deviate from maximizing profits of shareholders.

The role of the 'internal capital market', based on the main bank relationship in mitigating pressure to contest corporate control, is intended to strengthen incentives for incumbent managers and employees to accumulate capital specific to their own companies. In particular, as pointed out by Hoshi, Kashyap and Scharfstein (1990b), Packer and Ryser (1992), and Sheard (1993), the 'internal capital market' provides the valuable service of monitoring client firms in financial distress. This role is likely to promote the efficiency of a firm as a going concern.

Our investigation in this chapter, however, suggests that the 'internal capital market' was not so effective in monitoring management as to prevent the seeking of 'free cash flow'. Rather, it seems to have contributed to strengthening the discretion of incumbent managers, and made it possible for them to pursue managerial objectives which were inconsistent with maximizing the profits for shareholders.

NOTES

1. For example, see Aoki (1990), Aoki and Sheard (1992), Kester (1991) and Sheard (1993).
2. This argument may lead to a rather extreme conclusion that the effective workings of the 'internal capital market' make external pressure from open capital markets unnecessary. See Mayer (1993).
3. See Aoki and Sheard (1992).
4. See Horiuchi (1993) for an overview of this kind of sceptical argument about the efficiency of Japanese firms' management. But this chapter does not argue that the 'perquisites' of incumbent managers necessarily decrease the competitiveness of their companies. On the contrary, they could survive fierce competition from their rivals, particularly in international markets, because they are to some extent allowed to follow managerial strategies which do not directly increase profits for shareholders.
5. See Jensen (1986) as for the definition of 'free cash flow'.
6. There are some analyses that investigate empirically the relationship between the financial structure of individual firms and their managerial performance. See Horiuchi and Okazaki (1993), Hoshi, Kashyap and Scharfstein (1990a and 1990b), Kaplan and Minton (1993), Kester (1991), Lichtenberg and Pushner (1992), and Prowse (1990). The analysis in this chapter is closely related to them.
7. The Bank of Japan (BOJ) (1993) explains that, contrary to the claim by many managers, the cost of capital associated with issuing equity-related bonds was not low during the late 1980s. The BOJ, however, does not explain why Japanese managers did not pay attention to 'the standard cost of capital'.
8. See Brealey and Myers (1991, pp. 547–9). If corporate managers and some current shareholders believe that investors overestimate future share prices of their specific companies, they have an incentive to issue equity-related bonds to exploit the asymmetric information between them and outside investors. But, in this situation, to issue equity-related bonds is very likely to signal overestimation by investors and would lead to correcting the prices of securities in those companies. Moreover, this kind of asymmetric information would be less important for those firms that are closely monitored through financial institutions such as their

main banks, than those that are relatively independent from influence of big institutional investors. Therefore, if this asymmetric information is relevant for the recent surge of equity-related bonds, we could observe that the latter firms were much more active in issuing those bonds than were the former firms. As the investigation in Section 3.4 later shows, we cannot obtain results supporting this argument.

9. Jensen (1986) defines cash flow left after the firm has exhausted its positive net present value projects as 'free cash flow'.

10. This model assumes that the firm has exhausted its opportunity to issue equity. This assumption is too restrictive. In fact, the issuing of equity may be an effective method for managers to increase the amount of 'free cash flow'. In Japan, we have a very interesting history of self-imposed rules in the stock market concerning returning 'premiums' accrued to the firms issuing equities at market prices to their shareholders. Since, from the viewpoint of neo-classical theory, the issuing of equities at market prices will not return 'premiums' to anybody at all, the rules seem to be a strange matter produced because of a misunderstanding by related agents such as securities companies. But we may regard the rules about the 'premiums' associated with issuing equities at market prices as reflecting the interests of investors wishing to prevent managers from increasing the amount of 'free cash flow'.

This chapter also assumes that managers do not manipulate dividend policy in order to maximize the amount of 'free cash flow' in the first period. This assumption may seem to be too restrictive. But we should note the fact that firms almost always pay a predetermined annual dividend to their shareholders in Japan. Some authors go so far as to say that the policy adopted by Japanese firms of paying predetermined dividends have changed their equity into *de facto* fixed income debentures for shareholders. See Kurasawa (1993).

11. As will be seen later, the eligibility rules allows only those firms that are relatively large-scale and have histories of good performance to issue corporate bonds. For the managers of those companies, the default costs seem to be extremely high.

12. For a detailed explanation of the eligibility rules of bonds issue, see Committee on the Working of the Bond and Stock Markets (1977).

13. This chapter relies on the database provided by NEEDS.TS.COMPANY. This database contains statistics both of the total amount of various bonds and of convertible bonds issued by individual firms. The statistics of warrant bonds, however, are not available. Traditionally, electric companies have been overwhelmingly important as issuers of straight bonds in Japan. In contrast, manufacturing firms rarely issued straight bonds until around 1990, when those firms started issuing a large amount of straight bonds because the sharp decline in stock prices made it impossible for them to issue equity-related bonds.

14. See Miwa (1985) and Weinstein and Yafeh (1993) for difficulties with identifying main banks.

15. See, for example, Sunamura (1993).

16. When we utilized the data of the *Keizai Chosa Kai*, the most recent data about the main bank relationship was that of fiscal year 1988.

17. The data concerning the shareholding by the main bank is not sufficient, in the following sense. The data prepared by the *Keizai Chosa Kai* presents a table of the top ten largest shareholders of individual firms. Although the main bank is listed in this table in most cases, there are some exceptional situations in which the main bank holds some shares but the number is not sufficient to list the main bank in the table of the top ten largest shareholders. In this case, since the percentage of shareholding by the main bank is not available to us, this paper assigns 0 per cent to the shareholding of the main bank. Therefore there are some cases in which this chapter underrates the relative share of the main bank shareholding. However, we suppose that the number of such cases is not so large as to distort our statistical analysis.

REFERENCES

Aoki, Masahiko 1990. 'Towards an Economic Model of the Japanese Firm', *Journal of Economic Literature*, 28, pp. 1–27.

Aoki, Masahiko and Paul Sheard 1992. 'The Role of the Main Bank in the Corporate Governance Structure in Japan', Working Paper, Stanford, California: Stanford University, May.

Bank of Japan 1993. 'On the Function of the Stock Market: Its Relation to Corporate Behavior' (in Japanese), *The Bank of Japan Monthly Bulletin*, January.

Brealey, Richard A. and Stewart C. Myers 1991. *Principles of Corporate Finance*, 4th edn, New York: McGraw Hill.

Committee on the Working of the Bond and Stock Markets, Securities Exchange Council, 1977, *Report on the Desirable Bond Market for Japan*.

Horiuchi, Akiyoshi 1989. 'Informational Properties of the Japanese Financial System', *Japan and the World Economy*, 1, pp. 255–78.

Horiuchi, Akiyoshi 1993. 'Functions of the Japanese Capital Markets', *Japanese Economic Studies*, Spring, pp. 66–95.

Horiuchi, Akiyoshi and Ryoko Okazaki 1994. Capital Markets and the Banking Sector: The Efficiency of Japanese Banks in Reducing Agency Costs, in R. M. Levich, R. Ramachandran and R. Sato (eds.), *Japan and International Financial Markets: Analytical and Empirical Perspectives*, Cambridge University Press.

Hoshi, Takeo, Anil Kashyap and David Scharfstein 1990a. 'Corporate Structure, Liquidity and Investment: Evidence from Japanese Panel Data', *Quarterly Journal of Economics*, 106, pp. 33–60.

Hoshi, Takeo, Anil Kashyap and David Scharfstein 1990b. 'The Role of Banks in Reducing the Costs of Financial Distress in Japan', *Journal of Financial Economics*, 27, pp. 67–88.

Jensen, Michael 1986. 'Agency Costs of Free Cash Flow, Corporate Finance, and Takeovers', *American Economic Review*, 86, pp. 323–9.

Jensen, Michael and William Meckling 1976. 'Theory of the Firm: Managerial Behavior, Agency Costs and Ownership Structure', *Journal of Financial Economics*, 3, pp. 305–60.

Kaplan, Steven N. and Bernadette A. Minton 1993. '"Outside" Intervention in Japanese Companies: Its Determinants and Implications for Managers', Cambridge, Mass.: National Bureau of Economic Research Working Paper No. 4276, February.

Kester, W. Carl 1991. *Japanese Takeovers: The Global Contest for Corporate Control*, Cambridge, Mass.: Harvard Business School Press.

Kurasawa, Motonari 1993. 'Takeover Threats, Cross Shareholdings, and Managerial Behavior' (in Japanese), *Japan Financial Review*, 16, pp. 1–18.

Lichtenberg, Frank R. and George M. Pushner 1992. 'Ownership Structure and Corporate Performance in Japan', Cambridge, Mass.: National Bureau of Economic Research Working Paper No. 4092.

Mayer, Colin 1993. 'Ownership, An Inaugural Lecture', Department of Economics, University of Warwick.

Miwa, Yoshiro 1985. 'The Main Bank and its Functions' (in Japanese), in Takafusa Nakamura, Yutaka Kosai and Shunsaku Nishikawa (eds.), *The Economic System in Japan*, Tōkyō: University of Tōkyō Press.

Myers, Stewart C. and Nicholas C. Majluf (1984. 'Corporate Financing and Investment Decisions when Firms have Information that Managers Do Not Have', *Journal of Financial Economics*, 13, pp. 187–222.

Packer, Frank and Marc Ryser 1992. 'The Governance of Failure: An Anatomy of Corporate Bankruptcy in Japan', Working Paper no. 62, New York, N.Y.: Center on Japanese Economy and Business, Graduate School of Business, Columbia University.

Prowse, Stephen 1990. 'Institutional Investment Patterns and Corporate Financial Behaviour in the US and Japan', Journal of Financial Economics, 29, pp. 43–66..

Sheard, Paul 1994. 'Interlocking Shareholdings and Corporate Governance in Japan', in Masahiko Aoki and Ronald Dore (eds), *The Japanese Firms: Sources of Competitive Strength*, Oxford University Press.

Sunamura, Satoshi 1993. 'Main Banks as Effective Agents for Corporate Growth: How Managerial Capacity Can Be Built Up and Employed in the Development Process', A paper presented at the joint Stanford University-Columbia University-World Bank research project on *The Japanese Main Bank System and its Relevance for Developing Market and Transforming Socialist Economies*.

Weinstein, David E. and Yishay Yafeh 1993. 'Japan's Corporate Groups: Collusive or Competitive? An Empirical Investigation of Keiretsu Behavior', Cambridge, Mass.: Harvard Institute of Economic Research Working Paper No. 1623.

4 An Analysis of Labour Mobility in Japan

Atsuhiro Taki
and Toshiaki Tachibanaki*

4.1 INTRODUCTION

This chapter attempts to investigate changes in labour force status and labour turnover by using the *Employment Status Survey*, examining (i) the estimation of transition probabilities among several labour force statuses; (ii) the estimation of the determination in transition probabilities; and (iii) the estimation of labour turnover functions. It is emphasized that these three subjects are related, and provide complementary information.

The first subject has already been extensively investigated by Mizuno (1982, 1983). This chapter attempts to show what has previously been unknown in the analysis of the transition probabilities in Japan and is partly feasible because the data source is new, namely the *Employment Status Survey* of 1982. The most commonly used data source in the past has been the *Labour Force Survey*. Another aim is to emphasize the role of self-employed workers and of employees in different sizes of firm in the Japanese labour market.

Transition probabilities among various labour force statuses are different not only in personal characteristics but also in other economic variables. The second section investigates how these transition probabilities are determined or influenced by several economic variables, and gives economic interpretations. Thus this section attempts to estimate the causes of obtaining different transition probabilities among the several labour force statuses presented in the first part.

The third section presents the estimated results of labour turnover functions. A change in labour force status and labour turnover are

* An earlier version of this chapter was presented as a paper at the First Conference on the Contemporary Japanese Economy held in March 1993, hosted by the Centre for Japanese Economic Studies, Macquarie University, Sydney. The authors would like to thank Ms Monica Byrnes, School of Economic and Financial Studies, Macquarie University for her assistance with proofreading and corrections in this paper.

conceptually different. Labour turnover is defined as a separation from a previous employment, and the worker obtaining another job in a different firm during the previous year. Whereas the first and second sections of the chapter do not separate the cause of turnover between voluntary separations and involuntary separations, this third section attempts to do so, and to draw out economic implications. Emphasis is placed upon investigating any differences by adopting different procedure from that of Mincer and Higuchi (1988), who have estimated labour turnover functions in Japan.

As noted previously, the main data source of this work is the *Employment Status Survey*. The number of original observations is about 800 000, and the survey contains a large amount of useful information. Since it would be extremely costly to use all the observations, the number was reduced to one-tenth of the total, which was randomly selected. It is noted that even when the sample number is reduced to about 40 000 each for males and females, it is still very large as a cross-section data source.

4.2 ESTIMATED TRANSITION PROBABILITIES

Mizuno (1982, 1983) made a pioneering contribution to the analysis of transition probabilities among (i) employees, (ii) unemployed, and (ii) those not in the labour force, and provided several interesting insights into the Japanese labour market. The transition probability is given by p_{ij} where p_{ij} denotes the probability of changing the status from class i to class j,

$$P = \begin{bmatrix} P_{11} & P_{12} & \cdots & P_{lk} \\ P_{21} & P_{22} & & \\ P_{kl} & & \cdots & P_{kk} \end{bmatrix}$$

where $\sum_{j=1}^{k} p_{ij} = 1$ is satisfied, and k is the number of class. P is the matrix of transition probabilities. In the case of the above three labour force statuses, $j = 1$ signifies (i) employees; $j = 2$ signifies (ii) unemployed; and $j = 3$ signifies (iii) not in the labour force. For example, P_{12} indicates the probability from employees to unemployed. If the number of flows from one status to another and the total aggregate figure of each status are available, it is possible to estimate the transition matrix of P. Mizuno paid particular attention to the effect of the difference in the size of firms on the transition probabilities. This is quite natural in view of the fact that the difference in the size of firms is an important element in Japan.

This chapter emphasizes the importance of self-employed workers in interpreting the working of the Japanese labour market, by considering 'self-employed' as being an additional labour force status. Economists have tended to ignore the role of self-employed workers when analyzing the issues of employment and unemployment. A typical example is given by the fact that the analysis of labour turnover investigates all new hiring, quitting, laying-off and discharging of staff, and so on. Those phenomena arise largely from relationships between employers and employees. No serious consideration has been given to workers who are self-employed, and change their labour force status willingly or unwillingly.

The following data show the ratios of self-employed workers, including family workers, to the total labour force for various countries: Japan 0.250, the USA 0.084, the UK 0.108, West Germany 0.119, France 0.188, Italy 0.293 and Canada 0.095. These figures were taken from the *White Paper on the World Labour Market* published by the Ministry of Labour in Japan, and are largely the totals for 1985 or 1986. Japan and Italy show the highest ratios among the industrialized countries, and their figures are much higher than for other countries. This suggests that the analysis of self-employed workers is likely to give new clues to the understanding of the Japanese labour market, which is assumed to be quite different from that of other countries.

As noted earlier, the *Employment Status Survey* is used as the main data source, unlike other studies such as Mizuno (1982, 1983) which have used the *Labour Force Survey*. There are several notable differences between the two sources. One of them is the difference in observation periods. While the *Employment Status Survey* asks the status on the usual basis, the *Labour Force Survey* asks the status on the actual basis (that is, the status in the specific week, namely the last week of March each year). This distinction is crucial in measuring the number of unemployed people. Although some of those sampled in the *Employment Status Survey* may declare that they are unemployed, it is possible that they are not actively looking for jobs. However, they may not declare that they are out of the labour force. Those samples are somewhere between strictly unemployed and strictly not-in-the-labour-force. In other words, the *Employment Status Survey* measures unemployment and 'not-in-labour-force' somewhat ambiguously. Also, disguised unemployment may belong to this category. The *Labour Force*

Survey, on the other hand, asks the actual status for the particular week, and therefore the definition of unemployment is more rigorous and exact. In combining the above facts, it is quite natural that the rate of unemployment in the *Labour Force Survey* is much lower than that in the *Employment Status Survey*. See, for example, Tomita (1984).

Which data source is preferable? This chapter does not discuss this subject seriously, but it is believed that the usual state is preferable if the previous year's status and the current year's status are compared. This does not necessarily imply that the actual state is useless. A monthly or weekly transition should be measured on the basis of the actual state. Another reason for adopting the *Employment Status Survey* comes from the fact that the labour market condition in Japan, especially the rate of unemployment, is not defined well by the *Labour Force Survey*, as it does not include disguised unemployment (see Tachibanaki (1987), for example). One difficulty remains, however, in the *Employment Status Survey* because of the ignorance of multiple changes in labour force status within the observation period, which is not solved by any data source. In sum, the *Employment Status Survey* and the *Labour Force Survey* both have advantages and disadvantages. Which is better depends upon the purpose of the study. However, it is worthwhile to repeat that the estimation of transition probabilities in this chapter is made for labour force status measured on the basis of the usual state rather than the actual state, and is presented for the purpose of a comparison with the result on the basis of the actual state.

Table 4.1 shows the estimated transition probabilities based on nine classifications of labour force statuses, namely:

   (i) employed;
  (ii) unemployed; and
 (iii) not in the labour force.

Employed consists of the following seven statuses:

(a) firms with 1–9 employees;
(b) firms with 10–29 employees;
(c) firms with 30–99 employees;
(d) firms with 100–999 employees;
(e) firms with 1000 and more employees;
(f) employees in public sectors; and
(g) self-employed.

TABLE 4.1 Estimated transition probabilities among nine labour force statuses in 1982

Male (all age class)	1–9 employees	10–29 employees	30–99 employees	100–999 employees	1000 + employees	Public sector	Self-employed	Unemployed	Not in labour force
1–9 employees	0.9393	0.0104	0.0050	0.0052	0.0016	0.0005	0.0073	0.0240	0.0068
10–29 employees	0.0102	0.9324	0.0054	0.0057	0.0020	0.0011	0.0068	0.0322	0.0042
30–99 employees	0.0063	0.0077	0.9419	0.0052	0.0036	0.0006	0.0028	0.0275	0.0044
100–999 employees	0.0050	0.0043	0.0058	0.9573	0.0017	0.0006	0.0028	0.0192	0.0032
1000 + employees	0.0020	0.0035	0.0029	0.0033	0.9631	0.0007	0.0022	0.0176	0.0048
Public sector	0.0009	0.0003	0.0021	0.0027	0.0006	0.9771	0.0030	0.0060	0.0072
Self-employed	0.0023	0.0021	0.0017	0.0021	0.0005	0.0001	0.9810	0.0043	0.0059
Unemployed	0.1475	0.1177	0.1103	0.0790	0.0238	0.0149	0.0477	0.3994	0.0596
Not in labour force	0.0735	0.0382	0.0603	0.0382	0.0147	0.0176	0.0662	0.1956	0.4956

Female (all age class)	1–9 employees	10–29 employees	30–99 employees	100–999 employees	1000 + employees	Public sector	Self-employed	Unemployed	Not in labour force
1–9 employees	0.8690	0.0077	0.0066	0.0045	0.0038	0.0010	0.0073	0.0808	0.0192
10–29 employees	0.0106	0.8628	0.0081	0.0030	0.0034	0.0030	0.0042	0.0811	0.0238
30–99 employees	0.0069	0.0065	0.8825	0.0061	0.0039	0.0013	0.0056	0.0681	0.0191
100–999 employees	0.0086	0.0086	0.0098	0.8551	0.0031	0.0020	0.0078	0.0789	0.0262
1000 + employees	0.0090	0.0032	0.0051	0.0051	0.8536	0.0026	0.0051	0.812	0.0352
Public sector	0.0006	0.0048	0.0018	0.0006	0.0	0.9275	0.0012	0.0371	0.0222
Self-employed	0.0013	0.0013	0.0010	0.0006	0.0011	0.0003	0.9696	0.0150	0.0099
Unemployed	0.1331	0.1016	0.0867	0.0630	0.0374	0.0238	0.1064	0.3440	0.1040
Not in labour force	0.0208	0.0155	0.0127	0.0107	0.0059	0.0024	0.0243	0.2325	0.6751

Note: The underlined numbers are the diagonal elements.

Source: *Employment Status Survey, 1982.*

Since it is somewhat difficult to understand the data in Table 4.1, Table 4.2, which consists of five classifications (that is, employment consists of only two classifications), is presented. The data in Table 4.2 are the ones used mainly in this text. The economic interpretations, however, are made mainly on the basis of the figures shown in Table 4.1.

Observations on males of all age classes are initially discussed. There are a large number of findings, and these are presented item by item without much explanation. First, the probability of staying at the same status (that is, from *employed* to *employed*, from *unemployed* to *unemployed*, and from *not in labour force* to *not in labour force*), which is indicated by the diagonal element, is normally the highest. This is, in particular, true in the case of *employed*, and the probability of keeping the same employment is over 90 per cent. It should be pointed out, however, that in some cases (all age classes and by age classes) the diagonal element is smaller than the off-diagonal elements with respect to the numbers in rows of *unemployed* and *not in labour force*, that is, if the previous year's status is *unemployed* or *not in labour force*. This is different from the finding obtained by the *Labour Force Survey*.

Second, extremely low rates are observed with respect to the change from *employed* to *not in labour force*. The probabilities from *employed* to *unemployed* are three or five times higher than those from *employed* to *not in labour force*. It should be emphasized, however, that the probabilities from *employed* to *unemployed* for both self-employed and public-sector employees are extremely low (that is, 0.0043 and 0.0060, respectively).

By combining the above data, two interesting interpretations of the Japanese labour market emerge. It is noted again that these are revealed because the *Employment Status Survey* is used as the data source. One is that moving into the category *not in labour force* directly from *employment* is relatively rare; it occurs largely through *unemployment* after *employment*. One possible reason is that a large number of employees, if entitled, would opt to receive unemployment compensation before leaving the labour market. The channel from *employment* to *not in labour force* through *unemployment* is encouraged by the existence of the unemployment compensation system. The other reason is that there must be a non-negligible number of discouraged workers, even for males, if they are older. The channel from *employment* to *not in labour force* through *unemployment* is also explained by the so-called 'discouraged effect'.

Returning to the second economic interpretation, it is possible to conclude that the Japanese labour market is unable by its intrinsic nature to have a higher rate of unemployment. As already mentioned, the

TABLE 4.2 Estimated transition probabilities among five labour force statuses in 1982

Male (all age class)

This year (1982) Last year (1981)	Smaller firms (1–99 employees)	Larger firms (100 + employees) and public sector	Self-employed	Unemployed	Not in labour force
Smaller firms (1–99 employees)	0.9529	0.0085	0.0056	0.0278	0.0052
Larger firms (100 + employees) and public sector	0.0095	0.9679	0.0026	0.0151	0.0049
Self-employed	0.0061	0.0027	0.9810	0.0043	0.0059
Unemployed	0.3756	0.1177	0.0477	0.3994	0.0596
Not in labour force	0.1721	0.0706	0.0662	0.1956	0.4956

Female (all age class)

This year (1982) Last year (1981)	Smaller firms (1–99 employees)	Larger firms (100 + employees) and public sector	Self-employed	Unemployed	Not in labour force
Smaller firms (1–99 employees)	0.8866	0.0100	0.0058	0.0770	0.0206
Larger firms (100 + employees) and public sector	0.0186	0.8813	0.0052	0.0675	0.0274
Self-employed	0.0036	0.0020	0.9696	0.0150	0.0099
Unemployed	0.3215	0.1242	0.1064	0.3440	0.1040
Not in labour force	0.0491	0.0190	0.0243	0.2325	0.6751

Source: *Employment Status Survey*, 1982

Male (ages 15–29)

This year (1982) / Last year (1981)	Smaller firms (1–99 employees)	Larger firms (100 + employees) and public sector	Self-employed	Unemployed	Not in labour force
Smaller firms (1–99 employees)	0.9430	0.0174	0.0094	0.0285	0.0017
Larger firms (100 + employees) and public sector	0.0218	0.9612	0.0030	0.0137	0.0004
Self-employed	0.0092	0.0129	0.9761	0.0018	0.0
Unemployed	0.5964	0.1928	0.0241	0.1687	0.0181
Not in labour force	0.3965	0.1466	0.0603	0.2500	0.1466

Female (ages 15–29)

This year (1982) / Last year (1981)	Smaller firms (1–99 employees)	Larger firms (100 + employees) and public sector	Self-employed	Unemployed	Not in labour force
Smaller firms (1–99 employees)	0.8016	0.0170	0.0071	0.1315	0.0428
Larger firms (100 + employees) and public sector	0.0346	0.8251	0.0054	0.0980	0.0368
Self-employed	0.0088	0.0110	0.9011	0.0440	0.0352
Unemployed	0.4353	0.1971	0.0941	0.2147	0.0589
Not in labour force	0.0572	0.0308	0.0273	0.1909	0.6940

Male (ages 30–49)

This year (1982) / Last year (1981)	Smaller firms (1–99 employees)	Larger firms (100 + employees) and public sector	Self-employed	Unemployed	Not in labour force
Smaller firms (1–99 employees)	0.9687	0.0077	0.0045	0.0182	0.0009
Larger firms (100 + employees) and public sector	0.0055	0.9883	0.0013	0.0048	0.0001
Self-employed	0.0088	0.0034	0.9836	0.0040	0.0003
Unemployed	0.4306	0.1250	0.1065	0.3194	0.0185
Not in labour force	0.2558	0.0756	0.1337	0.2384	0.2965

Female (ages 30–49)

This year (1982) / Last year (1981)	Smaller firms (1–99 employees)	Larger firms (100 + employees) and public sector	Self-employed	Unemployed	Not in labour force
Smaller firms (1–99 employees)	0.9170	0.0103	0.0049	0.0578	0.0101
Larger firms (100 + employees) and public sector	0.0108	0.9277	0.0046	0.0464	0.0104
Self-employed	0.0048	0.0029	0.9691	0.0186	0.0045
Unemployed	0.3477	0.1307	0.1265	0.3140	0.0811
Not in labour force	0.0539	0.0196	0.0236	0.2565	0.6463

Male (ages 50 and over)

This year (1982) / Last year (1981)	Smaller firms (1–99 employees)	Larger firms (100 + employees) and public sector	Self-employed	Unemployed	Not in labour force
Smaller firms (1–99 employees)	0.9317	0.0029	0.0049	0.0448	0.0157
Larger firms (100 + employees) and public sector	0.0077	0.9249	0.0056	0.0414	0.0205
Self-employed	0.0033	0.0008	0.9796	0.0049	0.0115
Unemployed	0.2076	0.0692	0.0173	0.5917	0.1142
Not in labour force	0.0689	0.0459	0.0383	0.1607	0.6862

Female (ages 50 and over)

This year (1982) / Last year (1981)	Smaller firms (1–99 employees)	Larger firms (100 + employees) and public sector	Self-employed	Unemployed	Not in labour force
Smaller firms (1–99 employees)	0.9070	0.0022	0.0066	0.0635	0.0208
Larger firms (100 + employees) and public sector	0.0031	0.8861	0.0061	0.0539	0.0509
Self-employed	0.0016	0.0	0.9785	0.0076	0.0122
Unemployed	0.1599	0.0457	0.0685	0.5279	0.1980
Not in labour force	0.0244	0.0039	0.0235	0.2024	0.7459

probability for self-employed workers of either becoming *unemployed* or *leaving the labour force* is very low, and the ratio of self-employed workers to total labour force in Japan is much higher than in other industrialized nations. Since the Euro-American countries normally have a higher share of employed people to total labour force, their possibility of observing a higher rate of unemployment is greater. It would be possible to see a narrower gap of the rates of unemployment between Japan and the Euro-American countries, if the contribution of self-employed workers were controlled. In sum, the number of unemployable people is much lower in Japan, and this is one of the causes of a lower unemployment rate.

When the difference in the size of firms is examined, the following findings are obtained:

(i) Becoming *unemployed* or *not in labour force* from *employed* is higher in smaller firms than in larger firms. The figures in Table 4.2 are 0.0278 versus 0.0151 for *unemployed*, and 0.0052 versus 0.0049 for *not in labour force*.

(ii) Becoming *employed in firms* from *self-employed* status is concentrated on smaller-sized firms. The numbers in Table 4.2 are 0.0061 (smaller firms) versus 0.0027 (larger firms). In other words, if self-employed workers wanted to change their labour force status from *self-employed* to *employment*, the majority would have to work in smaller firms rather than in larger firms.

(iii) A similar story is observed for unemployed workers who want to find jobs. The figures in Table 4.2 are 0.3756 versus 0.1177. More concretely, the possibility of finding jobs is a decreasing function of the size of firm for unemployed people. The majority of unemployed workers have to work in smaller firms at least after being unemployed.

(iv) It is interesting to note that the probability of becoming *self-employed* from *unemployed* is also low, 0.0477. This is of a symmetrical nature, with the low possibility of becoming *unemployed* for self-employed workers. In other words, transition between *self-employed* and *unemployed* in both directions is limited.

(v) With respect to the change from *not in labour force* to *employed*, the role of the difference in firm sizes is smaller in comparison with the change from *unemployed* to *employed*. However, it is noted that the possibility of becoming *self-employed* from *not in labour force* is higher than that from *unemployed*. The numbers in Table 4.1 and 4.2 are 0.0662 versus 0.0477.

In summarizing the above arguments, emphasis is placed on the importance of self-employed workers as well as on the role of firm sizes in understanding the Japanese labour market. Self-employed workers show unique behaviour, judging from the transition probabilities both from *self-employed* to the other statuses and from the other statuses to *self-employed*. In other words, it would be possible to obtain a misleading judgement if the role of self-employed workers were ignored in analysing the Japanese labour market.

Next, the result for females is reviewed. Emphasis is placed upon a comparison with males in order to avoid repetition. Both the probability from *employed* to *unemployed* and the probability from *employed* to *not in labour force* is much higher for females than for males. The numbers in Table 4.2 suggest 0.0675 (females) versus 0.0151 (males) from larger firms, and 0.0770 versus 0.0278 from smaller firms with respect to becoming *unemployed*; and 0.0274 versus 0.0049 from larger firms, and 0.0206 versus 0.0052 from smaller firms with respect to becoming *not in labour force*. This suggests in general that the change in labour force status is much higher for females than for males. It is interesting to note, however, that the difference in firm sizes is relatively minor when examining the female transition probabilities from *employed* both to *unemployed* and to *not in labour force*, if public sector and self-employed are excluded. Although male observations gave a considerably different effect according to the size of firms (that is, stable employment in larger firms and unstable employment in smaller firms), female employees become *unemployed* or *not in labour force* regardless of the size of firms where they were employed; see Table 4.1 for detail.

With respect to the diagonal elements of the transition matrix, the probabilities of staying at the same status are higher than those of changing status. This was true also for males. It should be pointed out, however, that the female probabilities of keeping employment are considerably lower than the male ones. The figures in Table 4.2 are 0.8866 (females) to 0.9529 (males) for smaller firms, and 0.8813 to 0.9679 for larger firms. With respect to from *unemployed* to *unemployed* the female rate is slightly lower than the male one (0.3440 to 0.3994), while the female rate of staying at *not in labour force* is much higher than the male one (0.6751 to 0.4956). The above male–female difference is easily justified in view of the 'discouraged effect' for females and the lower rate of female labour force participation, as will be explained later.

As was true in the case of male observations, the possibility of finding jobs at smaller firms from *unemployed* is higher than that at larger firms. However, the possibility of leaving the labour market from *unemployed* is twice as high for females than for males (0.1040 to 0.0596). Two reasons are possible for a higher rate of the 'discouraged effect'. One is due to the data source. The *Employment Status Survey* adopts the usual state for measuring unemployment, as was explained previously. The other is due to the fact that females are discouraged more strongly than males, as pointed out by, for example Tachibanaki (1987), and Tachibanaki and Sakurai (1991).

The probability of finding a job from either *unemployed* or *not in labour force* is a decreasing function of the size of firms. In other words, females tend to find their jobs more easily in smaller firms than in larger ones. This is in contrast to the case of a worker leaving, because the difference in firm sizes had no effect on the transition probabilities of leaving employment. A quasi-asymmetry is observed for females between finding jobs and leaving jobs with respect to the effect of the size of firms. This is an interesting observation which distinguishes between the male and female labour markets.

The transition probabilities by age classes is now examined, namely (i) younger generation (ages 15–29), (ii) middle generation (ages 30–49) and (iii) older generation (ages 50 and over). Since most of the statements given previously in the case of all age classes are valid in the case of divided age classes, only the findings which are quite different from the findings for all age classes are described. The numbers in Tables 4.1 and 4.2 are not reproduced in the text to avoid being cumbersome.

(i) Younger generation – ages 15–29

Since recent graduates from schools are excluded from the sample, the number of adopted samples is considerably smaller. This does not necessarily affect the estimated transition probabilities of younger generation. However, new graduates who joined *not in labour force* straight from school are included in the sample. There is a significant difference between males and females with respect to the probability of leaving the labour market (that is, from either *unemployed* or *employed* to *not in labour force*). Very few males leave the labour market, compared with a large number of young females. The female result confirms the M-shaped curve of the labour force participation rate by ages in Japan. Staying unemployed is considerably lower in the younger generation than in all age classes. This is due to the fact that the duration of youth unemployment is shorter than that of the other generations. See Tachibanaki (1984a) on youth unemployment in Japan. Related to this fact, the diagonal elements show the probabilities of keeping the same status are considerably lower in the younger generation, in general, than all age classes. This implies that the change in labour force status among the younger generation is more frequent, and thus there is more instability than in the other generations. Finally, the effect of the size of firms on labour force status is not so prominent in comparison with the other generations, although detailed explanations are not provided. It is, however, impossible to deny the effect of size completely.

(ii) Middle generation – ages 30–49

This generation, in particular the male observations, shows the highest stability in labour force statuses. The diagonal elements of the transition probabilities, including public sector and self-employed, are quite high. Staying in employment is very pronounced. This is quite natural in view of the ages and careers of the respondents. However, there are some minor movements in the middle generation, in particular in the female observations. The examples are as follows: from *employed* to *self-employed*, from *unemployed* to *employed*, from *not in labour force* to *employed*, and several others. The important thing in these movements is the fact that smaller firms are the main sources of movement. Employees in larger firms are not associated with movement.

(iii) Older generation – ages 50 and over

This generation shows a considerably different picture in comparison with the other generations. Some examples unique to the older generation are as follows. First, although the probabilities of keeping employment are still high, the probability of staying *unemployed* or *not in labour force* becomes significantly higher in comparison with the other generations. Second, employees in larger firms as well as in the public sector change their labour force statuses, unlike the other generations. Related to this, it is interesting to note that the probability of becoming *unemployed* or *not in labour force* is higher for male employees in larger firms than for males in smaller firms, and this is also true for female employees who become *not in labour force*. Third, the transition probability from *unemployed* to *not in labour force* is extremely high. This arises partly because some workers of the older generation retire from the labour market voluntarily after receiving unemployment compensation, and partly because some of the older generation are forced to retire as discouraged workers in the face of the difficulty in finding jobs.

4.3 THE DETERMINATION OF TRANSITION PROBABILITIES

The previous section examined the estimated transition probabilities among various labour force statuses, with emphasis on the influence among employees of male–female differences, ages, occupations (namely employees versus the self-employed), and firm sizes. This section investigates the way in which the estimated transition probabilities are different among people who have different personal characteristics and economic conditions, or how the transition probabilities are determined.

There are two methodologies for investigating this. The first is to estimate each transition probability equation, which is explained by several explanatory variables, using time-series data. This approach was adopted by Toikka and Holt (1976) in the USA, and Mizuno (1983) in Japan. The second approach, which is used in this chapter, attempts to use cross-section data rather than time-series data. There is a trade-off between the above two data sources. While time-series data are able to take account of a change in several general economic conditions such as the tightness of the labour market and others, cross-section data are unable to give such information unless panel data are available. However, cross-section data are normally rich in information on social and economic characteristics of individual samples, therefore emphasis is placed on those individual social and economic conditions in determining the values of the estimated transition probabilities.

The statistical method in this section is fairly simple: multinomial logit analysis. Maximum likelihood estimation procedure is applied. Importance is placed upon investigating whether individual social and economic conditions are influential in the determination of the values of the estimated transition probabilities. Since it is too cumbersome to consider a large number of labour force statuses, only five were considered, namely (i) employees in smaller firms (the number of employees between 1–99); (ii) employees in larger firms (the number of employees over 100) and in the public sector; (iii) self-employed, (iv) unemployed, and (v) not in labour force. Even with only five labour force statuses the number of logit equations and parameters is still very large, so all the estimated equations and parameters are not shown, just a selection of interesting results.

Table 4.3 shows the estimated results of the logit equations, (24 in total – 12 male and 12 female). The probability P_{ij} indicates the transition from the ith status to the jth status. The exact meaning of the ith status corresponds to the status written by the arabic numeral above. For example, $i = 1$ means employees in smaller firms (the number of

TABLE 4.3 Estimated logit equations

Males

Last year's (1981) status	Dependent variables	Const	Wage	Education	Tenure	Number of children	Married	White-collar	Blue-collar	Equation number
Smaller firms	$\log_e \dfrac{P_{13}}{P_{12}}$	0.612 (1.136)	1.254* (0.043)	0.007 (0.078)	-0.181* (0.035)	-0.106 (0.155)	-0.804 (0.429)	0.772 (0.612)	0.509 (0.395)	(1)
Smaller firms	$\log_e \dfrac{P_{15}}{P_{14}}$	1.035 (0.825)	2.303* (0.013)	0.123 (0.065)	-0.669* (0.061)	0.174 (0.140)	-0.919* (0.431)			(2)
Larger firms and public sector	$\log_e \dfrac{P_{23}}{P_{21}}$	2.907* (1.438)		-0.184 (0.103)	-0.161* (0.016)	-0.374* (0.144)	-0.338 (0.530)	1.582* (0.782)	-0.255 (0.511)	(3)
Larger firms and public sector	$\log_e \dfrac{P_{25}}{P_{24}}$	2.365 (1.268)		0.129 (0.072)	-0.326* (0.023)	-0.045 (0.411)	-2.774* (1.028)			(4)
Self-employed	$\log_e \dfrac{P_{32}}{P_{31}}$	1.175 (2.103)	-0.384* (0.156)	-0.062 (0.149)	0.062 (0.038)	-0.335 (0.242)	0.378 (0.690)	1.754 (1.814)	0.265 (0.665)	(5)
Self-employed	$\log_e \dfrac{P_{35}}{P_{34}}$	-4.164 (2.094)		0.511* (0.168)	-0.243* (0.076)	-0.196 (0.234)	-1.120 (1.232)			(6)
Unemployed	$\log_e \dfrac{P_{42}}{P_{41}}$	2.804* (0.878)	-0.119 (0.136)	-0.138* (0.064)		0.040 (0.120)	-0.343 (0.281)	0.064 (0.437)	0.365 (0.317)	(7)

Unemployed	$\log_e \dfrac{P_{43}}{P_{41}}$	4.358* (1.462)	0.568* (0.074)	−0.112 (0.101)	−0.399* (0.152)	−2.035* (0.638)	0.726 (0.714)	0.915* (0.444)	(8)
Unemployed	$\log_e \dfrac{P_{43}}{P_{42}}$	1.554 (1.579)	0.687* (0.086)	0.026 (0.109)	−0.439* (0.176)	−1.692* (0.668)	0.662 (0.758)	0.550 (0.494)	(9)
Not in labour force	$\log_e \dfrac{P_{52}}{P_{51}}$	3.558* (1.291)	−0.066 (0.119)	−0.169 (0.092)	0.105 (0.155)	−0.314 (0.426)	−1.343* (0.578)	−0.206 (0.536)	(10)
Not in labour force	$\log_e \dfrac{P_{53}}{P_{51}}$	1.172 (1.242)	−0.012 (0.115)	0.049 (0.102)	0.228 (0.169)	−0.569 (0.435)	1.191 (0.729)	0.442 (0.424)	(11)
Not in labour force	$\log_e \dfrac{P_{53}}{P_{52}}$	−3.386* (1.597)	0.054 (0.085)	0.218 (0.122)	0.123 (0.207)	−0.255 (0.560)	2.534* (0.813)	0.648 (0.596)	(12)

Females

Last year's (1981) status	Dependent variables	Const	Wage	Education	Tenure	Number of children	Married	White-collar	Blue-collar	Equation number
Smaller firms	$\log_e \dfrac{P_{13}}{P_{12}}$	2.274 (1.694)	0.947* (0.411)	-0.143 (0.129)	-0.056 (0.040)	0.329 (0.239)	-0.857 (0.582)	1.053 (0.681)	-0.904 (0.556)	(13)
Smaller firms	$\log_e \dfrac{P_{15}}{P_{14}}$	2.795* (0.638)		-0.084 (0.047)	-0.344* (0.030)	0.217* (0.097)	0.800* (0.281)			(14)
Larger firms and public sector	$\log_e \dfrac{P_{23}}{P_{21}}$	4.805* (1.758)	4.553* (0.598)	-0.331* (0.132)	-0.682* (0.055)	-0.607* (0.200)	0.553 (0.532)	0.008 (0.679)	-1.964* (0.576)	(15)
Larger firms and public sector	$\log_e \dfrac{P_{25}}{P_{24}}$	2.149* (0.678)		-0.041 (0.050)	-0.560* (0.112)	0.184 (0.111)	-1.107* (0.272)			(16)
Self-employed	$\log_e \dfrac{P_{32}}{P_{31}}$	-1.255 (1.602)	0.005 (0.047)	0.088 (0.102)	0.067* (0.027)	-0.013 (0.089)	-0.043 (0.995)	0.542* (0.243)	0.833* (0.383)	(17)
Self-employed	$\log_e \dfrac{P_{35}}{P_{34}}$	9.099 (44.290)		-0.006 (0.087)	-0.202* (0.016)	0.307 (0.324)	-9.087 (44.283)			(18)
Unemployed	$\log_e \dfrac{P_{42}}{P_{41}}$	2.029* (0.627)	0.056* (0.028)	-0.090 (0.049)		-0.035 (0.075)	0.048 (0.219)	-0.306 (0.212)	0.043 (0.204)	(19)

Unemployed	$\log_e \dfrac{P_{43}}{P_{41}}$	4.133* (0.742)	0.174 (0.121)	-0.160* (0.053)	-0.097 (0.082)	-1.022* (0.375)	1.388* (0.389)	-0.850* (0.207)	(20)
Unemployed	$\log_e \dfrac{P_{43}}{P_{42}}$	2.105* (0.861)	0.118 (0.112)	-0.070 (0.063)	-0.062 (0.097)	-1.070* (0.402)	1.695* (0.411)	-0.892* (0.251)	(21)
Not in labour force	$\log_e \dfrac{P_{52}}{P_{51}}$	2.611* (0.892)	0.227* (0.014)	-0.134 (0.068)	-0.187 (0.110)	0.191 (0.335)	-0.161 (0.298)	0.199 (0.298)	(22)
Not in labour force	$\log_e \dfrac{P_{53}}{P_{51}}$	4.143* (0.977)	0.035 (0.076)	-0.112 (0.062)	-0.072 (0.105)	-1.673* (0.618)	-0.088 (0.323)	-0.751* (0.274)	(23)
Not in labour force	$\log_e \dfrac{P_{53}}{P_{52}}$	1.532 (1.165)	-0.191* (0.065)	0.022 (0.079)	0.114 (0.129)	-1.863* (0.654)	0.074 (0.372)	-0.950* (0.343)	(24)

Notes: 1. The numbers in parentheses are asymptotic standard errors.
2. The sign (*) shows statistical significance at 5 per cent level.

employees is between 1 and 99), and $i = 2, 3, 4$ and 5 follow the same correspondence. There are six equations for the case in which employment (that is, $i = 1, 2,$ and 3) is the origin of the status (that is, the previous year's status), while there are respectively three equations for the case in which the origin is both *unemployed* and *not in labour force*. The interpretation of the estimated results is made largely on the basis of statistical significance, and the sign of the parameters rather than the estimated numerical values of these. The explanatory variables in the logit equations are wages, educational attainment, tenure (years of working in one firm), number of children, marital status (a dummy variable), and occupational status (dummies indicating blue-collar or white-collar). Needless to say, these variables are expected to be influential in various ways on the determination of transition probabilities.

Following are several general findings about the determination of the transition probabilities in Japan, beginning with observations of male. First, both wages and, particularly tenure variables are statistically significant when *employed* is the origin of the status. With respect to the effect of tenure it is concluded that when the tenure is longer, employees tend again to choose employee status rather than becoming *self-employed* as equations (1) and (3) indicate, and also tend to become *unemployed* rather than entering the *not in labour force*, as equations (2) and (4) show. Second, wage (income) shows a somewhat surprising result, namely that employees (even unemployed) wish to or are obliged to choose *self-employed* status rather than becoming employees, if wage (income) is higher and other conditions are common. Those results are given by equations (1), (3), (8) and (9). It is not easy to explain this. Third, the result on the transition from *not in labour force* is basically poor, as none of the estimated parameters is statistically significant. There must be several unobservable variables which determine the transition from *not in labour force* to the other statuses.

There are several worthwhile points which can be applied to specific equations. If employees are married, they become *unemployed* rather than becoming *not in labour force* as given by equations (2) and (4). However, married people tend to be *employed* rather than becoming *self-employed*, when they were *unemployed* or *not in labour force* in the previous year. When the number of children is larger, people tend to be *employed* rather than becoming *self-employed*. Equations (1), (3), (8) and (9) refer to this. Equation (3) suggests that white-collar workers tend to move to *self-employed*, while the coefficient of blue-collar workers is statistically insignificant. Equation (8) suggests that *unemployed* blue-collar workers tend to become *self-employed* rather than becoming *employed*. Equation (10) suggests that white-collar workers *not in labour force* tend to work in smaller firms rather than in larger firms. It should be pointed out, however, that the effect of occupation, namely white-collar versus blue-collar, is not significant in determining the transition probabilities in general. Education is not so important in determining the transition probabilities in all equations except for equations (6) and (7), in which *self-employed* was the previous year's status. In other words, workers' transition probabilities are not influenced by their level of educational attainment. It is, however, interesting to note that while educated female employees tend to prefer *unemployed* to being *not in labour force*, educated male employees prefer *not in labour force* to *unemployment*.

Next, the female result is reviewed. Emphasis is placed upon the similarities and differences in comparison with males. With respect to the effect of the duration of employment (that is, tenure) females show a similar result to males. Female employees with longer tenure tend to become employees again rather than becoming *self-employed*. They also tend to become *unemployed* when both *unemployed* and *not in labour force* are available categories after being *employed*. The effect of wage (income) is less prominent in female observations than in males. However, the previous result for males, namely 'the higher the wage (income) level, the higher the probability of becoming *self-employed* rather than of becoming *employed*' is also supported for female observations. Unlike the male observations, the empirical result in the transition from *not in labour force* to the other statuses is better in the female observations. In fact, some of the variables such as wage (income), marital status and occupation are statistically significant, as given by equations (22), (23) and (24). This is an interesting contrast with males, and is fairly reasonable and understandable in view of the particularities in female labour supply behaviour. A similar result is observed in the case in which *unemployed* was the origin of the status, namely, some of the variables such as wage (income), education, marital status and occupation are statistically significant, as given by equations (19), (20) and (21).

Some other variables are reviewed briefly here. First, when the number of children is larger, female employees become *not in labour force* rather than becoming *unemployed* as given by equations (14) and (16), where females were working. Second, with respect to marital status, the difference between employees in smaller firms and employees in larger firms is evident, namely, female married employees in smaller firms tend to leave the labour market rather than becoming *unemployed*, while the opposite is true for female employees in larger firms. Third, the effect of occupations (white-collar workers versus blue-collar workers) does not provide any systematic impact on the change in labour force status in the case of female observations.

4.4 LABOUR TURNOVER

This section presents the estimated results of labour turnover functions by using the same data set as the previous sections. Labour turnover is defined here as a separation from the previous employer, and the worker obtaining another job in a different firm during the previous twelve months. It differs from the change in labour force status which was analyzed previously. An important distinction is made, however, with respect to the reasons for the separation, namely whether it is voluntary or involuntary. Since the original data source asked about the reasons for the separation, it is possible to distinguish between voluntary and involuntary reasons.

Since separations from employers are analyzed in this section, the only status in the previous year which can be used as data is employees in industries. It is impossible to consider the self-employed. Therefore, this section analyses only employees. Also, only male observations are considered. The reason for this is that it would be necessary to take account of information or variables which are not available in the *Employment Status Survey*, if female labour turnover functions are estimated. Labour turnover status is identified by 1 if a worker separated from the previous employer during the sample period (one year), and by 0 if a worker stayed in the same company. Thus, the dependent variable is basically a discrete one. The estimation procedure is the maximum likelihood method with the logistic transformation.

Mincer and Higuchi (1988) reported labour turnover equations which adopted similar approaches using the same data set. Their regression analyses have ignored the discrete nature of the dependent variable, and thus it is suspected that some of their estimated probabilities may be less than 0 or greater than 1. This section attempts to improve it slightly.

Two equations are provided in Tables 4.4a, 4.4b and 4.4c, namely total labour turnover (both voluntary and involuntary) and voluntary separations. Although equations for involuntary separations were attempted, the estimated results turned out to be unsatisfactory, partly

TABLE 4.4a   The estimated parameters of male labour turnover functions (both total separations and voluntary separations) for all age classes

	White-collar		Blue-collar		Sales and services	
	Total	Voluntary	Total	Voluntary	Total	Voluntary
Constant	−2.852	−2.754	−0.244	−0.363	−0.915	−0.825
	(1.090)	(1.467)	(0.495)	(0.570)	(0.600)	(0.728)
Tenure	−0.115	−0.193	−0.121	−0.192	−0.163	−0.222
	(0.024)	(0.042)	(0.015)	(0.021)	(0.024)	(0.035)
Experience	0.062	0.061	−0.017	−0.023	0.014	0.009
	(0.018)	(0.023)	(0.009)	(0.010)	(0.014)	(0.017)
Education	0.038	−0.023	−0.047	−0.057	−0.038	−0.056
	(0.070)	(0.095)	(0.040)	(0.046)	(0.044)	(0.054)
Size	−0.005	0.012	−0.151	−0.186	−0.092	−0.093
	(0.055)	(0.075)	(0.032)	(0.038)	(0.044)	(0.050)
Wage	−0.001	−0.001	−0.001	−0.000	−0.000	−0.000
	(0.000)	(0.000)	(0.000)	(0.000)	(0.000)	(0.000)
Number of	−0.189	0.003	−0.027	−0.017	−0.062	−0.007
children	(0.139)	(0.186)	(0.061)	(0.070)	(0.087)	(0.107)
Number of	−0.159	−0.111	−0.091	−0.064	−0.029	−0.050
earners	(0.139)	(0.191)	(0.064)	(0.074)	(0.084)	(0.104)
Married	−0.342	0.124	0.283	0.307	0.018	−0.185
	(0.374)	(0.532)	(0.174)	(0.201)	(0.223)	(0.273)
Urban	0.047	0.647	0.304	0.431	0.057	0.206
	(0.269)	(0.372)	(0.140)	(0.160)	(0.182)	(0.220)

Notes:
1. Married and Urban variables are dummy variables, indicating Married = 1.0 and 0.0 otherwise, and Urban = 1.0 and 0.0 otherwise.
2. Number of Earners excludes a family head.
3. Experience is the total labour force experience, measured by the formula (age minus schooling years minus 6).
4. The dependent variable is measured by the mover = 1.0, and by the non-mover = 0.0. The estimation method is the logit transformation.

TABLE 4.4b   The estimated parameters of male labour turnover functions (both voluntary and involuntary separations) by age class

	White-collar		Blue-collar		Sales and services	
	15–34	35–55	15–34	35–55	15–34	35–55
Constant	−1.579	−9.842	−0.500	−1.237	−0.994	−3.305
	(1.586)	(26.237)	(0.612)	(1.298)	(0.773)	(1.772)
Tenure	−0.283	−0.088	−0.266	−0.054	−0.344	−0.059
	(0.071)	(0.024)	(0.029)	(0.015)	(0.045)	(0.025)
Experience	0.047	0.057	0.022	0.008	0.048	0.057
	(0.054)	(0.034)	(0.019)	(0.024)	(0.028)	(0.036)

continued on page 104

TABLE 4.4b continued

	White-collar		Blue-collar		Sales and services	
	15–34	35–55	15–34	35–55	15–34	35–55
Education	−0.026	0.100	−0.044	−0.011	−0.014	0.031
	(0.099)	(0.105)	(0.047)	(0.084)	(0.054)	(0.099)
Size	−0.077	0.095	−0.124	−0.218	−0.074	−0.075
	(0.073)	(0.083)	(0.037)	(0.071)	(0.047)	(0.089)
Wage	−0.000	−0.001	−0.001	−0.001	−0.000	−0.000
	(0.000)	(0.000)	(0.000)	(0.000)	(0.000)	(0.000)
Number of	−0.023	−0.417	−0.020	−0.014	−0.036	−0.338
children	(0.196)	(0.207)	(0.073)	(0.124)	(0.098)	(0.206)
Numbers of	−0.244	−0.070	−0.046	−0.277	−0.041	−0.031
earners	(0.191)	(0.234)	(0.073)	(0.154)	(0.097)	(0.212)
Married	−0.387	6.249	0.317	0.336	0.200	−0.642
	(0.460)	(−)	(0.193)	(0.568)	(0.242)	(0.725)
Urban	0.035	0.000	0.332	0.205	−0.113	0.523
	(0.362)	(0.409)	(0.167)	(0.268)	(0.213)	(0.391)

Note: See notes to Table 4.4a.

TABLE 4.4c The estimated parameters of male labour turnover functions (voluntary separations only) by age class

	White-collar		Blue-collar		Sales and services	
	15–34	35–55	15–34	35–55	15–34	35–55
Constant	−1.752	−8.189	−0.717	−1.576	−0.910	−1.001
	(2.226)	(50.873)	(0.683)	(1.698)	(0.909)	(2.256)
Tenure	−0.414	−0.155	−0.368	−0.089	−0.465	−0.077
	(0.119)	(0.042)	(0.041)	(0.021)	(0.067)	(0.035)
Experience	0.068	0.011	0.012	0.028	0.033	0.016
	(0.076)	(0.045)	(0.022)	(0.030)	(0.032)	(0.048)
Education	−0.056	−0.027	−0.033	−0.100	−0.029	−0.065
	(0.140)	(0.137)	(0.052)	(0.115)	(0.063)	(0.129)
Size	−0.096	0.158	−0.153	−0.328	−0.054	−0.175
	(0.103)	(0.110)	(0.042)	(0.098)	(0.056)	(0.131)
Wage	−0.000	−0.001	−0.000	−0.001	0.000	−0.000
	(0.000)	(0.000)	(0.000)	(0.000)	(0.000)	(0.000)
Number of	−0.072	−0.035	−0.020	0.058	0.057	−0.279
children	(0.282)	(0.271)	(0.082)	(0.153)	(0.118)	(0.266)
Number of	−0.167	0.076	−0.026	−0.315	−0.038	−0.112
earners	(0.263)	(0.294)	(0.083)	(0.195)	(0.117)	(0.281)
Married	−0.168	7.025	0.362	0.553	0.045	−0.907
	(0.664)	(−)	(0.220)	(0.782)	(0.295)	(0.799)
Urban	0.412	0.951	0.429	0.433	0.005	0.737
	(0.515)	(0.552)	(0.186)	(0.323)	(0.252)	(0.509)

Note: See notes to Table 4.4a.

because it is hard to estimate involuntary separation functions based only on the supply side (that is, the information on individual workers). It is quite natural to suppose that involuntary separations would be influenced strongly by factors other than the supply side. In particular, the considerations for the demand factor are necessary. In view of this difficulty, the results for involuntary separations are not reported here. In any case it is a difficult subject to combine individual survey data and demand factors which are hardly matched with individual cross-section data, statistically speaking.

The equations are estimated for all age classes (that is, ages 15–55), ages 15–34 and ages 35–55 separately, and also for white-collar workers, blue-collar workers, and sales and services workers separately. It is anticipated that labour turnover is considerably different by both workers' ages and occupations. In addition to the usual independent variables such as job tenure, wages and education, several social and economic variables which are supposed to be influential on labour turnover are included. Those are:

 (i) size of firm;
 (ii) experience as a total civilian labour force;
(iii) number of children;
(iv) number of earners in the family;
 (v) marital status; and
(vi) living area (urban or rural area of residence).

The economic implications of these variables on labour turnover are fairly simple and straightforward. Regarding the size of firm, it is expected that the larger the size of firm, the higher the probability of staying (that is, the lower the probability of labour turnover); see, for example, Tachibanaki (1984b). This has been partly supported in different contexts in the previous sections. Experience does not have a strong implication, but it indicates the total labour force experience, which has a similar implication to age. Number of children is expected to have a negative effect on labour turnover because a family with many children may be more risk averse. Number of earners in the family does not have a strong *a priori* expectation. Urban variable indicates a job perspective, namely that an employment opportunity is higher in an urban area than in a rural area. This is expected to indicate a demand factor. Marital status shows the degree of the risk-averse parameter similar to that of the number of children.

Several observations are possible on the basis of the results in Tables 4.4a, 4.4b and 4.4c. First, the most influential variable is job tenure, which has a negative effect on labour turnover. The longer the job tenure, the less likely the degree of labour turnover. This is true regardless of the worker's age, occupation or the reason for separation. In view of the highly significant negative coefficients of job tenure, it may not be an exaggeration to conclude that job tenure dominates the story of labour turnover in Japan. This is consistent with Tachibanaki (1984b), who found a negative duration dependence on labour turnover. Needless to say, it is largely consistent with the results obtained in the previous sections of this chapter with respect to the effect of tenure, although they dealt with changes in labour force status rather than labour turnover. Second, labour market experience shows a somewhat ambiguous result (positive or negative) in the presence of the job tenure variable; however, job tenure is a much more important variable in determining labour turnover than total labour market experience. Third, wage level does not have any effect on labour turnover, and this is true even for voluntary separations. Japanese workers do not evaluate pecuniary factors at all when they consider the possibility of separation. This is an interesting contrast to American labour turnover, which normally suggests that the wage is one of the most important motivations for separation. A simultaneous equation bias due to wages and labour turnover may be a serious problem. Fourth, with respect to the size of firm it is recognized that sales and service workers, and in particular blue-collar workers, are influenced negatively: in other words, the bigger the size of firm, the less likely the labour turnover. There is an interesting contrast between blue-collar workers and white-collar workers because the effect of the size of firm is almost negligible for the latter. Fifth, all the variables which indicate individual characteristics such as number of children, number of earners, marital status and urban status do not have any systematic effects on labour turnover, judging from the estimated significance of the parameters and the sign of the coefficients.

In sum, the empirical results in Tables 4.4a, b and c propose that labour turnover in Japan is dominated by the strong negative effect of job tenure, and the other variables show only minor effects. The insignificant effect of the wage variable on labour turnover is worth noting. The results in this section are consistent with those in the previous sections to a considerable extent, although the two previous sections performed different tasks.

4.5 CONCLUDING REMARKS

This chapter has investigated changes in labour force status and the issue of labour turnover in Japan. Three main sections were presented in order to analyze the above issues. The first section estimated the transition probabilities among several labour force statuses, with emphasis on the role of self-employed workers, the difference in firm size and the male–female difference in the analysis of the Japanese labour market. The second section investigated how the transition probabilities estimated in the first section were determined or influenced by several social and economic variables. The third section presented the estimated labour turnover functions. It is noted that a change in labour force status and a labour turnover are conceptually different.

A common data source was used for all three sections, namely the *Employment Status Survey*. It has been emphasized that the data source is different from the *Labour Force Survey* which is commonly used in the analysis of transition probabilities of labour force statuses. Emphasis was placed upon the difference in the estimated results due to the different data sources. It is not an easy task to summarize all the results obtained. It is worthwhile, however, to suggest the following observations for the working of the Japanese labour market:

1. Self-employed workers are considerably different from employed workers with respect to their behaviour, judging from the transition probabilities.
2. The male–female difference, the difference in the size of firms, and the difference in ages are quite significant in the working of the Japanese labour market.
3. The wage level (or income) is important in several cases among changes in labour force status, while it is not important in the case of labour turnover.
4. Education is not an important variable in differentiating the behaviour of the Japanese labour force.
5. Job tenure is the most important and possibly the only significant variable in determining the degree of labour turnover.

It should be added that the above summary is somewhat over-simplified. Qualifications, exceptions and reservations were described in the main text.

REFERENCES

Mincer, Y. and Y. Higuchi 1988. 'Wage Structures and Labor Turnover in the United States and Japan', *Journal of the Japanese and International Economies*, 2, pp. 97–133.

Mizuno, A. 1982. 'Unemployment in Japan: A Flow Analysis' (in Japanese), *Kikan Gendai Keizai*, 51, pp. 4–19.

Mizuno, A. 1983. 'Employment, Unemployment and Labour Market Dynamics' (in Japanese), *Keizaigaku Ronsan*, 24, pp. 37–61.

Tachibanaki, T. 1984a. 'The Youth Unemployment Problem' (in Japanese), *Nihon Rodo Kyokai Zassi (The Monthly Journal of the Japanese Institute of Labour)*, 26, December, pp. 12–22.

Tachibanaki, T. 1984b. 'Labour Mobility and Job Tenure', in M. Aoki, ed., *The Economic Analysis of the Japanese Firm*, Amsterdam: North-Holland.

Tachibanaki, T. 1987. 'Labour Market Flexibility in Japan in Comparison with Europe and the US', *European Economic Review*, 31, pp. 647–84.

Tachibanaki, T. and K. Sakurai 1991. 'Labour Supply and Unemployment in Japan', *European Economic Review*, 35, pp. 1575–87.

Toikka, R. S. and C. C. Holt 1976. 'Labor Force Participation and Earnings in a Demographic Model of the Labor Market', *American Economic Review*, 66, pp. 295–301.

Tomita, Y. 1984. 'Unemployment Statistics in Japan: Frequency of Job Search and Persons Who Desire to Work Mainly or Partly' (in Japanese), in K. Koike, ed., *Contemporary Unemployment*, Tōkyō: Dobunkan, pp. 117–42.

5 Is the Tenure-Earning Curve Really Steeper in Japan? A Re-examination Based on UK–Japan Comparison

Giorgio Brunello
and Kenn Ariga*

5.1 INTRODUCTION

Empirical earnings functions stress the relationship between earnings, seniority, labour market experience and education. In modern labour economics, these functions are an important tool for the description of different labour market institutions. In an influential paper, for instance, Hashimoto and Raisian (1985) compare the results from estimates of similar earnings functions in Japan and in the USA and conclude that the labour markets in the two countries differ rather sharply in the relative importance of the accumulation of firm-specific human capital. In particular, they find that 'growth rates in earnings attributable to tenure are far greater in Japan than in the United States' (p. 732).

In another paper, Collier and Knight (1985) compare earnings profiles in Japan and the UK. They chose Japan 'as the country most commonly identified with institutionalized seniority pay and lifetime

* This chapter was written while the first author was visiting the Institute for Economic Research, Kyōto University. The authors are grateful to the Murata Science Foundation and to Consiglio Nazionale delle Ricerche for financial support. The English data used in this paper were kindly provided by the ESRC Data Archive, Essex University. Earlier versions of the chapter were presented as a paper at Macquarie University, Australian National University, University of Western Australia and also at the 1993 Far Eastern Meeting of the Econometric Society held in Taipei. We are grateful to Leslie Stein, Gerald Garvey, Bruce Chapman, Michael McAleer and Mari Sako for their comments and suggestions, and to Kathy Sayer and Dino Rizzi for help with the British data. We wish to also thank Misuaki Okabe for many editorial suggestions and advice. The usual caveats apply.

employment, and Britain as a country which has not attracted particular attention in this respect' (p. 19). Their main finding is that the seniority premium, defined as the percentage difference between the pay of those who have completed ten years of tenure with the same employer, and the pay of those with less than one year of service, is about twice as large in Japan than in Britain. Additional evidence for Britain is provided by Marsden (1989), who compares the four major European countries and find that the seniority premium is lowest in the UK and highest in France.[1]

The human capital interpretation of these differences in earnings profiles is that they reflect differences in the accumulation of firm-specific human capital.[2] According to this interpretation, steeper wage trajectories are a result of growth of skills within firms that put greater emphasis on training and retraining. Differences in the growth of skills and in the accumulation of human capital are widely regarded as being a critical factor in the explanation of international differences in productivity levels and productivity growth.[3]

There are two problems with this interpretation of earnings functions, estimated using various forms of cross-section data. First, positive age/tenure slopes of earnings function can be consistent with theories that have little to do with human capital explanation. Leading candidates are the theories of agency and matching. Second, there are important econometric issues that makes inference from standard estimates problematic. As we shall see shortly, these two problems are intertwined with each other.

The purpose of this chapter is to investigate differences in earnings profiles between Japan and the UK by taking these two problems explicitly into account. Our main innovation is the introduction into standard earnings functions of an additional variable, rank, or the position filled by an employee in the firm hierarchy. We believe that this additional variable serves two purposes well. First, it provides information that is closely related to the agency approach but not immediately explicable by the human capital approach. Second, it gives a new and simple solution to some of the econometric issues raised by standard earnings profiles.

By including a variable measuring the position filled by an employee in the firm hierarchy, our chapter is close to previous important work by Abraham and Medoff (1980), who are concerned with sorting out the relationship between performance and earnings. This chapter provides additional evidence in support of Abraham and Medoff's findings, based on two comparable data-sets from Japan and the UK, and adds to this a more detailed discussion on the role played by rank in standard earnings functions.

The material of the paper is organized as follows. Section 5.2 discusses the theoretical background of earnings functions; Section 5.3 posits the problem in a simple regression model; Section 5.4 presents the data; and Section 5.5 shows the results. Conclusions follow in Sections 5.6.

5.2 COMPETING THEORIES OF EARNINGS PROFILE

The positive correlation between age and tenure, on the one hand, and earnings on the other is admittedly one of the most important and robust empirical regularities in labour economics. It is important because no theoretical modeling of the wage determination can ignore the correlations which typically explain roughly 60–70 per cent of total cross-section variations in earnings. The correlation between age/tenure and earnings is quite strong over many labour markets with diverse institutional settings. Human capital theory explains this positive correlation with the accumulation of general and firm-specific human capital. The former is proxied by age and the latter is associated with the number of years spent at the current firm.

As we explained briefly in the Introduction, the correlation between age/tenure and earnings does not constitute sufficient evidence for the accumulation of firm-specific human capital. There are two fundamental problems in this interpretation. First, tenure is endogenous. Second, wages and productivity can differ. In this section, we will take up each of these issues in turn.

5.2.1 Bias in measured effects of tenure on wages

It is well known that ordinary least squares regressions of earnings on tenure (and other attributes) that use cross-section data give a biased estimate of the tenure effect on earnings. This is because longer job spells are likely to be of better matches, yielding higher pay. As Topel (1986) argues, however, the direction of the bias is not necessarily upwards. The true culprit is not the match (job-, individual-) specific productivity effect *per se* but rather the unobservable information gathering on current and alternative jobs and consequent job changes, which we shall simply refer to as 'job search', in a broad sense. Without further information, cross-section data cannot differentiate the effect of tenure on productivity from the effect of search on wage offers. By the same token, the data cannot differentiate the effect of general experience on wages from the effect of search on the distribution of wage offers received by a worker in the past. Depending upon the nature of job search and the relative efficacy of search activities on current and outside job opportunities, the bias can go in either direction. This unobservable information-gathering activity makes tenure endogenous, and causes the problem underlying the bias in the tenure effect on productivity.

The most well-known example of such bias is Jovanovic's model (Jovanovic, 1979). In this model, it is the evolution of the conditional expectation of the current match quality that determines the quit/stay decision. In Jovanovic's model, the true productivity is never observable but the employer–employee pair can observe current output, drawn from a known distribution. Hence output is informative but a noisy statistic of the true (and unobservable) productivity. They compute expected (match-specific) productivity by conditioning on the current and the past draws of output. It is this evolution of the conditional expectation of true productivity that drives the quit/stay decision. On average, better jobs last longer because the unconditional mean of new jobs is the same, and the probability of quits declines over tenure (see Figure 5.1). In this model, we get the extreme result that the expected gain from repeated draws of new offers is zero because all the new jobs offer the same wage, which is equal to the unconditional mean of the match-specific productivity. To put it simply, expected return from search (for outside opportunities) is smaller for those with better matches and hence they will eventually stop searching. Consequently, the measured effect of tenure on earnings is biased upward.

This need not be the case if the true productivity can be observed when the match is formed. In this case, there is no information gain on current productivity from accumulation of tenure. Information gains are represented, instead, by the total number of outside wage offers received. If there is no genuine effect of tenure on productivity, there will be a positive correlation between total experience and earnings but no correlation between tenure and earnings. General experience in this case simply measures the effect of a search for alternative jobs, and has nothing to do with the productivity gain from experience.[4]

Endogeneity can arise in many other different ways. It is possible that the tenure has a positive effect on productivity at the current firm. Without any other factor influencing the productivity, quitters are those who receive a higher wage offer from outside. To put it another way,

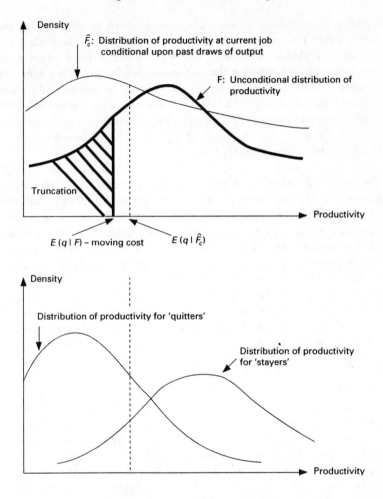

FIGURE 5.1   Matching model

there is a positive correlation between the frequency of quits and earnings growth: in this case, the measured effect of tenure on productivity *understates* the true effect. The mechanism behind this is the evolution of the conditional expectation of earnings, both in the current and in outside jobs, which occur concurrently with the accumulation of tenure and general experience. In Jovanovic's model, general experience does not matter, because the unconditional expectation of productivity is common to all the workers and is constant.

To sum up the discussion so far, endogeneity of tenure arises because tenure represents two different kinds of activity, both of which are unobservable but can be usefully approximated by tenure. On the one hand, tenure represents the accumulation of skills with the current employer. On the other, tenure also represents the collection of information, related either to the quality of the current match or to the availability and quality of alternative job matches.

5.2.2 Three competing theories

The economic implications of the correlation between the tenure and earnings are equally diverse depending upon which of the competing theories is used. The most straightforward interpretation is the one based upon the accumulation of specific human capital. The main problem of this interpretation is that recent empirical studies on the relationship between training and wages suggest relatively limited scope and effects of (either on- or off-the-job) training. Topel (1986), Topel and Ward (1992), and Matsushige (1989) all investigate this relationship among relatively young workers with short tenures. Although the approaches taken and samples used differ in these papers, they are unanimous in limiting the magnitude and the scope of firm-specific training on these workers.[5] On the other hand, there are several studies indicating the importance of training after major job changes within firms, especially job changes associated with promotion. There are also numerous studies indicating that the scope and depth of training vary widely across firms, jobs, and countries.[6] First, the scope of job changes is narrower among blue-collar workers. Second, the scope of job changes within firms is positively related to promotion. 'High flyers' tend to shop around quite frequently over a variety of jobs before they reach top management.[7] Third, frequency of job changes closely mirrors the width and depth of the internal labour market. In some specialized professions (such as university professor), a particular job stands by itself with very limited linkages to other jobs within an organization. Viewed from this perspective, the human capital explanation of earnings profiles is at best a crude approximation of the degree of development of internal labour markets. We shall come back to this point later on.

The second candidate is 'job matching' theory, partly discussed in the previous section. The main problem with the matching model is that this model essentially captures the job shopping in the early stages of a worker's career. Job shopping processes typically last three to five years after entry into the labour market. A typical estimate of the tenure effect on wages shows significant positive effects well beyond ten years of tenure. This point is especially important in interpreting the econometric studies below, where the focus is on the earnings profile of mature male workers.[8] Notice, however, that there is nothing wrong with combining matching theory with human capital aspects, or with combining the human capital model with job search. In fact, human capital and match-specific effects on productivity are likely to exhibit strong complementarity because 'good' matches reduce the expected benefit from the search for alternative jobs which in turn would reduce the probability of future separation. Reduction in the future probability of separation in turn reinforces the investment in firm-specific human capital, for obvious reasons. In fact, this complementarity is the major reason why the empirical decomposition of tenure effects into 'match', 'human capital' and 'search' components has proved to be so difficult.

So far, we have treated productivity and wages more or less as being synonymous because 'equilibrium' wage is assumed to be determined by productivity, net of training costs. In the agency explanation, the causality runs in the opposite direction. It is a particular wage policy that induces a particular level of productivity of a worker within a firm, rather than the other way around. To be precise, the focus here is the effect on productivity of a particular wage profile over the worker's career. E. P. Lazear was the first to present a formal analysis of this causality. The 'bonding' explanation in Lazear (1979) is shown quite simply in Figure 5.2. An employee can work up to two periods. For simplicity, innate ability (hence potential productivity) is assumed to be constant over the two periods. If a firm pays this worker according to this potential, the worker has no strong incentive to work hard, or to 'live up to his potential'. He can simply be idle or make minimum effort. A firm can condition his employment in the second period on good performance in his first period. With this condition, if the firm sets the earnings profile shown in Figure 5.2, a worker has a strong incentive to work hard to secure employment in his second period, when he will receive a wage above his productivity (as well as above his outside opportunity).

In a very sophisticated model, MacLeod and Malcomson (1988) combine moral hazard and adverse selection to show that the optimal wage policy looks very much like the one we commonly observe in well-developed internal labour markets. First of all, only a finite number of pay grades, or ranks, exists in equilibrium, even though the model

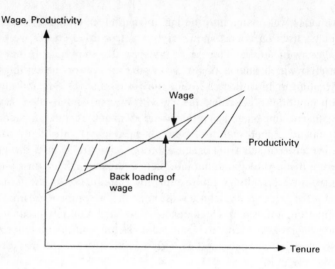

FIGURE 5.2   Bonding model

assumes a continuum of worker quality and effort. The optimal policy
is such that workers within the same rank will be paid the same wage
irrespective of the actual performance, which is not verifiable but is
observed by workers as well as by the firm. Promotion to a higher
rank is the major incentive device to induce effort, in the same way as
in Lazear's model. The model is important because it demonstrates the
underlying logic behind the agency theory of wage determination. In a
nutshell, the wage policy is a device to elicit private information held
by the worker. In some cases, such a policy can be designated for the
workers to self-select; in other cases, 'ranks' are used to induce particular levels of (otherwise unobservable or unverifiable) effort. The
positive correlation between tenure and wage arises because the tenure
slope of wage is used as the key device both in self-selection and in
effort elicitation.

   Like other theories, there is no compelling reason to believe that
agency theories and the others are mutually exclusive. Empirical test
of agency theory is so far close to non-existent. Hence we do not have
even a rough idea of how serious agency costs are, or of how important these costs are in explaining observed tenure earnings profiles. It
is unlikely, however, that agency theory by itself is the whole story.
This is so because if private information is the only reason, there are
many other alternative and cheaper devices to overcome the problem.

Primarily, various monitoring and evaluation of workers' performances can be used. Second, whenever we observe a large tenure effect on wages, we also find successive systematic selection processes at work through which only a fraction of entering workers survive to experience long tenure. Clearly, tenure–earnings profiles are closely linked to promotion as a screening device. This elaborate system seems too expensive unless the selection process is reasonably successful in distinguishing 'good matches' from 'bad matches'.

Therefore it seems unreasonable to single out any one of these competing theories as the dominant factor explaining the observed positive slopes in age/tenure wage profiles. This point is especially important when the bulk of available evidence cannot usefully discriminate skill formation, information gathering and reverse causality, all of which show up as the positive correlation between tenure and earnings.

Our preferred alternative is to take account of factors that are largely neglected in the previous empirical research. We believe that the most important information missing in these studies is the design of the internal labour market where the observed earnings profiles are placed.[9]

5.3 EARNINGS, SENIORITY AND RANK: A SIMPLE MODEL

Human capital earnings functions are based on the idea that labour market entrants start with a stock of human capital and accumulate it over time during their working life. Depending on the nature of the human capital being accumulated, tenure within a firm and labour market experience are the crucial explanatory variables (see Willis (1986) for further details). With accumulation increasing at a constant speed, for instance, the empirical earnings profile suggested by this theory is

$$\ln W = a_0 + a_1 A + a_2 T + \mu + v \tag{1}$$

where $\ln W$ is the logarithm of nominal earnings, A is age, T is tenure with the firm, μ is a fixed individual effect that captures unobserved individual quality or ability, v is residual noise and the following restrictions hold

$$a_1, a_2 > 0.$$

Since earnings reflect productivity, and since productivity is a function of the accumulation of general and firm-specific human capital, this theory has little to say on the relationship between rank and earnings.[10] On the other hand, this relationship is crucial in the agency explanation, where the prevailing factor is that firms organized as ranking hierarchies design earnings to tackle both moral hazard and adverse selection problems. The crucial issue here is not the accumulation of firm-specific human capital but the design of adequate measures to avoid the effort spent being less than contracted and to induce workers of different abilities to self-select.

With asymmetric information, the ability of potential employees cannot be observed by the firm. Abler employees must be induced to self-select to their appropriate rank by means of a promotion mechanism.

A convenient way of introducing the implications of agency theory into standard earnings profiles is to realize that unobserved productivity μ in equation (1) is not orthogonal to tenure. Hence, ordinary least squares estimates of equation (1) are biased (see Levine and Kiefer (1991) and Garen (1988) for a detailed survey of the literature on this issue). The simple reason is that abler employees can get better wages independently of tenure. They end up with longer tenure simply because they are less likely to break a good match with the firm.

Next, consider the MacLeod and Malcomson model. A crucial feature of this model is that, in equilibrium, there exists a correspondence between unobserved ability and observed rank. Thus, suppose that the firm as a ranking hierarchy succeeds in the design of a wage profile which induces both optimal effort and the self-selection of workers of different (unknown) abilities to their appropriate rank and rank-dependant wage. In this case, workers of higher ability self-select to higher ranks.[11]

The outcome of the selection process taking place within firms can be described as follows

$$R = \psi_0 \mu \tag{2}$$

where $\psi_0 > 0$. Replacing this equation into (1) allows us to get rid of μ and obtain

$$\ln W = c_0 + c_1 A + c_2 T + c_3 R + v, \tag{3}$$

where $c_3 = \dfrac{1}{\psi_0}$

If the model in equation (3) is the 'true' model, OLS estimates of the parameters in equation (1) are biased and the bias in the estimate of parameter c_2 is

$$E(\hat{a}_2) - c_2 = \hat{d}_2 c_3, \tag{4}$$

where '$\hat{a}_2$' indicates OLS estimates and the parameter d_2 is defined by the following equation

$$R = d_2 FT^* + \omega_2, \tag{5}$$

where FT^* are the residuals from the regression of tenure on age. If tenure, conditional on age, is positively correlated with rank, $\hat{d}_2$ is positive. Since c_3 is also positive, the right hand side of (4) is positive and OLS estimates of the effects of tenure on earnings are biased upwards. In this case, the inclusion of rank in equation (1) should lead to a reduction in the effect of tenure on earnings. An analogous argument holds for the estimate of parameter c_1.

In the derivation of (3), we have assumed that the accumulation of human capital is constant over age and experience. This is overly restrictive. If human capital is accumulated at a decreasing speed, equation (3) should be replaced by

$$\ln W = c_0 + c_1 A + c_2 T + c_3 R + c_4 A^2 + c_5 T^2 + v \tag{6}$$

where $c_4 < 0$, $c_5 < 0$

In the rest of the chapter we shall focus on equation (6).

5.4   THE DATA

To estimate equation (6), we need a data-set that includes information on rank. To this end we have selected the *Japanese Survey on Wage Structure* and the UK's *New Earnings Survey* and focused only on male workers. The Japanese data are cell means of earnings (gross of bonuses), years of tenure and age of worker, cross-classified by firm size, age group, industry and rank. In these data, a rank corresponds closely to the position occupied by the employee in the organizational hierarchy. The top rank is department director and the other ranks are, respectively, division director, sub-division director, foreman and unranked. Needless to say, this classification by rank has the merit of tracking closely the hierarchical structure within Japanese firms and the demerit of being rather gross, since it ignores all the grades within each rank.

The British data are also cell means of earnings (gross of incentive pay), years of tenure and age of workers, cross-classified by age group, industry and socioeconomic group. Socioeconomic groups in the ESRC Data Archive data-set are obtained by reclassifying the original data by occupation with the purpose of capturing in a broad way the elements of social and economic hierarchy within firms (see Gregory and Thomson, 1990). These groups are: managers, professionals, intermediate non-manuals, junior non-manuals, foremen, skilled manuals, semi-skilled manuals and unskilled manuals. For both countries, we measure the variable R (rank) by attaching to each rank a dummy variable.

Both data-sets provide information on rank that can be used to capture, at least in part, the effects of unobserved ability. Unfortunately, both the Japanese and the British data classifications are too broad to be fully satisfactory. Each rank is composed of several grades, but we have no data for grades. The implication is that the detailed grading system within a firm is measured with error. If this error is correlated with age and tenure, our estimates are bound to be biased even after controlling for observed rank. This important shortcoming cannot be avoided and must be kept in mind when interpreting our results.

The Japanese data are available for the whole period 1976–89. On the other hand, British data that include explicit information on tenure are limited to the years 1975, 1976 and 1979. For this reason, we focus our empirical analysis on two overlapping periods, 1976–79 for Japan and the three available years for Britain, and pool the time-series and cross-sectional information in each country. We restrict our attention to male workers in the age range 20–59 for Japan and 21–59 for Britain, to avoid plaguing the estimates with differences in the degree of labour market attachment exhibited by different segments of the labour force. Furthermore, we focus on three industries: manufacturing, distribution and finance, and, for Japan only, on two sizes of firm: those with 100–999 employees and those with more than 1000 employees. A more detailed discussion of the data-set is to be found in the Data Appendix. A summary of the main variables used in the chapter is given in Table 5.1, where we present means and standard deviations of age, tenure and the nominal wage in the two years where information is available for both countries. The summary statistics show that average tenure in the UK is about half the average tenure in Japan. In addition, average age is only slightly less in the UK compared to Japan. These data suggest that, on average, British workers included in the sample have joined their current firm at a much later age than have their Japanese counterparts.

TABLE 5.1 Means and standard deviations of age, tenure and wages over the whole sample, Japan and the UK, standard deviations within parentheses

Means and standard deviations	1976		1979		Pooled	
	UK	Japan	UK	Japan	UK	Japan
Tenure	7.68	15.10	7.97	15.87	7.79	15.51
	(4.99)	(7.12)	(5.19)	(7.48)	(5.10)	(7.30)
Age	36.72	40.43	36.76	40.44	36.73	40.46
	(11.55)	(11.06)	(11.69)	(11.07)	(11.58)	(11.05)
Wage	66.84	43 066	98.18	52 293	–	–
	(16.95)	(16 069)	(23.80)	(19 461)		

Note: British earnings are gross weekly pay in sterling, inclusive of incentive, overtime and shift pay. Japanese earnings are monthly wages in yen, inclusive of bonuses and overtime.

5.5 RESULTS AND DISCUSSIONS

5.5.1 Regression results

We estimate two versions of equation (6), one including rank dummies and the other excluding them. The estimation method is weighted least squares, with weights given by the number of observations within each cell. Results are given in Table 5.2. The first important finding is that, for both countries, we cannot reject the hypothesis that rank is significantly different from zero in the earnings equations.[12]

Turning to tenure effects on earnings, these are significantly different from zero both in general and conditional on age. At the bottom of Table 5.2 we present the average percentage growth of earnings with respect to tenure.[13] Our findings suggest that this value is almost halved, in both countries, by the inclusion of rank in the regression.

Since the slope of earnings profiles changes as tenure increases, a simple comparison of average earnings growth in the two countries is not very informative. Complementary information is provided by simulating relative earnings profiles for both countries under alternative assumptions about the age of entry in the current firm. Relative earnings are obtained by normalizing earnings at tenure T and age At, with

TABLE 5.2 Estimated earnings profiles, United Kingdom 1975, 1976 and 1979, Japan 1976–79. Dependent variable: $\ln W$

	UK		Japan	
T	0.056	0.078	0.032	0.102
	(7.42)	(7.41)	(4.46)	(13.88)
$T*T$	−0.00086	−0.0009	−0.00035	−0.0016
	(−3.77)	(−2.49)	(−2.07)	(−8.64)
A	0.030	0.034	0.062	−0.005
	(6.99)	(4.67)	(7.99)	(−0.58)
$A*A$	−0.0005	−0.0007	−0.00076	−0.00007
	(−12.39)	(−8.61)	(−8.84)	(−0.75)
R^2	0.96	0.87	0.90	0.84
N	356	356	1166	1166
Rank dummies	yes	no	yes	no
Significance of rank	$F(6,340) = 52.8$[§]		$F(4,1150) = 89.5$[§]	
Significance of tenure	$F(2,340) = 101$[§]		$F(2,1150) = 52.7$[§]	
Significance of tenure and age	$F(4,340) = 166$[§]		$F(4,1150) = 798$[§]	
$\dfrac{\partial \ln W}{\partial T} \mid (A - T)$	0.033	0.047	0.022	0.040

Notes: N = number of observations. Each regression includes a constant and two industry dummies. The pooled equation includes also year dummies. T-values within parentheses. The sign § indicates that the F-test rejects the null hypothesis (no effects) at the 5 per cent level of confidence.

earnings at tenure 1 and age $A1$. In order to stress the role played by the variable rank in the determination of earnings growth, we distinguish between *gross* and *net earnings growth*. The *gross earnings growth* is based on the estimate of equation (6) without rank dummies and combines, as a consequence, between-ranks and within-ranks earnings growth. The *net earnings growth* is based on the estimate of equation (6) and focuses only on within-ranks earnings growth.

A useful summary of seniority premia is provided in Tables 5.3 and Figures 3.5 and 5.4. Notice first that earnings growth is much lower when between-ranks effects are netted out.[14] Next, if we focus on gross earnings, the figures show that relative earnings growth is much larger in Japan than in the UK for any starting age. The gap between the two countries is often substantial. For instance, the earnings of a Japanese employee who entered the firm at age 30 and accumulated 15 years of

TABLE 5.3 Seniority premia in Japan and the UK

$$\frac{W_{T=10,\,A=A_0+T}}{W_{T=1,\,A=A_0+1}}$$

	Japan		UK	
	R	NR	R	NR
$A_0 = 20$	1.60	1.97	1.56	1.83
$A_0 = 30$	1.40	1.94	1.41	1.61
$A_0 = 40$	1.22	1.92	1.28	1.42

$$\frac{W_{T=20,\,A=A_0+T}}{W_{T=1,\,A=A_0+1}}$$

$A_0 = 20$	2.18	3.04	1.95	2.64
$A_0 = 30$	1.64	2.96	1.59	2.02
$A_0 = 40$	1.23	2.87	1.29	1.56

Note: R = rank dummies included; NR = rank dummies excluded; A_0 = age of entry into the firm.

tenure are about 2.5 times larger than the earnings of an employee aged 30 and with 1 year of tenure. In Britain, this ratio is less than 2. If we focus on net earnings, however, the story is rather different: the earnings ratio is about 1.6 in both countries. The difference between gross and net relative earnings becomes sharper as starting age increases. The overall impression that can be derived from the table is that the difference in seniority premia between the two countries is much smaller when tenure effects on earnings profiles are estimated correctly, that is, when we focus on regressions including rank.

The description of earnings profiles provided by Table 5.3 captures the total effect of tenure on earnings growth, because it includes both the direct and indirect effects induced by the fact that an increase in tenure increases age by the same amount. Another way of looking at earnings profiles is to compare workers with similar characteristics who differ only in accumulated tenure. This is equivalent to focusing only on the direct tenure effects and to ignoring the indirect effects operating through changes in age.[15] To do so, we focus on earnings profiles where age is constant at 40. The simulated gross and net earnings profiles are presented in Figures 5.3 and 5.4. The contrast between gross and net profiles is even sharper than before. In both cases, gross earnings profiles are steeper in Japan and net earnings profiles are steeper in Britain.

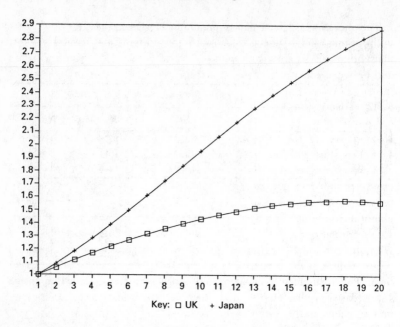

FIGURE 5.3   Gross earnings profiles, age varying, starting at 40

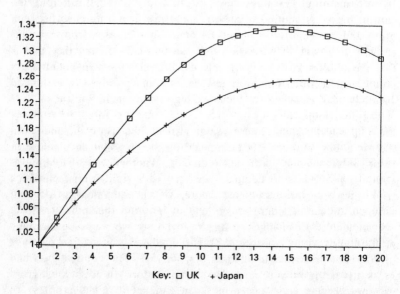

FIGURE 5.4   Net earnings profiles, age varying, starting at 40

The message is clear. If we decompose total earnings growth into within-ranks and between-ranks earnings growth, our results suggest that within-ranks earnings growth is relatively more important in Britain and between-ranks growth is relatively more important in Japan.

5.5.2 Discussions

How do we interpret the results in light of the discussion in Section 1? Let us start with the 'matching model'. Our results can be regarded as fairly strong evidence of heterogeneity bias in estimates based on cross-section data that excludes rank, since rank is obviously an important signal of worker quality. Is it then true that the only reason an elaborate ranking and promotion system exists is to uncover this private information? Circumstantial evidence suggests otherwise. To begin with, the empirical counterpart of 'tenure' in the matching model should be the tenure at the current job, not necessarily tenure with the current firm. The former is typically much shorter: in the case of Japan, as short as two years. Hence the 'matching' story is at best incomplete: and it needs to be supplemented with a theory explaining *interjob*, *intrafirm mobility*. Moreover, a direct test of 'matching models' must look at the data on 'stayers' in order to investigate the correlation between earnings and job tenures *within a firm*. If we limit our attention to the beginning of a worker's career (as we must if we directly apply the model to the data), the theory can at best explain earnings growth of young workers with only a few years of experience. The last, but not the least, problem with 'matching' the explanations of our result is the nature of the data-set. Our data is not particularly suitable for detecting effects of tenure on the earnings of young workers with little labour market experience, mainly because most of the variations in earnings and tenure originate from long tenure spells and a wide range of ages. Thus our preferred explanation is the agency model augmented by endogenously determined investment in human capital.

Why do we need agency explanation? Because incentive aspects of compensation policy seem to be of such paramount concern among management and it is hard to believe that such an issue does not arise in training/teaching activities among the employees.

Why do we believe at the same time that investment in human capital is also part of the story? Because otherwise it is hard to understand why we observe a clear association (clustering) of particular types of jobs experienced by an employee over his/her career. It can only be so because designing such a spiral pattern of promotion enhances the productivity growth of a worker.

The remaining question is why the same pattern cannot be accomplished by *interfirm* labour mobility? It seems that there are two potential factors at work here. First, repeated training can be used for investment in firm-specific human capital. One of the main tasks of higher-ranked workers is supervision. This function clearly entails a large amount of relation-specific and firm-specific information on the subordinates. Understanding the intricate workings of corporate hierarchy and its decision-making processes is also very firm-specific.

Without discounting the importance of this factor, we believe a second factor is really crucial to explain the advantage of *intrafirm* mobility over *interfirm* mobility. In a different paper, we showed that corporate hierarchy is largely insensitive to cyclical fluctuations either in the product market or in the external labour market.[16] This is consistent with the prevailing view that, although not completely rigid, a hierarchical structure cannot be costlessly adjusted to meet the conditions required by the minimization of agency costs. This constraint makes it impossible to design the corporate hierarchy wholly for the purpose of achieving the optimal promotion-ranking policy as suggested by MacLeod and Malcomson (1988). We believe that widespread use of long-term monitoring and evaluation to select management is prima-facie evidence indicating that interfirm arrangements are inefficient because of the loss of critical personnel information. Moreover, to the extent that the design of corporate hierarchy cannot be completely independent from the concern with production efficiency, it is not obvious at all that market mediated 'promotion' patterns replicate exactly what an internal labour market does.

In a nutshell, our empirical results add to an already voluminous literature indicating the important role played by job changes (within or across firms), especially promotions (within or across firms), in the determination of earnings. Our results also show the systemic influence on earnings and training by structural differences in the internal labour markets in the two countries. In particular, our findings are consistent with the view that, in the UK, each job within a firm is relatively independent, so that less emphasis is placed placed on promotion as an incentive device. This pattern is also consistent with less on-the-job training across jobs within a firm, which seems so important in career ladders in large Japanese firms. If these tendencies are as robust and important as we believe, not only pay but also the type and amount of training are strongly correlated with the job in a corporate hierarchy.

In conclusion, our econometric results indicate that the research on earnings profiles should incorporate explicitly interactions between compensation policy and monitoring and evaluation activity within internal labour markets. The large variations in earnings attributable to ranks found in this chapter suggest that investigations of earnings profiles should focus on career patterns rather than on job tenure.

5.6 CONCLUSION

This chapter investigated Japanese and British earnings profiles by introducing into standard earnings functions an additional variable, rank, or the position filled by an employee in a firm's hierarchy.

Agency theory establishes a clear link between observed allocation of workers to ranks and unobserved worker quality. The self-selection of workers to their appropriate positions provides a useful proxy to unobserved worker quality and a simple solution to the econometric problems that plague standard earnings functions.

Once rank is included in the earnings function, we find that the frequently mentioned view that Japanese earnings profiles are steeper than British earnings profiles is borne out only partially by the data. It is difficult to take this finding as evidence in support of the human capital interpretation of differences in earnings profiles. A more promising approach should combine the human capital story with the need to provide adequate incentives and to sort heterogeneous employees into their proper positions.

DATA APPENDIX

Japanese data

The source is the Annual Survey on the Wage Structure (*Chingin Kozo Kihon Tokei Chosa*), vol. 3. The survey, sponsored by the Ministry of Labour, focuses on the private sector and on firms with more than 100 employees. Published data are cell means cross-classified by age, industry, rank and firm size. Medium and large firms are firms with their number of employees respectively between 100 to 999 and more than 1000. The main variables used in the chapter are:

A = average age.
T = average tenure.
R = a group of five dummy variables in the manufacturing industry and of four dummy variables in the remaining two sectors. Each dummy

corresponds to a rank. The rank of foreman is available only in manufacturing.

W = gross yearly earnings, inclusive of overtime, allowances and bonuses.

English data

The English data are from the *New Earnings Survey*. The data, provided by ESRC Data Archive at Essex University, are 'minimal aggregations' of individual data. Each record in the tapes contains information on aggregates of at least three similar individuals. We used the macrofile 04, where aggregation is based on age groups. We have aggregated the original records to reproduce as closely as possible the format provided by the published Japanese data.

Compared with the Japanese data, the UK data include public corporations in the manufacturing sector and these are not disaggregated by firm size. Contrary to Japanese data, UK information is disaggregated into manual and non-manual occupations. Macrofile 04 provides information already classified into 8 socioeconomic groups. These groups are obtained by aggregating the original data organized by the KOS/CODOT system of occupations. We refer to Gregory and Thomson (1990) for further details. The main variables used in the chapter are:

A = average age.
T = average tenure.
R = a group of seven dummy variables.
W = gross weekly pay, inclusive of overtime, fringe benefits and bonuses. For a more detailed definition, the reader is referred to Gregory and Thomson (1990), p. 9.

NOTES

1. Marsden's definition is slightly different from Collier and Knight's definition of seniority premium. He uses this evidence to corroborate his view of the British labour market as an occupational market that differs sharply from the internal labour markets prevailing in France and Japan.
2. See Hashimoto and Raisian (1985), Mincer and Higuchi (1988) and Hashimoto (1989).
3. See Bean and Symons (1988) for a comparison of productivity growth rates in the largest developed economies. The relationship between the accumulation of human capital, productivity levels and productivity growth is stressed by the new growth economics. See Crafts (1992), Mankiew, Romer and Weil (1990) and the references therein.
4. In this example, we are assuming that on- and off-job search are equally productive and that workers accept any wage offer exceeding the current one. In this case, it is the total number of draws that matter; that is, general experience (number of offers received preceding this job) and current tenure (number of offers received during this job) have exactly the same effect on expected wage growth.

5. Topel (1986) jointly estimates the 'tenure decision and earnings profiles using US panel data. He finds strong 'match' effects that reduce the quit hazard rapidly. He concludes that the estimated pure effect of tenure on wage growth is virtually zero. Topel and Ward (1992) find the same negligible effect of tenure on earnings by estimating the earnings–loss-associated job changes. Matsushige (1989) investigates a large Australian motor vehicle firm and finds that the training specific to the firm is virtually completed within the first six weeks.

6. See Marsden (1989), Rosenbaum (1984) and Koike (1992).

7. See, for example, Rosenbaum (1984) and Koike (1988).

8. For example, Topel (1986) and Farber (1993) both find that the 'matching' effect on quits virtually dies out by the end of the first year.

9. We believe that the design of internal labour market in each particular firm gives us far more comprehensive information on the difference between jobs within and outside the current firm. In other explanations, the distinction between current and alternative jobs, on the one hand, and current and alternative employers on the other is often blurred.

10. See Abraham & Medoff (1980). The underlying model is

$$\ln W = g_0 + g_1 P + \varepsilon_1$$
$$P = \delta_0 + \delta_1 A + \delta_2 T + \varepsilon_2$$

where P is productivity.

11. See McLeod and Malcomson (1988) and Rosen (1982) for models of assignment of workers to ranks.

12. An implication of the agency model is that earnings increase as rank increases. We find that this is generally true in Japan and in the United Kingdom. Interestingly, the monotonic and positive relationship between rank and earnings is preserved in Britain only in so far as we separate manual from non-manual workers. This evidence is suggestive of the fact that hierarchical structures within British firms maintain a clear distinction between white- and blue-collar workers. Such a demarcation does not appear in the Japanese data. The coefficients of the rank dummies are available from the authors on request.

13. The numbers are calculated using the following formula

$$\frac{\partial \ln W}{\partial T}\bigg|_{\partial T = \partial A} = c_2 + 2c_5 T + c_1 + 2c_4 A$$

where T and A are evaluated at their sample averages.

14. Baker *et al.* (1993) also concluded '[rank] dummies are the most important explanatory variables for pay data. If they do not advance beyond lower levels, they eventually suffer a decline in real earnings' (p. 378).

15. Hashimoto and Raisian (1985) also make a similar distinction. The direct effects of tenure are computed as follows

$$\frac{\partial \ln W}{\partial T}\bigg|_{A = A_0} = c_2 + 2c_5 T$$

16. See Brunello and Ariga (1993) and Ariga *et al.* (1992). Baker *et al.* (1993) also find a surprisingly stable hierarchical structure using a large panel data of pay and grades in a large American firm.

REFERENCES

Abraham, K. and J. Medoff, 1980. 'Experience, Performance and Earnings', *Quarterly Journal of Economics*, 95, 4, pp. 701–35.

Aoki, M. 1988. *Information, Incentives and Bargaining in the Japanese Economy*, Cambridge University Press.

Ariga, K., G. Brunello, Y. Ohkusa and Y. Nishiyama 1992. 'Promotion, Hierarchy and Firm Growth: Japanese Internal Labor Market in Transition', *Journal of the Japanese and International Economies*, 7, 4.

Baker, G., M. Jensen and K. Murphy 1988. 'Compensation and Incentives: Practice versus Theory', *Journal of Finance*, 43, 3, pp. 593–616.

Baker, G., M. Gibbs and B. Holmstrom 1993. 'Hierarchies and Compensation: A Case Study', *European Economic Review*, 37, pp. 366–78.

Bean, C. and J. Symons 1988. 'The Thatcher Experiment', in S. Fischer (ed.), *NBER Macroeconomics Annual*, Cambridge, Mass.: MIT Press.

Brunello, G. and K. Ariga 1993. 'Promotion Policy and Hierarchic Structure of Japanese Firms', in C. Czerkawski (ed.), *Japanese Management: Challenges and Applications For Business Executives*, Hong Kong: Academic Press.

Carmichael, L. 1983. 'Firm Specific Human Capital and Promotion Ladders', *Bell Journal of Economics*, 14, 3, pp. 251–8.

Collier, P. and J. Knight 1985. 'Seniority Payments, Quit Rates and Internal Labour Markets in Britain and Japan', *Oxford Bulletin of Economics and Statistics*, 47, pp. 19–32.

Crafts, N. 1992. 'Productivity Growth Reconsidered', *Economic Policy*, 15.

Dore, R. and M. Sako 1988. 'Teaching or Testing: The Role of the State in Japan', *Oxford Review of Economic Policy*, 4, 3, pp. 72–81.

Farber, H. S. 1993. 'The Incidence and Costs of Job Loss: 1982–91', *Brookings Papers on Economic Activity*, 1, Washington, D. C.: Brookings Institution, pp. 73–132.

Garen, J. 1988. 'Empirical Studies of the Job Matching Hypothesis', *Research in Labor Economics*, 9, pp. 187–224.

Gregory, M. and A. Thomson 1990. *A Portrait of Pay*, Oxford: Clarendon Press.

Hashimoto, M. 1989. *The Japanese Labor Market*, Kalamazoo, Michigan: The Upjohn Institute.

Hashimoto, M. and J. Raisian 1985. 'Employment Tenure and Earnings Profiles in Japan and the United States', *American Economic Review*, 75, 4, pp. 721–35.

Jovanovic, B. 1979. 'Job Matching and Labor Turnover', *Journal of Political Economy*, 87, pp. 972–990.

Koike, K. 1988. *Understanding Industrial Relations in Modern Japan*, London: Macmillan.

Koike, K. 1992. *Daisotsu White Collar No Jinzai Keisei (Human Resources*

Development of White Collar University Graduates), Tokyo: Toyokeizai.

Lazear, E. P. 1979. 'Why is there Mandatory Retirement?, *Journal of Political Economy*, 87, pp. 1261–84.

Lazear, E. 1982. 'Agency, Earnings Profiles, Productivity and Hours Restrictions', *American Economic Review*, 71, 4, pp. 606–20.

Lazear, E. and E. Kandel 1992. 'Peer Pressure and Partnerships', *Journal of Political Economy*, 100, 4, pp. 801–17.

Levine, D. and N. Kiefer 1991. *Empirical Labour Economics*, Oxford University Press.

Mankiw, G., D. Romer and D. Weil 1990. 'A Contribution to the Empirics of Economic Growth', NBER Working Paper no. 3541. Cambridge, Mass.: National Bureau of Economic Research.

Marsden,D. 1989. 'Institutions and Labour Mobility: Occupational and Internal Labour Markets in Britain, France, Italy and the UK', in C. Dell'Aringa and R. Brunetta (eds.) *Markets, Institutions and Cooperation: Labour Relations and Economic Performance*, London: Macmillan.

Matsushige,H. 1989. *The Internalization of the Labour Market in the Australian Vehicle Building Industry*. PhD. dissertation, Australian National University.

MacLeod, B. and J. Malcomson 1988. 'Reputation and Hierarchy in Dynamic Models of Employment', *Journal of Political Economy*, 96, 4, pp. 832–54.

OECD 1992. *Employment Outlook*, Paris: OECO.

Mincer, J. and Y. Higuchi 1988. 'Wage Structures and Labor Turnover in the United States and in Japan', *Journal of the Japanese and International Economies*, 3, pp. 1–23.

Rosen, S. 1982. 'Authority, Control, and the Distribution of Earnings', *Bell Journal of Economics*, 13, 2, pp. 311–23.

Rosenbaum, J. E. 1984. *Career Mobility in a Corporate Economy*, New York: Academic Press.

Topel, R. 1986. 'Job Mobility, Search and Earnings Growth: A Reinterpretation of Human Capital Earnings Function', R. G. Ehrenberg, ed., in *Research in Labor Economics*, vol. 8 pt. A, Greenwich, CT: JAI Press.

Topel, R. and M. P. Ward 1992. 'Job Mobility and the Career of Young Men', *Quarterly Journal of Economics*, 107, 2, pp. 407–38.

Willis, R. 1986. 'Wage Determinants: A Survey and Reinterpretation of Human Capital Earnings Functions', in R. Layard and O. Ashenfelter (eds), *Handbook of Labor Economics*, Amsterdam: North-Holland, pp. 525–602.

Part II

Consumption, Saving, Investment and Growth

6 Consumer Behaviour in Japan under Financial Liberalization and Demographic Change

Wataru Takahashi
and Yukinobu Kitamura*

6.1 INTRODUCTION

The Japanese economy has been experiencing a long and wide-swinging business cycle since the mid-1980s. This cycle has some particular characteristics. First, it was led by a capital spending cycle; and second, it was accompanied by a swing in the external imbalance. These two features are common to all previous business cycles, but the magnitude is unprecedented. For example, capital spending accounted for over 40 per cent of gross national product (GNP) growth in the expansionary period of the latter half of the 1980s, exceeding the level during the high growth period of the late 1960s. The current account surplus to GDP was a record high 4.4 per cent in fiscal year (FY) 1986, then dropped to 1.1 per cent in FY 1990 and climbed again to about 3.5 per cent in FY 1993 (a forecast by the Japan Center for Economic Research). Third, asset price fluctuations under this cycle were enormous. While CPI inflation remained low (3.3 per cent in FY 1991, the

* This chapter was presented as a paper at the Second Conference on the Japanese Economy at Macquarie University, Sydney, Australia, 19–20 August 1993. We are grateful for comments from participants, in particular Jonathan Batten, Robert Dekle, Akiyoshi Horiuchi, Mitsuaki Okabe and Hiroshi Yoshikawa. The paper was also presented at the annual meeting of the Japanese Association of Monetary and Financial Studies at Nagasaki University on 13–14 November 1993 and at a seminar at the University of Tsukuba on 19 November 1993. We are grateful for comments from Junji Narita, Hiroshi Atsumi, Makoto Ohota, Yoshiaki Shikano and Hiroyuki Toda. We thank Michael Hutchison for his valuable comments on an earlier draft. We are also grateful to Michiko Matsumoto and Yuhko Ason for their statistical and editorial assistance. This paper represents the views of the authors and should not be interpreted as reflecting the views of the Bank of Japan.

highest during this cycle), land prices rose by more than 17.0 per cent in 1990 and rapidly dropped to −5.6 per cent in 1992. Fourth, unlike normal cycles, household consumption deepened (rather than alleviated) the economic slump, partly because of the balance sheet problem in the household sector (the debt–wealth ratio rose from below 12 per cent in 1989 to above 14 per cent in 1992). This fact has forced policy-makers and economists to recognize the importance of consumer behaviour in Japan.

This chapter conducts an empirical analysis of consumer behaviour in Japan based on a theoretical model, with emphasis on structural changes such as financial liberalization and demographic change. The motivation behind this chapter lies not only in these questions concerning the latest business cycle, but also in the following policy controversies.

Lawrence Summers, the Under-Secretary of the US Treasury, urges the Japanese government to pursue consumption-led growth assisted by expansionary fiscal policy (*Financial Times*, 1993). According to a similar argument, excess savings, or under-consumption, is said to be the primary source of Japan's current-account surplus. Indeed, although the recent acceleration of the current account surplus can be largely explained by reduced budget deficits in the government sector and borrowing by the corporate sector, the high savings of the household sector is the fundamental source of the surplus. On theoretical issues, so far as household savings are made optimally according to time preferences, no welfare loss is expected. If, on the other hand, proper consumption opportunities are distorted and, as a consequence, enforced savings occur owing to monopolistically high domestic prices and liquidity constraints because of imperfect financial markets, such distortions should be removed for the purpose of welfare improvement. In this respect, removal of monopoly power and deregulation of markets would induce competitive prices, and consumer credit expansion under financial liberalization in the 1980s was supposed to ease liquidity constraints on the household sector. Could these policy actions substantially improve welfare or be appropriate answers to reduce Japan's current account surplus? All these questions will be addressed in this chapter.

The following sections are organized in this way: Section 6.2 lays the theoretical foundations of the empirical models. After a brief survey of the recent literature in subsection 6.2.1, subsection 6.2.2 presents the theoretical model in which durable, non-durable and savings are simultaneously solved. Section 6.3 discusses the data and data transformation from an equilibrium theory model to a dynamic empirical model. In Section 6.4, general empirical models are formulated with some econometric discussion, including the model selection procedure. Section 6.5 evaluates the results. Propensities to consume and save, and income elasticities are calculated. With these results, model validity is examined by means of microeconomic theory. Policy implications are also discussed, especially in relation to monetary policy. A brief conclusion is given in Section 6.6.

6.2 THEORETICAL FOUNDATIONS

6.2.1 The recent literature

The recent literature on consumption is well surveyed in Deaton (1992) and Hall (1990). Hall (1990), who initially launched the permanent income-cum-rational-expectations model (known as the Euler equation approach) with constant expected real interest rate, now admits that such a model is inconsistent with the data. He wrote that the rate of change of consumption can be predicted by past values of real income and past values of number of financial variables (p. 152). Indeed, the Euler equation approach can test intertemporal efficiency, but an institutionally distorted economy, as is usually the case, cannot be explained by this approach (see Yoshikawa (1992), pp. 182–9).

Recent research interests are basically twofold. One is concerned with the microeconomic data analysis of consumer behaviour. For example, Deaton (1992) argues that 'I believe that future progress is most likely to come when aggregation is taken seriously, and when macroeconomic questions are addressed in a way that uses increasingly plentiful and informative microeconomic data' (p. 221). For Japan, Takayama and Kitamura (1994) conduct a fact-finding analysis based on the microeconomic data of the National Survey of Family Income and Expenditure (over 50 000 samples). The other is concerned with structural models which chiefly incorporate market imperfections and risk factors. This research also well suits microeconomic data. But it does not necessarily exclude macroeconomic time-series analysis. We will discuss briefly the major topics of recent interest in consumer behaviour.

Durables and durability of consumption goods[1]

Consumers do not change durable stock as frequently as they change expenditure on non-durables such as food, clothes and services. When they purchases durables, these are large. This behaviour is not consistent with the smooth optimal consumption behaviour expected by neo-classical models. Some economists try to explain this fact by introducing adjustment costs. Others use microeconomic data such as the four-year panel data of automobile purchases to explain durable consumption behaviour in detail. In reality, however, non-durable and durable consumption interact and there is no reason to separate durable consumption a priori. As Bernanke (1985) and Muellbauer (1981) suggest, the separability of utility *vis-à-vis* durables and non-durables is to be tested rather than assumed.

Liquidity constraints[2]

According to Hayashi (1987), the most widely accepted definition is that consumers are liquidity constrained if they face quantity constraints on the amount of borrowing (credit rationing) or if the loan rates available are higher than the rate at which they could lend (differential interest rates) (p. 92). An important policy implication of liquidity constraints is that the effectiveness of macroeconomic stabilization policies on aggregate demand depends on their existence. This is why many economists are interested in identifying liquidity constraints. Among various approaches to liquidity constraints, Deaton (1992) warns 'one research strategy that will not be successful is to model average behaviour as if it were generated by a representative agent who cannot borrow' and that 'if liquidity constraints play a part in the story of consumption, that part must be elaborated at the level of individual households, and aggregation explicitly taken into account' (p. 207). Indeed, liquidity constraints as defined by Hayashi cannot be analyzed by macroeconomic data. An alternative approach, if macroeconomic data is to be used, is to examine consumer access to financial markets, as revealed by consumer credit and the interest rate spread between lending and deposit rates.

Precautionary savings[3]

The basic logic of precautionary savings is that, if the marginal utility of consumption function is convex, increases in the uncertainty of future consumption will prompt a reduction in current consumption and an increase in savings. In permanent income models in which marginal utility is linear, increases in future uncertainty do not by themselves affect saving. This point can be further clarified by the theoretical result of Kimball (1990) that risk-aversion is controlled by the degree of concavity of the utility function, but the degree of precaution (called *prudence*) is the degree of convexity of the marginal utility function.

As Deaton (1991) points out, precautionary motives interact with liquidity constraints because the inability to borrow when times are bad provides an additional motive for accumulating assets when times are good, even for impatient consumers (p. 1222). However, these two models behave differently. Borrowing is entirely consistent with the precautionary motive, although prudent consumers will generally borrow less than those who exhibit certainty equivalence. Liquidity constraints also interact with prudence, since the inability to borrow in a tight spot is an additional reason to accumulate precautionary balances. These two models together stand in opposition to the permanent income and life-cycle models.

In the following modelling, two of the above issues, namely durables and liquidity constraints, will be incorporated. Issues related to precautionary savings are ignored in this chapter.

6.2.2 The model

In general, economists, considering consumer behaviour, use a model in which a representative household faces a problem of life-time utility maximization subject to a life-time budget constraint. We will follow this tradition with a further assumption of an additively separable utility function over time and over states, then the life-time utility maximization problem can be reduced to a within-a-period subutility maximization subject to a within-a-period budget constraint. With this assumption of an additively separable utility function, the model becomes empirically tractable but theoretically somewhat restrictive.[4]

For simplicity, we use a variation of the linear expenditure system extended for durables which is very close to Muellbauer (1981). Our model differs from his in that it incorporates structural change factors.

Suppose the specific consumer's problem is to maximize the Cobb–Douglas utility function (1) subject to budget and stock adjustment constraints (2)–(4):

$$\text{Max } U_t = W_t^\alpha (NDC_t - \theta_t)^\beta (K_t - K_{t-1})^\gamma \tag{1}$$

$$\text{Subject to } DI_t = NDC_t + DC_t + S_t \tag{2}$$

$$DC_t = K_t - K_{t-1} + \delta K_{t-1} \tag{3}$$

$$S_t = W_t - (1 + r)(1 - \varphi)W_{t-1}$$
$$\quad - WfCG - WhCG \tag{4}$$

$$1 = \alpha + \beta + \gamma, \quad \alpha, \beta, \gamma > 0 \tag{5}$$

where W_t = wealth stock; NDC_t = non-durable consumption;
   θ_t = structural change variable; K_t = durable stock;
   DI_t = disposable income; DC_t = durable consumption;
   S_t = savings;
   δ = the depreciation rate on durables; r = the real rate of
   return from wealth;
   φ = the depreciation rate on wealth; $WfCG$ = capital gains
   from financial assets; and
   $WhCG$ = capital gains from housing assets.

W_t is the sum of financial assets (Wf) and housing assets (Wh) (i.e. $W_t = Wf_t + Wh_t$). Note that the depreciation of wealth occurs only on housing assets. The way in which the structural change variable enters into the model is not unusual for the extended linear expenditure system (LES), if, as a whole, it can be regarded as a proxy for minimal non-durable consumption. The idea behind this model is that the consumer receives utility from service flows from financial as well as housing wealth, and those from durables and utility from non-durable consumption. In the case of durables, the consumer forms a habit of consuming services from durable stock at least as much as the level of the previous year. With this setting, the model solves the optimal levels of non-durable and durable consumption and savings simultaneously.

$$NDC_t = (\alpha + \gamma)\theta_t + \beta \{DI_t - \delta K_{t-1} + (1 + r)(1 - \varphi)W_{t-1}$$
$$+ WfCG + WhCG\} \tag{6}$$

$$DC_t = (\alpha + \beta)\delta k_{t-1} + \gamma\{DI_t - \theta_t + (1 + r)(1 - \varphi)W_{t-1}$$
$$+ WfCG + WhCG\} \tag{7}$$

$$S_t = -(\gamma + \beta)\{(1 + r)(1 - \varphi)W_{t-1} + WfCG + WhCG\}$$
$$+ \alpha\{DI_t - \theta_t - \delta K_{t-1}\} \tag{8}$$

The above solutions imply that the first term of the right-hand side is a shift variable and the second term in braces { } is an extended budget constraint. As is clear from equations. (6)–(8), non-durable and durable consumption and savings face different budget constraints with different shift variables. These extended budget constraints are closely related to what Hicks (1946) defines as income: the maximum value which a man can consume during a week and still expect to be as well off at the end of the week as he was at the beginning (p. 172). The extended budget constraints in our system include not only current disposable income, but also wealth at the beginning and capital gains during the period minus durable depreciation and structural change (budget shift) factors. This implies that consumers can borrow freely against their wealth holdings as collateral. It is, however, essentially an empirical question whether consumers are bounded by liquidity constraints. Note also that adding up the right-hand side of equations (6)–(8) yields DI_t, which is equivalent to equation (2). Only two equations out of the three are independent.

Wealth effect

The optimal solutions (6)–(8) provide only static information on the wealth effect. Namely, positive effects on non-durable and durable consumption and a negative effect on savings. These static effects do not necessarily correspond to the dynamic wealth effect in which forward-looking consumer behaviour with expectations of capital gains on wealth determines consumption and savings. How dynamic wealth changes influence consumption and savings is essentially an empirical question.

The causal relationship between savings and housing purchase has been discussed intensively (see, for example, Yoshikawa (1992) and Horioka (1988)). It is not quite clear how housing wealth change, in turn, affects consumption and savings. Again, it is basically an empirical question for, in particular, microeconomic survey data, because a distinction between houseowner and non-houseowner is crucial. In the current study, such a distinction is not feasible; therefore, the influence, if any, of housing wealth on consumption and savings will be quite limited.

Structural change

We cannot determine which factors change consumer behaviour *a priori*, so that multiple variables are empirically tested. Two broad factors of structural change are considered here: demographic change and financial liberalization.

Japanese society is experiencing a rapid ageing of the population, together with a dissolution of extended families into small nuclear families. Although indicators of such changes abound, the following four variables are selected for empirical tests (for definitions and sources, see the Data Appendix on pp. 163–4):

1. Ratio of population aged 65 or over to those aged 20–64 (working population) (DEMG65).
2. Per household population (HOUPOP).
3. Total number of households (HOUS).
4. Amount of bequest transfers (RBQ).

Other aspects of structural change have been induced by financial liberalization, internationalization, technological change, and market booms in the Japanese economy.

1. Outstanding consumer credit (RCCL).
2. CPI inflation (Inflation).
3. Relative price of non-durable prices to durable prices (RPRI).

The above structural variables are all combined in linear for the proxy of θ_t such that,

$$\theta_t = \lambda_1 HOUS_t + \lambda_2 DEMG65_t + \lambda_3 RBQ_t + \lambda_4 HOUPOP_t$$
$$+ \lambda_5 RCCL_t + \lambda_6 Inflation_t + \lambda_7 RPRI_t \tag{9}$$

As some proxy variables may turn out to be 'true' structural change variables, we intend to identify such 'true' variables for structural changes by means of testing out multiple proxy variables. At the same time, we hope to avoid using dummy variables in econometric modelling below.

6.3   DATA ANALYSIS AND ECONOMETRIC MODELLING

This paper uses annual data on macroeconomic variables, mainly from *National Accounts* (see the Data Appendix on pp. 163–4). Annual data is used simply because wealth data as well as demographic data are only available annually. This implies that econometric modelling might suffer from a small sample bias in exchange for escaping from the seasonality problem.

Data analysis

Prior to econometric modelling, it is important to identify the right empirical questions to investigate. In so doing, primary data analysis is given below.

One of the most striking features of consumer behaviour is the steady decline in the propensity to save (that is, the saving rate) since the mid-1970s (see Figure 6.1). In addition to this long-run trend, durable consumption in the mid-1980s magnified economic expansion of the latest business cycle shown in Figure 6.2.

The steady decline in the saving rate is often explained by demographic change and lower economic growth. If this is the case, the rapid ageing of the population and the shift towards low economic growth caused by a shortage of labour would certainly reduce the saving rate and inevitably shrink the current account surplus. However, judging from Figure 6.3, it is obvious that the monotonically increasing ageing factor alone cannot explain why the saving rate reached its peak in 1975. Many economists, including Hayashi (1992), point out that a shift in the growth of real output would influence the saving rate. There seems to be a consensus that the high saving rate in the 1960s was mostly due to the high growth rate in that period. This view, however, cannot extend to explain the steadily declining saving rates under the relatively high growth experienced in the late 1980s. In other words, the steady decline in the saving rate cannot be explained by a change in economic growth in the late 1980s.

An alternative explanation is based on short-run structural changes, along with the long-run trend. In the case of the late 1980s, durable consumption and other structural changes seem to have prevented the saving rate from rising. A proper question to ask here is to what extent durable consumption can be explained by disposable income and the wealth effect. Considering the high income elasticity of durable consumption, it is reasonable that the high growth of durable consumption corresponds to high economic growth in the same period. Considering an increasing share of durable consumption in total consumption, the steady decline of the saving rate in this period is reflected in the disproportional growth of durable consumption (see Figure 6.4). Furthermore, the Economic Planning Agency (1993) points out in its White Paper the importance of the wealth effect on consumption. Consumption (and in particular, durable consumption) seems to follow a similar trend to the movement of asset prices in the late 1980s (see Figure 6.5).

Having recognized the importance of the wealth effect on consumption, the next empirical task is to identify the transmission channel of the wealth effect. A simple and thus often-used logic is to assume that asset price rises directly influence consumption because of an increase in life-time wealth. On the other hand, Muellbauer and Murphy (1990)

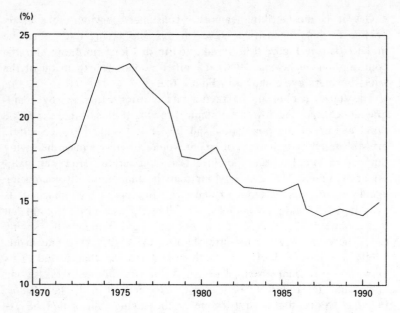

FIGURE 6.1   Household saving rate

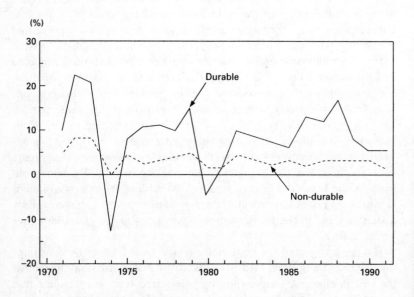

FIGURE 6.2   Consumption growth by types

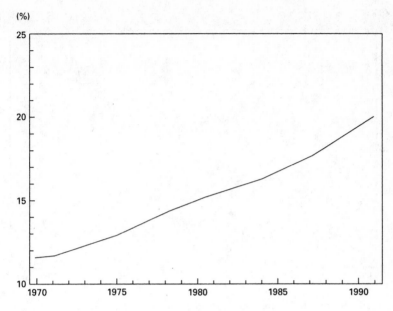

FIGURE 6.3   Share of age over 65 to age 20–64

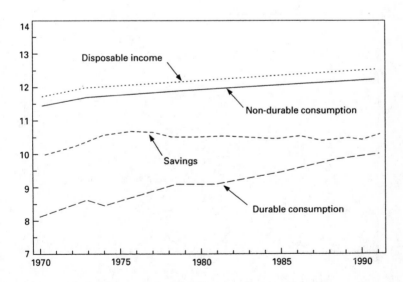

FIGURE 6.4   Plots of non-durable consumption, durable consumption savings and disposable income in logarithm

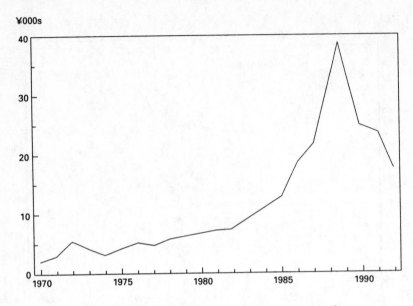

FIGURE 6.5   Stock price (Nikkei Index) at the end of year

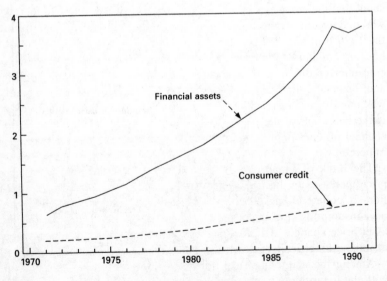

FIGURE 6.6   The ratio of household financial assets and consumer credit
to disposable income

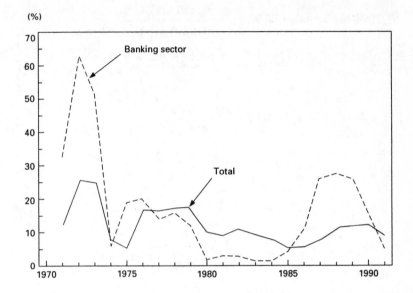

FIGURE 6.7   Growth rates of consumer credit

show that the consumer boom in the latter half of the 1980s in the UK was mainly due to the liberalization of domestic credit (especially by the 1986 Building Society Act) which, in turn, was made available by housing collateral. Similarly, banks in Japan developed and expanded consumer credit; in particular, non-housing credit backed by housing and financial collateral in the 1980s (see Figure 6.6). Such bank credit was mainly responsible for the expansion of overall consumer credit in the latter half of the 1980s (Figure 6.7). A wealth effect transmission channel on consumption via consumer credit seems to be increasingly important.

The Bank of Japan (1990) finds that a substantial portion of land price increases in the late 1980s were backed by bank credit. In addition, if collateral-backed consumer credit has a significant influence on consumption, the importance of monetary policy transmission via asset price changes will also increase. All the above questions will be examined empirically below.

Among the many empirical transformation possibilities, we end up with the logarithmic transformation of equilibrium solutions (equations (6)–(8)), employing the first order Taylor's series expansion, which yields basic empirical models:

$$\ln NDC_t = \ln\beta + \ln DI_t + \frac{(\alpha + \gamma)\theta_t}{\beta DI_t} - \frac{\delta K_{t-1}}{DI_t}$$

$$+ \frac{(1 + r)(1 - \varphi)W_{t-1} + WfCG + WhCG}{DI_t} \qquad (10)$$

$$\ln DC_t = \ln\gamma + \ln DI_t + \frac{(\alpha + \beta)\delta K_{t-1}}{\gamma DI_t} - \frac{\theta_t}{DI_t}$$

$$+ \frac{(1 + r)(1 - \varphi)W_{t-1} + WfCG + WhCG}{DI_t} \qquad (11)$$

$$\ln S_t = \ln\alpha + \ln DI_t - \frac{(\gamma + \beta)\{(1 + r)(1 - \varphi)W_{t-1} + WfCG}{\alpha DI_t}$$

$$+ \frac{WhCG\}}{\alpha DI_t} - \frac{\theta_t}{DI_t} - \frac{\delta K_{t-1}}{DI_t} \qquad (12)$$

The logarithmic versions of consumption and saving functions are, indeed, most frequently used in empirical modelling. The interpretation of the above empirical models is quite clear. The first two terms on the right-hand side are the fundamental variables (disposable income and a constant term), which can be called the 'Keynesian core' because they are the variables used in the usual Keynesian consumption function. The Keynesian core represents long-run equilibrium conditions. The next three terms (from the third to the fifth inclusive) on the right-hand side consist of the structural change and stock adjustment variables. Note that δK_{t-1} is the depreciation of durables and is equivalent to negative of real capital losses from durables. These represent disequilibrium dynamic conditions which are subject to business cycles and short-term fluctuations of the economy.

The above models are, however, not ready for empirical analysis because of non-stationality. As the recent development of time-series analysis suggests, the stationality of variables is a prerequisite for good econometric models. Figure 6.4 showed that dependent variables ($\ln NDC$, $\ln DC$, $\ln S$) and a major explanatory variable ($\ln DI$) in the above models (10)–(12) are non-stationary. A further model transformation is thus required.

If a structural change variable such as inflation rises rapidly, the models may over- (or under-) predict savings (consumption). This point was made by Pesaran and Evans (1984) and is known as the 'boundary problem'. As Taylor's series expansion implies that disequilibrium dynamic fluctuations around the long-run equilibrium path are infinitesimal, our models do not take account of the boundary problem by assuming structural change fluctuations are relatively small (as indeed they are).

6.4   ESTIMATION AND INFERENCE

The model selection strategy adopted in this chapter is the 'general to specific' approach. In brief, we start with a general model with a sufficient lag structure which is sequentially reduced by means of formal test procedures and diagnostics to finally arrive at the most appropriate specification within a class of model.[5] According to Harvey (1981), a good model must satisfy several selection criteria, which include: (i) theory consistency; (ii) parsimony; (iii) goodness of fit; (iv) predictive ability; and (v) robustness.

(i) Theory consistency requires that a good model be consistent with what is known *a priori*, in particular, economic theory. Plausibility of econometric modelling can be judged partly from sign conditions derived from economic theory. To put it the other way round, econometric modelling normally starts from a theoretical model at equilibrium (an optimal model). During the process of econometric specification, long-run equilibrium information from a theoretical model should be retained.

(ii) Parsimony is the statistical principle in which a good model contains the smallest possible number of parameters as long as it maintains reasonable explanatory power. In this way, a good deal is gained by focusing attention on the variables which really matter.

As to goodness of fit, predictive ability and robustness, only brief descriptions of diagnostic statistics are given. Detailed definitions and relevant references can be found in Hendry (1989).

(iii) Statistics for goodness of fit: The equation standard error (σ) and its percentage of error in a mean of dependent variable (σ/μ), together with usual statistics such as R^2 and *RSS* (the residual sum of squares), are recorded. Information criteria (*SC* = Schwarz, *HQ* = Hannan–Quinn, *EPE* = Final Prediction Error or Amemiya. For definitions of these statistics, see Judge *et al.* (1985), pp. 243–7) are used for model selection in the process of 'general to specific' research strategy. Parameter *t*-values are in parentheses ( ).

(iv) Statistics for predictive ability and parameter constancy: the idea is to examine the accuracy of predictions for observations arising in the post-sample period. The index of numerical parameter constancy for H forecasts (for the post-sample period) is calculated by the formula $Chi^2(H)/H$ which yields an approximate F-test. The Chow test of parameter constancy over the forecasting period H is also employed.

(v) Statistics for robustness: the Durbin–Watson test (DW) for serial correlation and the Chi-squared test for normality of residual distribution are used. Ramsey's RESET F-test for misspecification is also recorded (see also Godfrey (1988) for detail).

Among the above five criteria, we put the most emphasis on (iv) and, in particular, on (v). It is desirable and useful to select a robust model with stable parameters when economic policies are to be implemented under uncertainty. It is not recommended that a very delicate model, like a glassware in the Rococo period, is selected; it might have a high goodness of fit, but without robustness!

Prior to econometric model selection by means of the above mentioned diagnostic tests, usual econometric problems such as heteroskedasticity, multicollinearity and autocorrelation are, indeed, avoidable by a proper model transformation based on a proper theoretical model. The log-transformed models (equations (10)–(12)) are further differenced once (that is, the first difference) to make them fully dynamic as well as stationary (see Figures 6.8, 6.9 and 6.10), retaining the long-run equilibrium information on propensities to consume and save (that is $\ln\alpha$, $\ln\beta$, $\ln\gamma$ in equations (10)–(12)) in the form of an error correction model (ECM), for example, $\ln\alpha \approx \alpha_0 + \alpha_1(\ln S - \ln DI)_t = \alpha_0 + \alpha_1 \ln(S/DI)_t$, (see, for theoretical discussion on dynamic specification, Hendry (1993), ch. 4; and Benerjee *et al.*, (1993)). This way of introducing ECM terms is more convenient than the usual two-step estimates of the model with an ECM term (on this point, see Wickens and Breusch, 1988).

Three other modifications are made for model specifications. First, in the process of dynamic specification, parameter restrictions are removed. This implies that the simultaneity of the three equations no longer binds the system. Second, some structural change variables do not follow theoretically consistent data transformations because they are already quasi-stationary. These variables, incuding inflation and $dRPRI$ need not be further divided by DI. The capital gains variables, $WfCG$ and $WhCG$ on the other hand, are divided by wealth stock Wf

and *Wh* respectively. Third, a lagged durable depreciation divided by disposable income ($\delta K_{t-1}/DI_t$) is replaced by current capital losses from durables *WdCG* divided by durable stock (that is, $(WdCG/K)_t$).

$$
\begin{aligned}
d\ln NDC_t = {} & \beta_0 + \beta_1 \ln(NDC/DI)_{t-1} + \beta_2 d\ln DI_{t-1} \\
& + \beta_3 d(HOUS/DI)_t + \beta_4 d(DEMG65/DI)_t \\
& + \beta_5 d(RBQ/DI)_t + \beta_6 d(HOUPOP/DI)_t \\
& + \beta_7 d(RCCL/DI)_t + \beta_8 Inflation_t + \beta_9 dRPRI_t \\
& + \beta_{10}(WfCG/Wf)_t + \beta_{11}(WdCG/K)_t \\
& + \beta_{12}(WhCG/Wh)_t + \beta_{13} d(K_{t-1}/DI_t) \\
& + \beta_{14} d(Wf_{t-1}/DI_t) + \beta_{15} d(Wh_{t-1}/DI_t) + \varepsilon_t
\end{aligned}
\tag{13}
$$

$$
\begin{aligned}
d\ln DC_t = {} & \gamma_0 + \gamma_1 \ln(DC/DI)_{t-1} + \gamma_2 d\ln DI_{t-1} \\
& + \gamma_3 d(HOUS/DI)_t + \gamma_4 d(DEMG65/DI)_t \\
& + \gamma_5 d(RBQ/DI)_t + \gamma_6 d(HOUPOP/DI)_t \\
& + \gamma_7 d(RCCL/DI)_t + \gamma_8 Inflation_t + \gamma_9 dRPRI_t \\
& + \gamma_{10}(WfCG/Wf)_t + \gamma_{11}(WdCG/K)_t \\
& + \gamma_{12}(WhCG/Wh)_t + \gamma_{13} d(K_{t-1}/DI_t) \\
& + \gamma_{14} d(Wf_{t-1}/DI_t) + \gamma_{15} d(Wh_{t-1}/DI_t) + u_t
\end{aligned}
\tag{14}
$$

$$
\begin{aligned}
d\ln S_t = {} & \alpha_0 + \alpha_1 \ln(S/DI)_{t-1} + \alpha_2 d\ln DI_{t-1} + \alpha_3 d(HOUS/DI)_t \\
& + \alpha_4 d(DEMG65/DI)_t + \alpha_5 d(RBQ/DI)_t \\
& + \alpha_6 d(HOUPOP/DI)_t + \alpha_7 d(RCCL/DI)_t \\
& + \alpha_8 Inflation_t + \alpha_9 dRPRI_t + \alpha_{10}(WfCG/Wf)_t \\
& + \alpha_{11}(WdCG/K)_t + \alpha_{12}(WhCG/Wh)_t \\
& + \alpha_{13} d(K_{t-1}/DI_t) + \alpha_{14} d(Wf_{t-1}/DI_t) \\
& + \alpha_{15} d(Wh_{t-1}/DI_t) + v_t
\end{aligned}
\tag{15}
$$

The above specifications share the characteristics discussed in equations (10)–(12). The first three terms represent fundamental variables (long-run equilibrium information) and the rest structural changes and stock adjustments (short-run disequilibrium dynamic information). In general, the principal interest is in the long-run behaviour of the models, because this is what economic theory has most to say about, and because tests of the theory tend to focus on its long-run properties, such as propensity to consume, and income elasticities of consumption and savings. However, it is the short-run dynamic structure that would help in making forecasts. In other words, the above specification of the structural models with the short-run dynamic structure is a direct test against Hall's random walk hypothesis.

6.5 EVALUATION AND POLICY IMPLICATIONS

Regression results are reported in Tables 6.1 and 6.2, and Figures 6.8, 6.9 and 6.10. Calculated propensities to consume and save are presented in Table 6.3 on p. 159 and income elasticities are reported in Table 6.4 on p. 159.

Evaluation

Table 6.1 presents estimates of the general models. Although diagnostic statistics are fairly satisfactory, many estimated parameters are statistically insignificant. There is much room to improve the models by reducing the number of explanatory variables. The 'general to specific' approach of model selection works well in this case. With model selection, robustness of the estimated parameters increases. This implies that we can identify the 'true' models with the 'true' budget constraints within a class of model (that is, being based on a specific theoretical model with a set of explanatory variables).

Table 6.2 presents the finally specified models. These parsimonious models satisfy all diagnostic statistics. Namely, all information criteria show model improvement from the general models in Table 6.1. Neither the Chi-squared test for normality of residual distribution nor the RESET F-test for misspecification indicate any misspecification (including non-linearity) or omission of variables. Parameter constancy tests also imply that the models forecast fairly well during the bubble period (1989–91).

One of the most surprising and controversial findings of this chapter is that all wealth variables disappear from finally specified models, except the capital gains rate for durables (that is, a negative of the depreciation rate, $WdCG/K$) in the durable consumption model. This exception can be explained by a simple stock adjustment mechanism

TABLE 6.1 General models

Dependent variable (t-value)	Non-durable consumption $d \ln NDC_t$	Durable consumption $d \ln DC_t$	Savings $d \ln S_t$
Constant	−0.0646 (−0.8753)	−0.7399 (−3.9632)	−1.3350 (−3.1486)
$\ln(NDC/DI)_{t-1}$	−0.6137 (−2.2985)	—	—
$\ln(DC/DI)_{t-1}$	—	−0.2082 (−4.6031)	—
$\ln(S/DI)_{t-1}$	—	—	−0.6220 (−2.7772)
$d \ln DI_{t-1}$	0.0363 (0.0836)	1.4619 (2.2680)	−0.1637 (−0.0780)
$d(HOUS/DI)_t$	−0.4554 (−0.3448)	−1.1132 (−0.6314)	−15.0450 (−2.2751)
$d(DEMG65/DI)_t$	−1.4822 (−1.8758)	1.3035 (1.4409)	7.9095 (2.0743)
$d(RBQ/DI)_t$	0.4464 (0.3241)	−7.4072 (−4.3082)	−3.4692 (−0.5296)
$d(HOUPOP/DI)_t$	0.9633 (0.6289)	−5.0380 (−2.3959)	−16.5542 (−2.2651)
$d(RCCL/DI)_t$	−0.2433 (−0.5841)	0.9644 (2.5499)	1.1983 (0.6851)
Inflation rate	−0.3606 (−2.4072)	−1.9317 (−11.5652)	1.9951 (3.0080)
$d RPRI_t$	−0.1643 (−0.9906)	1.7412 (6.1289)	−0.1828 (−0.2749)
$(WfCG/Wf)_t$	−0.1127 (−1.0286)	0.0407 (0.2237)	0.9025 (1.5466)
$(WdCG/K)_t$	0.2990 (1.1285)	−0.6813 (−1.6244)	−0.7518 (−0.5821)
$(WhCG/Wh)_t$	0.0271 (0.7086)	−0.0040 (0.0767)	−0.1685 (−0.9225)
$d(K_{t-1}/DI_t)$	0.6030 (0.5748)	0.5729 (0.2867)	−5.9745 (−0.9987)
$d(Wf_{t-1}/DI_t)$	0.0091 (0.3504)	−0.0005 (−0.0123)	0.0097 (0.0763)
$d(Wh_{t-1}/DI_t)$	—	—	—
Diagnostics			
R^2	0.9915	0.9978	0.9529
σ	0.0076	0.0104	0.0362
σ/μ	0.2094	0.1228	1.2313
DW	2.6570	2.8640	2.8750
RSS	0.0003	0.0005	0.0066
Information criteria			
SC (Schwarz)	−8.9085	−8.2731	−5.7765
HQ (Hannan Quinn)	−9.5095	−8.8741	−6.3775
FRE (Amemiya)	0.0001	0.0002	0.0023
Normality			
Chi-squared Test	0.1940	0.3220	0.3880
Misspecification			
Reset F-test F(1.4)	0.0780	0.1610	0.0900
Parameter constancy over 1989–91			
Chi-squared Test	—	—	—
Chow Test $F(3, n)$	—	—	—

Note: Sample Period: 1972–1991 Estimation Method: OLS

TABLE 6.2 Finally specified models

Dependent variable (t-value)	Non-durable consumption $d \ln NDC_t$	Durable consumption $d \ln DC_t$	Savings $d \ln S_t$
Constant	−0.0944 (−3.4102)	−0.6990 (−5.7008)	−0.7090 (−4.3239)
$\ln(NDC/DI)_{t-1}$	−0.5530 (−4.4267)	—	—
$\ln(DC/DI)_{t-1}$	—	−0.2033 (−7.1411)	—
$\ln(S/DI)_{t-1}$	—	—	−0.3702 (−3.8924)
$d \ln DI_{t-1}$	0.0605 (0.3760)	1.7370 (5.6364)	−1.2315 (−1.4845)
$d(HOUS/DI)_t$	−1.3542 (−1.7286)	—	−3.3730 (−1.2656)
$d(DEMG65/DI)_t$	−0.7914 (−3.6159)	0.9866 (1.8920)	—
$d(RBQ/DI)_t$	—	−7.6324 (−4.4516)	—
$d(HOUPOP/DI)_t$	—	−4.3435 (−2.8888)	−5.6230 (−2.7147)
$d(RCCL/DI)_t$	—	0.9559 (3.5072)	—
Inflation rate	−0.3693 (−3.9298)	−2.0089 (−11.4079)	1.7448 (3.9246)
$d \, RPRI_t$	−0.2722 (−1.7123)	1.7023 (9.6099)	—
$(WfCG/Wf)_t$	—	—	—
$(WdCG/K)_t$	—	−0.5653 (−1.5651)	—
$(WhCG/Wh)_t$	—	—	—
$d(K_{t-1}/DI_t)$	—	—	—
$d(Wf_{t-1}/DI_t)$	—	—	—
$d(Wh_{t-1}/DI_t)$	—	—	—
Diagnostics			
R^2	0.9824	0.9975	0.8848
σ	0.0073	0.0925	0.0365
σ/μ	0.1968	0.1054	1.4258
DW	2.5850	2.5390	2.3480
RSS	0.0005	0.0006	0.0147
Information criteria			
SC (Schwarz)	−9.1923	−8.5872	−6.0567
HQ (Hannan Quinn)	−9.5013	−9.0286	−6.3215
FRE (Amemiya)	0.0001	0.0001	0.0018
Normality			
Chi-squared Test	0.2950	0.2050	0.6460
Misspecification			
Reset F-test $F(1.4)$	0.9220	0.5540	0.0820
Parameter constancy over 1989–91			
Chi-squared Test	0.4600	0.4000	0.7500
Chow Test $F(3, n)$	0.3300	0.2000	0.6500

Note: Sample Period: 1972–1991 Estimation Method: OLS

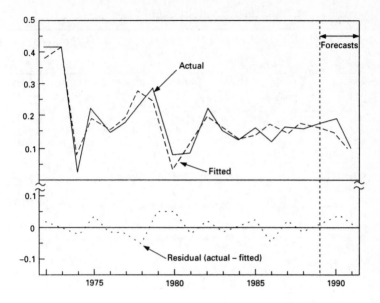

FIGURE 6.8   Estimation of non-durable consumption

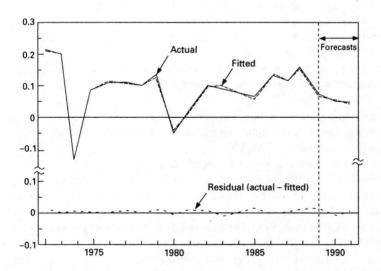

FIGURE 6.9   Estimation of durable consumption

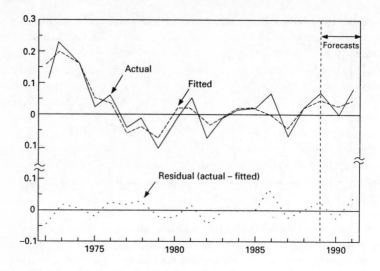

FIGURE 6.10   Estimation of savings

of durables. Therefore there is no evidence of the wealth effect on consumption in a conventional sense, contrary to what was argued in journals and the press in the late 1980s. The finally specified non-durable consumption model shares similarity with Davidson *et al.* (1978) (see also Hendry *et al.* (1990)). The saving model we come up with, on the other hand, is very similar to that of Deaton (1977), with some additional structural change variables.

Compared with non-durable consumption and saving, durable consumption faces a quite different budget constraint which is subject to various structural factors. Our study from Japanese macro data confirms Muellbauer's (1981) findings from UK evidence that non-durable and durable consumption are not consistent with the same neo-classical budget constraint (p. 232).[6]

As a proxy variable for financial liberalization, $d(RCCL/DI)_t$ is retained only in the durable consumption model. This implies that consumer credit expansion has a positive influence only on durable consumption, and therefore that a solo credit transmission in the household sector enters through durable consumption. We will return to the policy implications of this later. Other proxy financial variables such as (ex-post) real interest rate, interest rate spread (between the long-term average lending rate and one-year average deposit rate), and nominal long-term average lending rate were used in the earlier stage of this study. However, the negative real interest rate effect on consumption predicted by economic theory could not be statistically well identified because of unusually high inflation in the 1970s which made real interest rates negative for some years. At the same time, increased income uncertainty would have contributed to the reduction of consumption, rather than to an increase, even in the presence of negative real interest rates. Instead of using information on interest rates, CPI inflation is adopted. As is evident from Table 6.2, inflation has a significantly negative influence on non-durable and durable consumption and a significantly positive influence on savings (see also Horioka *et al.*, 1992). With all variables expressed in real terms, significant influences of inflation rate are indicative of money illusion in the household sector; in other words, the non-neutrality of money.

A change in relative price between non-durables and durables (defined as $d(P_{ndc}/P_{dc})_t$) induces demand for relatively cheaper goods, as price theory predicts, namely, demand shifts from non-durables to durables as the relative price $(P_{ndc}/P_{dc})_t$ goes up.

Undergoing demographic change is one of the major structural changes on behalf of the household sector which would certainly alter the structure of consumer demand. Tables 6.1 and 6.2 reveal some interesting facts about the influence of demographic change on consumption and savings. Because of the dominant role of the life-cycle theory in consumption function modelling, a variable representing age structure (for example, a dependent population ratio (that is, proportion of children and senior citizens to the working population) or an aged population ratio (that is, proportion of those aged over 65 to the working population)) is probably the most often used demographic variable in consumption function (see, for example, Horioka (1991), Muellbauer and Murphy (1989)). However, demographic change has also occurred in other dimensions, such as new family formation, the number of child-bearings, and family dissolution. In addition, intergenerational transfers (bequests) provide important information on the wealth of the aged and on family mergers between aged and young households. To take account of these demographic factors in consumption and saving functions, statistical inferences turn out to be quite contrary to what has been argued in the life-cycle theory. That is, the life-cycle theory expects the ageing process to discourage savings and encourage consumption. Both Tables 6.1 and 6.2 show that the ageing variable, $d(DEMG65/DI)_t$, has a negative influence on non-durable consumption and positive influences on durable consumption and saving shown in Table 6.1. Furthermore, it disappears altogether from the finally specified saving model.

An increase in the number of households factor, $d(HOUS/DI)_t$, reduces both consumption and savings. Newly-formed households normally consist of independent young people, newly-married couples, and divorced people. These households usually have lower purchasing power, thus contributing to negative influences on consumption and saving growth rates (that is, $d\ln NDC_t$, $d\ln DC_t$, $d\ln S_t$). Influences of an increase in per household population, $d(HOUPOP/DI)_t$, differ among non-durable consumption (positive) and durable consumption (significantly negative) and savings (significantly negative). This result can be interpreted as: a decrease in household members in recent years increases durable consumption and savings and decreases non-durable consumption.[7] The bequest factor, $d(RBQ/DI)_t$, has a significantly negative influence on durables. One interpretation is that substantial durable transfers would occur as bequests, although these transfers are regarded as being small amounts compared with housing and financial transfers. The bequest factor is known to have a significant influence on housing purchase decisions, but not so much on non-durable consumption and savings.

Table 6.3 shows average and marginal propensities to consume and save from disposable income. A notable finding is that propensities for durable consumption differ significantly between marginal and average ones, while those for non-durables and saving experience comparatively small changes. This implies that, although the level itself is low, durable consumption is very sensitive to structural changes. Indeed, judging from Table 6.2 on p. 154, structural change factors (that is, $d(DEMG65/DI)_t$, $d(RBQ/DI)_t$, $d(HOUPOP/DI)_t$, $d(RCCL/DI)_t$ and $d(RPRI)_t$) make the household sector consume 46.4 per cent more durables than those at the marginal level, in which no structural change is expected. Put differently, given that the saving rate is unaffected by structural changes, non-durable consumption decreases when durable consumption increases under structural change, along with the relative price change. Consumption substitution between durables and non-durables has taken place.

The propensities to consume and save are the concepts measuring marginal and average proportions of respective expenditures to given disposable income. Income elasticities, on the other hand, measure relative changes in consumption and savings when income increases marginally. Calculated income elasticities are reported in Table 6.4. The results are consistent with what economic theory expects. The income elasticity of non-durable consumption is normally less than unity. The value from Table 6.4 turns out to be as low as 0.0605.[8] Non-durables

TABLE 6.3 Propensity to consume or save

	Average propensity to consume or save (APC or APS)	Marginal propensity to consume or save (MPC or MPS)	Percentage change from MPC (or MPS) to APC (or APS)
NDC/DI	0.770	0.812	−5.20
DC/DI	0.041	0.028	46.40
S/DI	0.186	0.192	−3.10

Notes:
1. The average propensities to consume or save are calculated by solving the selected model in Table 6.2 for the long-run equilibrium. In the case of *NDC*, the following solution is given

$$\ln(NDC/DI)_{t-1} = \{-d\ln NDC_t - 0.0944 + 0.0605 d\ln DI_{t-1} \\ - 1.3542d(HOUS/DI)_t - 0.7914d(DEMG65/DI)_t \\ - 0.3693\text{Inflation} - 0.2722dRPRI_t\}/0.5530. \quad (N1)$$

Substituting average values for the right-hand side variables yields −0.2614. This figure has to be converted into average propensity to consume, i.e. *NDC/DI*, which becomes 0.770. The same procedure follows for *DC* and *S*.
2. The marginal propensities to consume are calculated from the level information (i.e. average value for inflation) and constant term in equation (N1), assuming all other first difference terms are zero. The same procedure follows for *DC* and *S*.

TABLE 6.4 Income elasticity

Item	Formula		Value
Non-durable consumption	$\dfrac{\partial NDC_t / \partial DI_{t-1}}{NDC_t / DI_{t-1}}$	$\approx \dfrac{\partial \ln NDC_t}{\partial \ln DI_{t-1}}$	0.0605
Durable consumption	$\dfrac{\partial DC_t / \partial DI_{t-1}}{DC_t / DI_{t-1}}$	$\approx \dfrac{\partial \ln DC_t}{\partial \ln DI_{t-1}}$	1.7370
Savings	$\dfrac{\partial S_t / \partial DI_{t-1}}{S_t / DI_{t-1}}$	$\approx \dfrac{\partial \ln S_t}{\partial \ln DI_{t-1}}$	−1.2315

Note:

1. By construction of the econometric models, income elasticities are calculated by using a lagged income (not by a current income).

here can be considered as typical *necessary goods*. The income elasticity of durable consumption, on the other hand, is 1.7370. Durables can be characterized as *luxury goods*. This significantly high value of income elasticity of durable consumption explains the high growth rate of durable consumption in the late 1980s, during which income growth rates were also high.

Policy implications

Some policy implications, especially in relation to household savings and the current account surplus, can be drawn from the above empirical analysis.

First, a significantly negative income elasticity of savings is particularly interesting. Many economists argue that Japan's high savings can be explained by the high economic growth of the 1960s and 1970s (for example, Hayashi (1989, 1992), Christiano (1989) and Yoshikawa (1992)). Hayashi (1992) concludes that 'we can be sure that the rapid aging of Japan's population will reduce national saving over the coming decades', also that 'today's young, fully aware of their income growth in this era of stable growth, will not contribute to national saving as much as yesterday's young did' (pp. 76–7). Both his claims contradict our econometric findings in the 1970s and 1980s: namely, the ageing process does not *per se* have any negative influence on savings, and the income elasticity of savings is significantly negative, rather than positive, as Hayashi and others implicitly assume. Apparently, the growth-led savings hypothesis of the 1960s and 1970s would not expain consumer behaviour in the 1980s. This might be due to the fact that many complex structural factors have been affecting consumer behaviour in recent years. An important policy implication of this result is that economic policy-making in the 1990s must take into account structural changes (in particular, the more complex aspects of demographic change in the 1980s) and must not singlemindedly base decisions on observations made in the 1960s and 1970s.

Second, our empirical result casts doubt on a commonly-held view that rapid ageing in Japan will reduce savings and eventually balance the current account. In fact, our finding is consistent with the recent empirical work on microeconomic data (for example, Takayama and Kitamura, 1994), showing that older generations keep saving until their late seventies. We believe that the current account surplus (that is, the *I–S* imbalance) will not easily be eliminated. Our result thus implies that some active policy action is called for to reduce the current account surplus.

Third, consumer credit is a significantly positive explanatory variable of the consumption of durables. This implies that bank credit to consumers increases durable consumption and, vice versa, a bank credit crunch would depress consumption. Consumption expansion might start from increases in asset (wealth) prices, which consequently raise collateral values, and then bank loans increase. If this is the case, our rejection of the wealth effect with respect to consumption and savings must be considered to be a refutation of *direct* influences, not as a refutation of an *indirect* channel.[9] Indeed, the transmission channels of monetary policy through asset prices have been strengthened in the other sectors of the economy (see, for example, Okabe, 1993), and the household sector may not be an exception. However, evaluating the expansion of consumer credit in the 1980s, special attention has to be paid to the fact that asset prices clearly exceeded fundamental values and thus bank credit expansion was not sustainable. Note, however, that a full analysis of the consequences of bank behaviour in the 1980s is yet to be made.

Fourth, inflation turns out to be the 'core' explanatory variable in the sense that it has significant influences on both consumption and savings. Price stability is a prerequisite for the steady growth of household consumption, which comprises the largest component of domestic demand. Resolution of price gaps between domestic and foreign markets via deregulation would contribute to consumption growth because of price stability, namely, a drop in consumer prices. Opening up domestic markets and improving the distribution system to assure exchange-rate pass-through can therefore be an important policy tool for boosting household consumption, and thus domestic aggregate demand.

6.6 CONCLUSION

This chapter has presented a theoretical model of consumption and saving, with special emphasis on structural changes, then conducted empirical tests for non-durables, durables, and saving based on the theoretical model. The virtues of structural models such as ours include being able to identify how each structural factor enters into consumption and saving behaviour and also to improve theoretical models by means of examining empirical results. Even after rigorous diagnostic tests for model selection, final validity of the model should be judged by the plausibility of values of fundamental parameters, such as propensity to consume or save and the income elasticity of consumption.

Our models satisfy all these requirements and turn out to be quite robust, as evidenced by the fact that they can forecast quite accurately for out-of-the-sample-period of the bubble economy in 1989–91.

The main results are summarized as follows:

1. there is no evidence of the wealth effect on consumption and saving in a conventional sense;
2. durable consumption faces quite a different budget constraint which is subject to various structural factors;
3. consumer credit expansion has a significantly positive influence on durable consumption;
4. significant influences of inflation on consumption and saving are indicative of money illusion in the household sector or imperfect financial markets; and
5. an often discussed demographic variable, the ageing population ratio variable does not *per se* show any clear sign of reducing saving.

Remaining problems and the future courses of research are briefly discussed below.

First, as policy effects are quite often judged in time-series, methodological as well as conceptual improvements in macroeconomic time-series analysis are called for. In this chapter, we presented a way in which inherently microeconomic structural change factors can be incorporated in macroeconomic data. As discussed, it is necessary to model a consumer credit expansion mechanism in which credit is endogenously determined, partly by household wealth as collateral. In so doing, the wealth effect on consumption can be identified, although there is no direct evidence of a wealth effect on consumption and saving.

Second, structural change effects must be analyzed with the aid of microeconomic survey data. For example, it is interesting to investigate the way in which endogenous decision-making occurs with respect to labour supply, marriage, child-bearing, education, retirement and inheritance over the life-cycle. With these analyses, economic effects of the rapid ageing of the population can be assessed quite differently from those based on comparative static analyses (that is, isolating the ageing factor alone). Two promising topics in the literature, as noted by Deaton (1992), are liquidity constraints and precautionary savings. Both topics should be pursued by microeconomic survey data. From our results, whether liquidity constraints on an aggregate basis exist in the household sector, remains an open question. Statistical influences of disposable income are insignificant *vis-à-vis* both non-durable consumption and savings which could be evidence of a non-liquidity constraint. On the other hand, disposable income, together with consumer credit, has a significantly positive influence on durable consumption, which could be evidence of liquidity constraint. Further analyses of liquidity constraints on Japanese microeconomic data are looked for.

Third, microeconomic survey data allows us to analyze how monetary policy affects wealth distribution, which is known to be more unequal than income distribution. Considering recent increases in wealth accumulation, characterized as a stock economy, the relationship between monetary policy and distribution of wealth is a potentially important policy issue which has to be explored.

DATA APPENDIX

Sources: *Annual Report on National Accounts* (Tōkyō: Economic Planning Agency), various years; *Japan Statistical Yearbook* (Tōkyō: Management and Coordination Agency, Statistics Bureau), various years, and *Annual Report of the Tax Bureau* (Tōkyō: Ministry of Finance, Tax Bureau), various years. All data is annual and real (deflated by 1985-based respective deflators). The sample period spans 1971–92. Statistical calculation is carried out by PC-GIVE v.6.1.

Definitions of variables

Data from National Accounts on the Household Sector

NDC	= Real non-durable consumption
DC	= Real durable consumption
S	= Real household saving
DI	= Real disposable income
RCCL	= Real total consumer credit outstanding (including the bank credits)
Wf	= Real financial assets
K	= Real durable stock
Wh	= Real land and housing assets
δK	= Real depreciation of durables[10]
WfCG	= Real capital gains from financial assets
WdCG	= Real capital losses from durables. This is equivalent to negative of δK
WhCG	= Real capital gains from land and housing assets
Inflation	= Year-to-year change of Consumer Price Index
RPRI	= Relative price of non-durable price deflator (*Pnd*) to durable price deflator (*Pd* (i.e. *Pnd/Pd*)

Data from Statistics Bureau

HOUS   = Number of households (in thousands)
DEMG65   = Proportion of population aged 65 or over to those aged 20–64
           multiplied by 1 000 000
HOUPOP   = Per household population multiplied by 10 000

Data from Tax Bureau

RBQ = Real bequest (net inheritance and gifts) transfers

NOTES

1. The recent literature on this topic includes Bar-Ilan and Blinder (1992), Bernanke (1985), Beaulieu (1993a, 1993b), Caballero (1990a, 1990b, 1993), Mankiw (1982), Muellbauer (1981) and Patterson (1985).
2. The recent literature on this topic includes Blundel-Wignall, *et al.* (1991), Deaton (1991, 1992), Hayashi (1982, 1985a, 1985b, 1987), Jappelli and Pagano (1989), Ogawa (1990) and Zeldes (1989b).
3. The recent literature on this topic includes Carroll (1992), Deaton (1991, 1992), Kimball (1991), Orphanides and Zervos (1993), Van Der Ploeg (1993), Weil (1993) and Zeldes (1989a).
4. We are fully aware of recent arguments against time-separable utility functions because of habit persistence and durability of consumer goods. See, for example, Beaulieu (1993a), Braun *et al.* (1993), and Heaton (1993). Furthermore, from a theoretical point of view, within-a-period utility maximization is not really dynamic, even though lagged variables are involved through budget constraints. Dynamic econometric modelling therefore needs some modifications from this theoretical model (see Sections 6.3 and 6.4). Note, however, that the primary reason for using a within-a-period utility maximization is that we use the data from the System of National Accounts (SNA) which are based on a within-a-period accounting. For a neo-classic dynamic model, intertemporally consistent statistical accounts, such as generational accounting advocated by Kotlikoff (1992), are to be used.
5. As for the statistical basis for model selection, see, for example, Harvey (1981), Spanos (1986) and Godfrey (1988).
6. 2SLS estimates without cross-equation restrictions of the simultaneous equations of durable and non-durable consumption and savings (note that in the dynamic model specification without cross-equation restrictions, the saving model is no longer identity endogenous) with nested explanatory variables (i.e. the same budget constraint) show apparent signs of misspecification and very poor forecasting power (e.g. the parameter constancy test of cumulative Chi-squared test with 9 degrees of freedom = 55.60 and the forecast F-test $F(9,5) = 16.35$). Thus no result of simultaneous equations is reported in this chapter.
7. This is closely related to the issue of *equivalence scale* or *adult equivalence*, in which required consumption standards vary with household

composition and number of household members. For details, see Deaton and Muellbauer (1980).
8. This could be due to an insignificant parameter value, as is evident from a low t-value (that is, 0.3760) in Table 6.2
9. In order to pursue this line of argument, consumer credit must be modelled as endogenous, being explained partly by household wealth as weakly exogenous or an instrumental variable.
10. National Accounts report durable *appreciation* (capital gains) in 1973 and 1974 which seems unreasonable. We re-estimated *depreciation* rates (i.e. $\delta K/K$): 0.1921 for 1973 and 0.1873 for 1974.

REFERENCES

Bank of Japan 1990. 'The Recent Rise in Japan's Land Prices: Its Background and Implications', Special Paper No. 193, December.

Bar-Ilan, A. and A. S. Blinder 1992. 'Consumer Durables: Evidence on The Optimality of Usually Doing Nothing', *Journal of Money, Credit, and Banking*, 24, 2, pp. 258–72.

Bernanke, B. 1985. 'Adjustment Costs, Durables, and Aggregate Consumption', *Journal of Monetary Economics*, 15, pp. 41–68.

Beaulieu, J. J. 1993a. 'Optimal Durable and Nondurable Consumption with Transaction Costs', Finance and Economics Discussion Series, Federal Reserve Board, no. 93–12.

Beaulieu, J. J. 1993b. 'Utilizing Cross-Sectional Evidence in Modeling Aggregate Time Series: Consumer Durables with Fixed Costs of Adjustment', Finance and Economics Discussion Series, Federal Reserve Board, no. 93–13.

Benerjee, A., J. Dolado, J. W. Galbraith, and D. F. Hendry 1993. *Co-Integration, Error-Correction, and The Econometric Analysis of Non-Stationary Data*, Oxford University Press.

Blundell-Wignall, A., F. Browne and S. Cavaglia 1991. 'Financial Liberalisation and Consumption Behaviour', Paris: OECD, Department of Economics and Statistics, Working Paper no. 81.

Braun, P. A., G. M. Constantinides and W. E. Ferson (1993. 'Time Nonseparability in Aggregate Consumption: International Evidence', *European Economic Review*, 37, pp. 897–920.

Caballero, R. J. 1990a. 'Expenditure on Durable Goods: A Case for Slow Adjustment', *Quarterly Journal of Economics*, 105, pp. 727–43.

Caballero, R. J. 1990b. 'Consumption Puzzles and Precautionary Savings', *Journal of Monetary Economics*, 25, pp. 113–36.

Caballero, R. J. 1993. 'Durable Goods: An Explanation for Their Slow Adjustment', *Journal of Political Economy*, 101, 2, pp. 351–84.

Carroll, C. D. 1992. 'The Buffer-Stock Theory of Saving: Some Macroeconomic Evidence', *Brookings Papers on Economic Activity*, 2, pp. 61–156.

Christiano, L. J. 1989. 'Understanding Japan's Saving Rate: The Reconstruction Hypothesis', *Quarterly Review*, Federal Reserve Bank of Minneapolis, Spring 1989, pp. 10–25.

Davidson, J. E., D. F. Hendry,, F. Srba and S. Yeo 1978. 'Econometric Modelling of The Aggregate Time-Series Relationship Between Consumers'

Expenditure and Income in The United Kingdom', *Economic Journal*, 88, pp. 661–92.

Deaton, A. 1977. 'Involuntary Saving Through Unanticipated Inflation', *American Economic Review*, 67, pp. 899–910.

Deaton, A. 1991. 'Saving and Liquidity Constraints', *Econometrica*, 59, 5, pp. 1221–48.

Deaton, A. 1992. *Understanding Consumption*, Oxford University Press.

Deaton, A. and J. Muellbauer 1980. *Economics and Consumer Behaviour*, Cambridge University Press.

Economic Planning Agency 1993. *The Economic White Paper*, Tōkyō: Government of Japan.

Financial Times, 29 June, 1993.

Godfrey, L. G. 1988. *Misspecification Tests in Econometrics*, Cambridge University Press.

Hall, R. E. 1990. *The Rational Consumer*, Cambridge, Mass.: The MIT Press.

Harvey, A. C. 1981. *The Econometric Analysis of Time Series*, Oxford: Philip Allan.

Hayashi, F. 1982. 'The Permanent Income Hypothesis: Estimation and Testing by Instrumental Variables', *Journal of Political Economy*, 90, 5, pp. 895–916.

Hayashi, F. 1985a. 'The Effect of Liquidity Constraints on Consumption: A Cross-Sectional Analysis', *Quarterly Journal of Economics*, 100, 1, pp. 183–206.

Hayashi, F. 1985b. 'The Permanent Income Hypothesis and Consumption Durability: Analysis Based on Japanese Panel Data', *Quarterly Journal of Economics*, 100, 4, pp. 1083–113.

Hayashi, F. 1987. 'Tests for Liquidity Constraints: A Critical Survey and Some New Observations', in F. F. Bewley (ed.), *Advances in Econometrics, 5th World Congress*, vol. II, pp. 91–120.

Hayashi, F. 1989. 'Is Japan's Saving Rate High?', *Quarterly Review*, Federal Reserve Bank of Minneapolis, Spring 1989, pp. 3–9.

Hayashi, F. 1992. 'Explaining Japan's Saving: A Review of Recent Literature', *Monetary and Economic Studies*, The Bank of Japan, 10, 2, pp. 63–78.

Heaton, J. 1993. 'The Interaction Between Time-Nonseparable Preferences and Time Aggregation', *Econometrica*, 61, 2, pp. 353–85.

Hendry, D. F. 1989. *PC-GIVE*, vol. 6.1, University of Oxford.

Hendry, D. F. 1993. *Econometrics: Alchemy or Science?*, Oxford: Blackwell.

Hendry, D. F., J. N. J. Muellbauer and A. Murphy 1990. 'The Econometrics of DHSY', in J. D. Hey and D. Winch (eds), *A Century of Economics: 100 Years of The Royal Economic Society and The Economic Journal*, Oxford: Blackwell, pp. 298–334.

Hicks, J. R. 1946. *Value and Capital*, 2nd edn, Oxford University Press.

Horioka, C. Y. 1988. 'Saving for Housing Purchase in Japan', *Journal of the Japanese and International Economies*, 2, 3, pp. 351–84.

Horioka, C. Y. 1991. 'Future Trends in Japan's Saving Rate and the Implications Thereof for Japan's External Imbalance', *Japan and The World Economy*, 3, pp. 307–30.

Horioka, C. Y., K. Ihara, K., Ochida and I. Nanbu 1992. 'The Levels and Determinants of the Japanese Saving Rate', *Financial Review*, December 1992, pp. 147–64 (in Japanese).

Jappelli, T. and M. Pagano 1989. 'Consumption and Capital Market Imperfections: An International Comparison', *American Economic Review*, 79, 5, pp. 1088–105.

Judge, G. G., W. E., Griffiths, R. Cartel Hill, H. Lütkepohl and T.-C. Lee 1985. *The Theory and Practice of Econometrics*, 2nd edn, New York: John Wiley.

Kimball, M. S. 1991. 'Precautionary Saving in the Small and in the Large', *Econometrica*, 58, pp. 53–73.

Kotlikoff, L. J. 1992. *Generational Accounting*, New York: The Free Press.

Mankiw, G. N. 1982. 'Hall's Consumption Hypothesis and Durable Goods', *Journal of Monetary Economics*, 10, pp. 417–25.

Muellbauer, J. 1981. 'Testing Neoclassical Models of the Demand for Consumer Durables' in A. Deaton, (ed.), *Essays in The Theory and Measurement of Consumer Behaviour in Honor of Sir Richard Stone*, Cambridge University Press.

Muellbauer, J. and A. Murphy 1989. 'Why Has UK Personal Saving Collapsed?' Credit Suisse First Boston, CSFB Economics, July.

Muellbauer, J. and A. Murphy 1990. 'The UK Current Account Deficit', *Economic Policy*, 5, pp. 347–95.

Ogawa, K. 1990. 'Cyclical Variations in Liquidity-Constrained Consumers: Evidence from Macro Data in Japan', *Journal of the Japanese and International Economies*, 4, 2, pp. 173–93.

Okabe, M. 1993. 'Transmission Channels of Monetary Policy in Japan: A Perspective', mimeo Sydney: Macquarie University.

Orphanides, A. and D. Zervos 1993. 'Optimal Consumption Dynamics with Non-Concave Habit Forming Utility', Finance and Economics Discussion Series, Federal Reserve Board, no. 93–15.

Patterson, K. D. 1985. 'Income Adjustments and the Role of Consumers' Durables in Some Leading Consumption Functions', *Economic Journal*, 95, pp. 469–79.

Pesaran, M. H. and R. A. Evans 1984. 'Inflation, Capital Gains and U.K. Personal Savings: 1953–1981', *Economic Journal*, 94, pp. 237–57.

Spanos, A. 1986. *Statistical Foundations of Econometric Modelling*, Cambridge University Press.

Takayama, N. and Y. Kitamura 1994. 'Household Saving Behavior in Japan' in J. Poterba (ed.), *International Comparisons of Household Saving*, Chicago: University of Chicago Press (forthcoming).

Van Der Ploeg, F. 1993. 'A Closed-form Solution for a Model of Precautionary Saving', *Review of Economic Studies*, 60, pp. 385–95.

Weil, P. 1993. 'Precautionary Savings and the Permanent Income Hypothesis', *Review of Economic Studies*, 60, pp. 367–83.

Wickens, M. R. and T. S. Breusch 1988. 'Dynamic Specification, the Long-Run and the Estimation of Transformed Regression Models', *Economic Journal*, 98, Supplement, pp. 189–205.

Yoshikawa, H. 1992. *The Japanese Economy and Macroeconomics*, Tōkyō: Toyo Keizai Shinposha (in Japanese), ch. 4.

Zeldes, S. P. 1989a. 'Optimal Consumption with Stochastic Income: Deviations from Certainty Equivalence', *Quarterly Journal of Economics*, 104, 2, pp. 275–98.

Zeldes, S. P. 1989b. 'Consumption and Liquidity Constraints: An Empirical Investigation', *Journal of Political Economy*, 97, 2, pp. 305–46.

7 Saving, Investment, and Capital Mobility: Lessons from Japanese Inter-regional Capital Flows

Robert Dekle*

7.1 INTRODUCTION

One of the most intriguing puzzles in international finance is the Feldstein–Horioka proposition (Feldstein and Horioka, 1980). As is well known, Feldstein and Horioka showed that in cross-country data, saving and investment rates have a correlation of nearly one. This, they interpret, is indicative of the international *immobility* of capital. If capital were fully mobile, then the level of investment in a (small) country should be largely determined by the international supply and demand for capital and not necessarily restricted by the domestic supply of capital, domestic saving. The increase in saving in one country should not change the international supply of capital noticeably; therefore, for a truly open economy, the level of investment in a country should not be affected greatly by its own saving rate. Feldstein and Bacchetta (1991) call the correlation coefficient of the investment rate on the saving rate, the 'savings retention coefficient'.

Subsequent estimates of the 'saving retention coefficient' using cross-country data up to 1990 by Feldstein and Bacchetta (1991) and Obstfeld (1993) were also close to unity. This is surprising, since the volume of international transactions has mushroomed in recent years. In April 1992, the average daily volume of foreign exchange trading was estimated at 1 trillion dollars a day, while as recently as 1988, it was only 600 billion dollars a day.

* I thank Professors M. Okabe and H. Yoshikawa and participants in the Second Conference on the Contemporary Japanese Economy held in August 1993 at Macquarie University, Sydney, for helpful comments.

If Feldstein and Horioka's *interpretation* is correct, then the high estimate of the 'savings retention coefficient' suggests that despite the recent volume of international financial transactions, domestic capital needs are still met by domestic savings. For cultural and sociological reasons, capital may not be highly internationally mobile; informational imperfections may limit cross-border investments.

During the 1980s, many papers were written criticizing the Feldstein and Horioka interpretation of the high 'savings retention coefficient'. These papers have argued essentially that a 'savings retention coefficient' estimate of close to unity can be explained by reasons other than international capital immobility. Several of these arguments are reviewed in Section 7.2.

In this chapter, we examine magnitudes of the 'saving retention coefficient' in a setting of *known*, (near) perfect, capital mobility, regions within Japan. If the saving and investment rates are highly positively correlated in Japanese regional data, then the Feldstein–Horioka interpretation of the 'saving retention coefficient' is misleading. Some reason other than imperfect capital mobility may account for the high international saving–investment correlation. Saving and investment rates should have a zero correlation under a setting of known, perfect capital mobility.

Our main conclusion is that, across Japanese regions, the saving and investment rates appear to be uncorrelated; the investment rate of each region is not restricted by its saving rate. Therefore, the Feldstein–Horioka use of the 'saving retention coefficient' as a benchmark to measure international capital immobility appears plausible.

There is, however, one qualification. The 'saving retention coefficient' should be estimated on data of *private* saving and *private* investment rates. This is because governments appear to be able to change the total saving and total investment rates, by changing the *government* saving and investment rates. The total saving (investment) rate is the sum of private saving (investment) and public saving (investment). Summers (1988) and Bayoumi (1990) are correct in suggesting that systematic current account balance targeting by the government can produce a strong cross-sectional association in the *total* saving and investment rates.

The estimation of the 'savings retention coefficient' on regional data is not new. Previously Thomas (1991), Bayoumi and Rose (1993) and Sinn (1992) have estimated the 'savings retention coefficient' on the regional data of Germany, the UK, Canada and the USA. Their results are summarized in Section 7.2.

Our work represents one of the first estimates of the 'savings retention coefficient' using Japanese regional data. Japanese regional accounts seem to be far superior to those of other nations. As described below, Japanese regional accounts are comparable to the national accounts of entire countries. For the regional data of other nations, various components of the national income accounting identity are missing and must be constructed from secondary sources. For example, for consumption in the American states and for the regions in the UK, only retail sales data are available.

Section 7.2 reviews the literature concerning the controversy surrounding the Feldstein–Horioka interpretation of the high 'savings retention coefficient'. Section 7.3 displays some suggestive saving–investment correlations. Private saving and investment rates are uncorrelated, but total saving and investment rates are negatively correlated. The negative correlation in the total saving and investment rates appears to be driven by the strong cross-regional negative correlation in the government saving and investment rates. Section 7.4 examines the interactions between the private and public components. It is concluded that there appears to be no relationship between private and public saving rates, and private and public investment rates. The independence of the private components from those of the government suggests that the private saving–investment correlation can be examined separately from the government components. Section 7.5 draws conclusions from the previous sections.

7.2   SAVING–INVESTMENT CORRELATION AND THEIR IMPLICATIONS FOR CAPITAL MOBILITY: A LITERATURE REVIEW

As mentioned in Section 7.1 Feldstein and Horioka (1980) proposed the size of the association between saving and investment as a barometer of capital mobility. They reasoned that if international capital markets were truly open, then the saving rate should have no correlation with the investment rate. In an open economy, the level of investment should be determined largely by the international supply of and demand for capital. An increase in the saving of one country should not noticeably affect the world capital supply; therefore, for a truly open economy, an increase in saving should not change the investment rate, or investment is not necessarily restricted by saving.

Feldstein and Horioka estimated the following equation:

$$(I/Y) = a + b*(S/Y) + u,$$

cross-sectionally on a sample of sixteen OECD countries, averaging data over sub-periods during 1960–74. Data averaged over 1960–74 led to an estimate of b, the 'savings retention coefficient', of 0.887, significant at the 1 per cent level. The authors interpreted the estimate of b as being close to one, as indicative of low capital mobility among industrialized countries.

International capital markets, especially among the industrialized nations, have been liberalized substantially since 1975. Feldstein and Bacchetta (1991) averaged data for twenty-three OECD nations for a more recent period, 1974–86, and found an estimate of b of 0.868, hardly different from estimates using earlier data. For twenty-one OECD countries with data averaged between 1973–90, Obstfeld (1993) found b to be 0.761. The high estimate of b is surprising, especially since capital market deregulation has proceeded among industrialized countries on a global scale since the mid-1970s.

Table 7.1 summarizes the estimates of the saving retention coefficient in the literature. The lower half of the table gives the total saving–total investment rate correlations estimated by previous authors on regional data. Apart from in the work of Thomas (1991), the authors have found a zero correlation in the rates. As pointed out in Section 7.1 the regional

TABLE 7.1   Previous estimates of the 'saving-retention' coefficient

On cross-country data	Economies	Time-averaged period	Saving-retention coefficient
Feldstein–Horioka (1980)	16 OECD	1964–70	0.887
Feldstein–Bacchetta (1991)	23 OECD	1974–86	0.868
Obstfeld (1993)	21 OECD	1977–90	0.761
On cross-regional data			
Thomas (1991)	10 British regions	1971–87	− 0.568
	10 Canadian provinces	1961–89	− 0.117
Sinn (1992)	48 US states	1957	0
Bayoumi–Rose (1993)	11 British regions	1971–85 regions	0

data used in previous studies appear to be far inferior to Japanese regional data.

Since the Feldstein–Horioka paper was published, there have been many studies criticizing Feldstein and Horioka's interpretation of the results. The papers have essentially argued that a cross-country estimate of b close to unity can be explained by reasons other than imperfect international capital mobility.

Some of the reasons proposed in the literature are as follows.

1. Growth rate of aggregate GDP   Obstfeld (1986, 1991) argues that a high rate of economic growth raises the growth of labour in efficiency units, and, in the steady-state, investment has to increase to keep the capital–efficiency labour ratio constant. If consumers behave according to the life-cycle hypothesis, a higher growth rate will result in higher saving as the young will be saving more than the old are dis-saving. The high positive correlation between the saving and investment rates could be a result of their common association with the growth rate.

However, Feldstein and Bacchetta (1991) show that the inclusion of the GDP growth rate as an additional variable does not affect their coefficient estimates. In Section 7.3 of this chapter, the GDP growth rate does not affect the coefficients either. Therefore, it appears that economic growth is not a viable explanation for the high saving–investment correlation.

2. Real interest rates   If non-traded goods exist, then purchasing-power parity will generally fail. Even if nominal interest rates are equated across countries, real interest rates may diverge, since countries may have different inflation rates. An increase in the saving of a country will then lower that country's real interest rate, stimulating local investment (Frankel, 1986, 1991). Saving and investment rates will therefore be positively correlated.

3. Government fiscal policy   Summers (1988) and Bayoumi (1990) have argued that systematic current account targeting by the government may cause aggregate saving and investment rates to be positively correlated. It may be politically difficult for a government to run persistent current account deficits or surpluses, and the government may try to bring the domestic saving rate into line with the domestic investment rate.

Advocates of Ricardian Equivalence (Barro, 1976) argue that changes in the government deficit are offset by changes in private saving, and in the absence of a relationship between private and public investment, government fiscal policy cannot affect the current account. Empirical evidence regarding the effectiveness of government policy in changing the current account balance is mixed (Artis and Bayoumi, 1989).

This chapter applies the Feldstein–Horioka approach to a setting of known, near perfect, capital mobility, Japanese regions. Japan has had a well-integrated national capital market since the early Meiji period (1870s). Branches of the major city-banks and securities firms exist in almost every prefecture. Funds are transferred between regional and city-banks through an active interbank market. If the saving and investment rates are highly positively correlated in Japanese regional data, then the Feldstein–Horioka interpretation will not be correct. Some reason other than imperfect capital mobility will account for the high international saving–investment correlation. Saving and investment rates should have zero correlation under a setting of known capital mobility such as that of Japanese prefectures.

We find that in all specifications, *private* saving and investment rates in Japanese time-averaged regional data have a correlation of zero. The implication may be that in testing the extent of international capital mobility, researchers should examine the correlation between *private* saving and investment rates; if the correlation between these is high, then international capital mobility is probably low. The Feldstein–Horioka benchmark should perhaps be applied only to private capital flows.

In Section 7.3, we also examine the correlation between *total* saving and investment rates. Total saving and total investment rates in Japanese regional data are negatively correlated. Total saving is private saving plus government saving; total investment is private investment plus government investment. The negative correlation in the total rates appears to be driven by the strong negative correlation in the government saving and investment rates. Even in a setting of known high capital mobility, the total saving and investment rates can have a nonzero correlation if government fiscal policy changes the regional current account balance. Summers (1988) and Bayoumi (1990) appear correct in arguing that government fiscal policy can affect the current account. The high positive correlation in the *total* saving and investment rates in international data may not only result from imperfect capital mobility, but also from systematic current-account targeting by the government. Accordingly, it may be difficult to judge the degree of capital mobility from the correlation of total saving and investment rates.

7.3 SAVING–INVESTMENT CORRELATIONS WITH JAPANESE PREFECTURAL DATA

7.3.1 The data

The primary data set we have used is the 1992 version of the *Annual Report on the Prefectural Accounts*, compiled by the Economic Research Institute of the Japanese Economic Planning Agency (EPA). The data set is a fourteen-year panel (1975–88) of the income accounts of Japan's forty-seven prefectures. As mentioned in Section 7.1, Japan is unique in that a set of income accounts comparable in detail and scope to that of entire countries exist for most of its regions.

Figure 7.1 shows a map of the prefectures of Japan. In compiling the *Accounts*, the EPA asked each of the prefectures to construct income accounts in accordance with the rules of the United Nations System of National Accounts (SNA). Typical items in the national accounts such as consumption, investment and government spending exist for most of the prefectures. For two prefectures, Niigata and Iwate, some items in the national income identity were missing. These two prefectures have been dropped from our working sample.

Total saving is defined as prefectural gross domestic product (GDP) minus consumption and government spending. *Private saving* is GDP minus consumption, minus household and corporate taxes.) Since the prefectural accounts do not include taxes, we had to construct the household and corporate taxes from the Asahi newspaper's *Minryoku* data base. Household saving is household income minus consumption, minus household taxes. Corporate saving is private saving minus household saving. Government saving is defined as the difference between total taxes and government spending, which in Japan excludes government investment.

In this section, we present illustrative scatter plots and correlations between the prefectural gross *saving rate* and the prefectural gross *investment rate*. To minimize the spurious correlation arising from the effects of transitory productivity shocks on both the saving and the investment rates, the data are averaged over long periods of time.

We will show that the prefectural *total* saving and *total* investment rates are negatively correlated, and this is attributed to the strong negative correlation between the prefectural government saving and investment rates. Private saving and investment rates are uncorrelated.

FIGURE 7.1 Districts and prefectures in Japan

7.3.2 Gross prefectural saving and investment: data

Table 7.2 (a) presents the *total* gross saving and investment rates and the ratio of the current account to GDP by prefecture. Saving rates are higher in the richer areas of Kantō, which includes Tōkyō; and Kinki, which includes Ōsaka and Hyōgo; and lower in the more isolated prefectures of Hokkaidō, Aomori, Akita, Kagoshima and Okinawa. Total investment ratios, however, are lower in the wealthier prefectures, resulting in large current account surpluses in these regions. Japan's large international current account surpluses are mainly generated by only a handful of prefectures: Tōkyō, Aichi (Nagoya), Kanagawa (Yokohama), Ōsaka, Hyōgo (Kobe), Okayama and Hiroshima.

Table 7.2 (b) depicts the ratios of *private* saving, *private* investment, *private* current account surplus, *government* saving and *government* investment to prefectural GDP. Private saving rates, again, are higher in the richer regions, but regional private investment rates tend not to greatly vary. The government saving rates are huge in Tōkyō, Aichi, Ōsaka and Hyōgo, and government deficits are large in the poorer Hokkaidō, Tōhoku, and Kyūshū districts. Prefectures with government deficits tend to have high rates of public investment. In Hokkaidō, Tōhoku, Shikoku and Kyūshū, public investment is often in excess of 33 per cent of total prefectural investment.

Most prefectures appear to be running a surplus of private saving over private investment, except for some prefectures in Tōhoku and Kyūshū.[1]

7.3.3 Gross total saving–investment correlations and government saving and investment

Figure 7.2 depicts scatter plots of total gross saving on investment rates. Total saving is the sum of private gross saving and government saving; total investment is the sum of private and public investment. The data are time-averaged between 1975 and 1988. The visual impression is confirmed by the regressions in Table 7.3.

Under perfect capital mobility, it may appear surprising that *total* saving and investment rates have a non-zero correlation. Summers (1988) and Bayoumi (1990) have suggested that total saving–investment correlations may be sensitive to government policy. If national governments can manipulate the total saving and investment rates to bring the current account into balance, then, even under perfect capital mobility, countries with high total saving rates will have high total investment

TABLE 7.2(a) Ratio of prefectural gross saving, investment, and the current account surplus to GNP (time-averaged data, 1975–1988)

Prefecture	Total Saving	Total Investment	Current Account
Hokkaidō	0.196	0.357	−0.162
Aomori	0.118	0.348	−0.230
Miyagi	0.235	0.341	−0.107
Akita	0.153	0.358	−0.205
Yamagata	0.198	0.338	−0.140
Fukushima	0.322	0.332	−0.010
Ibaragi	0.329	0.316	0.013
Tochigi	0.394	0.288	0.107
Gunma	0.318	0.289	0.028
Saitama	0.306	0.245	0.061
Chiba	0.339	0.280	0.059
Tōkyō	0.372	0.246	0.127
Kanagawa	0.349	0.251	0.098
Yamanashi	0.255	0.336	−0.081
Nagano	0.339	0.337	0.002
Shizuoka	0.374	0.277	0.098
Toyama	0.342	0.336	0.006
Ishikawa	0.275	0.320	−0.045
Gifu	0.307	0.283	0.024
Aichi	0.416	0.266	0.150
Mie	0.382	0.282	0.100
Fukui	0.313	0.405	−0.092
Shiga	0.354	0.315	0.039
Kyōto	0.289	0.293	−0.004
Ōsaka	0.396	0.242	0.154
Hyōgo	0.314	0.263	0.051
Nara	0.181	0.293	−0.112
Wakayama	0.283	0.339	−0.056
Tottori	0.210	0.322	−0.113
Shimane	0.178	0.377	−0.199
Okayama	0.332	0.313	0.019
Hiroshima	0.294	0.269	0.025
Yamaguchi	0.228	0.329	−0.101
Tokushima	0.204	0.312	−0.108
Kagawa	0.265	0.321	−0.056
Ehime	0.240	0.316	−0.076
Kōchi	0.115	0.343	−0.228
Fukuoka	0.286	0.317	−0.031
Saga	0.226	0.330	−0.103
Nagasaki	0.169	0.309	−0.140
Kumamoto	0.248	0.316	−0.067
Ōita	0.227	0.331	−0.104
Miyazaki	0.237	0.375	−0.138
Kagoshima	0.141	0.352	−0.211
Okinawa	0.157	0.392	−0.235

TABLE 7.2(b)   Ratio of prefectural private saving, investment, and the current account surplus to GDP (time-averaged data, 1975–88)

Prefecture	Private Saving	Private Investment	Government Deficit	Public Investment
Hokkaidō	0.235	0.209	−0.040	0.148
Aomori	0.185	0.207	−0.067	0.141
Miyagi	0.239	0.237	−0.004	0.104
Akita	0.184	0.220	−0.031	0.138
Yamagata	0.233	0.224	−0.034	0.114
Fukushima	0.338	0.232	−0.016	0.100
Ibaragi	0.315	0.223	0.014	0.093
Tochigi	0.361	0.213	0.034	0.075
Gunma	0.287	0.218	0.031	0.072
Saitama	0.258	0.186	0.047	0.059
Chiba	0.316	0.207	0.023	0.072
Tōkyō	0.225	0.195	0.147	0.051
Kanagawa	0.287	0.198	0.062	0.054
Yamanashi	0.251	0.221	0.004	0.115
Nagano	0.338	0.228	0.000	0.109
Shizuoka	0.327	0.216	0.048	0.060
Toyama	0.331	0.249	0.012	0.087
Ishikawa	0.265	0.222	0.010	0.098
Gifu	0.276	0.203	0.031	0.080
Aichi	0.317	0.209	0.099	0.056
Mie	0.349	0.213	0.033	0.069
Fukui	0.309	0.282	0.004	0.123
Shiga	0.327	0.246	0.027	0.069
Kyōto	0.253	0.233	0.036	0.060
Ōsaka	0.309	0.192	0.087	0.050
Hyōgo	0.250	0.190	0.064	0.073
Nara	0.183	0.205	−0.002	0.088
Wakayama	0.293	0.243	−0.010	0.096
Tottori	0.275	0.189	−0.065	0.133
Shimane	0.288	0.224	−0.110	0.153
Okayama	0.324	0.223	0.008	0.091
Hiroshima	0.284	0.189	0.010	0.080
Yamaguchi	0.243	0.229	−0.015	0.100
Tokushima	0.268	0.204	−0.064	0.108
Kagawa	0.251	0.220	0.013	0.101
Ehime	0.264	0.224	−0.024	0.92
Kōchi	0.153	0.197	−0.038	0.146
Fukuoka	0.277	0.241	0.009	0.077
Saga	0.249	0.203	−0.023	0.127
Nagasaki	0.249	0.199	−0.080	0.110
Kumamoto	0.302	0.219	−0.054	0.097
Ōita	0.248	0.229	−0.021	0.102
Miyazaki	0.266	0.243	−0.028	0.132
Kagoshima	0.190	0.222	−0.049	0.129
Okinawa	0.232	0.231	−0.075	0.162

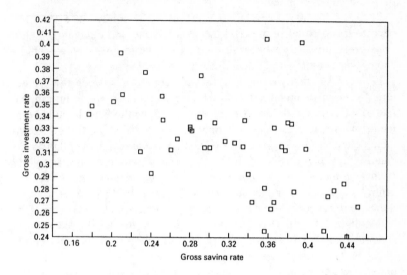

FIGURE 7.2   Plot of gross saving and investment rates (all prefectures)

TABLE 7.3   Cross-section estimates of 45 prefectures correlation between prefectural total investment and total saving rates, time-averaged periods

	1975–8	1975–9	1980–4	1985–8
Constant	0.47	0.52	0.44	0.40
	(15.78)	(11.95)	(13.2)	(22.9)
Total Saving/GDP	−0.35	−0.44	−0.31	−0.24
	(−4.52)	(−3.92)	(−3.50)	(−4.94)
R-square	0.24	0.23	0.20	0.20

Notes:
Dependent variable: total investment/GDP. T-statistics are in parentheses.
Ordinary Least Squares with Heteroskeskedasticity Correction.

rates. In cross-national data, total saving and investment will appear to be positively correlated.

In Japan, the stated central government social policy since 1970 has been to try to equalize regional incomes (Okuno and Futagami, 1990). Poor prefectures have been allowed to run large government deficits and invest heavily in public infrastructure projects.

Figure 7.3 depicts a strong negative correlation between the prefectural *government* saving rate and the prefectural *government* investment rate.[2] Prefectures with low government saving tend to have large government investment rates, and a variable correlated with both the government deficit and investment rates is the prefectural real per capita income (see Figures 4(a) and 4(b)). In Japan, regional public finance is tightly controlled by the central government, and large transfers occur between central and regional budget authorities (Ishihara, 1986).[3] In recent years, the central government has received tax revenues that exceed twice its expenditures. In contrast, the tax revenues of the local governments are much smaller than their needs. In prefectures with low per capita incomes, tax receipts are low and social welfare expenditure, such as unemployment benefits, are high, raising the deficit (Yonehara, 1986).

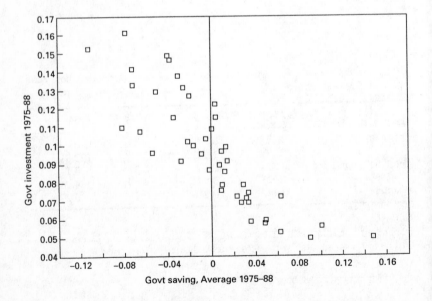

FIGURE 7.3   Negative correlation between government saving and investment rates

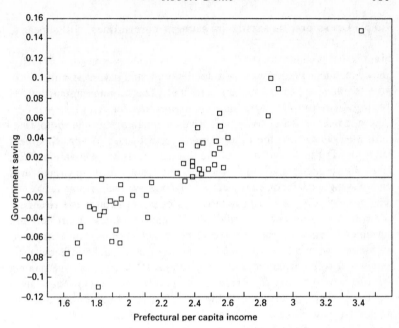

FIGURE 7.4 (a)   Per capita income and government saving average
1975–88

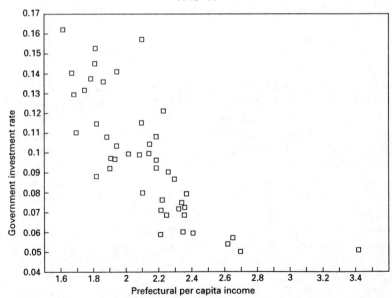

FIGURE 7.4 (b)   Per capita income and government investment, average
1975–88

7.3.3   Gross private saving–investment correlations

Figures 7.5 (a) and (b) are scatter plots of time-averaged *private* saving and investment rates. Unlike the total saving and investment rates, the private rates appear to be uncorrelated. The simple regressions in Table 7.4 confirm the impression. In all specifications and time-periods, time-averaged private saving and investment rates are uncorrelated.

In Specification 2, the time-averaged growth rate of aggregate prefectural GDP is included as an additional regressor. Obstfeld (1986, 1991) has argued that countries with rapid growth rates may have both high saving and investment rates. However, we see from Table 7.4 that the inclusion of GDP growth rates does not change the results.

A problem with both Specifications 1 and 2 is that if there are any variables in addition to the prefectural growth rate that are correlated with both the private saving and investment rates, the coefficient estimates will suffer from omitted variable bias (Dooley *et al.* 1987). One solution would be to use instrumental variables estimation. The instrument should be correlated with the private saving rate, but not directly with the private investment rate.

In Specification 3, we use two-stage least squares estimates, where in the first stage, the private saving rate is regressed on the following 'life-cycle' variables: (i) the proportion of the population under age 19; (ii) the proportion of the population over age 65; and (iii) the ratio of net social security receipts to prefectural GDP. We find that the two-stage least squares estimates do not differ from the ordinary least squares estimates.

In Specification 4, the private saving rate is divided into household and corporate saving. If, as Hoshi *et al.* (1991) argue, credit constrained firms rely on internally generated funds for financing, then the corporate saving rate should be correlated with the private investment rate. Hoshi *et al.* show that financing constraints are mitigated for Japanese firms affiliated with main banks. There are, however, many small corporations in Japan, especially in rural areas, that do not have main bank ties, and for these companies, internally-generated funds would appear to be important.[4] We find, however, that private investment is uncorrelated with neither household saving nor corporate saving rates. The results do not change when we use instrumental variables estimation.[5] Apparently, financing constraints are on average not severe for Japanese companies.

Baxter and Crucini (1993), Backus *et al.* (1992) and Tesar (1991), among others, have criticized the Feldstein–Horioka approach, essentially

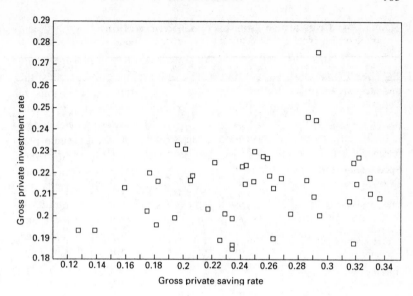

FIGURE 7.5 (a) Gross private saving and investment rates
(all prefectures)

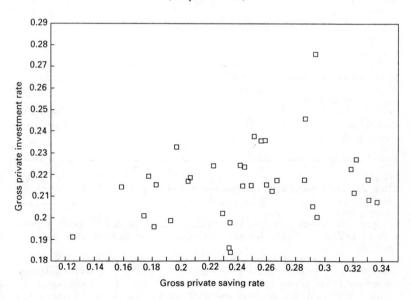

FIGURE 7.5 (b) Gross private saving and investment rates
(excluding Kantō and Kansai)

TABLE 7.4 Cross-section estimates of 45 prefectures correlation between prefectural private investment and saving rates, time-averaged periods

	1975–88	1975–9	1980–4	1985–8
Specification 1[a]				
Constant	0.21	0.24	0.20	0.21
	(12.1)	(11.0)	(14.2)	(20.1)
Private Saving/GDP	0.87	0.021	0.088	0.97
	(0.66)	(0.29)	(1.48)	(1.37)
R-square	0.022	0.014	0.031	0.026
Specification 2[b]				
Constant	0.22	0.23	0.20	0.22
	(14.67)	(8.93)	(12.56)	(7.78)
Private Saving/GDP	0.087	0.00098	0.084	0.13
	(0.84)	(0.012)	(0.99)	(0.66)
Growth rate of	−0.12	0.43	0.14	−0.68
prefectural GDP	(−0.25)	(1.13)	(0.40)	(−0.88)
R-square	0.033	0.045	0.28	0.078
Specification 3[c]				
Constant	0.20	0.27	0.25	0.22
	(5.93)	(3.92)	(2.75)	(7.78)
Private Saving/GDP	0.16	−0.15	−0.20	0.13
	(0.84)	(−0.60)	(−0.39)	(0.66)
Growth rate of	−0.36	0.55	0.90	−0.67
prefectural GDP	(−0.50)	(1.25)	(0.62)	(−0.88)
R-square	0.032	0.010	0.032	0.078
Specification 4[d]				
Constant	0.16			
	(2.55)			
Household savings/GDP	−0.018			
	(−0.08)			
Corporate savings/GDP	0.73			
	(0.70)			
Growth rate of	0.37			
prefectural GDP	(0.43)			
R-square	0.044			

Notes:
[a] Ordinary least squares with heteroskedasticity correction.
[b] Inclusion of average prefectural growth rates. Ordinary least squares with heteroskedasticity correction.
[c] Instrumental variables estimates; instruments for S/Y: proportion of population under age 19; proportion of population over age 65; ratio of net social security receipts to prefectural GDP.
[d] Private saving rate divided into household (HS/Y) and corporate saving (CS/Y) rates; two-stage least squares estimation. Instruments for HS/Y: proportion of population under age 19; proportion of population over age 65; ratio of net social security receipts to prefectural GDP. Instruments for CS/Y: number of prefectural capitals within three hours' travel from own prefectural capital.
Dependent variable: private investment/GDP T-statistics in parentheses.

arguing that the positive saving–investment correlations are uninformative about international capital mobility when there are temporary productivity shocks. When an economy experiences a temporary, unexpected surge in productivity, *private* saving rates rise, which is an implication of the permanent income hypothesis.[6] The increased aggregate demand will raise the market value of capital, raise Tobin's *q* ratio, and the rate of investment.

The above criticisms appear to be aimed more at the time-series, rather than the cross-section correlations. If private saving and investment rates both respond positively to positive transitory productivity shocks, then even with perfect capital mobility, private saving and investment will appear to be positively correlated. With data averaged over long time-periods, the impact of the transitory shocks are obviously less important unless the effect of the shocks are drawn out over long periods of time, due, say, to investment adjustment costs, as in the model produced by Cardia (1992). For each of the forty-five prefectures in our working sample, Table 7.5 presents time-series private saving–investment correlations using fourteen years (1975–88) of data. The correlations range from negatively to positively significant, suggesting that the nature or the effect of the productivity shocks differ by prefecture.

In this section, we have shown that the *total* saving and investment rates are negatively correlated and that the *private* rates are uncorrelated. Given the strong correlation in the government components, the lack of correlation in the private components is, in fact, surprising. If government saving affects private saving, and if public investment affects private investment, then the correlation in the government components should imply a correlation in the private components.

In the next section, we show that *government* and the *private* components in Japanese regional data are uncorrelated. This suggests either that public saving does not affect private saving (non-Ricardian equivalence) or that public investment is irrelevant to private investment. An implication of the results in both this section and the next is that government fiscal policy can affect the current account.

TABLE 7.5 Time-series estimates, annual data 1975–88

	Constant	Private saving rate	Growth rate of GDP
Hokkaidō	0.12	0.47	−0.015
	(5.0)	(4.9)	(−0.012)
Aomori	0.20	0.10	−0.36
	(12.1)	(1.2)	(−0.183)
Miyagi	0.27	0.25	−0.38
	(2.5)	(2.3)	(−1.86)
Akita	0.06	1.06	−0.37
	(0.59)	(2.2)	(−1.00)
Yamagata	0.44	−0.84	−0.092
	(1.5)	(−0.65)	(−0.92)
Fukushima	0.69	−1.26	−0.31
	(3.35)	(−2.10)	−1.59)
Ibaragi	−0.15	1.22	−0.13
	(−0.43)	(1.20)	(−0.30)
Tochigi	0.35	−0.33	−0.19
	(5.32)	(−1.80)	(−0.80)
Gunma	−0.42	2.04	0.85
	(−0.64)	(0.93)	(0.75)
Saitama	0.19	−0.10	0.67
	(1.99)	(−0.29)	(1.53)
Chiba	0.28	0.19	−0.076
	(4.45)	(1.45)	(−0.60)
Tōkyō	0.45	−0.96	−0.64
	(6.96)	(−2.70)	(−1.54)
Kanagawa	0.28	0.075	−0.11
	(1.96)	(0.12)	(−0.21)
Nagano	0.42	−0.52	0.035
	(3.58)	(−1.52)	(0.10)
Shizuoka	0.16	0.27	−0.32
	(1.52)	(0.85)	(−1.23)
Toyama	0.10	0.63	−1.16
	(2.05)	(4.24)	(−4.89)
Ishikawa	0.28	−0.13	−0.20
	(4.67)	(−0.60)	(−0.60)
Gifu	0.20	0.14	−0.61
	(3.22)	(0.60)	(−1.75)
Aichi	0.22	0.077	−0.44
	(2.00)	(0.22)	(−1.11)
Mie	−0.27	1.37	0.57
	(−2.98)	(5.52)	(2.33)
Fukui	0.37	−0.17	−0.32
	(1.91)	(−0.27)	(−0.98)
Shiga	0.12	0.40	0.074
	(0.70)	(0.85)	(0.28)
Kyōto	−0.13	1.55	−0.20
	(−1.59)	(4.33)	(−0.75)

	Constant	Private saving rate	Growth rate of GDP
Osaka	0.21	−0.026	−0.30
	(3.43)	(−0.14)	(−0.12)
Hyōgo	0.10	0.19	1.12
	(2.11)	(1.22)	(2.84)
Nara	0.24	−0.072	−0.99
	(12.0)	(−0.72)	(−0.60)
Wakayama	0.20	0.20	−0.094
	(2.84)	(0.87)	(−0.53)
Tottori	0.15	0.24	−0.38
	(3.99)	(1.74)	(−1.41)
Shimane	0.14	0.36	0.01
	(1.24)	(0.96)	(−0.38)
Okayama	−0.095	0.78	−0.20
	(−0.70)	(1.97)	(−0.038)
Hiroshima	0.26	−0.19	−0.14
	(4.65)	(−0.99)	(−0.24)
Yamaguchi	0.12	0.44	0.51
	(1.13)	(1.03)	(1.27)
Tokushima	0.15	0.30	−0.29
	(1.68)	(0.88)	(−0.095)
Kagawa	0.13	0.39	0.27
	(1.96)	(1.55)	(0.72)
Ehime	0.060	0.69	−0.32
	(0.56)	(1.55)	(−0.92)
Kōchi	0.21	0.016	0.26
	(9.99)	(0.012)	(1.12)
Fukuoka	0.08	0.67	−0.30
	(1.56)	(3.59)	(−0.81)
Saga	0.18	0.16	−0.088
	(2.49)	(0.53)	(−0.69)
Nagasaki	0.22	−0.035	0.018
	(4.91)	(−0.19)	(0.19)
Kumamoto	0.19	0.096	0.032
	(2.71)	(0.38)	(0.86)
Ōita	0.31	−0.36	0.67
	(0.97)	(−0.29)	(0.80)
Miyazaki	0.20	0.24	−0.13
	(5.72)	(1.77)	(−0.056)
Kagoshima	0.19	0.13	0.42
	(11.2)	(1.34)	(2.77)
Okinawa	0.15	0.50	−0.45
	(3.34)	(2.46)	(−3.30)

Notes:
Dependent variable: private investment rate. Cochrane–Orcutt correction for first-order serial correlation. T-statistics in parentheses.

7.4   INTERACTIONS BETWEEN PRIVATE AND GOVERNMENT SAVING AND INVESTMENT

One of the implications of Ricardian equivalence is that the level of government deficits does not change real aggregate spending in the economy (Barro, 1976). In an open economy, therefore, Ricardian equivalence will imply that government deficit policy will not change the current account. In fact, in simple infinite-horizon, open-economy models such as those of Sachs (1981) and Brock (1988), where Ricardian-equivalence holds, the steady-state current account surplus ratio is determined entirely by *initial* conditions, the initial level of net external debt. An open economy that is initially a net creditor will in the steady-state run a current account surplus equal to the rate of GDP growth times the initial stock of credit.[7] In these models, government spending and investment policy, therefore, cannot affect the steady-state level of the current account.

The steady-state invariance of the current account means that a change in the government saving rate implies an exactly offsetting response, collectively, in the private components. In this section, we show that private saving and investment rates have *zero* correlation with public saving and investment rates. The implication is that, at the regional level, government fiscal policy can change the current account. There is no private offset to a change in government fiscal policy.

In Section 7.3 we argued that the lack of correlation in the private saving and investment rates, despite the strong negative correlation in the government components, is a puzzle. The puzzle can be resolved if either (i) government saving and private saving are uncorrelated; or if (ii) public investment and private investment are uncorrelated. We show below that empirically, both (i) and (ii) appear to be true. If there is no private offset to a change in government saving and investment, then the private saving and investment rates can be independent of the government components.

In addition to the lack of correlation in public and private investment rates, we show further that the private and public capital stocks per capita are uncorrelated. In a per capita production function with both private and public capital stocks, the level of private capital per capita will be a function of the real interest rate and the level of per capita public capital. Under perfect capital mobility and negligible capital installation costs, if the production functions of all the regions are equal, the private capital stock per capita will depend only on the level of public capital per capita. The real interest rates are equated across regions.

That empirically, private and public capital per capita are uncorrelated suggests that public capital is separable from private capital in production, which means that the marginal productivity of private capital is unaffected by the level of public capital. In Japanese regions, the stock of public capital does not change the productivity of private capital. An increase in the public capital stock of a given prefecture will neither 'crowd-in' nor 'crowd-out' private capital.

In many countries, much of public infrastructure investment is justified on the grounds that public investment raises the productivity of private capital. Aschauer (1988) and Barro (1990), for example, present production functions with the property that the marginal productivity of private capital rises with an increased stock of public capital. The authors have in mind public capital that is complementary to private capital, such as railways, harbours and roads.

Lucas (1990) is sceptical of this view, arguing in the context of foreign aid that public capital drives out private capital. Public and private capital are close to being perfect substitutes. He argues that developing countries are poor, not because of international capital immobility, but because developing nations have low levels of human capital. The marginal product of private capital in developing countries is equal to that of the industrialized countries, and an increase in foreign aid, usually channelled to public infrastructure investment, only serves to drive private capital out of the poor country.

Under settings of imperfect capital mobility, it has been difficult to test whether public capital drives out private capital. The endogeneity of the real interest rate means that when the private capital stock changes, the real interest rate also changes, making the identification of the direct effect of public on private capital difficult. Under settings of known perfect capital mobility, such as that of the Japanese prefectures, the real interest rate is fixed, so the impact of an increase in public capital can be assessed directly. Our empirical finding that the public and private capital stocks per capita are uncorrelated calls into question the views of both Aschauer–Barro and Lucas.

7.4.1 Government–private interactions in regional saving and investment: the estimates

In this sub-section, we present correlations showing that, across Japanese regions, private saving and investment rates are uncorrelated with public saving and investment rates.

First, we show that conditional on the level of public saving and investment rates, the private saving and investment rates are uncorrelated. This result is what is expected under perfect capital mobility.

Second, there appears to be zero correlation between private and public investment, and private investment and government saving. The latter result is, again, what is expected under perfect capital mobility.

Third, private and public saving rates are uncorrelated; Ricardian equivalence does not seem to hold at the regional level.

Finally, we show, cross-regionally, that private capital per capita is uncorrelated with public capital per capita. In regional production, the stock of private capital is determined independently from the stock of public capital.

Since prefecture-specific unobservables may affect both the government saving and investment rates, the public components should be instrumented. Below we show that a certain indicator of the political strength of a prefecture's elected national politicians is highly correlated with the size of a prefecture's deficit and public investment rates.

7.4.2   Prefectural government saving and investment and the zoku politician: selecting the instrument

There is no commonly accepted definition of a *zoku* politician, except that he or she must belong to the Liberal Democratic Party (LDP).[8] Unlike a politician appointed to a congressional committee in the US, a Japanese Diet member is not appointed or elected to a *zoku*. One definition is a politician that has strong influence over a policy arena represented by a ministry (Inoguchi and Iwai, 1987).[9] The politician is expected to use his influence to help his constituents.

In the search for instruments correlated with a prefecture's deficit rate and public investment rate, we examined three *zoku*: 1. The Ministry of Finance; 2. Construction; and 3. Agriculture and Forestry. Recall that the Japanese central government (in Tōkyō) has the ability to redistribute funds from one prefecture to another. We showed earlier that to a large extent, a prefecture with a low income per capita is allowed to accumulate government deficits and receive subsidies from the central government to increase its public investment. We may expect that an influential national politician will be able to direct central government funds to a district in his prefecture. If a prefecture has one or more politicians who belongs to one of the above *zoku*, does that fact increase the size of the prefecture's public deficit and investment rates, even after controlling for the prefecture's per capita income?

To classify a given prefecture's national politicians into one of the three above *zoku*, we use the definitions of Sato and Matsuzaki (1985), which applied to both Lower and Upper House Diet members in 1983. Within each *zoku* category, Sato and Matsuzaki further sub-divide politicians into the powerful (*Kankei Yuryoku Giin*) and the less powerful *zoku*. All the 'powerful' Ministry of Finance *zoku* politicians, for example, have either been Finance ministers or have served as Chairmen of Research Councils (*Chosa Kaicho*).

We created dummy variables that equal unity when one or more of a prefecture's politicians is in one of two sub-categories (Powerful, Weak) of the three *zoku* (MOF, Agriculture, Construction). There are a total of six (2^*3) dummy variables.

Table 7.6 presents estimates of the effects of *zoku* affiliation on the prefectural government saving and investment rates, controlling for per capita income. We find that, as expected, per capita income is highly significant in all specifications. The only *zoku* affiliation dummy that is significant is the MOF-Powerful dummy.[10] If a prefecture has at least one politician who belongs to the MOF-Powerful category, then the prefecture is allowed to accumulate high government deficits and receive large amounts of public investment. Therefore, we use below the MOF-Powerful dummy as one of the instruments for the government saving and investment rates.

7.4.3 The estimates

The estimates below depict the lack of correlation between the private and public components in the regional current account.

Table 7.7 presents estimates of the correlation between the private investment and saving rates, conditional on the public saving and investment rates. The estimates measure the effect of private saving on the investment rate, given that the public saving and investment rates are held constant. Under perfect capital mobility, we would expect the coefficient on private saving, conditional on the public components, to be zero. This will be true regardless of the relationship between the public components and private investment, since, in the multiple regression, the relationship is held constant across prefectures. Even when the public components affect the private investment rate, the *conditional correlation* between private investment and saving should be zero under perfect capital mobility. The *unconditional correlation* between private saving and investment (examined in Section 7.2) will, as mentioned, generally be different from zero if public components affect the private investment rate.[11]

TABLE 7.6 Prefectural government deficits, public investment and Liberal Democratic Party *zoku* affiliation

	Power	Weak
Dependent variable: government saving/GDP		
Constant	−0.50	−0.54
	(−10.41)	(−10.2)
MOF-Powerful	−0.029	
	(−2.16)	
MOF-weak		0.0017
		(0.14)
Agriculture-power	0.00828	
	(0.55)	
Agriculture-weak		0.010
		(0.83)
Construction-power	−0.00029	
	(−0.030)	
Construction-weak		−0.0041
		(−0.50)
Per capita GDP	0.020	0.20
	(9.77)	(8.31)
R-square	0.80	0.80
Dependent variable: government investment/GDP		
Constant	0.23	0.23
	(7.70)	(7.67)
MOF-Powerful	0.012	
	(2.08)	
MOF-weak		0.85
		(1.39)
Agriculture-power	0.0014	
	(0.28)	
Agriculture-weak		0.035
		(0.52)
Construction-power	0.0058	
	(−1.03)	
Construction-weak		−0.010
		(−1.77)
Per capita GDP	−0.065	−0.071
	(−5.05)	(−6.11)
R-square	0.625	0.531

Notes:
Time-averaged data, 1975–88. Cross-section of 45 prefectures. T-statistics in parentheses.
MOF-Powerful, MOF-weak, Agriculture-Powerful, Agriculture-weak, Construction-Powerful, Construction-weak are dummy variables which take on a value of one for the prefecture if a National Diet lower or upper house politician from the prefecture is in the particular *zoku* category, as defined by Sato and Matsuzaki (1985).

TABLE 7.7 Cross-prefectural estimates of the effects of private saving, public saving and public investment rates on private investment rates

	All prefectures[c]	Prefectures excluding Kanto and Kansai[d]
Specification 1[a]		
Constant	0.13	0.13
	(3.29)	(3.40)
Private saving rate	0.16	0.12
	(2.58)	(2.11)
Public investment rate	0.34	0.39
	(1.51)	(1.83)
Government saving	0.032	0.11
	(0.34)	(1.14)
Growth rate of GDP	0.26	0.43
	(0.59)	(0.93)
R-square	0.21	0.19
Specification 2[b]		
Constant	0.15	0.15
	(2.52)	(2.62)
Private saving rate	0.044	0.44
	(0.38)	(0.35)
Government saving rate	0.038	0.034
	(0.21)	(0.19)
Public investment rate	0.42	0.25
	(0.66)	(0.71)
Growth rate of GDP	0.45	0.76
	(1.31)	(1.22)
R-square	0.16	0.16

Notes:
[a] Ordinary Least Squares with Heteroskedasticity Correction.
[b] Two-stage least squares estimates; instruments for private Saving/GDP: proportion of population under age 19; proportion of population over age 65; ratio of net social security receipts to prefectural GDP; instruments for public investment/GDP: MOF-Powerful, and the size of the land that could be used for building purposes. Instruments for government saving/GDP: MOF-Powerful.
[c] 45 prefectures.
[d] 37 prefectures.
Dependent variable: private investment rate. T-statistics in parentheses

In the Ordinary Least Squares estimates, in Table 7.7, the correlation between the private saving and investment rates is positive, but the correlation could be spurious, because of the influence of unmeasured variables. As instruments for the public saving/GDP ratio, we use the MOF-Powerful dummy defined earlier. As instruments for the public investment/GDP ratio, we use the MOF-Powerful dummy and the size of the land in the prefecture that could be used for building purposes (*takuchi*).[12] It appears obvious that other things being equal, a physically large area such as Hokkaidō would have more need for public infrastructure investment such as roads and railways. The demographic variables are used as instruments for the private saving rate. The Instrumental Variables estimates in Table 7 depict a *zero* correlation. Conditional on the public components, private saving has no effect on private investment, which is what is expected under perfect capital mobility.

The government deficit and public investment ratios also appear to have zero effects on the private investment rate (the Instrumental Variables results). When the sample excludes the 'large' prefectures in Kantō and Kinki, the results do not change.

The results in Table 7.7 suggest that, in Japanese regional data, private investment and saving rates are unaffected by the government components. The private investment-saving correlations, conditioned by the government components, do not differ from the unconditional estimates shown in Table 7.4 on p. 184. Even if the public saving and investment rates are negatively correlated, the private unconditional rates can be uncorrelated when the regional private and public sectors are independent.

Tables 7.8 (a), (b), (c) and (d) depict several correlations between the private and public components, conditioned only by the level of prefectural GDP per capita or the growth rate of prefectural GDP. Both the Ordinary Least Squares and the Instrumental Variables estimates are presented. The correlation between the public and private components is always zero.

Table 7.8 (a) shows the correlation between private saving and public saving rates. The correlation is positive but statistically insignificant. If Ricardian equivalence held at the regional level, the correlation should be negative and significant. A rise in government saving should entail a corresponding fall in private saving.

Table 7.8 (b) shows that the public and private investment rates are uncorrelated. Instead of examining the correlations in the changes (investments) in the public and private capital stocks, Table 7.8 (c) depicts

TABLE 7.8(a)   Cross-prefectural correlation between government and
private saving rates

	Ordinary least squares	Instrumental variables
Constant	0.16	0.18
	(5.11)	(4.99)
Government saving rate	0.11	0.26
	(0.70)	(1.61)
Growth rate of GDP	2.74	2.32
	(3.37)	(2.50)
R-square	0.26	0.25

Notes:
Instruments for the government saving rate: MOF-Powerful. 45 prefectures
Dependent variable: private saving rate. T-statistics in parentheses.

TABLE 7.8(b)   Cross-prefectural correlation between private and public
investment rates

	Ordinary least squares	Instrumental variables
Constant	0.17	0.18
	(6.38)	(7.15)
Public investment rate	0.21	0.19
	(1.86)	(1.54)
Growth rate of GDP	0.63	0.60
	(1.31)	(1.45)
R-square	0.10	0.10

Notes:
Instruments for the public investment rate: MOF-Powerful and the size of
the land that could be used for building purposes. 45 prefectures.
Dependent variable: private investment rate.

correlations in the per capita stocks of public and private capital. As
mentioned earlier, the stock of private capital per capita in equilibrium
(not necessarily in the steady state) is determined in an open economy
by the exogenous real rate of interest and, if public capital enters into
the production function, by the stock of public capital per capita. To
control for regional differences in total factor productivity, we include
the prefectural per capita GDP as an additional regressor. Some regions
may have higher per capita GDP, not because of a higher capital–labour
ratio, but because existing factors of production are more productive,
perhaps because of external economies or a higher educational level.

TABLE 7.8(c)   Cross-prefectural correlation between private and public capital per capita

	Ordinary least squares	Instrumental variables
Constant	−1.01	−3.43
	(−1.07)	(−0.93)
Public capital per capita	0.24	1.06
	(0.80)	(0.85)
GDP per capita	2.37	2.80
	(9.40)	(3.61)
R-square	0.74	0.65

Notes:
Instruments for public capital per capita: MOF-Powerful, Agriculture-Powerful, Construction-Powerful. 45 prefectures.
Dependent variable: private capital per person.

TABLE 7.8(d)   Cross-prefectural correlation between government saving and investment rates

	Ordinary least squares	Instrumental variables
Constant	−0.14	−0.13
	(−3.93)	(−2.16)
Public investment rate	−0.62	−0.67
	(−4.24)	(−3.00)
GDP per capita	0.094	0.09
	(8.68)	(5.03)
R-square	0.87	0.87

Notes:
Instruments for the public investment rate: MOF-Powerful, size of the land that could be used for building purposes. 45 prefectures.
Dependent variable: government saving/GDP. T-statistics in parentheses.

We find that the stock of public capital per capita is uncorrelated with the stock of private capital per capita. One interpretation of this result is that marginal productivity of private capital is unchanged by the stock of public capital.

The results in Tables 7.8 (b) and 7.8 (c) suggest that, at least since 1975, public investment in the Japanese regions has not changed the productivity of private investment. If public capital does not stimulate private capital formation, why do Japanese bureaucrats insist on channelling public investment to the poorer prefectures?

There are several possible explanations. First, as shown in Table 7.6 on p. 192, if a prefecture has a politician affiliated with the MOF-Powerful *zoku*, then the prefecture will tend to receive more public investment. Whether a politician will be able to gain the posts (of Minister of Finance or Chairman of the Ministry of Finance Research Council) that lead to the MOF-Powerful *zoku* depends on the electoral success of the politician. A politician needs to be elected close to a dozen times before he has a chance of being awarded the post of minister of a major ministry (Sato and Matsuzaki, 1985). As is well known, in Japan, in poor electoral districts, each vote carries more weight. A politician who establishes an electoral base in a poor district may have a larger chance of being elected repeatedly. Therefore, it is usually only the politicians from poor, rural districts who can achieve the desired *zoku* posts. An example of a highly influential MOF-Powerful *zoku* politician is Kakuei Tanaka, who hails from the poor, predominantly agricultural, Niigata Third District.

Second, the bureaucrats may be allocating public investment for reasons other than raising the marginal productivity of private capital. Even if public capital is separable from private capital in the production function, an increase in the public capital stock will raise the level of GDP in a given prefecture. The increase in public capital will raise employment as workers will be required to man the capital and raise the prefectural GDP level by an amount equalling the factor payments to labour. The regional allocation of public capital may simply be an income redistribution scheme from the cities to the rural areas.

Additionally, it has been argued that, since the early 1970s, public investment has been carried out mainly to raise the marginal utility of private consumption.[13] Japan does not have the quality of public parks, resorts and other amenities befitting a country of its international stature. Public capital of the type that has a direct consumption effect on utility may not have direct effects on the productivity of private capital.

Table 7.8 (d) reinforces the conclusion reached in Section 7.3 that the public investment rate is negatively correlated with the public saving rate. Even after controlling for the GDP per capita of a prefecture, a prefecture that has a high public investment rate has a high government deficit rate. This suggests that the regional public components are affected by factors other than the per capita GDP of the prefecture.

7.5 CONCLUSION

In this chapter we examined correlations between the different definitions of saving and investment under a setting of known capital mobility: Japanese regions. All our results are from cross-prefectural data
averaged over relatively long time-periods. The averaging process should
smooth out the effects of short-run shocks. Our results should therefore be interpreted as applying to a cross-section of economies in long-
run steady-state equilibrium. Our main results, and the implications
arising from them, are as follows.

1. Private saving and investment rates are uncorrelated. Under high
   capital mobility, a rise in a region's private saving rate will not
   change the region's private investment rate. Private investment is
   not restricted by private saving. We take this result to mean that
   the private saving–investment correlation coefficient is a good indicator of capital mobility. This is also true across countries. When
   capital mobility is very high, as in the Japanese regions, the correlation between the private saving and investment rates is expected
   to be zero, and this was shown in this chapter to be the case. The
   results for the Japanese regions are a clear indication that even up
   to the present time, national boundaries have placed limits on international capital flows. For example, there may be cultural or linguistic barriers across countries that do not exist within nations.
2. The correlation between total saving and investment rates, which is
   inclusive of public saving and investment, is significantly negative.
   The negative correlation in the total rates is driven by the strong
   negative correlation between regional government saving and investment. This result suggests that the public sector may be able to
   influence significantly regional current account imbalances.

   The applicability of this result to an entire national economy will
   depend on the economy's relative sizes of the public and private
   sectors. As mentioned earlier, in a Japanese region such as Hokkaidō,
   public investment accounts for over 33 per cent of total investment.
   The public sector can be large in a typical Japanese prefecture, since
   each prefectural government receives large transfers from central
   government.

   Perhaps our result will be more applicable to a group of nations
   that are highly integrated through fiscal transfers, such as the European
   Community, rather than to the entire sample of industrialized countries. In the European Community, there is a program of economic

assistance from the richer nations to the relatively poor countries of Greece and Portugal.

3. At the regional level, changes in the public saving and investment rates do not affect the private saving and investment rates. The statistical independence of the public and private components implies that the private saving and investment correlations may be examined separately from the public saving and investment correlations. The functional separability of private from public capital suggests that public capital neither 'crowds in' nor 'crowds out' private capital. Our results suggest that the rationale that public investment promotes private capital accumulation, or in turn that public investment hinders private investment, should be re-examined.

One fundamental question is the applicability of the evidence arising from an analysis of regional capital flows to international capital flows. In principle, as long as 'saving' and 'investment' can be defined, the Feldstein–Horioka approach can be used on data of any economic entity. For example, the correlation between saving and investment can be estimated with firm level data, since a company both saves and invests. It is not, however, convincing to use cross-company saving–investment correlations to draw conclusions about international capital mobility. A firm is much more specialized than an entire country. We would expect that even under perfect international capital mobility, the capital flows between countries will be much smaller than the flows between firms (both financial and non-financial). A country contains many types of firms and consumers, and much of the trade in financial claims can be performed intranationally.

The same criticism may apply to attempts to draw implications for international capital mobility from regional capital mobility. We feel, however, that most Japanese prefectures are fairly well diversified in the types of industries that they contain, so that the prefectures can at least approximate the capital market conditions existing in many small nations.

It is true that labour mobility is much higher between regions than between countries. Perhaps the failure of Ricardian equivalence at the prefectural level is partly related to the fact that people can move easily from one prefecture to another. Why be concerned about the external debt of one's prefecture if one can easily migrate to another? Again, perhaps our results on Ricardian equivalence best apply to a group of countries that are truly integrated, with both high capital and high labour mobility, plus a high level of fiscal transfers among group members. Perhaps our results will best apply to the European Community in the future.

NOTES

1. Nara is an anomaly in that it is a relatively rich prefecture, but it runs a private savings–investment deficit.
2. The negative correlation between total saving and investment can also be observed in the regional data of Canada, Great Britain and Germany (Thomas, 1991). As with Japanese prefectures, the results appear to be driven by the strong negative correlation between regional government saving and investment.
3. Of all the taxes received by the central government, 32 per cent are allocated, without discretion by central government, to the regional governments.
4. A firm can be incorporated with seven employees and 100 000 yen in capital, and take advantage of limited liability and generous physical capital depreciation tax allowances. To be listed on the stock exchange, a firm's equity must be above a given amount, be widely traded, and the firm must run a profit for two years in succession. In Japan, at the end of March 1990, there were 975 861 corporations, of which 4872 were listed on the two sections in Tōkyō, and the seven regional stock exchanges. Only a very small percentage of the unlisted firms will have main bank ties.
5. As instruments for the household saving rate, we use the same demographic and social security variables as in Specification 3. As an instrument for the corporate saving rate, we use the number of prefectural capitals that are within three hours' travel from the base prefectural capital. We would expect that financing constraints will be more severe, and the need to accumulate corporate saving greater in the more isolated prefectures such as Okinawa, Kagoshima and Hokkaidō.
6. A temporary rise in income caused by the productivity shock raises consumption, but consumption does not rise as much as the amount of the increase in current income, since individuals will want to transfer some of the increase in current income to future consumption. Saving therefore increases.
7. This level of the current account surplus will allow the stock of credit-GDP ratio to be constant.
8. This was true at least until the recent defeat in the lower house elections of the LDP.
9. Inoguchi and Iwai (1987) list the following *zoku*. Commerce and Industry, Agriculture and Forestry, Fishing, Transportation, Construction, Welfare, Labour, Education and Culture, Posts and Communications, Finance, Defence. All these policy areas have government ministries attached to them.
10. The MOF-Powerful category includes four former prime ministers, Tanaka, Fukuda, Takeshita and Miyazawa, and one potential prime minister, Michio Watanabe. Niigata is not in our sample, so the influence of Kakuei Tanaka (probably enormous) is excluded.

11. The difference between the conditional and unconditional correlations is similar to the difference between the total and the partial derivative. Under perfect capital mobility, the partial derivative of a change in private saving on private investment is zero. The total derivative, however, may not in general be zero if a change in private saving is related to a change in government saving and investment, which, in turn, affects the private investment rate.

12. As an additional instrument for both the government saving and investment rates, we also included per capita GDP. The per capita GDP level of a prefecture was, as expected, highly negatively correlated with the public investment ratio, and highly positively correlated with the deficit rate. The inclusion of per capita GDP did not affect the instrumental variables results.

13. I thank Professor Hiroshi Yoshikawa on this point.

REFERENCES

Artis, M. and T. Bayoumi 1989. 'Saving, Investment, Financial Integration, and the Balance of Payments', manuscripts, Research Department, International Monetary Fund.

Asahi Newspapers, *Minryoku*, various issues.

Aschauer, D. 1988. 'Is Public Expenditure Productive?' manuscript, Chicago: Federal Reserve Bank of Chicago.

Backus, D., P. Kehoe and F. Kydland 1992. 'International Real Business Cycles', *Journal of Political Economy*, 72.

Barro, R. 1976. 'Are Government Bonds Net Wealth?' *Journal of Political Economy*, 66.

Barro, R. 1990. 'Government Spending in a Simple Model of Endogenous Growth'. *Journal of Political Economy*, 70.

Barro, R., G. Mankiw and X. Sali-i-Martin 1992. 'Capital Mobility in Neoclassical Models of Growth', manuscript, Harvard University.

Bayoumi, T. 1990. 'Saving–Investment Correlations', *International Monetary Fund Staff Papers*, 37.

Bayoumi, T. and A. Rose 1993. 'Domestic Saving and Intra-National Capital Flows', *European Economic Review*, 21.

Baxter, M. and M. Crucini 1993. 'Explaining Saving–Investment Correlations', *American Economic Review*, 83.

Brock, P. 1988. 'Investment, the Current Account, and the Relative Price of Non-traded Goods in a Small Open Economy', *Journal of International Economics*, 18.

Cardia, J. 1992. 'Crowding Out in Open Economies: Results from a Simulation Study'. *Canadian Journal of Economics*, 25.

Dooley, M., J. Frankel and D. Matheson 1987. 'International Capital Mobility: What Do Saving–Investment Correlations Tell Us?', *International Monetary Fund Staff Papers*, 34.

Eaton, J. 1989. 'Foreign Public Capital Flows', in H. Chenery and T. N. Srinivasan (eds), *Handbook of Development Economics*, Amsterdam: Elsevier Science.

Economic Planning Agency, Government of Japan 1992. *Annual Report on* the *Prefectural Accounts*, Tōkyō: Ministry of Finance Printing Office.

Feldstein, M. and P. Bacchetta 1991. 'National Saving and International Investment', in B. Douglas Bernheim and John B. Shoven (eds), *National Saving and Economic Performance*, Chicago: University of Chicago Press.

Feldstein, M. and C. Y. Horioka 1980. 'Domestic Saving and International Capital Flows', *Economic Journal*, 30.

Frankel, J. 1986. 'International Capital Mobility and Crowding-Out in the U.S. Economy: Imperfect Integration of Financial Markets or of Goods Markets?', in R. W. Hafer (ed.), *How Open is the U.S. Economy?*, Lexington, Mass.: Heath.

Frankel, J. 1991. 'Quantifying International Capital Mobility in the 1980s', in B. Douglas Bernheim and John B. Shoven (eds), *National Saving and Economic Performance*, Chicago: University of Chicago Press.

Hoshi, T., A. Kasyhap and D. Scharfstein 1991. 'Corporate Structure, Liquidity, and Investment–Evidence from Japanese Industrial Groups', *Quarterly Journal of Economics*, 56.

Inoguchi, T. and T. Iwai 1987. *A Study of the Zoku Politician (Zoku Giin No Kenkyu)*, Tōkyō: Nihon Keizai Shimbun.

Ishihara, N. 1986. 'The Local Public Finance System', in Tokue Shibata (ed.), *Public Finance in Japan*, Tōkyō: University of Tōkyō Press.

Lucas, R. 1990. 'Why Doesn't Capital Flow from Rich to Poor Countries?', *American Economic Review*, 81.

Obstfeld, M. 1986. 'Capital Mobility in the World Economy: Theory and Measurement', *Carnegie–Rochester Conference Series on Public Policy*, 24.

Obstfeld, M. 1991. 'Comment', in B. Douglas Bernheim and John B. Shoven (eds), *National Saving and Economic Performance*, Chicago: University of Chicago Press.

Obstfeld, M. 1993. 'International Capital Mobility in the 1990s', manuscript, University of California, Berkeley.

Okuno, N. and R. Futagami, 1990. 'Regional Income Inequality and Allocation of Public Investment: The Experience of Japan, 1958–1986', Working Paper, Nagoya University.

Sachs, J. 1981. 'The Current Account and Macroeconomic Adjustment in the 1970s', *Brookings Papers on Economic Activity*, 21.

Sato, S. and T. Matsuzaki 1985. *The Liberal Democratic Party Regime (Jiminto Seiken)*, Tōkyō: Chuo Koron.

Sinn, S. 1992. 'Saving-Investment Correlations and Capital Mobility: On the Evidence from Annual Data', *Economic Journal*, 102.

Summers, L. 1988. 'Tax Policy and International Competitiveness', in Jacob A. Frenkel (ed.), *International Aspects of Fiscal Policies*, Chicago: University of Chicago Press.

Tesar, L. 1991. 'Saving-Investment Correlations: What Do They Tell Us?', *Journal of International Economics*, 21.

Thomas, A. 1991. 'Saving, Investment and the Regional Current Account: An Analysis of Canadian, West German, and British Regions', manuscript, Massachusetts Institute of Technology.

Yonehara, T. 1986. 'Financial Relations Between National and Local Governments', in Tokue Shibata (ed.), *Public Finance in Japan*, Tōkyō: Tōkyō University Press.

8 High Economic Growth and Its End in Japan: An Explanation by a Model of Demand-led Growth

Hiroshi Yoshikawa*

8.1 INTRODUCTION

The high economic growth of the Japanese economy during the 1950s and 1960s ended in the early 1970s. Glancing at virtually any time-series of Japan, one is, in fact, struck by a sharp break around 1970. For most variables, the 'structural' changes in the early 1970s seem to have been caused by the sharp deceleration of the growth rate. Even seemingly unrelated variables such as the female labour participation rate show a break around 1970, which can be explained by the growth rate (see Yoshikawa and Ohtake (1989) for the variable just mentioned). It is therefore essential to understand why the high growth of the Japanese economy ended around 1970. Many economists and casual observers, both in Japan and abroad, attribute the 'structural change' to the first oil shock in 1973. The present chapter takes issue with this standard view and maintains that the structural change was basically caused by domestic factors and that it preceded the 1973 oil embargo.

Our proposition regarding the end of high growth in Japan is based on a model which emphasizes the importance of demand in the process of economic growth. The standard theory of economic growth, based on Solow (1956, p. 57), analyzes the growth process by focusing on the supply side of the economy. In a steady state, the rate of growth is determined by population growth and exogenous technological progress.

* An earlier version of this chapter was presented as a paper at the Second Conference on the Contemporary Japanese Economy organised by the Centre for Japanese Economic Studies, Macquarie University, Sydney, on 19–20 August 1993. This chapter draws heavily on Yoshikawa (1995).

The new 'endogenous growth theory' such as described in Grossman and Helpman (1990) is no exception in that it focuses on the supply side. Endogenizing technological progress by focusing on the supply side leads us naturally to identify, apart from the time preference, the endowment of a factor used intensively in research and development (R&D) as the ultimate *exogenous* factor to explain economic growth. Thus in Grossman and Helpman (1990), for example, exogenously-given inputs that are used intensively in R&D are conducive to innovation and growth, while inputs that are used intensively in the manufacturing of traditional goods may discourage innovation and growth.

It is beyond doubt that capital accumulation and technological progress played vital roles in post-war Japanese economic growth; Kosai (1986), for example, describes vividly the technological progress during this period. These important supply-side issues, however, must be analyzed in conjunction with real demand constraints differently from the way it is ordinarily done. In particular, investment, which not only brings about capital accumulation but also carries embodied technological progress, is strongly conditioned by demand constraints. Investment is therefore the nexus of the supply and demand sides of the economy in growth. By analyzing investment and growth in relation to demand constraints, we can better understand Japan's high economic growth and its end.

Section 8.2 first describes the post-war high economic growth of the Japanese economy during the period 1955–70. Section 8.3 offers a model of demand-led growth, and interprets Japan's high growth and its end in Japan within this framework.

8.2 HIGH ECONOMIC GROWTH OF THE JAPANESE ECONOMY: 1955–70

Very rapid economic growth is perhaps the most important characteristic of the post-war Japanese economy. The growth rate accelerated in the post-war era compared to the pre-war period; 3.2 per cent for 1889–1938 as against 6.7 per cent for 1955–88. It is also high by international standards. Figure 8.1 shows the growth rate of real GNP for Japan in comparison with the USA. For a period spanning nearly three decades, the growth rate of the Japanese economy almost always exceeded that of the US economy.

Figure 8.1 also shows a very significant fact: that the growth rate of the Japanese economy fell from about 10 per cent to 4 per cent in the

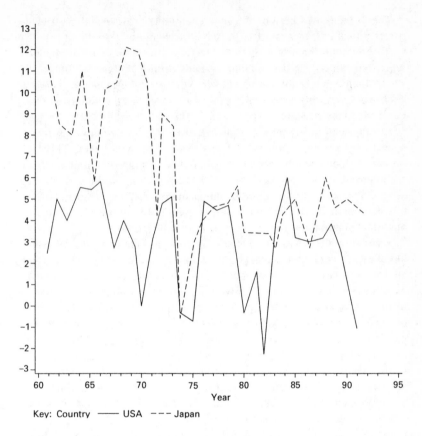

FIGURE 8.1   Growth rate of real GNP, Japan and USA.

early 1970s. This sharp decline in the growth rate is the most conspicuous phenomenon surrounding the post-war Japanese economy. At
the same time, measured by standard deviation, fluctuations of the
growth rate became much less volatile: 2.7 per cent for 1961–72 as
against 1.8 per cent for 1973–89. For the USA, on the other hand, the
average growth rate declined only slightly, and unlike Japan, its standard deviation became larger, beginning in the early 1970s. In fact,
Horie *et al.* (1987), using deviation from a trend estimated by the
Bayesian approach, demonstrate that despite all the attention paid to
stagnated productivity growth, in the USA and UK, there was no such
significant 'structural change' in growth rate of real GNP around the
early 1970s as they find for Japan.

The fifteen-year period of rapid economic growth and its subsequent rather abrupt cessation provide an excellent opportunity to investigate the mechanism of growth. This section explains the mechanism which sustained rapid economic growth during the period 1955–70. By so doing it also explains why the growth rate of the Japanese economy declined so sharply around the early 1970s, and at the same time became much more stable than it was in the 1950s and 1960s.

As was seen in Figure 8.1, growth of the Japanese economy was not necessarily a smooth process; rather, it was in growth cycles. This fact makes it necessary to consider simultaneously growth and cyclical fluctuations. As we will see shortly, a sharp decline in the growth rate around the early 1970s accompanies a major change in the nature of business cycles. An analysis of these changes therefore contributes to our understanding of the process of economic growth.

Analyzing the post-war business cycles in Japan, Yoshikawa and Ohtake (1987) conclude that the fluctuations in the 1960s were generated by investment *demand*, particularly construction. In fact, investment in the rapid economic growth behaved very differently from that in the 1970s and 1980s. Table 8.1, for example, shows the correlation of investment across industries for two periods. We observe strong parallels in investment across various sectors during the high growth period. This means that economy-wide rather than industry-specific factors spurred investment demand in the 1960s. We suggest that demographic trends played a particularly important role in this process.

Recall that the Japanese economy in the 1950s and 1960s was a two-sector economy consisting of a rural agricultural sector and an urban manufacturing sector. As of 1950, nearly half of the total labour force was still engaged in agriculture (see Table 8.2). This percentage is comparable to those of most developing Asian nations today: for example, 56 per cent for Indonesia in 1988. The population flowed continuously from agriculture into industry in the process of economic growth. The dual structure of the economy enabled the manufacturing sector to hire enough labour at the level of real wages which, determined by the agricultural sector with its 'disguised' unemployment, were lower than the marginal product in the industrial sector. The growth of the manufacturing sector therefore entailed high profits in the same sector rather than an increase in real wages. Then high profits, in turn, were supposed to induce high investment. All this is, of course, what Lewis (1954) describes as a typical process of growth in an underdeveloped dual economy.

The Lewisian model has been applied successfully by a number of

TABLE 8.1 Correlations of investment across industries

	Food	Textiles	Pulp & paper	Chemicals	Iron & steel	Non-ferrous metals	Fabricated metals	General machinery	Electrical machinery	Transportation equipment	Electricity	Service
(1966 I to 1972 IV)												
Food	1.00											
Textiles	-0.14	1.00										
Pulp & paper	0.06	0.50	1.00									
Chemicals	0.47	0.49	0.48	1.00								
Iron & steel	-0.14	0.15	0.10	0.22	1.00							
Non-ferrous metals	0.46	-0.15	0.27	0.46	0.30	1.00						
Fabricated metals	0.32	0.40	0.22	0.39	0.29	0.15	1.00					
General machinery	0.31	0.51	0.37	0.66	0.46	0.30	0.75	1.00				
Electrical machinery	0.23	0.51	0.31	0.59	0.61	0.37	0.67	0.84	1.00			
Transportation equipment	0.45	0.46	0.53	0.46	0.40	0.30	0.56	0.60	0.66	1.00		
Electricity	0.16	0.40	0.33	0.42	0.02	0.12	0.02	0.12	0.38	0.27	1.00	
Service	-0.30	0.24	0.06	0.10	-0.07	-0.20	-0.28	-0.09	0.19	-0.30	0.45	1.00
(1973 I to 1985 I)												
Food	1.00											
Textiles	0.12	1.00										
Pulp & paper	0.21	0.13	1.00									
Chemicals	0.03	-0.11	0.33	1.00								
Iron & steel	-0.12	0.08	-0.29	-0.04	1.00							
Non-ferrous metals	0.06	0.05	0.15	0.20	-0.14	1.00						
Fabricated metals	0.06	0.13	0.18	0.02	-0.28	0.18	1.00					
General machinery	0.20	0.28	0.10	0.12	-0.31	0.07	0.32	1.00				
Electrical machinery	0.16	0.30	-0.04	-0.16	-0.25	0.03	0.56	0.52	1.00			
Transportation equipment	0.20	-0.17	-0.01	-0.03	-0.21	0.20	0.24	0.36	0.51	1.00		
Electricity	-0.12	-0.05	0.02	-0.37	-0.05	-0.50	0.14	0.04	0.16	0.01	1.00	
Service	0.18	0.38	0.02	-0.10	-0.06	-0.31	0.26	0.34	0.53	0.22	-0.03	1.00

TABLE 8.2   Percentage composition of total employment between primary,
secondary and tertiary occupations

	Primary (Agriculture and Mining) (per cent)	Secondary (Manufacturing, Construction) (per cent)	Tertiary (Services) (per cent)
1950			
Japan	**48.3**	**21.9**	**29.7**
USA	12.4	35.3	49.7
UK	5.1	47.5	47.0
Germany	23.2	42.2	32.4
1989*			
Japan	**7.6**	**33.8**	**58.1**
US	2.9	25.9	71.1
UK	2.4	29.0	68.6
Germany	4.9	38.4	55.3

* For UK and Germany, 1987.

economists to the century-long development of the Japanese economy
(see, for example, Ohkawa and Rosovsky (1973) and Minami (1970)).
In the Lewisian model, however, population flow between two sectors
is taken solely as a *result* of the growth of the modern manufacturing
sector. Umemura (1961), Minami (1970) and Ono (1972) demonstrate
that internal migration was in fact quite sensitive to the growth of the
manufacturing sector: more people left rural agricultural areas for urban industrial areas in times of economic expansion and vice versa.
Yearly fluctuations in the population flow were therefore a *result* of
industrial growth. In the Lewisian model, the key factor behind this
industrial growth is low real wages, made possible by the previously
noted existence of 'disguised' unemployment in the agricultural sector. In contrast to the Lewisian model, however, in what follows we
argue that in the case of the *post-war* Japanese economic growth (1955–
70), the population flow between the two sectors was the major factor
generating high demand for products of the industrial sector. In our
view, population flow was a *cause* as well as a result of economic
growth.

Because of the large-scale population flows (see Figure 8.2), household formation dramatically accelerated during the period of high economic growth, 1955–70 (see Figure 8.3). We underline the fact that in
this period, the growth rate of households formed a hump shape at a

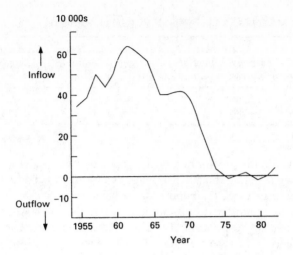

FIGURE 8.2   Population inflow into three largest city (Tōkyō, Ōsaka, and Nagoya) areas

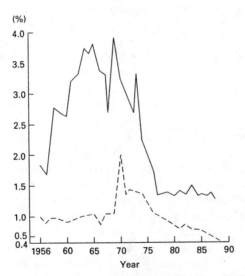

Key: ——— Growth rate of the number of households
       - - - Growth rate of population

Note: 1970 is an outlier. Okinawa prefecture (Ryukyu Island) was returned to Japan by the USA in 1970.

FIGURE 8.3   Growth rates of the number of households and population

TABLE 8.3   Growth of household, by type

Year	'Core' household: a married couple, possibly with unmarried children	Three-generation merged household	Unmarried single
1955	10 366	6 353	596
1975	19 980	6 988	4 236

high level, while the growth rate of the population was quite stable at a much lower level, at about 1 per cent. As a result, for the two decades beginning in 1955, the population in Japan increased by only 20 per cent – from 90 million to 110 million – while the number of households increased by 80 per cent. Table 8.3 shows household formation during this period, by type. Traditional three-generation merged households hardly increased, but the 'core' households, consisting of a married couple, possibly with unmarried children, and those of unmarried singles, dramatically increased, particularly in urban industrial areas. When three generations of a family kept a traditional single household in rural villages, they would have needed only one of each consumer durable such as a refrigerator, a television set, a washing machine and a car. But young people giving up agriculture left rural villages for urban industrial areas, where they formed new households. Household formation necessarily generated additional demand for houses, consumer durables and electricity. In this way, population flow sustained high domestic demand in the period of high economic growth, 1955–70.

Along with the creation of a large number of households, the high growth period was also characterized by the diffusion process of newly-available consumer durables. The diffusion of consumer durables was facilitated by steady declines in prices of products over time, and an increase in real income. Electric washing machines, for example, first appeared on the Japanese market in 1949. At the time, a machine cost ¥54 000, while the average annual income was about ¥50 000. Understandably, only twenty machines were sold each month! However, by 1955, only six years later, the price of a washing machine had been reduced to ¥20 000, while the average annual income had risen to above ¥200 000. About a third of households owned a washing machine in 1955. The same story also holds for other consumer durables. Since it was urban areas that led this diffusion process, urbanization, not only by creating new households, but also in itself sustained high demand for those consumer durables (see Table 8.4). At the same time, the

TABLE 8.4 Diffusion of consumer durables

	Year	Urban industrial area, per cent	Rural agricultural area, per cent
Refrigerator	1959	11.1	3.4
	64	77.6	57.7
	69	97.5	91.2
	74	107.2	108.2
Washing machine	1959	44.2	24.4
	64	85.9	76.5
	69	99.9	97.0
	74	101.8	102.9
Black & white television set	1959	42.9	23.5
(Colour television set)	64	110.5	101.4
	69	118.1 (27.0)	110.3 (22.7)
	74	– (107.2)	– (106.0)

diffusion of consumer durables naturally augmented household demand for electricity. By the end of the 1960s, however, most of the then available consumer durables had saturated in the domestic market.

This whole process of domestic demand-led high economic growth (1955–70) is schematically summarized in Figure 8.4. Channels 1 and 2 in the diagram have been well recognized: capital accumulation in the industrial sector raising labour demand brings about population flow from rural agricultural areas to urban industrial areas. In addition to these well-recognized channels, we emphasize the neglected and yet very important fact that *such population flow, in turn, by creating new households and raising demand for consumer durables and electricity, ultimately sustained the profitability of investment in manufacturing industry* (channels 3, 4, 5). We emphasize that the role of newly-available consumer durables was not confined to demand for those products themselves. Through the input–output interrelationship, they augmented demand for intermediate goods such as steel, and accordingly high investment in those sectors.

In this virtuous circle for high economic growth, low real wages were not as instrumental as Lewis (1954) has emphasized. Rather it was the growth of domestic demand that sustained the profitability of investment. And for the growth of consumption demand, a steady *rise* in real wages, rather than repressed wages, is a contributing factor. Figures 8.5 (a) and 8.5 (b) compare real wages in the pre-war and

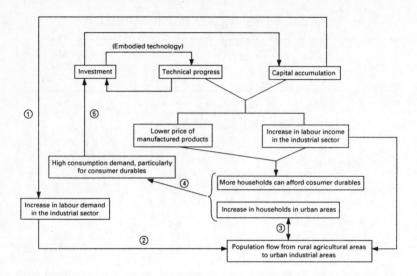

FIGURE 8.4　Domestic demand-led high economic growth of the Japanese economy, 1955–70

post-war periods. In the pre-war period, except for years 1920–21 and 1929–30, real wages saw little increase, while in the post-war period real wages enjoyed steady growth. A steady rise in real wages sustained effective demand for the post-war Japanese economy because the key product was consumer durables which, not as yet having enough international competitiveness, had to find a market domestically. On the other hand, the pre-war Japanese economy was a typical export-led economy (see Shinohara, 1961, and Yoshikawa and Shioji, 1990) where the key industry was cotton, and low real wages were instrumental for international competitiveness.

The domestic demand-led virtuous circle for economic growth based on the Lewisian dual structure is not unique to the post-war Japanese economy. Kindleberger (1967), for example, discusses in a Lewisian model the post-war growth of the European economy. On the other hand, and perhaps a little ironically for the Lewisian theory which purports to explain development, this mechanism is not necessarily observed in today's developing countries.

The relationship between household formation and economic growth is also well known. The so-called building cycle has a long tradition (see, for example, Hickman, 1974). However, in the case of the pre-war US economy, particularly prior to the restrictive immigration law

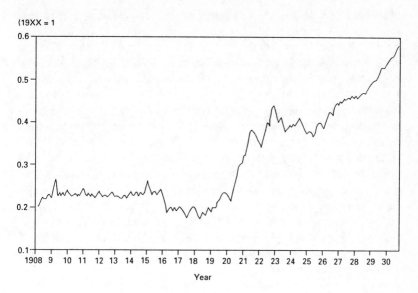

FIGURE 8.5(a)   Real wages in pre-war Japan

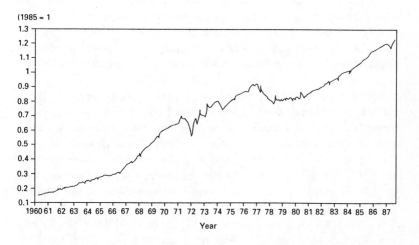

FIGURE 8.5(b)   Real wages in post-war Japan

of 1924, it was immigration rather than domestic population flow that endogenously responded to the growth of income and fuelled household formation. In the building cycle, it is residential construction that brings about a close relationship between household formation and economic growth. In contrast, in the post-war Japanese economy, it was a firm's fixed investment rather than residential construction that played a crucial role in growth and its fluctuations. In the 1960s, residential construction shared less than half the total of private construction. Its share eventually rose to above 70 per cent in the mid-1970s, when the growth rate fell sharply. Household formation, by way of diffusing consumer durables rather than residential construction, ultimately sustained high investment in the manufacturing industry. In this sense, our explanation of Japanese economic growth during the period 1955–70 is closer to Gordon (1951) than to the building cycle theory. Gordon argued that high investment, both residential and non-residential, in the USA in the 1920s was fuelled by urbanization and the diffusion of the automobile:

> Between 1923 and 1929 the growing *use* of automobiles and trucks had a more important impact on total investment and employment than did the expansion of motor vehicle output. Motor vehicle registrations in 1929 were about 75 percent greater than in 1923 and nearly three times the number in 1920 . . . large scale investment was necessary for roads and bridges, oil wells, pipe lines, garages and service stations, and tire and automobile supply stores, as well as for oil refining and tire manufacture. In addition, the automobile accelerated the trends toward urbanization and 'suburbanization,' stimulating thereby residential and commercial building.

In the Japanese economy during the period 1955–70, population flows and the consequent household formation by way of diffusing newly-available consumer durables stimulated continuously economy-wide investment demand, and fluctuations in investment demand were in turn the most important generating force of business cycles from the late 1950s through the 1960s. In the next section we shall explain this mechanism in an explicit growth model with endogenous investment.

The situation changed dramatically around 1970. By then the pool of the so-called 'disguised unemployed' in the agricultural sector had been largely exhausted. Therefore the population flow from the rural sector and its associated urban household formation decelerated sharply. At the same time, the then available consumer durables reached saturation point in the domestic market (see Table 8.4 on p. 211). In this way, the domestic-demand-led virtuous circle for high economic growth was over. Looking at Figures 8.2 and 8.3 on p. 209, we note that *this structural change occurred around 1970, a few years in advance of the first oil embargo in 1973.* More formally, Iwamoto and Kobayashi (1992), using the regression with a piecewise linear trend for real GNP, sought a turning point. Rolling the turning point from 1969.III to 1974.II, they found that the point which attains the minimum standard error is 1971.IV.

This structural change is seen clearly in individual industries as well as in the macroeconomy. Table 8.5 shows the time-series of capacity and investment in the petrochemical industry. By the end of the 1960s,

TABLE 8.5   Investment in the petrochemical industry

Year	Capacity for ethylene production (000s tons)	Investment (millions/yen)	Real investment (Index, 1970 = 100)
1956	0	8 349	3.3
1957	0	24 017	9.5
1958	43	23 396	9.9
1959	115	27 555	11.5
1960	115	38 494	15.9
1961	160	66 435	27.2
1962	316	55 904	23.3
1963	378	62 017	25.4
1964	633	91 229	37.3
1965	1 080	110 921	45.0
1966	1 190	77 202	30.6
1967	1 565	109 215	42.5
1968	1 970	202 837	78.3
1969	2 480	216 547	81.8
1970	4 010	274 299	100.0
1971	4 330	251 762	92.5
1972	4 980	152 467	55.6
1973	4 980	140 195	44.1
1974	5 065	240 818	57.7
1975	5 145	280 650	65.3
1976	5 185	226 853	50.0
1977	5 215	192 680	41.9
1978	5 235	110 643	24.7
1979	6 079	117 016	24.3
1980	6 257	200 614	35.4

Note: Real investment is investment deflated by WPI.

Source: Watanabe and Saeki, 1984, p. 99, table V–1.

the industry had faced a major turning point. This situation was typical, not exceptional. The first oil shock hit a Japanese economy which had already seen structural changes caused by the domestic factors explained above.

8.3   A MODEL OF DEMAND-LED ECONOMIC GROWTH

Section 8.2 described the domestic-demand-led high growth of the Japanese economy during the period 1955–70. High growth was brought about by high investment, but it in turn was ultimately sustained by high household formation and diffusion of consumer durables. Because the labour pool in the rural agricultural sector had been exhausted and the then available consumer durables had seen saturation in the domestic market by 1970, high growth necessarily ended. The representative alternatives to this view, such as Bruno and Sachs (1985) and Jorgenson (1988) attribute the end of high growth to the oil shock in 1973. Their formal analysis of possible effects of oil shocks on economic growth is summarized in the Appendix at the end of this chapter. Drawing on Yoshikawa (1995), this section provides an analytical framework for our own interpretation.

In a standard model of economic growth (Solow, 1956, 1957), supply factors such as population growth and the rate of technological progress ultimately determine the growth rate of the economy. Out of a steady state, an increase in the saving rate also accelerates growth. Growth in the population or the labour force, however, is not quite as fundamental in explaining economic growth. By itself, population increase will not suffice to fuel growth, as is amply illustrated both in history and in the world today. The same also applies to the saving rate.

As is often pointed out, what neo-classical theory lacks, is an the independent investment function (see Sen, 1965) and a role for demand therein. The post-war Japanese experience also demonstrates that investment is indeed the nexus of demand and supply in economic growth. It is essential to understand investment in relation to demand constraints.

8.3.1   The model

To introduce investment into the theory of growth, we consider the investment decisions of a firm. The model is standard, except for one thing: the firm is demand-constrained, but to some extent the growth of demand depends on current investment.

Investment is customarily identified as something which augments the production capacity of the firm on the supply side. We maintain, however, that investment embodying *demand-creating technological progress* also raises the demand for the firm's product to some extent. Specifically, investment would expand future demand for the firm's product, perhaps through the introduction of new products (product innovation), the improvement of quality of existing products, or the reduction of their prices (process innovation). At any rate, it must be emphasized that this *demand-creating* aspect of investment is conceptually different from the capacity-augmenting aspect of investment, since the former concerns the market for the product, and the latter the technology or production function. In reality, of course, the two would be related. Unless a part of the existing capacity is scrapped, investment necessarily accompanies an increase in capacity. Both product and process innovations are embodied in new investment, and therefore investment creates future demand while at the same time augmenting capacity.

The firm maximizes the following discounted sum of net cash flow:

$$\int_0^\infty \{D_t - w_t L_t - \phi(\alpha_t)K_t\}e^{-\rho t}dt \tag{1}$$

D_t, w_t, L_t, K_t and ρ are respectively demand for the firm's product, real wages, labour, capital stock and the discount rate; α_t is the growth rate of capital stock:

$$\alpha_t = \dot{K_t}/K_t \tag{2}$$

For simplicity, we have ignored depreciation.

As usual, the adjustment cost is assumed to be convex:

$$\phi'(\alpha) > 0, \ \phi''(\alpha) > 0$$

$$\phi(0) = 0, \ \phi'(0) = 1 \tag{3}$$

At each moment in time demand, D_t, is given. Demand grows exogenously at the rate of θ but its growth also depends on current investment:

$$\dot{D_t} = (\theta + \gamma\alpha_t)D_t \qquad (0 < \gamma < 1) \tag{4}$$

Equation (4) captures the demand-creating technological progress embodied in investment, its degree depending on parameter γ. The larger

γ is, the stronger the firm's product and process innovations are, and/or the responsiveness of the market.

Normalizing the units in such a way that $D_0 = K_0^\gamma$, we obtain

$$D_t = e^{\theta t} K_t^\gamma \tag{5}$$

On the supply side, output equal to D_t is assumed to be produced according to the Cobb–Douglas production function:

$$D_t = \Lambda_t L_t^a K_t^b \tag{6}$$

where Λ_t is the capacity-augmenting technological progress on the supply side. This production function does not have to exhibit constant returns to scale (a + b = 1). In fact, we underline the importance of increasing returns (a + b > 1). We do assume, however, that *b* is larger than γ: that capital elasticity is greater on the supply side than on the demand side. As γ approaches *b* from below, the demand constraint becomes virtually non-existent. Since we wish to stress the importance of the demand constraint here, the assumption is reasonable.

Since D_t and K_t are both given at time *t*, employment of labour is determined as follows:

$$L_t = \Lambda_t^{\frac{-1}{a}} D_t^{\frac{1}{a}} K_t^{\frac{-b}{a}} \tag{7}$$

The marginal product of labour at this level of employment is given by:

$$\frac{\partial D}{\partial L} = a\Lambda_t L_t^{a-1} K_t^b$$

$$= a\Lambda_t^{\frac{1}{a}} D_t^{\frac{a-1}{a}} K_t^{\frac{b}{a}} = a\Lambda_t^{\frac{1}{a}} e^{\frac{(a-1)\theta t}{a}} K_t^{\frac{b+(a-1)\gamma}{a}} \tag{8}$$

It is assumed to exceed the real wage since labour employment is constrained by demand for products. The neo-classical theory, in contrast, having no such demand constraint, equates real wages w_t to this marginal product of labour. If they are equal, $w_t L_t$ becomes aD_t and the labour's share is *a*. Therefore the factor share becomes independent of the technological progress Λ. This is the well-known result we obtain under the assumption of Hicks' neutral technological progress. We assume, however, that real wages grow in parallel with the marginal product of labour as capital accumulates but their *levels* are below the marginal product. In this case, the factor share depends on the technological progress Λ even though Λ is Hicks neutral.

Specifically, we assume:

$$w_t = w_0 \ e^{\frac{(a-1)\theta t}{a}} \ K_t^{\frac{b+(a-1)\gamma}{a}} \tag{9}$$

where w_0 is taken to be exogenous and is assumed to satisfy:

$$w_0 < a\Lambda_t^{\frac{1}{a}} \tag{10}$$

Given w_t, we obtain:

$$
\begin{aligned}
w_t L_t &= w_0 \Lambda_t^{-\frac{1}{a}} e^{\theta t} K_t^{\gamma} \\
&= w_0 \Lambda_t^{-\frac{1}{a}} D_t
\end{aligned} \tag{11}
$$

The capital share $R = 1 - w_0 \Lambda_t^{-\frac{1}{a}}$ is defined as a ratio of profits to sales. This capital share depends on w_0 and Λ_t. An increase in real wages with an unchanged Λ, of course, lowers the capital share. On the other hand, capacity-augmenting technological progress (an increase in Λ) raises the capital share *only to the extent that it is not fully reflected in an increase in real wages.*

Using (1), (5) and (11), we obtain:

$$\int_0^{\infty} \{Re^{\theta t}K_t^{\gamma} - \phi(\alpha_t)K_t\}e^{-\rho t}dt \tag{12}$$

as the objective function which the firm maximizes under constraint (2) and the initial stock of capital. Assuming the existence of the solution, we know that it is unique and can characterize it as follows.

The optimum level of investment $\alpha_t K_t$ satisfies

$$\phi'(\alpha_t) = q_t \tag{13}$$

where the marginal q_t is defined as

$$q_t = \int_t^{\infty} \{R\gamma K_{\tau}^{\gamma-1} - \phi(\alpha_{\tau})\} \exp\{-\int_t^{\tau}(\rho - \alpha_v)dv\}d\tau \tag{14}$$

q_t itself depends on the time path of α, or investment. On the assumption of the existence of optimum path, the simultaneous determination of q and investment can be analyzed as detailed below. For this purpose, we first define k_t by:

$$k_t = K_t^{1-\gamma} e^{-\theta t} \tag{15}$$

which is nothing but capital–output ratio or capital coefficient K_t/D_t. Then the necessary conditions for optimality consist of:

$$\dot{k}_t = [(1 - \gamma)\alpha(q_t) - \theta]k_t \tag{16}$$

and

$$\dot{q}_t = (\rho - \alpha(q_t))q_t - \frac{R\gamma}{k_t} + \phi(\alpha(q_t)) \tag{17}$$

The optimum path which satisfies the transversality condition is unique and is drawn by a bold line in the phase diagram (shown in Figure 8.6). *In the long-run stationary state, the growth rates of capital and output both converge to* $\dfrac{\theta}{1-\gamma}$. The long-run q is equal to:

$$q^* = \phi' \left(\frac{\theta}{1 - \gamma} \right) > 1 \tag{18}$$

The long-run capital-output ratio k^* satisfies:

$$\frac{R\gamma}{k^*} = \left(\rho - \frac{\theta}{1 - \gamma} \right) \phi' \left(\frac{\theta}{1 - \gamma} \right) + \phi \left(\frac{\theta}{1 - \gamma} \right) \tag{19}$$

The higher the long-run growth rate α^* *is, the lower the long-run capital–output ratio.* Some economists using the Harrod-Domar formula, argue that a rise in capital–output ratio in Japan during the 1970s is a cause of slower economic growth. The implication of the present model is, however, that low growth and high capital–output ratio are both the *result* of lower θ and/or γ. We also note that *the higher is the long-run growth rate* α^*, *the higher is the profit rate,* $\dfrac{R\gamma}{k^*}$.

The time paths of capital accumulation and output growth depend on θ, γ and R. Using the phase diagram, we can establish the following results. When θ decreased, for example, the $\dot{k} = 0$ schedule shifts down, while the $\dot{q} = 0$ schedule remains unchanged. As a result, given the current capital stock, investment declines. But in this process the growth of output falls short of capital accumulation and it leads to a higher capital–output ratio; recall the Japanese experiences during the

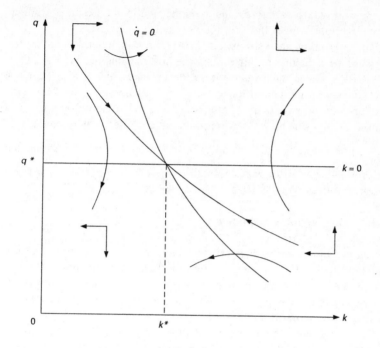

FIGURE 8.6 Determination of optimal path

1970s. Similarly, we can find that the higher γ or R, the higher is investment. When R increased, the long-run capital–output rises, which implies that the acceleration of capital accumulation is greater than that of output. The effect of an increase in γ on the long-run capital–output ratio is, however, ambiguous.

Changes in θ and γ affect the growth rates of capital and output permanently whereas the effect of changes in R on growth rate is only transitory. The main generating force of growth in this model is therefore the exogenous growth of demand θ and the demand-augmenting factor γ. In fact, *given demand conditions*, technological progress on the supply side (an increase in Λ) does not affect investment by itself if it is absorbed by an increase in real wages. One might expect that in the real economy technological progress would raise investment. This intuitively appealing result is obtained either if technical progress not only augments efficiency on the supply side but also augments the growth rate of demand (an increase in γ), or if it raises the capital share. The kind of new technology which brings about the introduction of new products or improvement in the quality of existing products would certainly meet the first requirement.

The preceding analysis of firm behaviour can naturally be carried forward to a theory of growth of the macroeconomy. Above all, it leads us to focus on investment as the key variable. It also suggests that the most important ultimate factors in explaining economic growth are growth of exogenous demand θ and the demand-augmenting power of investment γ. The long-run growth rate of the economy is $\frac{\theta}{1-\gamma}$. For simplicity, discussion of aggregation, labour market and the determination of real wages is omitted here. The interested reader is referred to Yoshikawa (1995).

8.3.2 The Japanese economy

Using this model, we explain post-war Japanese economic growth again. As described in the previous section, the Japanese economy in the late 1950s and 1960s enjoyed high θ, and, as a consequence, very high growth of the economy. The economic growth in this period was led basically by domestic demand.

To recapitulate the point, the factors behind high θ were (i) an unprecedentedly high growth of the number of households (much higher than population growth) which was generated by internal migration in the Lewisian dual economy; and (ii) the introduction of many consumer durables at progressively lower prices. As stated earlier, if three generations of a family lived in a traditional way within a single household, they would have needed only one of each consumer durable, for example, a refrigerator. But young people moved to urban areas and created new households, so they needed duplicate consumer durables. In this way, internal migration, by generating an unprecedentedly high growth of households, sustained high domestic demand.

As the pool of labour in the rural agricultural sector was exhausted, however, internal migration subsided and, accordingly, the increase in the number of households decelerated. Meanwhile, the domestic market for the then-existing consumer durables became saturated. It restrained not only growth of the industries producing consumer durables but also, through input–output channels, affected the whole manufacturing industry, including iron and steel and chemicals, which had led the rapid economic growth beginning in 1955. In this way, both θ and γ declined substantially. This explains the end of the rapid growth period around 1970.

This whole process can be illustrated by using a simple model explained above. The growth rate of the economy is $\frac{\theta}{1-\gamma}$. Noting that internal migration sustains high growth of domestic demand, we assume that:

$$\theta = g + \dot{f} \tag{20}$$

where g is a constant and f is the percentage of population in urban areas; f changes in a logistic way, but its rate of change depends positively on the growth rate of the economy. High growth accelerates migration from rural to urban areas (see Minami, 1970). Thus we have:

$$\dot{f} = [\beta + \delta \left(\frac{\theta}{1-\gamma} \right)] (1 - f)f \quad (0 < \delta < 1, 0 < \beta) \tag{21}$$

From (20) and (21), we obtain:

$$\theta = \frac{\beta(1 - f)f + g}{1 - \left(\dfrac{\delta}{1-\gamma} \right) (1 - f)f} \tag{22}$$

where:

$$\frac{\partial \theta}{\partial f} \gtreqless 0 \quad \text{as} \quad f \lesseqgtr \frac{1}{2} \tag{23}$$

and

$$\theta \to g \text{ as } f \to 1$$

Therefore, as f monotonically approaches unity, both internal migration and the growth rate of the economy first accelerate and then decelerate. This is shown in Figure 8.7. This is the basic mechanism of the high growth of the Japanese economy in the 1950s and 1960s, and it ended around 1970.

In growth accounting, the positive effect of contraction of agriculture on growth is often taken into account (see Denison, 1967; Maddison, 1987). This positive effect, however, arises only because of the different pace of technological progress from agricultural to industrial sectors. In contrast, we argue here that the unprecedently high growth of

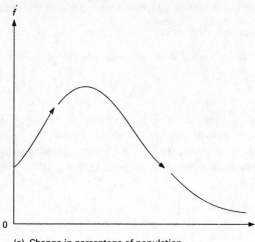

(a) Change in percentage of population
of urban areas

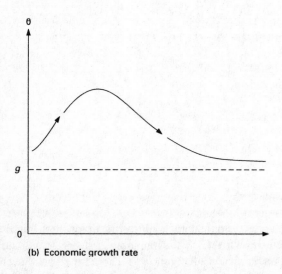

(b) Economic growth rate

FIGURE 8.7 Internal migration and economic growth

the number of households generated by internal migration sustained high growth of domestic *demand* in the post-war Japanese economy.

8.4 CONCLUDING REMARKS

This chapter explained the high economic growth of the Japanese economy in the 1950s and 1960s, and its end in the early 1970s because of changes in domestic factors. Particularly instrumental in the process of high economic growth were high household formation due to the population flow between rural agricultural and urban areas, and the diffusion of consumer durables.

The popular views such as Bruno and Sachs (1985) and Jorgenson (1988), attribute a fall in the rate of economic growth in the 1970s ultimately to the oil shock in 1973 (see Appendix for details of their analyses). These approaches cannot explain, however, why the second oil shock, which occurred in 1979, did not bring about a similar fall in the rate of economic growth; the average growth rates of real GNP for 1973–80 and and 1981–90 are 4.1 per cent and 4.2 per cent respectively. During the first oil crisis, the oil price quadrupled (in 1973–74), while in the second oil crisis it only doubled (in 1979–80). It might be argued that the first oil crisis naturally hit the Japanese economy harder than did the second oil crisis. But transfer payments to OPEC necessitated by an increase in the oil price, when seen as relative to GNP, were actually comparable during the two oil crises, at 3.8 per cent and 4.1 per cent respectively. The supply-side analyses, such as Bruno and Sachs (1985) and Jorgenson (1988), which attribute a fall in the rate of economic growth to the first oil crisis are therefore inconsistent with the fact that the second oil crisis did not entail a similar fall in the growth rate. Nor can they explain why the growth rate of the oil-importing Korean economy fell so sharply during the *second* oil crisis while the effect of the *first* oil crisis was relatively small, which contrasts with the Japanese case.

We do not mean to argue that the oil crisis did not affect the supply side of the Japanese economy. Importantly, two oil shocks in the 1970s were a strong stimulus to innovation in the Japanese manufacturing industry. Innovations were particularly vigorous in the machinery industries, and by the end of the 1970s the machinery sector began to dominate both growth and the cycles of the Japanese economy. The first oil shock, though it was an adverse supply shock to the economy as a whole, in fact had some *favourable* effects on machinery industries.

In the first place, an increase in costs because of the oil embargo was very slight in machinery industries when compared to other industries such as chemicals, paper and metals; the energy coefficients in the 1973 input–output table were 9.9 (chemicals), 7.2 (iron and steel), 4.7 (paper and pulp) and 1.4 (machinery) respectively. Therefore, when a sharp increase in the real price of oil, equivalent to terms of trade deterioration in Japan, brought about the 10 per cent depreciation of the yen, machinery industries benefited, gaining international competitiveness. During the period 1973–6, WPI (Wholesale Price Index) in machinery industries increased by 25.2 per cent in Japan as against the 40.3 per cent increase in the USA. And yet during the same period, the yen depreciated against the dollar by nearly 10 per cent. This means that the price competitiveness of the Japanese machinery industries improved by 25 per cent.

Beyond that, the oil embargo created a huge transfer of money from the oil importing countries to OPEC; about 16 billion dollars in the case of Japan. This newly-created oil money was then eventually loaned to developing countries through international financial intermediaries. To sustain domestic investment, growth-orientated developing countries needed to import machinery. In this way, machinery became the product which enjoyed exceptionally high demand, particularly by developing countries, in the generally depressed post-first-oil-shock world economy. Helped by price competitiveness, Japanese machinery industries emerged as the chief suppliers to meet this world-wide demand: the beginning of the 'Japan problem' of the 1980s and 1990s! All this is, however, different from the end of high growth in the early 1970s. We maintain that a permanent fall in the rate of economic growth beginning the early 1970s was caused by a *domestic* structural change, as explained in this chapter, rather than the first oil crisis. In this respect, we concur with Maddison (1987). By his careful growth accounting, Maddison finds that the growth rate of real GDP in Japan would have been 3.8 per cent during 1973–84 as against its actual value of 3.6 per cent, 'if it had been possible to maintain the relation between energy growth and GDP growth in the previous period' (his table 15b). In his view, the effect of the oil shocks on growth rate is plainly minor.

The post-war Japanese experience demonstrates that demand is crucial, not only for short-term but also for long-term economic growth. In the famous controversy on a decline in the British manufacturing industry in the late nineteenth century, Habakkuk (1962) argues that investment, and therefore also the pace of technological progress, slowed down in Britain because the growth rate of demand fell sharply. This chapter maintains that the Habakkuk thesis applies to the post-war Japanese economic growth as well.

APPENDIX: OTHER EXPLANATIONS FOR THE END OF RAPID ECONOMIC GROWTH

This chapter explained that the end of rapid growth during the period 1955–70 was caused by the domestic structural change of the Japanese economy which had occurred by the end of the 1960s *prior to the first oil embargo in 1973–74*. A popular view, on the other hand, attributes the end of high growth to the first oil shock. There are two slightly different explanations.

Bruno and Sachs (1985) explicitly introduce raw materials and energy into a gross production function. In this analysis, a firm is assumed to maximize the present value of the following net cash flow:

$$\int_0^\infty [Q_t - w_t L_t - \Pi_t R_t - \phi(\alpha_t) K_t] e^{-rt} dt \tag{1}$$

The gross output, including raw materials, Q, is produced according to the well-behaved production function:

$$Q = F(K, L, R) \tag{2}$$

Here K, L and R are capital, labour and raw materials/energy, respectively. The value added in the economy as a whole or GNP, Y is given by:

$$Y = Q - \Pi R \tag{3}$$

Π is the real price of raw materials/energy. W and r in (1) are real wages and the real interest rate. Finally, the rate of capital accumulation, $\alpha = \dot{K}/K$ is subject to the convex adjustment cost $\phi(\alpha)$:

$$\phi(\alpha) = 0, \ \phi'(0) = 1, \ \phi' > 0, \ \phi'' > 0 \tag{4}$$

Given the initial stock of capital K_0 and real factor prices, w, Π, r, the firm chooses the optimal time path of capital accumulation, and variable inputs L and R so as to maximize (1). The necessary conditions for optimality are:

$$\partial F/\partial L = W \tag{5}$$

$$\partial F/\partial R = \Pi \tag{6}$$

and

$$\phi'(\alpha_t) = q_t \tag{7}$$

$$q_t = \int_t^\infty \Delta_s \left[\frac{\partial F}{\partial K} - \theta(\alpha_s) \right] ds \tag{8}$$

where $\Delta_s = \int_t^s [r = \alpha_u] du$. Equations (7) and (8) imply Tobin's q theory of investment.

In this framework, the oil shock can be identified with an unanticipated permanent increase in Π at time 0. Our major concern is to see the effect of an increase in Π on the growth rate, α. Equation (7) shows that α depends on q while (8) shows q depends in turn on the marginal product of capital $\partial F/\partial K$.

The effect of an increase in Π on $\partial F/\partial K$ can be analyzed by the factor price frontier shown in Figure 8.8. A curve in the diagram corresponds to a particular Π. Point A is the equilibrium where both capital and labour are fully employed at the real raw material/energy price Π_0. On the assumption that production function (2) is weakly separable with respect to value added and raw materials/energy:

$$Q = F(V(K, L), R) \tag{9}$$

the factor price frontier homothetically shifts inwards when Π increased. The oil shock is therefore equivalent to a Hicks neutral technical regress. For K and L to be fully employed, both real wages and the marginal product of capital must decrease. A decrease in the marginal product of capital becomes larger if for any reason a decline in real wages is not realized to the extent indicated by point C in the diagram. In any case, a decline in the marginal product of capital caused by an increase in the real raw material/energy price entails a decline in q, and accordingly a decline in the growth rate, α, *as long as the real interest rate did not proportionately decline*. This is the Bruno–Sachs explanation for deceleration of growth in terms of the oil shock.

We note that, in this explanation, the basic reason for growth deceleration lies in the inflexibility of the real interest rate. If the real interest rate declined proportionately with the marginal product of capital,

Real wages

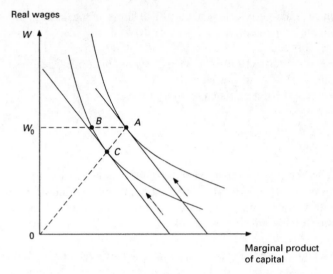

FIGURE 8.8   Factor price frontier

then an increase in the real material–energy price leaves the growth
rate intact. Bruno and Sachs (1985) emphasize the role of demand factors in their empirical analysis of world-wide stagflation in the 1970s,
but demand and supply sides are not fully integrated in their formal
analysis. As explained above, their analytical framework focuses only
on the supply side.

Another approach which focuses on the supply side of the economy
to explain deceleration of growth is Jorgenson (1988). Jorgenson emphasizes the bias of technical change. A technical change is defined
as $\partial F/\partial t$ in the following production function:

$$Q = F(X_1, \ldots, X_n, t) \tag{10}$$

where X_i is the i-th input, and t is time. A 'bias' of technical change
indicates how the technical change thus defined affects factor shares.
Since the factor share of the i-th input, σ_i is equal to:

$$\sigma_i = \partial \log Q / \partial \log X_i \tag{11}$$

in the neo-classical theory, a bias of technical change is defined as:

$$\partial \sigma_i / \partial t \gtreqless 0 \tag{12}$$

A technical change is called neutral, i-th input using, and finally i-th input saving, depending on the sign of $\partial\sigma_i/\partial t$ being zero, positive and negative, respectively. Jorgenson (1988) shows that in the post-war Japanese economy (1969–79), energy-using technical progress was dominant in almost all the industries.

Now energy-using technical progress means:

$$\frac{\partial(\partial\log Q/\partial t)}{\partial\log E} > 0 \qquad (13)$$

where E is the energy input. Therefore, an increase in the real energy price, by way of lowering the level of E makes the rate of technical change decelerate. This is the essence of the Jorgenson argument. The conclusion of his analysis is as follows:

> I have emphasized that there are important sources of the slowdown in Japan associated with the falloff in upgrading of the labor force. However, the most important single factor in the Japanese slowdown is the sharp decline in the rate of technical change. I have now succeeded in linking that decline directly to energy prices through the energy using bias of technical change in Japan.

Jorgenson's analysis rests entirely on traditional growth accounting. His result attributes nearly half of the fall in the rate of economic growth in the 1970s to capital input. And yet, noting that 'after the energy crisis as well as before, the growth rate of capital input was higher than that of output', Jorgenson argues that 'rather than causing the slowdown, the growth of capital after the energy crisis contributed to the continued growth of output at unsustainable levels'. Thus he concludes that 'the decline in the growth rate of capital is not the cause of the slowdown in Japanese economic growth'.

Capital accumulation is certainly not exogenous. But then, what brought about a fall in the rate of economic growth and thereby caused the decline in the growth rate of capital in the first place? Jorgenson's answer is, of course, a fall in the rate of technical change caused by the oil shock. In growth accounting, technical progress is identified as the part of the blossom of economic growth which cannot be explained by contributions of production factors, the so-called 'residual'. To say the least, however, whether the residual measured by the growth accounting method really captures technical progress or not is an open issue.

REFERENCES

Bruno, M. and J. Sachs 1985. *Economics of Worldwide Stagflation*, Cambridge, Mass.: Harvard University Press.

Denison, E. 1967. *Why Growth Rates Differ*, Washington, DC: Brookings Institution.

Gordon, R. A. 1951. 'Cyclical Experience in the Interwar Period: The Investment Boom of the Twenties', in Conference on Business Cycles, New York: *National Bureau of Economic Research*.

Grossman, G. and E. Helpman 1990. 'Comparative Advantage and Long-Run Growth', *American Economic Review*, September.

Habakkuk, H. 1962. *American and British Technology in the Nineteenth Century*, Cambridge University Press.

Hickman, B. 1974. 'What Became of the Building Cycle?', in P. David and M. Reder (eds), *Nations and Households in Economic Growth*, New York: Academic Press.

Horie, Y., S. Naniwa and S. Ishihara. 1987. 'The Changes of Japanese Business Cycles', *Bank of Japan Monetary and Economic Studies*, 5, 3, December.

Iwamoto, Y. and H. Kobayashi 1992. 'Testing for a Unit Root in Japanese GNP', *Japan and the World Economy*, 4–1.

Jorgenson, D. 1988. 'Productivity and Economic Growth in Japan and the United States', *American Economic Review*, May.

Kindleberger, C. 1967. *Europe's Postwar Growth*, Cambridge, Mass.: Harvard University Press.

Kosai, Y. 1986. *The Era of High-Speed Growth*, Tōkyō: University of Tokyo Press.

Lewis, W. Arthur 1954. 'Economic Development with Unlimited Supplies of Labour', *Manchester School of Economic and Social Studies*, 5, May.

Maddison, A. 1987. 'Growth and Slowdown in Advanced Capitalist Economies: Techniques of Quantitative Assessment', *Journal of Economic Literature*, June.

Minami, R. 1970. *The Turning Point of the Japanese Economy* (in Japanese), Tōkyō: Sobunsha.

Ohkawa, K. and H. Rosovsky 1973. *Japanese Economic Growth*, Palo Alto, Calif.: Stanford University Press.

Ono, A. 1972. 'Labor Mobility in Prewar and Postwar Japan' (in Japanese), *Gendai Keziai*, November.

Sen, A. 1965. 'The Money Rate of Interest in the Pure Theory of Growth', in F. Hahn and F. Brechling (eds), *The Theory of Interest Rates*, London: Macmillan.

Shinohara, M. 1961. *Growth and Cycles of the Japanese Economy* (in Japanese), Tōkyō: Sobunsha.

Solow, R. 1956. 'A Contribution to the Theory of Economic Growth', *Quarterly Journal of Economics*, February.

Solow, R. 1957. 'Technical Change and the Aggregate Production Function', *Review of Economics and Statistics*, August.

Umemura, M. 1961. *Wages, Employment and Agriculture* (in Japanese), Tōkyō: Taimeido.

Watanabe, T. and K. Satki 1984. *The Turning Point of the Japanese Petro-*

chemical Industry (in Japanese) Tōkyō: Iwanami.

Yoshikawa, H. 1995. *Macroeconomics and the Japanese Economy*, Oxford: Oxford University Press.

Yoshikawa, H. and F. Ohtake 1987. 'Postwar Business Cycles in Japan: A Quest for the Right Explanation', *Journal of the Japanese and International Economies*, 1, December.

Yoshikawa, H. and F. Ohtake 1989. 'An Analysis of Female Labor Supply, Housing Demand and the Saving Rate in Japan', *European Economic Review*, May.

Yoshikawa, H. and E. Shioji 1990. 'A Macroeconomic Analysis of the Prewar Japanese Economy', in H. Yoshikawa and T. Okazaki (eds), *Economic Theory in Historical Perspectives* (in Japanese) Tōkyō: University of Tōkyō Press.

Part III

The Financial Markets, Monetary Policy and the Policy Institutions

9 The Rise and Fall of the Bubble Economy: An Analysis of the Performance and Structure of the Japanese Stock Market

Fumiko Kon-ya*

Japanese stock prices have shown quite dramatic fluctuations since the early 1980s. After reaching an all time high of 38 915 yen in December 1989, the Nikkei Stock Price Average plummeted to 14 309 yen in August 1992. In the seven years up to December 1989 there was a 5.7–fold rise, and in the following two or three years the stock price dropped sharply, to only 37 per cent of the peak period. The Japanese stock market, which recovered relatively quickly after the world-wide crash of stock prices on Black Monday in October 1987, hovered around 16 000–21 000 yen during 1992–3 and seems now to be in a long-term slump when compared with previous levels during the boom period of the late 1980s.

The large swing of the stock price average, one of the most commonly-watched and important financial variables, has been the result of various domestic and international market forces, as well as an outcome of public policies. The effects of the fluctuation in financial markets and the Japanese economy have been analyzed enormously in many ways. This chapter intends to review the developments, the reasons, and the various effects of the Japanese stock price fluctuations

* An earlier version of this chapter was presented as a paper at the First Conference on the Contemporary Japanese Economy organized by the Centre for Japanese Economic Studies, Macquarie University, Sydney on 25–26 March 1993. The author greatly appreciates the useful advice given by Professor Mitsuaki Okabe in completing this paper. The author also thanks Professors Bill Norton, Richard Tress and Roger Tuckwell and the participants at the Conference for their helpful comments.

since the late 1980s and tries to analyze how the structure of the Japanese stock market has been responsible in substantial part for the wide swing of the market.

Section 9.1 reviews the increase in stock prices in the late 1980s and discusses the reasons. Section 9.2 deals with the effects of the stock market crash of 1990. Section 9.3 analyzes the structure and workings of the Japanese stock market. Section 9.4 examines a number of ways to improve the structure and the functioning of the market. Section 9.5 is the conclusion.

9.1   THE INCREASE IN STOCK PRICES IN THE LATE 1980S

9.1.1   The bubble

In 1992, Japanese stock prices experienced the heaviest fall in post-Second World War history. After reaching an all-time high of 38 915 yen in December 1989, the Nikkei Average plunged to 14 309 yen in August 1992, representing a drop of 63.2 per cent, or the price level reaching only 37 per cent of its peak level (see Figure 9.1). This 63.2 per cent drop was even more dramatic than the drop of 44.2 per cent registered during the Securities Depression of 1972, which had hitherto been considered as the most serious fall of Japan's stock prices since the Second World War.

In Japan, as well as in other industrialized nations, this dramatic crash of the index was identified as the bursting of the 'bubble' of Japan's booming economy. Many observers in Japan, as well as observers around the world, saw the rapid rise in Japanese stock prices up to 1989 as an abnormality. The rapid rise in stock prices was thought to be incongruous with both the history of the Japanese stock market and the condition of other markets around the world. In other words, it was thought to be a 'bubble'. However, this hypothesis does not seem to have been tested conclusively. If we say that a dramatic rise in stock prices is a 'bubble' which is not related to fundamentals, then it is very difficult to assess which part of, or to what extent, any rise in stock prices constitutes a 'bubble'. There is a basic difficulty in determining stock prices which truly reflect those determined by fundamental factors.

However, it seems to be incorrect to say that this rapid increase in Japanese stock prices was abnormal. Japanese stock prices rose over a period of nearly seven years, growing 5.7-fold in the period from autumn

Level of Nikkei Average
(in thousand yen)

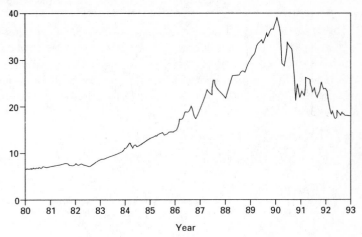

FIGURE 9.1   Monthly Nikkei Stock Average, January 1980 to
February 1993

1982 to the end of 1989. This was in fact the fourth time that such an increase in stock prices had taken place in the Japanese stock market. There is an established pattern whereby stock prices grew five- or six-fold over a period of seven or eight years, then lost around 40 per cent of that value (see Figure 9.2). If we compare the growth of stock prices internationally, we can see that in the 1980s, countries such as the UK and France experienced equal, or even larger, increases in stock price levels than did Japan. A similar phenomenon can be seen in other Asian nations as well. Further, it is misleading if, in making international comparisons between the stock index and those of other nations, too much emphasis is placed on comparisons with the Dow Jones Index. The growth in stock prices in the USA over the aforementioned period was substantially lower than that seen in many other nations, including Japan. If we compare the growth of Japan's stock index with those of other nations, excluding the USA, then we can see that it was not unreasonably high.

Some fundamentals that determine stock prices are: levels and rates of growth of corporate profits; interest rates; and the risk premiums required by investors. However, it is very important to note that these factors are not observable. The fundamental value of stock prices is not determined by the observable past value of both growth and interest

log (Level of
Nikkei Average)

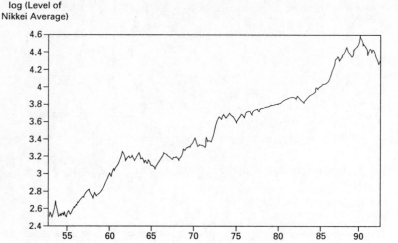

FIGURE 9.2　Monthly Nikkei Stock Average, January 1953 to
February 1993

rates, but rather by the investors' expectations of the future value of
these factors, which cannot be observed. The amount of risk premiums
required by investors cannot be observed either. As we cannot know
what investors' expectations for the future are, it is impossible to calculate accurately the fundamental value of stocks. Interest rates and
risk premiums, which form the basis for calculating the discount rate
for future corporate profits, are determined by the market. Even though
these interest rates and risk premiums are obtainable, the discount rate
is indispensable in order to estimate a stock price. But the discount
rate is also determined by the market. Only if the market, which determines the rate, is rational, is it possible to determine whether rising
stock prices are leading to a 'bubble' or not. At the same time, the
market determines the stock price. So, it is contradictory to say that
the market, which determines the rate, is rational, while the same market,
which determines the stock price, is not rational.

There is no rigorous test for determining which stock prices are
determined rationally on fundamentals, and which are not. A rough
regression analysis suggests that the rising stock prices in the latter
half of the 1980s were possibly a 'bubble'. However, a large part of
the growth of the rising stock prices can be explained by both the low
interest rates and GNP of that period:

$$SP = + 3.75 - 0.196 \, LI + 1.22 \, GNP + 0.013 \, PI$$
$$\quad (15.52) \quad (4.06) \quad\quad (8.46) \quad\quad (0.84)$$

$$R^2 = 0.917$$

where SP = log stock price
$\quad\quad LI$ = long-term interest rate
$\quad\quad GNP$ = log GNP
$\quad\quad PI$ = log price index (GNP deflator)

9.1.2 Interest rates and corporate growth

An important factor in the rapid rise in Japanese stock prices was the existence of prevailing low interest rates. In August 1980, the Central Bank reduced its official discount rate from 9 per cent to 8.25 per cent. After that period, it reduced the rates ten times over seven consecutive years. By February 1987, following a further nine reductions, the discount rate stood at 2.5 per cent (see Figure 9.3). As a result of these reductions, interest rates hit their lowest point in Japanese history. At that time, Japanese interest rates were also the lowest worldwide. Interest rates remained low until the discount rate was increased, for the first time in over nine years, in May 1989. This was the first time in history that interest rates had remained so low for such a long

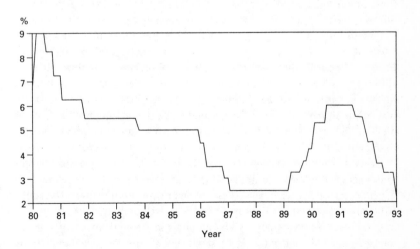

FIGURE 9.3 Official discount rate, January 1980 to February 1993

period of time. The long-term rise in stock prices can be directly linked to this long period of prevailing low interest rates.

After the crash of Black Monday, in October 1987, American and European stock markets entered a long-term price slump. In Japan, however, stock prices recovered much more quickly, and continued to progress on these early gains. The principal reasons for this growth were prevailing low interest rates, and the anticipation of an expected high rate of growth for Japanese companies. Japanese companies had entered a prosperous period of record duration which can be attributed to changes in the industrial structure of Japan's economy, such as a shift in emphasis towards the service and high-technology sectors. Thus, corporate restructuring coupled with an abundant money supply fuelled corporate growth.

9.1.3 Reduced risk premiums

The reduction of risk premiums required by investors was another important factor that drove up stock prices in the 1980s.

In the 1980s, substantial increases in pension funds heated up competition among financial institutions engaged in investment management activities. Deregulation caused changes in the so-called 'peer group' behaviour among Japanese financial institutions. In the investment sphere, the introduction of free market principles, brought about by deregulation, increased competition among institutional investors. Along with the enlarged framework for equity investment, the new financial instruments increased the degree of freedom involved in fund management. Two examples of specified money trusts, called *Tokkin* and *Fantora*, reduced the costs of realizing capital gains, made it easier to show them in financial statements, and thus contributed to stimulating further equity investment. Before the introduction of those trusts, it was difficult for life insurance companies, for example, to disclose their profits from portfolio appreciation. As a result, portfolio managers in Japan were seldom evaluated in terms of performance.

However, with increased levels of financial disclosure, mutual funds, insurance companies and financial institutions began to publish records of their performance, intensifying competition among fund managers. It became impossible to compete using fixed-interest, risk-free investments alone. Fund managers abandoned the strategy of passive holdings of securities and moved into more active fund management, trying to realize more profits from rising stock prices. This shift in strategy towards increased investment in the stock market by fund managers

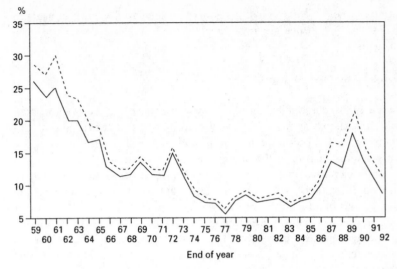

FIGURE 9.4   The ratio of stock holding to the total financial assets of household

greatly increased the overall amount of money invested by financial institutions in stocks overall.

In addition, individual investors became more willing to take higher risks for higher return potential, and increased their holdings of high-risk assets, such as stocks (see Figure 9.4). Net financial assets held by households exceeded 13 billion yen. When wealth holdings are low, investors tend to choose low-risk investment opportunities. However, as savings increase, risk tolerance grows, and investors pursue higher returns on their investments. This tendency explains why wealth accumulation is accompanied by an increased percentage of total savings invested in stocks. In Japan, the percentage of the population approaching old age is increasing gradually. So households, with their increased saving, tend to seek high-return investments in order to ensure their future financial security. Therefore, we can predict a long-term trend towards increased investment in the stock market. The overall decrease in the percentage of equity held by individual investors in the Japanese stock market has been viewed as a serious problem. In contrast, the percentage of stock market investment within the investment portfolios of individuals had doubled by the 1980s. The reason why the percentage of stocks held by individual investors has decreased overall is because the stock market has grown too rapidly for individual investors to keep up with it.

9.1.4   The cost of capital

In the 1980s, corporations increased their investments in the stock market, which is known as *zaitech*. However, it seemed that the trend did continue for a long-term period. It is undeniable that *zaitech* played a very important role in the sharp rise of stock prices in the 1980s.

With increases in the level of stock prices, many firms started to use equity finance very actively by issuing new stocks, convertible bonds, and bonds with warrants. Growth was observed in the number of corporations using raised funds for *zaitech*, and a cycle developed whereby investment demand pushed up stock prices. Higher stock prices subsequently facilitated fund-raising by corporations. However, this situation, whereby non-financial corporations invest in securities through raised funds instead of via surplus ones, can only arise in an inefficient financial market. Financial institutions, who specialize in managing financial assets, were restricted by many regulations in their financial activities. On the other hand, there was no restriction in corporations' financial activities: the corporations had opportunites to participate in *zaitech*. Thus in the 1980s, either financial institutions failed to carry out their role to the fullest, because of inadequate legislation, or corporations ignored the high costs involved in participating in *zaitech*. Perhaps both these factors played a role in explaining the spread of *zaitech* among corporations.

It is true that financial institutions are subject to many regulations, while other business corporations enjoy a substantial degree of freedom in their financial activities. Within this context, *zaitech* activities can be very lucrative ventures for business corporations. However, the success of *zaitech* activities cannot be explained only by the regulation of financial institutions. If this were so, one would have expected *zaitech* abilities to diminish rather than increase with the process of deregulation during the 1980s.

If we accept the argument that corporations do not regard stockholders' required rates of return as the cost of capital, the aforementioned factors explain why *zaitech* spread so widely. Facts lead us to the opinion that corporations did not fully acknowledge all the aspects of the cost of capital. An example of this can be seen in managerial decisions regarding the raising of capital. Their main consideration was in the nominal cost of equity financing, such as interest paid on convertible bonds or warranted bonds, instead of the cost of capital. Corporate managers are often quoted as saying that the financial costs of convertible bonds are very low. The low rates can be attributed to investors' high expectations for future stock appreciation. In the boom of latter half of the 1980s, investors expected the high rise of stock prices which made them rush to purchase the newly issued stocks, giving free hand to the corporate management to do the fund-raising, and utilize the raised money for *zaitech* (due to the lack of restrictions on the corporate management by the shareholders, the raised money was often used for the purchase of the financial assets, which is called *zaitech*, or financial technology).

9.2 THE CRASH IN 1990–93

9.2.1 The stock market crash and asset deflation

Worried about overheating of the market and inflation, the Bank of Japan (BOJ) adopted the policy of interest-rate raising. The BOJ raised the official discount rate five times in rapid succession between May 1989 and August 1990. Within fifteen months the rate went up from 2.5 per cent to 6.2 per cent, representing an increase of 140 per cent. In March 1991, the economy hit a recession. The real economic growth rate, expected to reach 4 per cent or 5 per cent in 1992, in fact fell to 1 per cent, and concern for the state of the Japanese economy intensified. Increasing interest rates rapidly deflated the price of land and other assets, as well as stocks. At this point, no counter-measures were taken, so land and stock prices fell even further. As a result, financial institutions faced the possibility of a very serious crisis.

One factor behind the crisis involved the Bank for International Settlements' (BIS) regulations requiring banks to increase their capital to an assets ratio of 8 per cent by the end of March 1993. In Japan, banks are allowed to hold stocks. However, BIS regulations allow banks to add only 45 per cent of unrealized capital gains from stocks to the total valuation of their equity capital. This is why the drop of stock prices had a double effect on the banks' asset and risk management. The drop in stock prices not only increased risks for financial institutions, as it lowered their capital ratio, it also decreased their capital, thereby restricting credit expansion. The lack of money subsequently intensified the recession, by pushing stock prices even lower in a vicious spiral.

Opinions concerning the influence of asset deflation on the rest of the economy are divided. One point of view holds that while asset deflation delays economic recovery, it does not contribute directly towards deepening a recession beyond the normal business cycle. On the other hand, some believe that asset deflation contributes directly to financial instability, and therefore deepens the effects of a recession. Those who support the former point of view must now accept the fact that the effect of asset deflation on the real economy is somewhat greater than previously believed. In spring 1993, the fall in individual consumption was the largest on record. There remains a great deal of concern that the real economy will itself enter a vicious circle, when companies adjust employment downward to compensate for decreased consumption. Decreased employment levels will cause further reductions in personal consumption, worsening the overall condition of the economy.

9.2.2   Growth of the 'money economy'

One major change in Japan's economy that must not be overlooked is the increased weight of its 'money economy'. In other words, the ratio of 'stock' (that is, assets) to 'flow' (that is, income or products) has increased within the economy, and the role and influence of the assets market in the economy has increased. In the ten-year period up to 1991, nominal GNP grew 1.8 times, while the value of financial assets, excluding equity stock, grew 2.3 times, and the value of listed stocks grew 4.1 times (see Figures 9.5 and 9.6). Only a short time ago, 'stock economy' was the name given to this trend. However, after the bursting of the 'bubble', both economic authorities and the public seem to have forgotten about this basic change within the Japanese economy. Instead, they focus solely on the 'bubble'. It is even possible to say that stock accumulation brought about by asset inflation, or the so-called 'bubble', was an 'illusion' with no relevance to the real economy.

However, as a 'stock economy' with a large weighting of assets, the wealth effect, caused by changes in asset prices, has had a strong impact. In Japan, after significant growth of the assets market in the second half of the 1980s, low interest rates pushed up asset prices and created enormous capital gains on assets. For the four-year period 1986–9 inclusive, capital gains from land and equity stocks exceeded, or were on a level close to annual GNP. However, since 1990, capital loss from land and stocks has approached the 100 trillion yen mark (see Table 9.1). The figures are not yet available for 1992, but even larger capital losses are expected to be recorded.

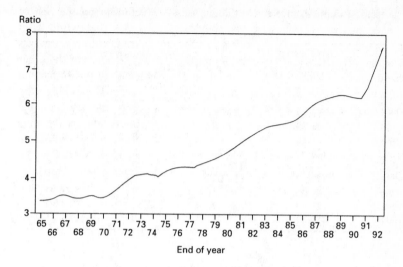

FIGURE 9.5   Ratio of total financial assets excluding stocks to GNP at current prices

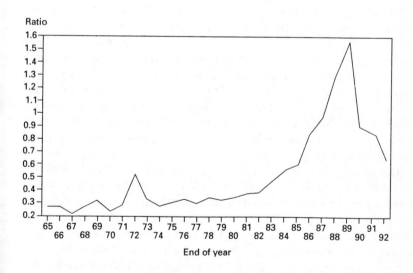

FIGURE 9.6   Ratio of total stock market value to GNP at current prices

TABLE 9.1   GNP, capital gain (loss) on land and stock
(¥ trillions)

Year	GNP	Capital gains (losses)		
		Land	Stock	Land & Stock
1982	270.67	57.83	−7.03	50.80
1983	282.08	34.99	30.18	65.17
1984	301.05	37.69	37.07	74.76
1985	321.56	76.22	33.78	110.00
1986	335.84	255.26	121.38	376.64
1987	350.48	416.48	76.05	492.53
1988	373.73	168.03	177.49	345.52
1989	399.05	315.81	193.59	509.40
1990	428.67	186.97	−306.57	−119.60
1991	456.11	−111.44	−7.00	−118.44

In addition to the wealth effect, changes in asset prices affect the real economy in various ways. The crash of stock and land prices made not only banks, but also other financial institutions, corporations and householders much more reticent about new investment.

Expansion of the money economy is not a phenomenon limited to Japan. Economic data from all countries supports the conclusion that with overall growth in the economy, the weight of the money economy increases. An expanded money economy contributes to the instability and volatility of the overall economy for two reasons. First, very high liquidity of financial markets leads to a greater degree of speculation, and second, psychological factors play a greater role. In any asset market where trading is based on the anticipation of future profits, there is a great deal of scope for speculation and other activities based on psychological factors.

Incidentally, the size of Japan's equity market also increased as its importance to the Japanese economy grew. Before the 1970s, indirect finance through financial intermediaries was the most important means of corporate finance. In Japan, the stock market was given only a limited role as a means of finance, and was not given nearly as significant a role for investment opportunity as it is today. Since the 1980s, the role of the stock market, in terms of raising and managing funds, has expanded at a consistently high rate. This rapid growth was based on the increase in stock prices as well as the increased importance of the stock market to Japan's economy. The stock market in Japan now carries as much significance within the economy as in other nations.

9.2.3 The increased instability of stock prices

Figure 9.7 plots the frequency of the drastic rise and drop in the Nikkei Average for the 44-year period following the Second World War. We can see clearly when abnormal fluctuations occurred. Out of 12 600 trading days, there were 200 days (less than 1.6 per cent of the total) with large price fluctuations. As time passed, economic growth stabilized and instances of abnormal price fluctuations decreased. However, from about the time of Black Monday in October 1987, the frequency of abnormal price fluctuations increased rapidly. This increase in the frequency of price swings illustrates the instability of stock prices at this time. Even though the stock market became efficient due to its innovations in the latter half of the 1980s, stock prices became more unstable. This is a very important fact to remember. In the three years after 1990, stock prices showed the greatest amount of volatility in the entire post-war history of the Japanese stock market. In this three-year period, the Nikkei recorded abnormal price fluctuations on 44 per cent of the total number of days.

Since 1985, the rest of Japan's economy has been stable. We cannot see any extraordinary fluctuations or volatility. We can even say that the world economy, as well as Japan's, experienced a degree of stability never before achieved. Therefore, the increased volatility in stock prices was not the result of fundamental changes in the economy at large. There must be some other explanations behind the rise in volatility in Japan's stock market.

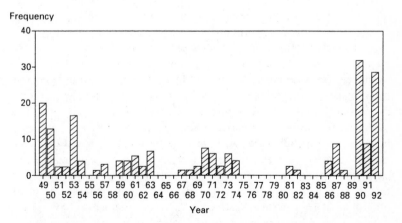

FIGURE 9.7   The frequency of abnormal change of stock prices

9.2.4   The suspension of new stock issues

As stock prices became unstable in the secondary market, authorities were so concerned that they actually ordered private and public corporations to suspend new stock issues – a very serious situation considering the importance of the role played by the stock market in Japan's economy. The sharp drop in the Nikkei average affected not only the credit expansion of banks, but also resulted in new issues being suspended as authorities worried that excessive supply would depress prices further. New issues through public offerings by both listed companies and companies wishing to go public were halted from April 1990 up until April 1994. Due to the fall in stock prices, Japanese companies have been limited in their financing through both banks and capital markets as well.

9.3   CHANGES IN THE STRUCTURE OF THE STOCK MARKET

9.3.1   Institutionalization

Why did the stock market gravitate towards further instability, instead of stabilizing? The stock market environment has undergone many rapid changes since the latter half of the 1980s. In particular, Japanese institutional investment has been transformed during this period (see Figure 9.8 and 9.9).

Initially, an excessive money supply arising from lowered interest rates, coupled with the deregulation of the financial market, heated up competition between institutional investors, increasing the weight of high-risk, high-return equity investments within their portfolios. This competition was further fuelled by improved disclosure of their performance. Because annual reports published by these firms contained performance evaluations, they promoted trading for short-term profits. Given the tendency of stock prices to fluctuate in the short term, coupled with the pressure to realize profits annually, many fund managers began to find it difficult to wait for long-term profits based on fundamental factors. As a result, there emerged a tendency to make short-term investments in an attempt to secure profits from the short-term fluctuations in stock prices. Although there is no guarantee as to the reliability of short-term investments, investors seemed to have gained too much confidence in this type of strategy in the low-interest period after the Plaza Accord of 1985. The introduction of new financial in-

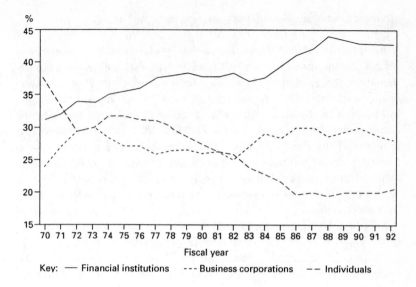

FIGURE 9.8   Share ownership by type of investors, by market value

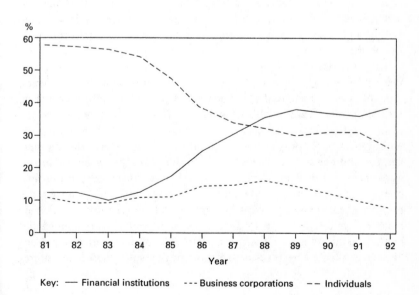

FIGURE 9.9   Percentage shares of stock trading

struments, such as *Tokkin* and *Fantora* increased incentives for making investments orientated towards high, and short-term gains.

In order to realize short-term capital gains, greater emphasis was placed on monitoring the short-term movements of prices than reliance on the fundamentals of long-term investment. Thus investors began to speculate how the other investors in the market would interpret information in the short run, rather than interpreting the fundamental implications; that is, how it would really affect the economy in the long run. Thus the 'psychology of the market' became the focus of attention, as the winner in the market is one who can read this 'psychology' more quickly and more exactly, and act on it before all others. As a result the market became ruled by investor psychology rather than fundamentals.

So while the market could have become more liquid, more flexible, and with lower costs, it became more vulnerable to the influence of psychological factors and speculative activities. The introduction of computer-based trading systems and the futures and options markets made it technically possible to respond very quickly to new information. This also contributed to the growth in short-term transactions. Originally, deregulation and technological innovations were expected to add reasonable stability and rationality to the price formation mechanism. However, these innovations increased the number of speculative investment transactions targeting profits through short-term price fluctuations.

The rapid rise towards an information-based society was another factor that promoted this upward trend in the psychological market. Many thought that the increased speed and volume of information made price formation more reasonable. However, this is not really true. On the contrary, the market has become dominated by psychological factors, with traders vacillating between optimism and pessimism for the market, as different pieces of news come to light. In such an environment, stock index manipulation has become possible. Although some see today's market as impossible to manipulate, with no one entity having the necessary vast funds, if we take into consideration the technique of market psychology, it no longer seems impossible to manipulate the market in this manner. It seems that the degree to which the present market is affected by investor psychology is greater than ever before.

9.3.2 Market psychology and 'peer group' actions among institutional investors

It is ironic that as the market develops and becomes more complex, it becomes more susceptible to irrational forces such as market psychology. 'Black Monday' illustrated the trap of the technological revolution in financial markets, and the psychology of the market. It is difficult to say whether the Japanese market has experienced such a clear lesson until now. It can be said that because of the lack of safeguards in the market place, the stock market has failed to function as efficiently as it is supposed since 1990. Of course, market innovations must be promoted, but it must be fully understood that market innovations are double-edged swords, otherwise the possibility of collapse would become much greater.

The instability of stock prices is a result of the increase in the role of psychological and speculative factors in investment decisions. In other words, if we pull up the anchor of fundamentals in the market, the danger of dramatic price fluctuations increases greatly. Attention should be paid to the fact that during the Middle East crisis of 1990, Japanese stock prices plummeted to far lower levels than those of other nations. The Japanese economy is greatly dependent on oil imported from the Gulf countries and as a result, it holds substantial oil reserves in case of shortages. Additionally, after the oil crisis in 1973, Japanese industry made an effort to reduce oil consumption, so Japan's dependency on oil is now the lowest among the industrial countries. The Japanese economy was running at a higher level of prosperity than any other nation during that period; therefore it seems that the huge drop in Japanese stock prices was based largely on psychological factors.

Psychological factors can have a great impact on the market when the majority of market participants share the same psychological perceptions. People react similarly to similar information when they share similar opinions. From this point, a group market psychology develops and the market becomes very responsive to this group psychology. Once this psychology develops, it has an amplified effect on the fluctuation of stock prices. The market tends to be very one-sided, being either a buyers' or a sellers' market. If the existing trend in the market is so strong, any action taken to the contrary creates only losers. Even if fundamentals lead one market participant to move in a different direction, using fundamentals in such a situation will not bring profits. Only when one determines in which direction psychological factors will move the market, and moves in that direction first, is there an opportunity to make profits.

Not only psychological factors are influential in moving investors to act in the same way. Regulations that restrict investors' actions also, technically, force investors to act in similar ways. One example of this is the system of reporting performance results at the end of each period. In order to secure a certain level of performance by the end of each reporting period, institutional investors sell securities to realize profits or reduce possible risks. Because all institutional investors must publish their results by the same date, a situation in which they are all buying or all selling at the same time is very likely to arise.

In addition to the technical reasons given above, there is the notion of a 'peer group consciousness' in Japanese society that puts an emphasis on 'being together with others'. For example, a climate exists whereby losses are tolerated in light of the fact that if everybody suffered losses at that time, they would not be seen as very serious. Fund managers themselves are 'salarymen' and do not personally bear risks in relation to their clients, nor do they run much risk within their firms. Therefore institutional investors act in accordance with the actions of other institutional investors because of a structural factor, which has its roots in the basic Japanese business culture. Once decisions are influenced by such psychological factors, and once the market becomes affected by decisions influenced by psychological factors, the overall effect of this distortion is amplified. The combined actions of multiple actors moving in the same direction amplifies the effect of the original fluctuation that motivated them to act in the first place. In a market controlled by psychological factors it is very difficult to make investment decisions that contradict the psychology of the market. Price formation in such a market becomes very unstable, as small decreases in price levels result in market depressions, and slight increases in price levels result in market rallies.

In this sense, what is important is the fact that the character of the stock market today has changed. It is no longer a textbookish market of individual buyers and sellers with no power to influence prices, but rather a market dominated by a few large institutional investors with the power to influence greatly each other's decisions. Institutionalization is a sign of the times that has increased the market's vulnerability to the influence of psychological factors. Accordingly one of the most important tasks for the future is to introduce some measures that control market psychology and thus make it possible to maintain a reasonable price formation mechanism with fundamentals as its key determinant.

9.4 SEVERAL PROPOSALS FOR THE NORMALIZATION OF THE PRICE FORMATION MECHANISM

If market psychology and the narrow regulation of investment activities are said to be the main factors behind the instability of price formation, then lessening market psychology distortions and making investors' decisions more reasonable are the basic measures necessary for correcting the price formation mechanism.

9.4.1 Public disclosure of market information

If stock prices tend to be influenced by investor psychology, then the most important step to take in order to lessen this effect is to provide ample information to investors.

Insufficient information is already fully recognized as one of the main reasons why arbitrage trading had a negative impact on the market. And counter-measures have already been taken. There were also rumours that trading concentrating on the highest valued issues making up the Nikkei greatly influenced investor psychology. If there were public disclosure of such transactions, market participants could surmise the real source of price distortions; at least, distress would not arise without proper cause. There have been very urgent calls for this kind of disclosure. Lately there have been some efforts to implement wider disclosure, though these have been only partially successful. However, there is a point of view that full public disclosure of trading information may lead to a 'beauty contest' effect on stock prices: investors would not take into account fundamentals, but just speculate on the way their fellow investors would act in the market. They also point out that there are many countries that do not disclose such information. However, because there are differences in pricing mechanisms and market making among stock markets, the fact that other stock markets do not fully disclose trading information cannot be used as an argument for Japan to also restrict access to trading information. Clearly, any information affecting stock trading being accessible to only a few market participants is not desirable. If we ever reach the stage where all trading is computer-based, without market participants perusing the stock market display board, then perhaps at such a time it would be worthwhile to reopen the debate as to whether or not there should be full public disclosure.

We have already learnt that increased speed and volume of information do not automatically lead to increased efficiency in stock price formation. However, maldistribution of information is a somewhat larger problem. Of course, the disclosure of information that can disrupt the market unnecessarily must be avoided. However, the possibility that maldistribution of information can cause disorder must be considered strongly. The maldistribution of information is not only unfair in itself, but it can also cause extreme bias, and lead to back-door manipulations.

9.4.2 Increasing the degree of freedom among institutional investors

Institutional investors enjoy far greater privileges over individual investors because they can collect and analyze larger amounts of information and diversify risk more widely, because of the large amounts of money they control, as well as having more efficient fund management. However, we cannot say that Japanese institutional investors were ever able to make full use of their advantages in the past. It was only when market liberalization and deregulation spurred greater competition among institutional investors that they made use of their advantages of scale and specialization. The result of their success in utilizing these advantages promoted further institutionalization of financial markets.

Having said this, some steps must be taken to guard against the widespread uniformity of action among institutional investors. There are problems in the way reforms of the Japanese financial market have been instituted in the past. Those reforms promoted 'peer group' uniform action among institutional investors. Market reforms broadened the actions of institutional investors within the framework defined by each institutional level; large institutions, medium-sized institutions, and smaller institutions: each acted within the context of similar-sized institutions. When looking for new investment opportunities, financial institutions were not creative beyond the scope of these limitations. Thus these reforms did not add up to increased business opportunities. If they had, they might have led to more long-term-investment-orientated strategies, influenced by increased competition.

As investment performances of institutional investors are assessed in the short-term period, they are short-term trading in the stock market for long-term investment. The deregulation of investment activities for financial institutions is necessary. At the same time, there is a need for a certain level of stability to insure that funds originally intended for long-term investment are not diverted to efforts for fast, short-term profit. We must examine the possibility that regulations which reduce investor freedom lead to increased risks. If institutional investors were freed from such narrow regulations, and started to act more independently of others on the same level, this phenomenon of 'peer group' actions would dissolve naturally. If we could create an environment in which investor ingenuity is necessary not only to make profits, but just to survive, then the actions of each individual institutional investor would naturally come into conflict with the present practice of 'peer group' actions. Freedom and self-responsibility come together; we cannot expect investors to act reasonably without giving them freedom. If we give them freedom, they will naturally develop a sense of self-responsibility.

Again, it should be stressed that there is a need to deepen the understanding that risk management must be based on a long-term investment strategy. Wider disclosure, a policy agenda already mentioned above, is one means of enlightening investors.

9.4.3 Counter-measures against stock index trading and other block trading

The process of institutionalization changed the basic nature of stock trading. Instead of many small investors determining prices through competition, the situation has changed to one in which a few large institutional investors play an increasingly important role in the formation of stock prices. We cannot say that this is necessarily inefficient, however it is clear that it has contributed to the problem of speculation based on the 'beauty contest' effect, as well as the problem of market liquidity caused by block trading. That is, a large trading lot has a strong influence on the stock market. Therefore, there is a need for an open discussion about the problems of, and possible counter-measures against, the price formation mechanism and manipulation of it by a few very large institutional investors. Trading such large volumes of shares and exceeding the liquidity of the market can too easily enlarge market fluctuations. Such transactions may have the effect of either initiating instability in the market or being a factor contributing to such instability. Thus there is a need to discuss how we can soften the effects of such large transactions on the volatility of the price. In addition, there is the need to secure the interests of smaller demands; to ensure that they do not suffer unjustifiable losses.

We can think in terms of two possible ways to counter the effects of large-volume trading. First, we can introduce a 'market maker' system into high-volume trading. Second, we could attempt a *de facto* separation of high-volume and low-volume trading. One of the purposes underlying the introduction of futures and options trading was to create a new vehicle for high-volume trading. Nevertheless, it has become clear that improvements are needed in the futures and options markets. There are several problems, including the composition of shares making up the stock price index, and the gaps that have emerged in brokerage commissions. If we can solve these problems, price formation in the futures market may stabilize, becoming more fair and reasonable over time.

One possible measure might be the introduction of 'basket purchases' on the spot market. The importance of the role of the futures market in Japan lies mainly in the practice of trading 'baskets' of shares. The spot trading of 'baskets' of shares, with no expiration dates, may eliminate some of the problems related to futures trading, which has been affected by the existence of expiration dates.

We can also avoid market disruptions caused by arbitrage nullification occurring at the end of expiration periods. Many market observers believe that the existence of uncovered arbitrage positions is also a factor contributing to market disruption. Contrarily, some point it out as a false belief because if the market mechanism functioned properly, selling shares in order to close open positions (simply a technical operation) would bring about a movement in the opposite direction to buy these shares. Therefore, stock prices would not suffer any loss in value as a result of arbitrage nullification. However, in the real world, the market mechanism does not function as efficiently as in theory. So it is possible that uncovered arbitrage positions could be a factor in influencing investor psychology negatively, thus producing a market downturn. Small drops in the market can cause alarm among investors, leading to a further depression of stock prices. Many market experts point out that spot 'basket' purchases with no expiration dates do not resolve the problems arising from having different prices for the same product. Basically, this situation can be solved without arbitrage trading. In so-called 'arbitrage transactions', pure arbitrage, in the strictest sense of the word, cannot solve the problem of the existence of more than one price for a single product. This situation can be solved simply through buyers gathering at levels where the price is low, and sellers gathering at levels where the price is high.

As long as the institutionalization develops, the institutional investors still continue index trading such as stock price index futures. We see this trend will be continuous in the future. Investors who select index investment do not usually evaluate corporate value. Strategy of index investment can be effective only on the condition that others evaluate corporate value. Actions of investors who pick up under-valued companies in order to make profits will reflect the correct corporate value on stock prices. Index investment by institutional investors who are the major investors leading stock market will lead to malfunctioning of allocation of funds.

However, the comprehensive solution depends on efficient functioning of market mechanism for institutional investors. If deregulation of finance and free competition occur in the Japanese market, the institutional investors will lose their competitiveness against foreign money managers, unless they make a better performance than before. Index investment is a passive strategy which may not lose against market but will never win. Thus introduction of market mechanism is inevitable in order to reduce peer activities, and to promote the stock market's function of fund allocation while prices reflect corporates' fundamentals.

9.4.4 The problem of individual investors

It is important to create a market in which individual investors may participate easily. There are two reasons to encourage the participation of individual investors.

First, participation by many investors in the market is a necessary element in the stable formation of prices. Because there are investors with varying preferences and conditions for choosing stocks, there are many possible ways to respond to the problem of their participation in the market. The fact that the role of institutional investors has grown is important to recognize, but it is also important to insure the continued participation of smaller investors. Deregulation has rationalized the actions of institutional investors to some degree. However, they are not yet free from the effects of 'peer group' actions. As long as institutional investors are merely fiduciaries, who obtain their invest funds from clients, they will be subject to regulations to protect those clients. These regulations prevent institutional investors from acting freely. As long as institutions exist, they will be regulated by the existence of defined performance periods and performance evaluations that naturally affect their activities. Therefore, even under further deregulation of the market, the important role played by individual investors will by no means disappear.

Second, the increased ratio of financial asset holdings by individuals has increased the desire on the part of the individual investors themselves to participate more fully in the market. Many people see shrinking participation levels of individual investors (see Figure 9.8 on p. 249) as a major problem. The main reason for this decline is that the equity market as a whole grew much faster than did individual equity holdings. However, the share of equity holdings in individual portfolios, in fact, grew. If we consider the development of Japan's stock market, and also the 'greying' or 'ageing' of Japan, we must come to the conclusion that the need for individual shareholding is likely to increase. In spite of the improved efficiency of investment management, and the improved portfolio performance of institutional investors, the need for individuals to invest in stocks independently of investment funds will not disappear. Given the increased financial asset accumulation by individuals, the need for individual participation in the stock market can only grow.

In this case, it will become very important to create an environment in which all investors can stand on an equal footing. Creating such an environment is an important policy goal for the sake of individual investors. Such an environment must guarantee the survival of individual investors as a group who are at a disadvantage in terms of information resources, and also the volume of funds available for investing – they should not suffer unjustifiable losses. Such an environment will contribute to a more stable price formation mechanism. Because individual investors possess comparatively small amounts of funds for investment, transaction costs are relatively high for them. Stock scandals have increased the level of distrust and uncertainty among individual investors. Therefore, if we do promote further participation of individuals in the stock market, we must sweep away the reasons for these feelings of distrust and uncertainty. Such feelings underlying the market will only serve to damage the prospects for broader participation in the stock market. It is important to convince potential investors that Japan's stock market is a safe place for investment. In order to accomplish this, it is essential to create a system in which individual investors who are at a disadvantage, do not lose out even more. Of course, there will be costs involved in developing and instituting such a system. However, since the benefits of such a system: namely, a stable price formation mechanism as well as increased fairness in the market, are so great, these costs are relatively small. Above all, however, we must hold the individual investors themselves responsible for their own investment decisions. For this to happen, individual investors must be more broadly educated.

In order to promote further participation of individual investors in the market, we should promote greater disclosure and design new financial instruments that meet the needs of individuals. For example, one new financial instrument which may promote greater participation would combine stocks and options. One measure we might take to reduce risks for individual investors might be to make it possible for individuals to participate in index-based trading. Recalling the idea of selling 'baskets' of stocks on the spot market, we could assemble 'baskets' small enough for purchase by individuals. Though some may point out that individuals are already able to participate in index-based trading through mutual funds created specifically for this purpose, such mutual funds do not provide an avenue for direct participation, which is necessary to enable individual investors to have some effect on price formation. Broader opportunities for participation make price formation more stable and equitable for all market participants, while at the same time meeting the needs of those individual investors who want to participate directly in the market.

9.5 CONCLUSIONS

Following the upsurge of the early 1980s, the Japanese stock price recorded a dramatic crash at the end of that decade. This is commonly identified as the bursting of the 'bubble' in Japan's overheating economy. However, the increase in stock prices up to 1989 is neither something very unusual for the history of Japan's stock market, nor strange in terms of international comparison. The main reason for a world-wide rally of stock prices in the 1980s was the prevailing low interest rates in major industrialized countries. In these countries, higher interest rates since the late 1980s played an important role in the market slump at the beginning of the 1990s. The Japanese stock market was not necessarily an exception. A greater part of the Japanese stock price behaviour over that period can be explained by fundamental factors, although the sky-rocketing and slumping of prices did sometimes exceed the boundaries of fundamental reasoning.

The first in a line of fundamentals is interest rates, whose rise led directly to the crash of the stock market at the beginning of the 1990s. During the latter half of the 1980s, yearly capital gains from the rise of land and equity prices in Japan were enormous and they were on a level close to or exceeding that of the annual GNP. But the 1990s turned capital gains sharply into capital losses, amounting to 110 trillion yen (about a quarter of GNP) each for 1990 and 1991. Because the size of the Japanese assets market increased enormously, it was not difficult to imagine what a large impact the (negative) wealth effect, due to asset price declines, would have on the economy. However, financial policies which seem to have been aimed at bringing down land and stock prices have failed to take into account the magnitude of the impact this effect might have had on the economy.

In Japan, land usually acts as security for bank loans. Increased competition between banks brought about by financial deregulation processes loosened the requirements for bank lending on the one hand, and the inflated land values made collateral evaluation increase on the other, hence the enormous expansion of bank lending. But after the crash, these expanded loans turned into bad debts and have become a heavy burden for banks trying to maintain sound banking operations. In addition to the resulting suspension of new stock issues, the fall in stock prices resulted subsequently in reduced bank lending and hindered banks from maintaining adequate capital. Ultimately, it harmed the real economy by restricting bank lending and at the same time has brought an element of instability to the financial system.

Another important factor behind the increase in stock prices was the reduction of risk premiums required of investors. Asset accumulation and financial deregulation both seemed to have increased the risk tolerance of investors. Moreover, in the course of continued economic growth, investors began to have higher expectation of a growth in corporate profits. This became an added cause for low interest rates and risk tolerance to rising stock prices during the second half of the boom period. The reversal occurred; that is, higher interest rates, risk aversion, and lower-than-expected corporate profits emerged, and this caused the market to fall.

The third important factor for the stock price movements was market psychology/market structure. It would be impossible to deny the role of investor psychology in explaining market volatility or the fluctuation beyond the limits determined by fundamentals. But the larger problem for Japan has been the market structure, which, combined with the market psychology, was mainly responsible for the price fluctuations. Institutionalization of the stock market, that is, increased shareholding by institutional investors and increased cross-corporate shareholding, has led to increased price instability. This institutionalization in Japan took place in two stages. First, the 1960s saw a liberalization of capital markets which accelerated cross-shareholding because of the fear of a take-over by foreign investors. In this period, institutional investors accepted a so-called 'buy and hold' policy in order to become 'stable shareholders'; those shares were rarely traded. Second, the second half of the 1980s saw a growth in pension funds, accelerated by a deregulation of financial markets. This resulted in increased competition between institutional investors, and the period was characterized by aggressive trading. Japan's stock market was thus transformed into the speculative market as is depicted by J. M. Keynes's 'beauty contest'. Accordingly, the market price fluctuates significantly because of the actions of a small number of institutional investors.

In deciding the behaviour of Japanese institutional investors, the characteristic conduct of Japanese fund managers has been of importance. They are strongly inclined towards uniform actions, rather than being a 'maverick', because of the system within which they work (including the long-time employment system), and for other reasons valued in Japanese business culture associated with the system. Therefore, a situation is possible where investors follow each other's leads, resulting in the selling and buying of stocks *en masse*.

The problem of Japanese stock markets is one of instability of price formation rather than one of level of stock prices, which broadly reflect the fundamentals, except for some periods. The Japanese stock market, along with some other financial markets, tends to show wide swings in prices. The increase in daily price fluctuations is not serious, but it is important to avoid such volatility or swings in stock prices that are not warranted on the grounds of economic fundamentals, since it causes instability in the whole financial system. The instability of Japanese stock prices is closely related to the above-mentioned institutionalization of the secondary market. This has an additional effect of influencing the investment mood of the market, especially in periods of stock market depression, where distrust is easily brought about in official policies, thus making the investment mood extremely reluctant.

To rectify the structural problem of the dominance of institutional investors in the Japanese stock market, which has been a source of price destabilization, a host of measures need to be implemented, including such measures as increased public disclosure of market information; further liberalization of the activities of institutional investors; introduction of counter-measures against stock index futures trading and other large-volume trading; and easier access to the market for individual investors. The financial sectors of the Japanese economy not only have an important share as an industry, but also the performance of these markets has an enormous effect for the whole economy, as witnessed in recent years. Without structural improvements in financial sectors, it will be difficult for the Japanese economy as a whole to achieve a stable growth in future.

REFERENCES

Bank of Japan 1993. 'The Function of Japan's Stock Market' (in Japanese), *The Bank of Japan Monthly Bulletin*, January.

Kon-ya, F. 1988. 'Reconsidering Japan's Stock Prices', *Report on Japan's Stock Price Level*, Japan Securities Research Institute, October.

Kon-ya, F. 1991. 'What Individual Investors Seek' (in Japanese), *Report on Instability of Stock Price in Japan*, Japan Securities Research Institute, July.

Kon-ya, F. 1991. 'Instability of Stock Price and Market Innovation' (in Japanese), *Investment*, Ōsaka Securities Exchange, August.

Kon-ya, F. 1993. 'Situation and View of Stock Market' (in Japanese), *Business and Cycles*, Japan Association of Business Cycles, June.

Nishimura, K. and Y. Miwa 1990. *Land Price and Stock Price in Japan* (in Japanese), Tōkyō: University of Tōkyō Press.

Shiller, R., F. Kon-ya and Y. Tsutsui 1988. 'Investor Behavior in the October 1987 Stock Market Crash: The Case of Japan', NBER Working Paper No. 2684, August.

Shiller, R., F. Kon-ya and Y. Tsutsui 1991 'Speculative Behavior in the Stock Markets: Evidence from the United States and Japan', NBER Working Paper No. 3613, February.

Wakasugi, T., K. Nishina, F. Kon-ya and M. Tsuchiya 1984. 'Measuring the Profitability of the Nonfinancial Sector in Japan', in Daniel M. Holland (ed.), *Measuring Profitability and Capital Costs*, Lexington, Mass.: Lexington Books.

Wakasugi, T. and F. Kon-ya 1991. 'Increased Instability of Stock Prices and Problems of the Stock Market' (in Japanese), *Report on Instability of Stock Prices in Japan*, Japan Securities Research Institute, July.

10 Bubbles, Bursts and Bail-outs: A Comparison of Three Episodes of Financial Crises in Japan

Koichi Hamada*

10.1 INTRODUCTION

If we look back at the modern economic history of Japan over almost a century and a half since Japan came out of isolation in 1854, we encounter many dramatic transitions, confusions and even catastrophes in the national economy. There have been several periods of serious inflation: inflation during the 1860s just after the 'opening up' of Japan; inflation during 1877–81 caused by a large issue of fiat money and contained by the Matsukata deflation policy; hyper-inflation (1945–9) after the Second World War calmed down by the Dodge plan; and the 'frenzied price' period (1973–4) that followed the first oil crisis. Related are several episodes of foreign exchange abnormalities: a large outflow of gold accompanied by a tremendous inflow of Mexican dollars during the 1860s; the economic and political drama relating to the return to the gold standard (1929) followed shortly afterwards by the re-embargo of gold (1931); the adherence to the fixed yen–dollar parity that was broken by President Richard Nixon's New Economic Policy (1971) and finally led to the adoption of the flexible exchange rate (1973); and the recent excessive co-operative effort to maintain the value of the dollar after the Louvre Accord (1987).

* This chapter was presented at the National Taiwan University (National Science Council Lecture) on 11 March 1993 and at the Second Conference on the Contemporary Japanese Economy organized by the Centre for Japanese Economic Studies, Macquarie University, Sydney, Australia on 19–20 August 1993. I benefited greatly from my discussions with Munehisa Kasuya, Sam Nakagama, Frank Packer and, in particular, Mitsuaki Okabe for his thoughtful suggestions. I am also thankful for the research assistance of Wan-Jung Kuo and Yoshio Mamiya, and the stylistic advice of Carolyn M. Beaudin.

In the past – even though we cannot yet readily talk about the present (1990s) recession – the Japanese economy somehow survived these crises and built the foundation of its remarkable economic growth path. It is at least as interesting to study qualitatively these dramatic events of Japan's economic history as to reveal quantitatively the long-term laws governing its economic development.

In this chapter I would like to compare the three historical episodes of stock market crashes and financial crises – or disorders if you do not like the Marxian connotation of crises – in Japan: (i) the stock market crashes and bank runs that culminated in the financial crisis in 1927; (ii) the bail-out of Yamaichi Securities in 1965 after the stock market decline; and (iii) the on-going recession triggered by the bursting of the stock market and real estate market bubbles.

Needless to say, there have been other episodes of stock market crashes and financial disorders in Japanese economic history. Even if we limit our attention to the post-Second World War period, we find such occasions as the (post-) Stalin stock market crash in 1953, and the 'cold turkey' stabilization process after the frenzied price period following the first oil crisis. However, as far as the magnitude or impact of events was concerned, the above two episodes we are dealing with here: namely, the financial crisis of 1927, and the security market recession that led to the bail out of Yamaichi Securities, were the most serious. Moreover, the present decline of the stock market and the instability of the credit markets are comparable in scale with these major dramas in the Japanese economic history.

10.2   COURSE OF EVENTS

Let us start by reviewing the chronology of events in these three episodes (for further detail on the first two episodes, see, among others, Bank of Japan (BOJ) 1982–6, vols. 3, 4; Goto (1990); Takahashi and Morigaki (1968); Nakamura (1967, 1986); Yabushita and Inoue (1993)).

10.2.1   Financial crisis of 1927

After the Meiji Restoration (of the Emperor's Government) in 1868, Japan started a development that could be called 'modern economic growth' around 1885. It established a unified currency (1871), a central bank – the Bank of Japan (1882), adopted the gold standard (1897), and gradually developed its financial and stock markets.

The First World War (1914–18) brought Japan a period of prosperity via the demand for exports that was followed by a stock market boom. The boom was interrupted by a stock market crash in March 1920. On 15 March the Tōkyō Stock Exchange prices lost their values, as if 'autumn leaves were driven by wind' (Tōkyō Stock Exchange, 1928). The Tōkyō Stock Exchange closed its operation for the following two days. On 7 April, Masuda Broker Bank – a bank that financed stock brokers – suspended its payments, and, consequently, the Tōkyō as well as the Ōsaka Exchange had to cancel trading. Seven commercial banks, including Konoike and Sumitomo Bank, agreed to finance the rescue by lending to Masuda Broker Bank. Each stock market, when reopened on 13 April continued to decline, and triggered decline in commodity markets, notably those of cotton and silk. Many small banks were under the attack of deposit withdrawals and suspended business. In May a substantially large bank, Shichiju-yon (Seventy-fourth) Ginko went bankrupt. The stock price index was not ready at that time, but the stock of the Tōkyō Stock Exchange declined almost 50 per cent between between the beginning of March and the middle of April. From April to July, 169 bank offices were under bank runs, and 21 banks had to suspend business; 233 firms became bankrupt during the period from May to the middle of July.

To cope with the financial crisis and the collapse of the credit system, the BOJ extended loans amounting to ¥240m (exchange rate at that time was about ¥2 = $1) in order to provide reserves and sufficient liquidity for troubled banks as well as for brokers and dealers in the stock and commodity markets. Most of them were paid back to the BOJ in two years. These loans signalled to the public the role of the central bank as the lender of last resort, and they were in fact repeated in the succeeding financial squeeze, on a smaller scale, in 1922.

On 1 September 1923, the eastern part of Japan was hit by a devastating earthquake that registered about 7.9–8.2 on the Richter scale. Three-quarters of the residents in Tokyo and 95 per cent of those in Yokohama suffered from earthquake and resulting fires. More than 140 000 people died. The total physical damage caused by the earthquake was estimated to be 5.5 bn (equivalent to $2.2 bn) which was 42 per cent of the GNP of the year. (We rely on the GNP estimates by Ohkawa and Yamada.) Banks and financial institutions were seriously affected as well.

The government tried to provide necessities to the devastated area. It issued the Ordinance of Moratorium that allowed the postponement for thirty days of the payments of debt, except for the payments of

wages, salaries and deposits under a certain amount. It was also stipulated that the BOJ would rediscount 'Earthquake bills' until the end of
March 1924. 'Earthquake bills' were defined as the commercial bills
that were either bank bills due for payments in the affected areas. The
Moratorium was discontinued after thirty days, but the large accumulation
of these earthquake bills set the stage for the financial crisis of 1927.

In 1926, the ailing Taisho Emperor died. The new name of the era
was chosen from one of the Chinese classics as 'Showa' (*jau-he*) *Yaodian*
(The Documents of Yao) the first chapter of *hujing* (Book of History)
– meaning that the emperor, as well as the people, co-operate for world
peace (Goto, 1990). But the first half of the Showa era turned out to
be, rather than the beginning of a peaceful era, a period of economic
depression and Japan's militaristic aggression in Asia.

The main drama of the 1927 (the second year of Showa) financial
crisis started on 14 March when, in the Diet that was discussing the
process of redeeming the earthquake bills, the Finance Minister, Naoharu
Kataoka, said, 'Today at noon, Watanabe Bank in Tōkyō finally failed
to meet the demand for deposit withdrawals'. It is now known, that
the Watanabe Bank got into financial difficulties in the morning, but
through concerted efforts it managed to deal with customers in the
afternoon. However, these words by the Finance Minister at the Diet
created a reaction of distrust and fright among depositors. Many banks
that were rumoured to be unsound faced bank runs for withdrawal by
depositors.

At that time, the Taiwan Bank was considered most insecure in terms
of delinquent debts in its operation with Suzuki & Company who operated aggressively in Asian trade and had a monopoly on the cam-
phor trade with Taiwan. Suzuki & Company held a large amount of
earthquake bills amounting to ¥430m 26 per cent of which was financed by loans from the Taiwan Bank.

As well as the Taiwan Bank, the Ohmi Bank, which was instrumental in the Western cloth trade, suspended their business. The chain
reaction of rumours created a panic situation in Japan, and on 23 and
24 April all the banks were closed by their, allegedly voluntary, co-
ordinated action. To order a moratorium, special imperial ordinance
was needed. If this plan had been leaked to the public, it would have
caused panic. That was the reason why voluntary actions were requested
from the Bank. After these closing days, a moratorium of three weeks
was announced, and the BOJ started supplying money by lending to
the banks that were dealing with unprecedented bank runs. Thirty-two
banks suspended operation in April and May, and forty-five followed

suit during 1927. Thus the BOJ acted the lender of last resort. The BOJ had to print banknotes so rapidly that they issued ¥ 200 bills with white backs – that is, without any printing on the reverse. Incidentally, the degree of stock market crash during that year was about 20 percent and milder than that in 1920.

In the meantime, Japan was contemplating a return to the gold standard that had been abandoned after the outbreak of the First World War. The new Finance Minister, Junnosuke Inoue, strongly believed that returning to the gold standard was a necessary step to making Japan a respectable member of the club of industrialized nations. He staged the return to the gold standard with a substantially appreciated value of the yen of about 18 per cent. The Japanese economy went into a severe depression. Prices dropped precipitously; output declined by only about 10 per cent, but the consumer price and the investment goods price declined by 27 per cent and 33 per cent respectively during 1926– 31. The rural sector was severely depressed by the decline of the relative price of agricultural products to industrial products. It was certainly one of the factors that promoted the Fascist movements that led Japan into the reckless Second World War.

The rescue lendings by the BOJ amounted to ¥679m, almost 5 per cent of the national income for 1927. It was not until 1952 – 25 years later – that banks were able to repay to the BOJ all their liability related to this emergency measure. This alone demonstrates the magnitude and the gravity of the Showa financial crisis.

10.2.2 The Yamaichi rescue operation

The Japanese economy grew, alternating recessions and booms mainly generated by the 'stop and go' policy of the Japanese government that was constrained by the balance of payments under the fixed exchange rate. In the late 1950s, the economy grew faster and the stock market advanced; the motto of security companies was, 'Goodbye to the banks and welcome to the security companies.' The government encouraged newly-introduced mutual funds and, in particular, public bonds mutual funds that would facilitate the issue of bonds of public electric companies. Many customers also thronged around stockbrokers in order to buy the newly-introduced mutual funds.

Starting in 1961, however, the stock market began to decline. The stock market index declined by about 40 per cent from the peak in July 1961 to the through in July 1965. Difficulties developed in the security companies: many clients sold mutual funds, and they began to withdraw securities from the 'broker-managed' accounts. The broker-managed account was the account of customers in security companies which consisted of deposits of securities and were managed by security companies. In many cases, security companies had already sold the securities that were supposed to be in the account. In particular, the Yamaichi Securities company and the Oi Securities company were in deep trouble.

As difficulties developed, commercial banks started helping security companies by building the Nihon Kyodo Shoken (Japan Co-operative Securities), a stock holding company. Two hundred billion yen (at that time the exchanged rate was $1 = ¥360) were provided as relief funds for the stock market. Security companies, which were afraid of increased control by banks in the future, built another institution called Nihon Shoken Hoyu Kumiai (Japan Securities Holding Union) that engaged in price-supporting operations in the stock market. Banks like Fuji, Mitsubishi and JIB were trying hard to rescue the Yamaichi and the Oi.

The Ministry of Finance (MOF hereafter) had asked major presses in Tōkyō to refrain from leaking the news that there might be securities and financial difficulties – the fact that MOF had such an influence may be a favorite topic for an author like van Wolferen (1989). However, Nishi Nippon Press (The Western Japan Press), which was not a member of the major press club, leaked the news that Yamaichi Securities were in serious financial difficulties. Customers who held management accounts in the Yamaichi and other security companies started runs to withdraw from their accounts. The BOJ was reluctant to engage in an extensive relief operation. On 28 May 1965 the Finance Minister, Kakuei Tanaka,[1] a very interesting, down-to-earth politician, was meeting the responsible central bankers and commercial bankers. Tanaka came to join the meeting by the President of the Industrial Bank of Japan (IBJ), Fuji, Mitsubishi and Vice-Governor of the BOJ, from the very Diet that passed the licensing system of security companies. A commercial bank president said that they should proceed in a gradual, conservative way. Another suggested the closing of the security market for a few days in order to reduce public anxieties. According to the political scientist A. Kusano (1986; see also Goto, 1990), Tanaka shouted, 'Shut up! How can you be a responsible president of a large bank?' Kusano interprets this as a ritual to save the face of the BOJ Vice-Governor. It was not the commercial banks, but rather the BOJ that was reluctant. However, if the Finance Minister had scolded the BOJ Vice-Governor, then it would have been a disgrace to the Central

Bank and accordingly an embarrassment. Consequently, a commercial bank president took the blame as a scapegoat in place of the Vice-Governor of the central bank. This is surprising even to me, for it is an incredible way of subtle and ambiguous communication with gaps between words and actual intention that reminds me of the best seller *The Rising Sun* by Crichton.

Consequently, the BOJ agreed to lend indirectly about ¥28.2bn to Yamaichi Securities. Fortunately, the Japanese economy returned to a rapid growth path very soon, and the relief was repaid in just four years. The MOF obtained more power by the enactment of the licensing system. After that, approval of a license became mandatory before establishing a security company. This system may work as a good device for monitoring and controlling security companies. On the other hand, the licensing system is criticized by foreigners as another form of non-tariff barriers.

10.2.3 Current financial recession

At the turn of the new decade of the 1990s, in January of the second year of Heisei, '*ping chen*' again from *Shujing*, the era of peace and accomplishment, the new era after the death of the Showa emperor, the Tōkyō stock market, which enjoyed its glorious record during the 1980s, started a precipitous decline. You may remember that the financial crisis of the first episode started in the second year of the Showa era. The Nikkei-Dow Index lost about 63 per cent of its value in two and a half years. At the same time, soaring land prices ceased to appreciate and started to decline substantially almost for the first time in post-war history.

Security brokerage firms are struggling to recover from the loss of their public image that was caused by troubles with loss-offset practices; banks are trying to reorganize their operations in face of the increased incidence of unsound loans. Commercial banks and other major financial institutions will be under stricter capital-asset requirement that is proposed by the Bank for International Settlements (BIS). For some of these institutions, the requirement could become a substantial constraint for business. Mists of uncertainty prevail in the future of the Japanese financial and security market. Some people even suspect that the declining stock market and failures of some financial institutions might trigger chain reactions that could undermine the systemic stability of Japan's financial market.

There are still some comforting aspects in the real side of the Japanese economy. The unemployment rate is still only slightly above 2.2. per cent. The ratio of job offers to job applicants fell below unity in the fall of 1992, and was news to the Japanese public; but the fact that it was news shows the overall tightness of Japan's labour market. However, we find troubling aspects as well. Sales in department stores, equipment investment, and industrial production are all declining; expectations for the future are pessimistic and the plans of firms for future investment have become conservative.

This is the current picture of the Japanese economy, and we do not know exactly where it is heading in the future. So let us look back to the recent history of macroeconomic policy and describe how this process took place.

There was a long period of excess liquidity, and land and stock price booms during the late 1980s. From 1987 to 1989, the BOJ kept its discount rate to an historical low of 2.5 per cent over a period of two years. Because of the appreciation of the yen, the price of the consumer price index and the wholesale price index were relatively stable. However, there were tremendous land price booms or 'bubbles'; the total value of land in Japan was estimated to be four times as great as land value in the spacious USA. The enormous growth of the stock market continued until the end of 1989. After Yasushi Mieno became governor of the BOJ at the end of 1989, he tightened monetary policy by raising the discount rate several times in order to recover the role of and independent and traditional central bank.

In the meantime, stock market 'scandals' concerning loss offset practices and cases of bad debts from banks, even from many respectable banks, erupted. Land prices showed a substantial decline, unprecedented in the land-scarce Japanese economy. The Nikkei Index, approaching almost ¥39 000 in 1989 plunged to ¥15 000. The BOJ and the government watched the situation, hoping in vain that the decline would be short-lived, and that the decline in asset prices would be good medicine to cure the 'bubble' psychology on land and stock prices.

The impact of disturbances to the financial sector was enormous. The number of bankruptcies exceeded 6000 in the first half of 1992. The magnitude of liabilities of bankrupt firms during fiscal year 1991 (91/4–92/3) was ¥8137bn. It was estimated, in one of the most pessimistic scenarios (Kenji Uchida, *Toyo Keizai*, 25 July 1992), that the credit of about ¥68 000bn held by banks might be unsound. The Japanese deposit insurance system charges only about 0.012 per cent of the value of deposits, and its standby credit line from the BOJ is only ¥0.5bn. Thus, unless the BOJ acts as the lender of last resort, the Japanese financial system may well be threatened by a very uncertain future.

In August 1992, the government finally turned to an expansionary macroeconomic policy as an emergency relief measure. This time, the government relied on a fiscal expansion package. Amazingly, there is still some room for government expenditure in Japan, because the flow of funds account shows a recent surplus in the I–S balance of the government sector that includes social security. The stock market temporarily rebounded at this fiscal package, taking it as an encouraging signal for future economic activities, but the rebound was short-lived. The stock market continues to linger within a low range owing to the uncertainty that was reinforced by the loss of leadership of the Liberal Democratic party (LDP). Thus the long-run consequences of this emergency measure are yet to be seen.

One structural policy in the fiscal package is even amusing to notice. The MOF asked for commercial banks to refrain from selling stocks. This could not be truly effective because it implies the postponement of supply, and unsold stocks can be a factor for the excess supply for the future. This is typically Japanese, however, because this kind of moral persuasion has been popular there and was as well used by the Ministry of International Trade and Industry (MITI) as an emergency measure to help declining industries such as aluminum (see Dore, 1986).

10.3 RELATIVE MAGNITUDE OF DISTURBANCES

I have constructed tables (Table 10.1) comparing several indicators such as the decline of stock market indexes, the relative scale of the BOJ relief loans, the relative sale of the supplementary fiscal package, and the number of bankruptcies during these three financial crises. (The growth of money supply was not given because of the wide discrepancies among several money supply data series in the first episode.) Possible causes and consequences that I will discuss in the next section are also summarized. From Table 10.1 we can see that the scale of relief operations in terms of the BOJ relief in the first episode and the sum of fiscal packages currently proposed to be needed to recover from a crisis or a financial disorder, even though they are of quite different character, are nevertheless of comparable magnitude as far as their relative magnitude to the economy is concerned. Japan is currently suffering financial turbulence of almost the same degree as that of the late 1920s. On the other hand, even though the Yamaichi rescue by the BOJ was aided by a co-ordinated syndicate of loans

TABLE 10.1 Qualitative comparison of three episodes

(i) Financial Crisis of 1927

Year started	1927
Anticipated by	Stock market crash of 1920
Followed by	Depression caused by the return to the gold standard (Jan. 1929 to 1930), and simultaneous worldwide depression
Stock market decline	73% (1927–31) 20%(Feb.–July, 1927)
BOJ relief	¥679 million
Exchange rate	$47 = ¥100 ($1 = ¥2.2)
GNP	¥13.1bn (Yamada est.; Ohkawa est.)
Relief as percentage of GNP	5 per cent
Relief repaid	1952 (in 25 years)
Supplementary budget as % of GNP	n.a.
Number of banks suspending business	45 (32 during March–April)
Number of bankruptcies	3 155
Causes	Ending wartime boom; Great Earthquake (1923); Easy BOJ rescuing operations; Chain of rumours (blunder of Finance Minister)
Policy measures	Moratorium; Rediscounting of Earthquake Bill; BOJ as lender of last resort
Effects	Great depression; Reogranization of banking sector; the Bank Law (30 March 1927); Fascism

(ii) Bail Out of the Yamaichi Securities

Year started	1965
Anticipated by	
Followed by	High growth era
Stock market decline	22%(1961–6)
BOJ relief	¥28.2bn (Yamaichi); ¥5.3bn (Oi)
Exchange rate	$1 = ¥360
GNP	¥32.7 trillion
Relief as percentage of GNP	0.08 per cent
Relief repaid	By 1969 (in 4 years)
Supplementary budget	¥259bn in terms of public debt
As % of GNP	0.7 per cent

Number of banks
  suspending business n.a.
Number of   6 060, bad debt ¥464bn
  bankruptcies
Causes   Overexpansion of security industry;
                    Contracting budget under the balanced budget
                    legislation;
                    Rumour leaked by *Nishi Nippon Shinbun*
Policy measures   Bail out by BOJ lending
Effects   Establishment of the licence system of security
                    company membership

(iii) The Current Situation

Year started   1990
Anticipated by   Land and stock price boom
Followed by   ?
Stock market   63 per cent (Dec. 1989–Aug. 1992)
  decline
BOJ relief   n.a.
Exchange rate $1 = ¥125
GNP   ¥484 trillion
Relief as percentage
  of GNP   n.a.   { 10.3 1992
                                      { 13.2 1993
Relief repaid   n.a.   5.0 1993
Fiscal Package   { ¥10.7 trilion   ($87bn)   August 1992
               { ¥13.2   April 1993
As percentage of GNP 2.3 (1992)
                    2.8 (1993)
                    5.1 Total
                    Approximately 6.2 per cent (total)
Number of banks
  suspending business n.a.
Number of   10 723, bad debt ¥8 148bn (1991)
  bankruptcies   8 928,   ¥4 587bn (Jan.–Aug. 1992)
                              ¥ 427bn (August 1993)
Causes   Lack of discipline in banks and security industry;
                    excess liquidity created by low-interest policies
                    because of international policy co-ordination to
                    keep the value of the dollar.
Remedies   Fiscal stimulus; tax incentives for investment;
                    deregulation of bank dividend policy; moral
                    persuasion to financial institutions not sell the
                    holding stocks.

from a group of commercial banks, the relative magnitude of the loans delivered as a relief to the two security companies was much smaller than the corresponding macroeconomic magnitude involved in the first and the present episodes. If we use the analogy of the Richter Scale, the first and the last have a similar magnitude of turbulence.

Thus the seriousness of current financial troubles can be regarded as being historically unprecedented since the financial crisis of 1927. This is why the present cabinet appealed to a powerful fiscal measure of $87bn to encourage aggregate demand.

10.4   CAUSES AND EFFECTS OF FINANCIAL CRISES

Many factors contributed to the occurrence of financial crises. Some factors were real and often outside the control of government; some were nominal and often created by the mishandling of monetary or fiscal policy; some were related to the behaviour of private economic agents such as the lack of discipline in lending and the contagious spread of panicky expectations.

10.4.2   Financial crisis of 1927

For the financial crisis of the 1920s, among real factors, the export boom during the first World War used aggressive lending practices in colonial Japan (like Taiwan). Both countries should have used more restraint with the lenders' financial checks. The BOJ played the role of the lender of last resort, and a moratorium was announced for the stock market crash of 1919. This might well have weakened the discipline of banks and left reckless lending and borrowing behaviour unchecked. The most significant factor was, of course, the Great Earthquake of 1923.

The importance of the public's expectations was well illustrated by the impact of Minister Kataoka's statement, based on a half truth. Recently, however, Yabushita and Inoue (1993) have argued that fundamentals were more important than the vicious circle of panicky expectations, because only those banks with poor performance were faced with the demand for deposit withdrawals. They claim that econometric tests do not find the evidence that there existed such a form of expectation crisis as was analyzed by Diamond and Dybvig (1983). (The theoretical implication of the Diamond–Dybvig model will be explained in section 10.5.)

The financial crisis of 1927 was a forerunner of the world-wide Great Depression. The BOJ's lending and the Moratorium Ordinance restored financial stability, but Japan's return to the gold standard, at the worst time of January 1930, with the old parity that prevailed before the First World War, drove the Japanese economy into a severe depression. Employment and output did not decrease much, but prices went down dramatically. The relative price of agricultural commodities plummeted – 'fifty cabbages for a package of cigarettes' was a symbolic, popular phrase; and both farmers and tenants had to send their daughters to work in textile factories under unhealthy conditions. Behind brutal coups and assassinations of politicians and business leaders by Fascists, who eventually led Japan into the Second World War, were hidden the frustration of peasants over poverty and the anger against the profit-making speculation of *zaibatsu* trading companies taking advantage of the confusion before and after Japan's return to the gold standard. Principal actors such as Junnosuke Inoue and the somewhat Keynesian Finance Minister, Korekiyo Takakashi, were assassinated by the coups (Nakamura, 1967).

10.4.2 Yamaichi rescue operation

In the second episode of the Yamaichi incident, a major factor was (as explained above) the rapid increase in the mutual fund of both equities and public bonds. At that time, these mutual funds were newly-introduced into Japan, and security companies managed aggressive sales campaigns for them. The government encouraged these activities because they helped its public debt issues. However, the stock market went down. Clients were dissatisfied and they took money out of the mutual funds. Also security companies speculated unsuccessfully with the securities that they received from clients as deposits in 'broker-managed' accounts. Thus security companies could not accommodate the clients' demand for withdrawal from those accounts. This created a financial crisis very similar to the fear of bank failure.

There were also in progress macroeconomic factors related to the business cycles. At that time, under the Bretton Woods regimes, Japan did not possess ample international reserves so the government had to pursue 'stop and go' policies depending on current-account deficits. In 1963 and 1964 the balance of payments was in deficit and accordingly a tight monetary policy was followed. The reduction of tax revenues made the proposed budget of fiscal year 1965 10 per cent smaller than the budget for 1964. This incident was instrumental in changing the strictly balanced budget requirement on the Japanese fiscal system.

Fortunately, 1965 turned out to be the only exceptionally weak year for the Japanese economy during the rapid growth era from 1960 through 1973. The Japanese economy returned to its high growth trajectory again after 1965, and after that it was no longer limited by foreign reserve considerations. As mentioned above, the debt of Yamaichi and Oi Securities were repaid in just four years.

10.4.3   Present bursting of bubbles

In contrast to the causes of the 1927 financial crisis, which were primarily real shocks owing to the Great Earthquake, principal factors that triggered the present recession are monetary in nature. In short, in spite of Japan's adoption of the flexible exchange-rate regime that in principle allows her to block monetary shocks from abroad, the Japanese monetary authorities used monetary policy to stabilize the dollar–yen exchange rate rather than to stabilize her domestic economy. In the name of international monetary co-ordination, Japan assigned her monetary policy to the objective of defending the dollar. This policy error and the following adjustment were, in my opinion, the basic causes of the present recession.

I pointed out in my book (Hamada, 1985) that monetary co-ordination is helpful and often indispensable under the fixed exchange rate. Industrial nations are, however, under the flexible exchange-rate regime now. The advantage of flexible exchange rates is that each nation can pursue more or less independently its autonomous monetary policy in order to achieve the different macroeconomic objectives that circumstances necessitate. The present turmoil related to the monetary integration of the European Community (EC) clearly demonstrates the difficulties involved in the pursuit of a unified monetary policy across nations that have different real economic conditions.

In fact, empirical analysis of the effectiveness of policy co-ordination, by Oudiz and Sachs (1984) and many others, did not find a large gain in policy co-ordination under the flexible exchange rate. Also, if the reduction of the current account was the policy objective, the co-ordination of fiscal policies would have been much more effective than the co-ordination of monetary policies – as is pointed out in the work of Mundell (1968) and Dornbusch (1976).

Because of the excuse of international policy co-ordination, the political balance between the MOF and the BOJ seems to have been influenced in favour of the MOF. The MOF was reluctant, because of the goal of deficit reduction that they strongly adhered to, to use the fiscal policy for international co-ordination, and shifted all the burden to the monetary policy. Thus Japan's experience of the late 1980s presents a typical example of the unfavourable effect of policy co-ordination when there is a conflict of interest within a country (see, for example, Rogoff, 1984). The policy co-ordination by means of monetary policies to maintain the value of the dollar created, on one side of the Pacific, speculative bubbles of asset prices followed by a severe recession in Japan, and, on the other, a lack of export demand owing to the higher value of the dollar in the USA.

In fact, during 1987–9, using the excuse of international co-ordination to keep the value of the dollar from depreciating imposed an extremely easy monetary policy that fuelled the land and asset price bubbles. The US government did not want a further rise in the yen. This compromise caused the Japanese government to pressure the BOJ to sustain an easy money policy. The BOJ seemed to have learned a lesson during the frenzied price period after the first oil crisis (1973–4) – when panicked housewives ran for toilet tissue out of fear of the disappearance of petroleum products – that monetary policy should be assigned, not to maintain the exchange rate but to stabilize the domestic economy. Ryutaro Komiya was an articulate critic of the monetary policy during that period (Komiya, 1988, ch. 8). After the first oil crisis, the monetary policy of the BOJ had been stable and quite reasonable until the first half of the 1980s. In the second half of that decade, the BOJ might have forgotten the bitter lesson.

In October 1986, US Secretary, James Baker, and the then Finance Minister of Japan, Kiichi Miyazawa, issued a statement with the co-operative intention of stabilizing the dollar. After the Louvre Accord in February 1987, the BOJ reduced its discount rate to an historic low of 2.5 per cent, and kept it there until the end of May 1989. The real GNP of Japan was growing at around 4.4 to 6.6 per cent, the money supply (M2 plus CD) grew at around 10 to 11 per cent. The BOJ was once fairly influenced by monetarism, but it did not seem to have worried about the high growth rate of money during that period. Since both the consumer index and the wholesale price index were quite stable, neither private journalists nor academic economists alerted the public to the danger of this extremely easy monetary policy. (I do not claim to have an alibi for this neglect of attention just because I was abroad.)

The BOJ was not keenly concerned about the rise in asset prices because of the price stability in flow of goods. It did not recognize

the fact – in fact, there were papers in the BOJ by Kumiharu Shigehara
and by an IMF economist, Hiroshi Shibuya, that pointed it out – that
the asset-price spiral could be interpreted even in the rational expectations market economy as a signal that people expected the continuation of an easy money policy in the future. Or, even if the BOJ had
been aware of the problem, it could not have coped with the pressure
from the MOF to make the easy money policy abide by international
commitment.

In October 1987, the New York Stock Exchange had a record decline – on 'Black Monday'. Also, Japanese business people worried
about the recessionary effect of the appreciation of the yen. Hence the
easy money policy during 1987 may be justified. However, the BOJ
continued to keep the low discount rate even after Germany and the
USA started to raise the discount rate. Indeed, it did continue to do so
even after the speculative spiral of land and stock markets became
apparent and after the job offers–applicants ratio exceeded the value
of 1.4 in the labour market.

The Governor of the BOJ at that time, Satoshi Sumita, conceded
later (in November 1991) that the BOJ should have requested more
disciplined loan attitudes at that time, but still maintained that the easy
money policy was inevitable because of the recessionary pressure because of the yen appreciation and expanding current account surpluses.
He did not seem to understand, even afterwards, that the primary responsibility of the central bank lies in quantitative control of money
and credit conditions and not in its power of moral persuasion.

Thus, the present situation of the Japanese economy is like a car,
driven by an upset driver, braking to a sudden stop. Since the monetary authorities neglected both the yellow and red lights, and kept
pushing the accelerator, it had to stop precipitately, barely keeping its
balance against the shock of such a sudden braking.

10.5   ECONOMICS OF A FINANCIAL CRISIS

It will be useful here to summarize some of the recent developments
in economic theory that analyze the financial crisis.

A traditional approach in the post-Keynesian tradition is taken by
Minsky (1986) and applied by Kindleberger (1989) to many historical
instances. These studies contain interesting historical examples of financial manias, panics and crashes, staring from the tulip mania in
Holland in the seventeenth century and including the South Sea Bub-

ble in London in the eighteenth century. The theory of financial crisis expounded by these authors draws a general pattern of the course of events in a financial crisis. The sequence goes from displacement (exogenous shock), to speculative mania (with euphoria, overtrading and excessive gearing), to monetary contraction, to financial distress, and finally ends in catastrophe. During the process of overheating, the increase in prices generates expectations of further increases in the future. The theory recognizes explicitly the importance of explosive expectations and group psychology in the critical stage of a financial crisis. I am ready to admit that people, particularly in a critical setting, behave differently from the way in which most rational-expectations-orientated economists would postulate. Rational expectations macro-economic models (or at least their standardized version of homogeneous expectations) are useful in understanding the normal course of economic affairs, in which the nature of disturbances and the rules of monetary policy are well understood by the public. These presumptions do not apply to panics. The future task for economists is to find, in a more or less systematic fashion, how differently economic agents under financial crises behave from the way the neo-classical rational expectations theory predicts.

Theoretical development of the economics of incomplete and asymmetric information provides a new analytical framework within which to study financial crises. For example, Diamond and Dybvig (1983) constructed a bank-run model in which perceptions held by the public of the possibility of a bank failure will indeed realize bank-runs and a crisis even in the absence of weakness in the economic fundamentals in the bank. In other words, the lack of co-ordination of expectation among people – or, one might say, the presence of *wrong* co-ordination of expectations – will lead to the trap of the prisoners' dilemma, which is, in fact, a self-fulfilling rational expectations equilibrium. Yabushita and Inoue (1993) maintain that bank runs during the financial crisis of 1927 were not a pure form of this type of equilibrium caused by the miscoordination of expectations because not all the banks, but only those banks with weak fundamentals, were attacked by withdrawals.

However, in my opinion, one should not underestimate the role of rumour and expectation. Minister Kataoka's slip of the tongue triggered the bank-runs in 1927; and the 'scoop' reported by a newspaper accelerated the trouble of the Yamaichi Securities. These episodes tell us the utmost importance of maintaining the public's confidence in the safety of financial institutions and also in the effectiveness of fail-safe mechanisms.

Another issue that the economics of asymmetric information sheds light on is the trade-off relationship between the *ex ante* incentive mechanism to maintain credit discipline and the *ex post* salvage operation to relieve the system. Since the fail-safe mechanism is a kind of insurance for financial activities, the moral-hazard problem, inherent to any insurance scheme, can always arise.

If banks expect that the lender of last resort will bail them out, then the discipline of lending in terms of screening and monitoring may be impaired. The same applies to the behaviour of borrowers, who expect the possibility of relief financing in adversity. Since at least a part of risk-taking behaviour is not perfectly observable, the insurance system cannot penalize moral hazard behaviour completely.

A related issue, viewed from the time dimension, is the dilemma of time inconsistency. Once a crisis develops, the central bank usually has no choice but to rescue ailing banks, financial institutions, and even business enterprises. Let us take the example of banks. So long as this central-bank behaviour is expected by banks, they will count on the lender-of-last-resort function and may accordingly indulge in unsound lending. After a critical situation develops, it is often the best for the central bank to engage in relief operations. In the moral hazard problem, the information asymmetry is crucial; in the time-consistency issue the sequence of time makes the reneging on previous commitment too tempting.

One suggested solution to the time inconsistency problem is the trembling hand equilibrium (Selten, 1975), or the sequential equilibrium (Kreps and Wilson, 1982). In our context, the solution would be that the central bank leaves room for doubt that under certain circumstances it may behave as a cold-blooded disciplinarian and not rescue failing banks.

In retrospect, the generous attitude of the BOJ in the stock market crisis of 1919 might have promoted easy-going lending activities before the Great Earthquake, and thus aggravated the financial crisis in 1927. The easy-money policy during 1987–9 certainly worked against the strict discipline of bank lending behaviour during the bubble of ascending stock and real-estate prices.

10.6 POLITICAL ECONOMY

Behind the scenes of each drama is hidden the interaction of politics and economics. A certain group of people benefit from booms and

market already entertains so many foreign agents that do not conform to the Japanese norm, based on the long-term relationship between a firm and the MOF, rules should now be written to be transparent, open to any participant, and consistent with the incentive compatibility of economic participants. Otherwise, implicit control through the administrative guidance of the MOF presents additional grounds for the argument of revisionists, such as van Wolferen's *The Enigma of Japanese Power* (1989). It is a challenge to Japan's financial markets whether or not they can be opened under a transparent set of rules without impairing the merit of security under mutual trust.

10.7 CONCLUDING REMARKS

In this chapter, I have compared three episodes of financial crises (or at least, financial difficulties) in Japan's economic history. Among many possible lessons, I would like to emphasize the following. First, there is always a dilemma between incentive mechanisms and security after a financial emergency develops. Fail-safe mechanisms are indispensable in order not to drive the national economy into chaos, but too much protection, as well as the expectation of it, impair economic incentives and financial discipline. Second, the maintenance of public confidence in the financial system is crucially important. If rumours create rumours, if panic psychology becomes contagious, then the financial system collapses in a process of a self-fulfilling prophecy. Third, institutions develop as political economic responses to impasses, influence the economic outcome of succeeding years and, in particular, that of the next financial difficulty.

These episodes all point to the crucial importance of the multiple role of the BOJ, that is, the role as the lender of last resort as well as the executive of appropriate monetary policy. In the first episode, too easy bail-outs of the banks before 1927 might have created the lack of discipline in banks and might have triggered the real financial crash. In the present episode, the amplitude of business cycles would have been much reduced if the BOJ had not succumbed to pressure for the defense of the dollar.

In place of any further summary and concluding statements, I would like in passing to raise the following question of macroeconomic policy. In Europe as well as in the USA, the Keynesian idea of stimulating the economy through government spending fell out of favour. Now economists in the Clinton Administration have revived interest in the short-run effect of fiscal stimulus, but governments in Europe and in the USA cannot afford to exercise government spending policies on a substantial scale. Nor is public opinion very much in favour of big-spending policies.

In Japan, the Keynesian thinking among economists has a strong tradition (for example, Hamada, 1986). Belief in the price mechanism is, on the other hand, not so universal as in the USA or Europe. Moreover, in Japan, the overall government sector, including the social security account, has been running at a surplus over the past few years, so Japan can implement Keynesian short-term measures. According to the flow of funds statistics, the I–S balance of the Japanese government sector had an approximate $60 bn surplus in 1991. There is still room for the short-term shot-in-the-arm measure, which the Japanese call a 'camphor injection'.

There is strong resistance to deficit spending in the MOF. People, of course, do not like tax increases. Pressure from the public for reducing taxes is, however, not very strong, so that a substantial package of government spending can be attempted, provided that the leadership of the government holds its own. Thus the phantom of Keynesian economics seems still to be haunting Japan. It remains to be seen whether Keynes is still effective as a short-term relief, or merely a ghost of the past.

Exported commodities from Japan: televisions, personal computers and automobiles, advertised their own quality. The current turmoil indicates that Japanese financial industries have yet to prove the quality of their service on the international scene, in spite of a large flow of funds from Japan to the world because of her current-account surpluses. Japanese financial activities have a strong influence on the world market, not so much because of their financial entrepreneurship as for the mere size of surplus savings. The second half of the Showa era was the age of proving the quality of Japan's industrial products. Whether the Heisei era may become the age of proving her financial entrepreneurship depends on the way in which Japan can transform her financial system to an incentive compatible one without losing the advantage in its insurance features.

NOTE

1. He was only an elementary school graduate, who became the Prime Minister later. But his career came to an abrupt halt by the bribery charge related to the Lockheed-All Nippon Airline (ANA) airbus procurement scandal.

REFERENCES

Bank of Japan 1982–86. *Nihon Ginko Hyakunen Shi* (The Hundred-Year History of the Bank of Japan), Tōkyō: Bank of Japan.
Diamond, D. and P. Dybvig 1983. 'Bank Runs, Deposit Insurance and Liquidity', *Journal of Political Economy*, 91, pp. 401–19.
Dore, R. P. 1986. *Flexible Rigidities: Industrial Policy and Structural Adjustment in Japan 1970–80*, London: Athlone Press.
Dornbusch, R. 1976. 'Expectations and Exchange Rate Dynamics', *Journal of Political Economy*, 84, pp. 1161–76.
Goto, Shin-ichi 1990. *Showa Kinyu-shi* (Financial History of Showa), Tōkyō: Jijitsushin-sha.
Hamada, Koichi 1985. *The Political Economy of International Monetary Interdependence*, Cambridge, Mass.: MIT Press.
Hamada, Koichi 1986. 'The Impact of the General Theory in Japan', *Eastern Economic Review*, October/November.
Kindleberger, C. P. 1989. *Manias, Panics and Crashes: A History of Financial Crises* (revised edn), New York: Basic Books.
Komiya, R. 1988, *The Japanese Economy: Trade, Industry and Government*, Tōkyō: University of Tōkyō Press.
Kreps, D. M. and R. Wilson 1982. 'Sequential Equilibria', *Econometrica*, 50, pp. 863–94.
Kusano, A. 1986. *Showa 40-nen 5-gatsu 28-nichi Yamaichi Jiken to Nichigin Tokuyu* (The Yamaichi Incident and the Bank of Japan Relief Loans), Tōkyō: Nihonkeizai Shinbun.
Minsky, H. P. 1986. *Stabilizing an Unstable Economy*, New Haven, Conn.: Yale University Press.
Mundell, R. A. 1968. *International Economics*, New York: Macmillan.
Nakamura, Takafusa 1967. *Keizai Seisaku no Unmei* (The Destiny of Economic Policy) Tōkyō: Nihonkeizai.
Nakamura, Takafusa 1986. *Showa Keizai-shi* (Economic History of Showa) Tōkyō: Iwanami-Shoten.
Oudiz, G. and J. Sachs 1984. 'Macroeconomic Coordination Among the Industrial Economies', *Brookings Papers on Economic Activities*, 1, pp. 1–64.
Rogoff, K. 1984. 'Can International Monetary Coordination be Counter Productive? *Journal of International Economics*, 18, 3/4 (May), pp. 199–217.
Selten, R. 1975. 'Re-examination of the Perfectness Concept for Equilibrium Points in Extensive Games', *International Journal of Game Theory*, 4, pp. 25–55.
Suzuki, Yoshiro 1992. 'When a Recession is not a Recession', *Japan Scope*.
Shibuya, Hiroshi 1992. 'Dynamic Equilibrium Price Index: Asset Price and

Indexation', *Bank of Japan Monetary and Economic Studies*, February.

Shigehara, Kumiharu 1990. 'Asset Price Fluctuations and Inflation' (in Japanese) *Kinyu Kenkyu*, Bank of Japan, July.

Takahashi, Kamekichi and Toshi Morigaki 1968. *Showa Kinyu Kyoko shi* (History of the Showa Financial Crisis) Tōkyō: Seimeikai, (paperback edition, Tōkyō: Kodansha 1993).

Tokyo Stock Exchange 1928. *The Fifty Year History of the Tokyo Stock Exchange*.

Wolferen, Karel van 1989. *The Enigma of Japanese Power*, New York: Knopfs.

Yabushita, Shiro and Atsushi Inoue 1993. 'The Stability of the Japanese Banking System: A Historical Perspective', presented at the NBER–TCER Conference, Tōkyō, January 1993.

11 Evolution of the Main Bank System in Japan

Takeo Hoshi*

In Japan, the largest provider of bank loans to a firm is usually identified as the firm's main bank. A main bank and its client are typically linked in several ways. For instance, the main bank provides cash management and other financial services for the firm, is often a major shareholder, and sometimes sends its employees to serve as directors of the firm. The main bank is expected to be responsible for monitoring the firm and, if the firm gets into trouble, the main bank often intervenes in the firm's management and tries to rescue it. This set of ties between banks and firms is called the main bank system.

There are a growing number of papers that discuss the main bank system and its economic implications.[1] The main bank is considered to be responsible for monitoring firms for other lenders (Schoenholtz and Takeda, 1985; Horiuchi, 1989; and Sheard, 1991). By delegating monitoring to the main bank, the creditors as a whole can economize on monitoring costs. From the viewpoint of corporations, the main bank system may provide an insurance mechanism (Nakatani, 1984; Horiuchi et al., 1988; Hirota, 1990). If industrial firms are more risk-averse than their main banks, the main banks can offer an implicit contract to smooth out the firm's profit by changing the loan rate according to the business condition of the firm. The main bank system can also mitigate the problem of financing constraint (Hoshi et al., 1991). Close ties and smooth informational flows between firms and their main banks reduce informational and incentive problems in the funds market. For a firm in financial trouble, the main bank system provides another advantage by reducing the costs of financial distress (Hoshi et al., 1990). A so-called 'rescue' package is often put together by a main bank to help its financially-troubled client. This rescue, however, does

* The first draft of this chapter was written while the author was a visiting scholar at the Centre for Japanese Economic Studies at Macquarie University, Sydney. I thank the Centre for its support and hospitality. I also thank Anil Kashyap, Mitsuaki Okabe and Hugh Patrick for helpful comments.

287

not come without cost to the firm: the main bank often sends its employees to take over the management of the firm (Pascale and Rohlen, 1983; Sheard, 1989, 1992). Thus the main banks also play an active role in disciplining the management. Kaplan and Minton (1993) find that firms with poor performance are more likely to have board members appointed by their main bank.

The objective of this chapter is to study how such a system of corporate finance developed in Japan. We argue that the main bank system emerged from the financial system during the Second World War. In particular, several key factors in the development of Japanese corporate finance from the 1930s to the 1950s that contributed to the evolution of the main bank system are highlighted.

For many large firms, the main bank system is a part of a larger alliance called *keiretsu*, or corporate groups. Some *keiretsu* have their origins in pre-war conglomerates called *zaibatsu*, but there are some important differences between *zaibatsu* and *keiretsu*, especially in their financial arrangement. By focusing on the evolution of bank–firm relations from the pre-war to the post-war periods, this chapter also describes how the pre-war *zaibatsu* were transformed into the post-war *keiretsu*.

The chapter starts with an examination of the corporate financing of Japanese firms before the Second World War, in Section 11.1. It shows that the pre-war way of financing Japanese corporations was very different from the post-war one. The main bank system as we know it today did not emerge instantly after the war. Rather, the system evolved gradually from the wartime system of corporate finance. Section 11.2 studies major changes in corporate financing during the fifteen years when Japan was at war, first with China, and then with the United States. We argue that those changes led to the creation of the prototype of the post-war main bank system. Although the wartime financial system already exhibited some characteristics of the main bank system, there was one key difference: the banks under wartime controls were not able to reject loan requests from munitions companies. Thus, unlike the modern main bank system, bank monitoring played no role in selecting investment projects. Section 11.3 studies how the banks acquired the monitoring capability during the post-war period of reconstruction. This section also discusses why banks and firms were able to retain close ties established before the end of the war. The final section contains a brief conclusion.

11.1 PRE-WAR CORPORATE FINANCE

Japanese firms relied heavily on bank borrowings during periods of rapid economic growth, but this was not the case during the pre-war period. The dependence on external funds was often quite low, and even when firms could not finance themselves with retained earnings, new share issues and bond issues were the dominant form of external financing. Figure 11.1 shows the capital structure for major Japanese corporations during the pre-war period. The data are from Bank of Japan Statistics Bureau (1966, table 124), and the sample includes 60–70 large firms. Bank loans accounted for only about 20 per cent of total assets throughout the period, and were much less important than the amount of paid-in capital for major corporations.

The dominance of financing through equities and bonds rather than bank borrowings is more clearly observed for the *zaibatsu* firms. Table 11.1, which was created using the data in Kasuga (1987), shows the proportion of major capital and liability items for a sample of Mitsui firms. The proportion of paid-in capital in total assets was high for all the firms, and borrowings were not important for many firms. Patrick (1981) examined the financing of Mitsubishi companies in the 1930s, and found that most of the funds were raised inside the *zaibatsu*: the companies most often raised their funds by selling shares to affiliates. Subsidiaries of the Mitsubishi companies also showed a similar composition of sources of funds: funds from the parent companies in the form of paid-in capital were most important for them.

Another characteristic that distinguishes the pre-war financial system from the post-war one is the presence of a large number of small banks. Teranishi (1982, p. 303) reports that there were 1521 banks in 1904, but only 63 of them had equity larger than ¥1 million. Moreover the total value of the equity of these 63 banks accounted for 43 per cent of all the bank equity in Japan. In contrast, many of the remaining 1458 banks were very small: 390 banks had equity of less than ¥100 000, and another 528 had equity of between ¥100 000 and ¥300 000. The situation did not change much by 1925. Teranishi (1982, table 5-6) shows that only 85 out of 1515 banks had equity larger than ¥3 million.[2] Most of the remaining banks were small: 823 had equity of less than ¥300 000 and another 451 had equity of between ¥300 000 and ¥1 million. Not surprisingly, bank failures were relatively common. On average, 25 banks per year failed during the period 1902–19, and 44 banks per year during the period 1920–32 (Teranishi 1982, p. 300, 311).

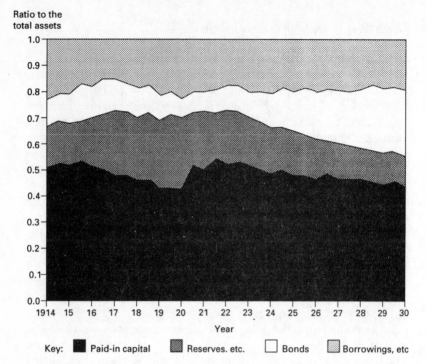

Note: The original data are from Toyo Keizai Shimpo-sha (1932), *Jigyo Gaisha Keiei Koritsu no Kenkyu.* The sample includes 60–70 large companies.

Source: Bank of Japan Statistics Bureau (1966), pp. 334–5.

FIGURE 11.1   Capital structure for large corporations

In contrast to the post-war norm, in which banks play a central role in corporate control, in the early twentieth century, shareholders were the main monitors of firms. As Okazaki (1993b) shows, the fraction of equity owned by the largest shareholders was often high, dividend payout ratios were generally high, and managers typically were rewarded with bonus payments that were closely tied to profits.

Shareholders were also actively involved in management. Many large shareholders of non-*zaibatsu* firms sat on the board and directly monitored the firms. According to Okazaki (1993b, table 4.4), on average more than 20 per cent of board members of ten non-*zaibatsu* companies in his sample were representatives of the ten largest shareholders.

TABLE 11.1   Capital structure for Mitsui Zaibatsu companies in 1920,
per cent

| Company | Major capital items | | Major liability items | | |
	Paid-in capital	Reserves	Borrowings	Trade credits	Bonds
Mitsui & Co. (Honsha)	68.1	20.4	6.1	0.0	0.0
Mitsui Mining	66.7	14.3	0.0	6.9	0.0
Hokkaido Tanko Kisen	54.8	10.4	3.1	1.1	16.6
Shibaura Seisakusho	39.0	20.8	5.3		0.0
Nihon Seiko-sho	41.7	6.4	1.2	10.6	18.8
Oji Paper	46.2	14.2	11.1	2.0	12.9
Dai Nihon Celluloid	70.0	1.6	4.6	15.3	0.0
Kanefuchi Boseki	21.0	31.9	0.0	0.0	3.7
Denki Kagaku Kogyo	46.9	6.4	0.0	18.9	0.0
Onoda Cement	48.2	18.0	8.8	5.1	10.7

Source: Kasuga (1987), tables 1–7, 1–11, 1–14, and 1–21.

The average number of board members placed by the ten largest shareholders (23) is comparable to the average number of inside board members (32) in 1935.

A different framework for monitoring was used by *zaibatsu* companies. In Okazaki's sample of ten *zaibatsu* companies, an average of only six board members were sent by the ten largest shareholders and the *zaibatsu* family in 1935, compared to an average of 38 inside. The average number of directors sent by the *zaibatsu honsha* (holding company) was fifteen. Instead of placing many board members, *zaibatsu* established organizational rules to allow the *honsha* to monitor closely the operation of each *zaibatsu* firm.

For example, consider the monitoring mechanism at the Sumitomo *zaibatsu*.[3] The Sumitomo House Accounting Rule, which was added to the Sumitomo House Constitution in 1900, established the monitoring procedures. Although the House Constitution was modified to become the Company Regulations when Sumitomo & Co. (the holding company of Sumitomo) was established in 1928, the change left the accounting rule virtually intact. According to the rule, each Sumitomo company was required to submit its budget estimates and actual expenses to Sumitomo & Co. (*honsha*) and obliged to explain any discrepancies between the two reports. Thus the *honsha* was positioned to receive both the *ex ante* plans and *ex post* analyses of their members' activities. Monitoring of capital investment was especially strict; a Sumitomo firm had to submit a detailed report which included the estimated date of completion and expenditure for each year to Sumitomo & Co. and get approval. Moreover, when there was a change in any part of the project, the firm had to consult the *honsha*. These monitoring activities were mainly carried out by the Accounting Department of Sumitomo & Co.

Hashimoto (1992, pp. 120–1) includes an interesting case that shows the effectiveness of the monitoring process at the Sumitomo *zaibatsu*. In 1928, Sumitomo Fertilizer planned to enter ammonium sulphate production and submitted a budget estimate to Sumitomo & Co. The Accounting Bureau of Sumitomo & Co. opposed this plan and sent it back to Sumitomo Fertilizer, which later came up with a less risky plan than the initial one. The revised plan was approved in 1929, but the final budget that Sumitomo Fertilizer submitted far exceeded the estimate. Sumitomo & Co. intervened at this point and replaced the Sumitomo Fertilizer director who had been in charge of the project.

Mitsui and Mitsubishi had similar frameworks, although not as comprehensive as Sumitomo's, to monitor their affiliates (Kasuga 1987 and Asajima 1986, 1987a); organizations similar to the Accounting Department of Sumitomo & Co. existed in the *honsha* of both Mitsui and Mitsubishi *zaibatsu*, and the affiliates were required to consult the *honsha* on many occasions, especially when considering capital investment.

To summarize, the characteristics of Japanese corporate finance in the pre-war period were very different from those of the post-war financial system. Bank borrowing was not an important source of funds for many firms, including both *zaibatsu* and non-*zaibatsu* firms. There were a large number of small banks, and they frequently failed. As a result of these characteristics, banks could not be prominent players in corporate control. Instead, shareholders had tight controls on Japanese companies and monitored managers closely. In Section 11.2, we discuss how the pre-war system of corporate finance changed drastically during the Second World War.

11.2   WARTIME ECONOMY: ORIGINS OF THE MAIN BANK SYSTEM

The pre-war system of corporate finance, which was briefly described in Section 11.1, went through a major transformation during the war. Some changes already started during the inter-war period and com-

pleted during the war. This section identifies four changes that under-
lay the origins of the main bank system. These changes include: (i) a
concentration of the banking industry; (ii) a higher dependence on bank
borrowings; (iii) the development and affirmation of close bank–firm
ties through wartime financial controls; and (iv) the decline of shareholders' power.

11.2.1 Concentration of banking industry

In order for banks to play an important role in corporate governance
as required by the main bank system, they themselves must be financially solvent. Thus the emergence of large and financially healthy
banks is a necessary condition for the main bank system. If one accepts Sheard's (1991) interpretation of the main bank system as an
elaborate mechanism of mutual delegation of monitoring among banks,
then it seems to be important to have a relatively small number of
banks, because such a co-operative delegation mechanism would be
difficult to implement with a large number of participants.

The concentration of the banking sector, which took place during
the inter-war period and during the war, produced a small number of
large banks. Figure 11.2 shows the number of banks in Japan between
1901 and 1945: there were 1890 banks in Japan at the end of 1901,
but only 61 by the end of 1945. We can identify two episodes of large
negative growth rate for several years: one in the late 1920s and the
other in the 1940s.

The concentration during the 1920s had several causes. First, financial crises in 1920, 1922 and 1927 forced smaller and weaker banks to
go bankrupt or to be acquired by larger banks (Fujino, 1965, p. 79).
So called 'organ banks' were especially vulnerable to business cycles
and many of them disappeared during this period of concentration. An
organ bank is a bank that shares directors or shareholders with a group
of industrial firms (Teranishi, 1982, pp. 304–8). Many organ banks
were, in fact, established by industrial firms to raise funds. As a result, an organ bank often limited its lendings to a specific group of
firms and ignored diversification of risk. Although an organ bank probably had good information about the firms, it was not in a position to
use such information for effective monitoring because it was too dependent on the firms. Thus organ banks did not play an important role
in corporate governance, as the main banks today do, and they often
failed when their industrial firms went down.

Second, government policies also encouraged mergers. The Banking

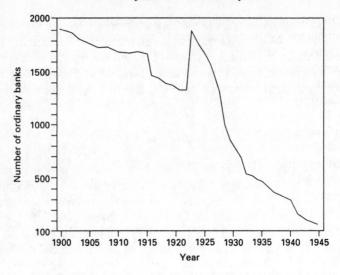

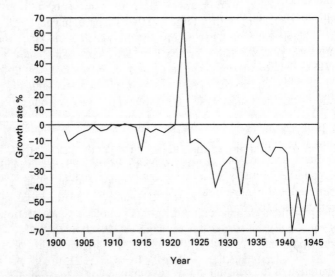

Note: In 1922, following the implementation of new Savings Bank Law,
which prohibited the ordinary bank business by savings banks, many
savings banks switched to ordinary banks, recording one shot increase
of the number of ordinary banks.

Source: Goto (1991), tables 4, 7, 15, 16, 22, 23 and 24.

FIGURE 11.2   Decline of the number of ordinary banks
(actual number and growth rate)

Law implemented in January 1928 was particularly important. This law stipulated a minimum amount of required capital (¥1 million for most banks; ¥2 million for banks in urban areas), and pressured those banks which did not satisfy the requirement to merge before 1932 (Teranishi, 1982, p. 332). The effect of this law is seen clearly in the sustained growth rate of less than -10 per cent during the period of 1928–32 shown in Figure 11.2.

The concentration during the 1940s was mainly due to wartime financial controls which aimed to allocate funds preferentially to war-related industries. These industries were located in metropolitan areas and regional centres, so that by discriminating against firms outside war-related industries, the wartime controls generally hurt firms that were located in rural areas. As these companies declined, so too did the regional banks that had them as customers. Thus many regional banks eventually found that merging with larger banks was their best choice.

Table 11.2 reports the five largest banks' share, which is a measure of concentration in the banking sector. The table suggests that the large banks grew larger during this period by acquiring smaller firms. The wartime controls seem to have been particularly advantageous to the largest banks. Even between 1940 and 1945 (roughly the period of the Second World War), shares of the five largest banks in the banking business increased considerably.

Finally, the Ministry of Finance and the Bank of Japan often directly proposed mergers between banks in the name of efficiency. The pressure was especially strong for regional banks. Finance Minister Eiichi Baba declared the goal of 'one prefecture–one bank' in May 1936, and the Ministry of Finance aggressively advocated mergers between regional banks (Goto, 1991). By the end of the war, 34 of the 46 prefectures had no more than one bank.

11.2.2 Greater dependence on Bank loans

Concentration of the banking industry through competition and aggressive government policies advocating mergers created a small number of large banks, and laid some of the ground work for the main bank system. At the same time, an important change was taking place in the composition of sources of industrial funds. The Japanese firms, which relied mainly on internal funds and new share issues to raise the funds, as we saw in Section 11.1 started to rely more on bank borrowings. Table 11.3 shows sources of industrial funds for the period 1934–44.

TABLE 11.2   Shares of the five largest banks in all ordinary and savings banks, per cent

End of year	Paid in capital	Deposits	Lending
1900	5.4	15.1	10.6
1910	10.2	17.4	15.1
1920	13.9	20.5	16.5
1930	24.1	31.0	27.6
1940	31.6	35.4	44.7 '
1945	40.4	45.7	58.6

Note: The five largest banks include Mitsui, Mitsubishi, Sumitomo, Daiichi and Yasuda until 1942; and Mitsubishi, Sumitomo, Yasuda and Teikoku from 1943. The Teikoku Bank was created by a merger between Mitsui and Daiichi in 1943. It absorbed the Juu-Go Bank in 1944, and broke up again into Mitsui and Daiichi in 1948.

Source: Teranishi (1982), p. 295.

TABLE 11.3   Source of industrial funds, per cent

Year	Internal funds	New shares	New bonds	Bank loans
1934	54.8	55.4	2.8	−11.4
1935	51.6	32.9	1.0	14.9
1936	47.4	33.5	−2.3	18.3
1937	33.3	35.5	−0.1	31.9
1938	30.5	34.6	5.4	29.9
1939	27.1	24.5	7.9	38.4
1940	30.4	26.7	5.5	38.3
1941	33.6	29.1	10.1	28.1
1942	31.2	25.7	8.9	32.8
1943	30.3	22.6	7.8	35.8
1944	24.2	9.1	8.3	57.8

Source: Ministry of Finance (1978), pp. 462–3.

The table shows clearly the increasing dependence on bank borrowing during this period.

The major cause of this change in corporate financing was heavy industrialization accelerated by the war effort. During the inter-war period, capital-intensive heavy industries grew much more rapidly than light industries, and the war effort reinforced this tendency. For example, Table 11.4 shows that between 1934 and 1942, the share of output coming from the steel/metals and machinery industries increased from

TABLE 11.4 Shares of manufacturing output 1924–42, private companies with more than five employees, per cent

Industry	1924	1929	1934	1939	1942
Steel & Metals	5.7	8.9	15.6	21.6	20.1
Machinery	6.7	8.8	11.5	20.0	28.7
Chemicals	11.0	14.0	16.1	18.4	17.2
Textiles	44.2	38.8	31.1	17.9	11.1
Food	16.3	14.6	11.1	9.3	7.6

Source: Ando (1979), p. 119.

TABLE 11.5 Industrial distribution of paid-in capital within *zaibatsu*

Zaibatsu	Industry	1937	1941	1946
Mitsui	Finance	11.5	5.4	5.5
	Mining	26.5	25.1	15.8
	Heavy/Chemical	22.1	39.9	56.6
	Light	13.8	12.2	8.9
	Other	26.0	17.4	13.2
Mitsubishi	Finance	22.1	10.6	6.2
	Mining	18.6	20.3	10.6
	Heavy/Chemical	27.1	36.5	57.5
	Light	11.5	7.7	2.5
	Other	20.7	24.9	23.3
Sumitomo	Finance	15.1	10.3	4.1
	Mining	8.8	6.1	7.2
	Heavy/Chemical	35.2	65.5	80.5
	Light	9.4	1.4	1.8
	Other	31.4	16.7	6.4

Source: Sawai (1992), pp. 154–5.

27 per cent to 49 per cent, while the fraction of production in the food and textiles industries declined from 42 per cent to 19 per cent. With the increasing importance of capital intensive sectors in the economy, firms were no longer able to rely on internal funds to finance their investment. They substantially increased their dependence on bank borrowings, as Table 11.3 showed.

The compositional shift toward heavy industries and the resulting change in corporate financing was more dramatic for *zaibatsu* companies. Table 11.5, which was taken from Sawai (1992), shows the shift in industrial composition from 1937 to 1946 for the three largest *zaibatsu*.

Since the table uses the amount of paid-in capital to calculate the share of each industry, the numbers are not directly comparable to those in Table 11.4, which are based on outputs. Yet the table shows a dramatic shift from light industries and non-manufacturing to heavy and chemical industries. For example, in the Mitsubishi *zaibatsu*, the share of heavy and chemical industries increased from 27 per cent in 1937 to 36 per cent in 1941, and to 58 per cent by the end of the war. The share of light industries declined from 12 per cent in 1937 to 8 per cent in 1941, and to only 3 per cent by the end of the war. The experience at Mitsui was similar: in Sumitomo, the shift was even more dramatic.

Although large *zaibatsu* traditionally financed most projects by selling shares to *honsha* and the affiliates, the rapid shift to capital-intensive heavy industry made it necessary for them to become dependent on external sources of funds. As *zaibatsu* expanded into heavy industries, they started to finance their investment by selling shares to the public and by borrowing from the financial institutions in the same *zaibatsu*. It is sometimes argued that *zaibatsu* started to offer shares to the public for the first time in the inter-war period in order to divert harsh criticism away from them. As Shibagaki (1974, pp. 42–5) points out, another, and perhaps more important, reason behind the decision to sell shares to the public appeared to be the increase in the demand for funds because of heavy industrialization.

Asajima (1986, pp. 329–39) classifies new share issues of Mitsubishi companies into two parts: those placed within the Mitsubishi *zaibatsu* and those offered to investors outside the *zaibatsu*. He calculates the ratio of internal placement for three periods and finds the ratio fell from 49 per cent in 1917–36 to 36 per cent in 1937–41, and 32 per cent in 1942–5. Asajima (1987a, pp. 202–7) performs a similar calculation for the Sumitomo *zaibatsu* and finds an even more dramatic shift. The ratio of internal placement dropped from 70 per cent in 1921–36 to 49 per cent in 1937–44. These numbers show that it became increasingly difficult to finance the *zaibatsu* operations internally as heavy industrialization accelerated during war-time and the *zaibatsu* had to seek outside funds.

The investment in heavy industries was also financed by increased borrowings from *zaibatsu* banks. Table 11.6 shows the time series for the total amount of *zaibatsu* firms' borrowings from *zaibatsu* financial institutions and the proportion to the total loans made by *zaibatsu* financial institutions. The numbers are for the Mitsubishi and Sumitomo *zaibatsu*. The table shows clearly that *zaibatsu* firms increased their dependence on bank borrowings during this period.

TABLE 11.6 Bank borrowings of *zaibatsu* companies

	Mitsubishi *zaibatsu*		Sumitomo *zaibatsu*	
Year	Total bank borrowings (¥10 000)	Loans of Mitsubishi fin. inst. (%)	Total Bank borrowings (¥10 000)	Loans of Sumitomo fin. inst. (%)
1932	4 921	9.3	3 834	6.5
1933	5 963	12.1	3 777	6.1
1934	3 699	7.7	3 650	6.2
1935	2 472	5.0	2 594	3.9
1936	2 974	5.2	1 731	2.2
1937	7 566	9.9	4 663	5.0
1938	16 047	18.3	10 956	9.8
1939	28 520	29.2	18 134	12.3
1940	27 232	21.8	28 478	14.9
1941	47 566	32.5	39 184	17.6
1942	45 734	27.7	45 322	18.4
1943	63 413	20.1	52 554	16.7
1944	196 285	40.2		

Sources: Asajima (1987a), table 2–18; and Asajima (1987b), table 3–18.

11.2.3 Direct wartime financial controls

War-time financial controls also affected directly the ways that individual companies arranged their financing. Major financial controls during this period are summarized in Table 11.7, which is created from Nakamura (1971, appendix to ch. 10), Ministry of Finance (1976, pp. 3–23) and Nakamura (1989, table 1-2). Soon after Japan initiated war with China in July 1937, the Temporary Funds Adjustment Law was promulgated and a series of war-time financial controls started. This law sought to control long-term funds, and preferentially allocate funds for war-related industries. Operationally this meant that each industry was classified into one of three categories: those which were expected to receive approval for most of their long-term funds requests; those which would sometimes get approval; and those which would generally not expect to get approval. Within six months, the government had passed a second law, the Total National Mobilization Law (TNML), which gave it the authority to control all the major aspects of the economy including labour, materials, facilities, firms, prices and credit. The Industrial Bank of Japan (IBJ) became a central agent in the control of credit. By April 1939, with the enactment of the Corporate

TABLE 11.7   War-time financial controls

1937	September	Temporary Funds Adjustment Law
1938	March	Total National Mobilization Law (TNML)
1939	April	Corporate Profits Distribution and Fund Raising Order (according to clause 11 of TNML)
1940	September	Zenkoku Kin'yu Kyogikai (National Conference on Finance)
	October	Bank Funds Application Order (according to clause 11 of TNML)
1941	August	Jikyoku Kyodo Yushi-dan (Emergency Co-operative Lending Consortium)
	December	Hijo-ji Kin'yu Taisaku (Emergency Finance Measures)
1942	February	Reform of Bank of Japan Law
	April	Establishment of Wartime Finance Corporation Establishment of Zenkoku Kin'yu Tosei-kai (National Committee on Financial Regulation)
1943	June	Kigyo Seibi Yoko (Outline for Corporate Restructuring)
	July	Kigyo Seibi Shikin Sochi-ho (Measures for Proceeds from Corporate Restructuring)
	October	Munitions Companies Act
	November	First Designation of Munitions Companies (150 companies)
1944	January	Munitions Companies Designated Financial Institutions System
	April	Second Designation of Munitions Companies (422 companies)
	December	Third Designation of Munitions Companies (109 companies)
1945	February	Special Law on Wartime Finance
	March	Co-operative Lending Bank (to mobilize the funds of regional banks)
	May	Fund Integration Bank (restructured Co-operative Lending Bank)

Sources: Nakamura (1971), Appendix to ch. 10; Ministry of Finance (1976), pp. 3–23; and Nakamura (1989), table 1–2.

Profits Distribution and Fund-Raising Order (which was justified on the basis of Clause 11 of the TNML), the government acquired the power to direct the IBJ to make loans to specific firms.[4]

In October 1940, again using clause 11 of TNML, the government passed the Bank Funds Application Order (BFAO), and advanced financial controls one step further. The scope of control now included short-term funds. Under the BFAO, the government acquired the right to direct lending by banks other than the IBJ. In order to respond to increasing demand for loans for war-related industries, commercial banks started to form lending consortia to share the risk and co-ordinate their lendings. The lending consortia later developed into the Emergency Co-operative Lending Consortia (August 1941) and eventually into Financial Control Associations (April 1942).

Teranishi (1993a) argues that these lending consortia developed into the main bank system in the post-war period. Although the wartime lending consortium was mainly a device for risk diversification, the post-war main bank system added another role, of delegated monitoring among banks. By letting a main bank be responsible for monitoring its clients and avoiding the duplication of monitoring by other lenders, the *de facto* lending consortium under the main bank system provided an efficient monitoring mechanism.

Financial controls reached the final phase when the government passed the Munitions Companies Act (October 1943), and the Munitions Companies Designated Financial Institutions System (January 1944) was implemented. The Munitions Companies Act put major companies which were considered strategically important under the direct control of the government, and the Munitions Companies Designated Financial Institutions System assigned a major bank to each munitions company to take care of the firm's financial needs.[5] In many cases, a lending consortium was formed around the designated bank to serve the munitions company.

About 150 companies were designated as munitions companies in the first round of designation of November 1943, and financial institutions were allocated to these firms in January 1944. Through the second-round and the third-round designations, the number of munitions companies reached about 680 by the end of 1944. Financial institutions were allocated to all these firms according to the Munitions Companies Designated Financial Institutions System. The Special Law on War-time Finance, stipulated in February 1945, enhanced the scope of financial institutions designation to about 1870 non-munitions companies (Teranishi 1993b, p. 78; Bank of Japan Research Bureau, 1973, p. 429). Thus virtually all Japanese firms were paired with banks by the end of the war.

As the Selection Policy for Munitions Companies Designated Financial Institutions declares, most designations are likely to have been based on past relations through loans, shareholdings, and directorship.[6] Thus assignments under the Munitions Companies Designated Financial Institutions System often served only to reinforce pre-existing ties between banks and firms, especially for *zaibatsu* firms and banks. But episodes of competition among banks to receive designations for munitions companies suggest that there were some degrees of freedom in the selection process (see Miyazaki and Ito 1989, p. 202). Mitsubishi Bank (1954, pp. 349–50) reports that banks lobbied to obtain as many designations as possible, because loans made to munitions companies were perceived to be riskless. For some banks, such as Sanwa, which began as a merger of three banks (Yamaguchi – in Ōsaka, Kamoike and San-Jū-Shi) in 1933 and grew as a result of several further mergers during the war, the assignments mainly created a new set of enduring ties.

Some non-*zaibatsu* firms also started to have close ties to *zaibatsu* banks as a result of designation. An example is Ajinomoto, which changed its name to Dai Nippon Kagaku Kogyo during the period of 1943–5, which was designated as a munitions company, and assigned to the Mitsubishi Bank. Ajinomoto does not appear to have had extensive relations with the Mitsubishi Bank before the war. In fact, its low debt–equity ratios during the pre-war periods suggest that close ties to any bank were unlikely (Ajinomoto 1971, appendix to vol. 1, pp. 10–11).[7] After the war, Ajinomoto gradually moved closer to the Mitsubishi group. For example, during the reconstruction period, Mitsuo Ogasawara of the Mitsubishi Bank served as one of five special managers responsible for planning the restructuring of the firm. By 1962, the Mitsubishi Bank was the largest lender to Ajinomoto, although it was not among the ten largest shareholders. By 1972, however, the Mitsubishi Bank had become both the largest lender and the largest shareholder of Ajinomoto.[8] In addition to the financial ties, Ajinomoto and the Mitsubishi Group developed close relations in the intermediate products markets. For example, Ajinomoto's Tokai factory purchased raw materials from Mitsubishi Chemicals, Mitsubishi Petro-Chemicals, and Mitsubishi Monsanto (Ajinomoto, 1989, p. 281). Thus, even for the former *zaibatsu* banks, there appears to have been new and long-lasting relationships formed because of the designation system.

To investigate systematically the importance of the relationships that were formalized by the Munitions Companies Designated Financial Institution System, the identity of a firm's main bank in the post-war period was compared with its designated lender during the war. The initial sample contains 157 munitions companies that were assigned designated financial institutions during the first round of designations in 1944. The list of such companies and their designated financial institutions is found in Bank of Japan Research Bureau, 1973, pp. 402–20. The designated financial institutions for those firms are compared with their largest lenders and shareholders in the post-war period. The relevant data in the post-war period were collected for two years: 1962, which is the first year that *Keiretsu no Kenkyu* shows the identities of large lenders and shareholders for all the companies listed in the first section of the Tokyo Stock Exchange (TSE); and 1974, which was chosen arbitrarily. *Shuyo Kigyo no Keifuzu*, compiled by Kōbe University's Research Institute of Economics and Management was used to follow name changes and reorganizations during the post-war period.

Table 11.8 shows a summary of the findings from the comparison. More detailed results are reported in the appendix to Hoshi (1993). In

TABLE 11.8   Financial institutions assignment for munitions companies and the post-war main bank relationship

	1962	1974
Number of companies where main bank relationship was checked	111	122
(A) Designated institution (DI) is the largest lender and one of the top 10 shareholders	70	64
(B) A financial institution in the same *keiretsu* as DI is the largest lender and one of the top 10 shareholders	11	21
(C) DI is the largest lender, but not one of the top 10 shareholders	13	7
(D) A financial institution in the same *keiretsu* as DI is the largest lender but not one of the top 10 shareholders	4	1
(A) + (B) + (C) + (D)	98	93
Number of companies which belonged to 4 largest *zaibatsu*	27	27
(E) DI is the largest lender and one of the top 10 shareholders	17	14
(F) A financial institution in the same *keiretsu* as DI is the largest lender and one of the top 10 shareholders	5	7
(G) DI is the largest lender but not one of the top 10 shareholders	4	1
(H) A financial institution in the same *keiretsu* as DI is the largest lender but it is not one of the top 10 shareholders	0	1
(E) + (F) + (G) + (H)	26	23

Keiretsu no Kenkyu for 1962, one finds the information for 111 companies that are descendants of the 157 munitions companies. In 70 (63 per cent) of these 111 cases, the designated financial institution was both the largest lender and one of the ten largest shareholders. Adding other cases such as the one where the trust bank or the life insurance company in the same *keiretsu* as the designated financial institution is the largest lender and one of the top ten shareholders or the one where the designated financial institution was the largest lender though not one of the top ten shareholders, the total number of cases which shows still-remaining effects of designation as of 1962 becomes 98 (88 per cent). Thus the main bank relations in 1962 were strongly influenced by the designated financial institutions system during the war.

The effects of the designated financial institutions system remained significant even in 1974: thirty years after the designation. For 1974, one can identify 122 companies as the descendant of 157 munitions companies using *Keiretsu no Kenkyu*. The number of companies increases to 122 mainly because *Keiretsu no Kenkyu* for 1974 allows us to track those firms listed only in the second section of the Tōkyō Stock Exchange and some unlisted companies. The designated financial institution was both the largest lender and one of the ten largest shareholders in 1974 in 64 cases (52 per cent) out of the 122. Adding other cases where we observe a weaker relationship, we find that, in 93 out of 122 cases (76 per cent), the companies still had close ties to the designated financial institutions even in 1974.

Of the 111 companies that can be tracked to 1962, 27 are considered to have had close links with the four largest *zaibatsu* (Mitsui, Mitsubishi, Sumitomo and Yasuda) even before the designation of financial institutions. The four *zaibatsu* owned the four largest ordinary banks at the end of the war (Teikoku, Mitsubishi, Sumitomo and Yasuda). As I have already argued, the designation of financial institutions for these *zaibatsu* firms may have been nothing more than an acknowledgement of some pre-existing ties. Thus it may not be surprising to find that in 1962 the designated financial institution or the trust bank in the same group was the largest lender in 26 out of 27 cases. A more important result, however, is that the ties through the designated financial institutions system were long-lasting even for the other 84 firms which did not have close ties to *zaibatsu*. Out of the 84, 72 companies (86 per cent) had a designated institution or a financial institution in the same group as the largest lender in 1962.

11.2.4 Decline of shareholders' power

The final important change to corporate finance during this period was the shift in corporate governance practices. Naturally, as the firms started to depend more on external funds, especially bank loans, the relative power of shareholders declined somewhat. However, there were also regulatory changes that further limited the power of shareholders. For example, the 1939 Corporate Profits Distribution and Fund-Raising Order required firms with a dividend pay-out ratio of more than 10 per cent to seek approval from the Ministry of Finance if they wanted to increase their dividend payments.[9] The order also required those firms with dividend pay-out ratio between 6 per cent and 10 per cent to seek approval from the Ministry of Finance if they wanted to increase the pay-out ratio by more than 2 per cent.

Thus the Corporate Profits Distribution and Fund-Raising Order severely restricted shareholders' rights to residual income. The payoffs to shareholders now resembled those to debt holders: their income was fixed in nominal terms and they were not residual claimants. Okazaki (1993a, table VIII) reports a regression analysis that supports stabilization of pay-out ratios during the war. He estimated the sensitivity of the dividend pay-out ratio to the profit ratio for a sample of 19 companies, which included both *zaibatsu* and non-*zaibatsu* firms. Comparing the estimated sensitivities for the period of 1921–36 to those for 1937–43, he finds that sensitivity declined significantly in 16 out of the 19 companies.

This restriction on shareholders' property rights must have reduced their incentive to influence and control management. Interestingly, this tendency for firms to pay a nominally fixed amount of dividends continued into the post-war period in the name of *antei haito seisaku*, or 'stable dividends policy'. Okazaki's (1993a) regression analysis shows the sensitivity of dividend pay-out ratios for the period of 1961–70 were as low as those for 1937–43. The shareholders do not seem to have regained their rights to residual income even in the post-war period.

It was not accidental that the government's financial controls reduced shareholders' power. Okazaki (1991) argues that the shift of corporate control away from shareholders was a result of deliberate government policy, which attempted to organize every aspect of the economy to work efficiently for war purposes. During the war, the government viewed self-interested shareholders, who cared more about profits than national priorities, as nuisances. The following statement by a government official vividly displays the government attitude toward shareholders during the period:

The majority of shareholders take profits by selling appreciated stocks, sell in times when the price is expected to fall, and often seek dividend increases without doing anything to deserve them. If these shareholders control the directors of companies, influence strategies, and seize a substantial amount of profits, then the system of joint stock corporations has serious flaws. (Munemasa Suzuki, 'Kojo no Rijun Bunpai Seido to Ko Chingin Taisaku' (Factories' Profit Distribution and Measures towards High Wages), *Shakai Seisaku Jiho*, April 1938, quoted by Okazaki, 1991, p. 382)

In addition to the financial regulations that heavily restricted the right of shareholders as residual claimants, the government passed other laws that more directly limited the scope of managerial control by shareholders. The first attempt (via *tosei-kai*, 'control associations') sought to forge a co-operative alliance between the government and managers in key industries. When these associations failed to provide the kind of tight control sought by the government, they passed the previously mentioned Munitions Companies Act. In addition to putting the companies under the direct control of the government, the Munitions Companies Act also allowed managers substantial autonomy as long as they were acting in the interests of the nation by trying to 'increase productivity' (Okazaki, 1991, pp. 392–3). Thus the power to control corporations was largely transferred from shareholders to managers during this period.

The shift of power from shareholders to managers is evident when one looks at the changes in the number of inside directors. Okazaki (1993b, table 4.4) shows that the average number of inside directors for ten non-*zaibatsu* firms in his sample increased from 32 in 1935 to 49 in 1945, while the average number of directors appointed by the top ten shareholders fell from 23 to 10 during this period.

The controlling families in the *zaibatsu* also lost some of their authority during this period. As it was pointed out in Section 11.2.2, *zaibatsu* companies raised funds by public sales of new shares (including those for the *honsha*) and by increased bank borrowings in order to finance their investment in heavy industries. The mechanism of direct monitoring by *honsha*, which was discussed in Section 11.1, also started to crumble. For example, at the Sumitomo *zaibatsu*, the elaborate monitoring mechanism of *honsha* was replaced by the Sumitomo Wartime Council (*Sumitomo Senji Soryoku Kaigi*) in 1944. The Council aimed to let each *zaibatsu* company do its business without any restrictions or impediments from *honsha* to contribute to the total war (Sawai,

1992, pp. 194–5). Thus, *zaibatsu honsha* was not able to control the affiliates as it did before. As Shibagaki (1974) argues, the *zaibatsu* may have been starting to disintegrate even before they were officially dissolved during the Occupation period.

11.2.5 Wartime banking as the prototype of the main bank system

The four changes discussed above laid the groundwork for the main bank system. As industrial companies shifted towards heavy capital-intensive industries, they became more dependent on bank borrowings. Larger banks that survived the concentration of the banking industry accommodated the increasing demand for funds, sometimes forming a lending consortium. The creation of a lending consortium was a response by commercial banks to wartime financial risk, and the government also found the consortium useful in directing loans to war-related industries. The Munitions Companies Designated Financial Institutions System developed or reaffirmed the strong ties between banks and industrial firms. As companies became more dependent on bank borrowings, shareholders' power declined somewhat.

The decline of shareholders' power was accelerated by explicit government interventions, and, by the end of the war, managers were effectively free from monitoring. Financial institutions were turned into organizations which merely followed the government's lending orders. The evaluation and monitoring of borrowers, which is central to a healthy banking system, was no longer the banks' concern under the wartime economy. The following quote taken from a banker's memoirs shows what the banking business was like during the war:

> I was in charge of the loan business for the companies connected with production of top secret bombs: balloon bombs. My name was registered at Army Headquarters for Weapons Administration, and my activities were a closely guarded secret. I dealt with all the loan documents related to balloon bombs, which was flagged by the letter 'fu', ['fu' for 'fusen', the Japanese word for balloon]. Incidentally, the documents with the letter 'ro' was for rocket bombs for Navy, and another person was in charge of these loans.

> My job was to make the loan immediately whenever a slip with the letter 'fu' came to my desk. Lots of companies, such as paper manufacturers, producers of percussion caps, and *konnyaku* paste-makers [paste made from arum root], took part in the production of balloon bombs. (Matsuzawa, 1985, p. 14)

The absence of bank monitoring is also reported in the corporate history of the Mitsubishi Bank published in 1954. For instance, the Mitsubishi Bank, (1954, pp. 351–3) notes that the managers of the munitions companies 'never had to worry about financing' and the banks 'could rarely use their own judgements regarding loan requests'.

After the war, the banks had to restart their monitoring activities, to enable the wartime financial system to develop into the main bank system. Section 11.3 discusses how this transformation took place.

11.3 POSTWAR RECONSTRUCTION AND THE EMERGENCE OF THE MAIN BANK SYSTEM

As the war ended, Japan inherited a financial system with large banks and close bank–firm relations. Although this inheritance from the war economy was a major reason why the main bank system emerged after the war, it was not the only one. The decline of shareholders' power during the war created a serious void in corporate governance: no one had the incentive or ability to monitor the managers of munitions companies. The absence of monitoring that characterized wartime financing had to be corrected, and the banks had to gain the power and ability to monitor companies before the main bank system fully developed. Thus, in order to understand how the wartime financial system was transformed into the main bank system, one must investigate why the pre-war and post-war Japanese financial systems showed remarkable continuity on the one hand and yet, on the other, the banks achieved power to monitor the industrial firms.

This section argues that (i) a special role that banks played in supervising reconstruction and reorganization of industrial firms, and (ii) the 'credit crunch' – especially after the Dodge Line of 1949 – were important in increasing the monitoring capacity of the banks, while (iii) the Occupational Forces' lack of commitment to fully break up the *zaibatsu*, and (iv) the exclusion of banks from anti-trust measures, insured a significant amount of continuity in the system.

11.3.1 Postwar restructuring of financial institutions and industrial firms

After the war, the balance sheets of munitions companies were filled with receivables of wartime compensation. The Japanese government initially planned to pay the compensation by collecting property taxes, but following pressure from the Allies, the government eventually decided to suspend completely compensation payments.[10] Since financial institutions obviously had high exposure to munitions companies, the suspension of wartime compensation also seriously damaged their balance sheets. To make matters worse, the government also decided to drop the guarantees on government guaranteed corporate bonds, most of which were held by financial institutions, and suspended compensation of losses of uncollectable government-ordered loans to munitions companies. The losses stemming from the suspension of wartime compensation were enormous. The government estimated the amount to be ¥66.9 bn.[11] If one adds the losses due to repudiation of government guaranteed bonds (¥19.8 bn) and the losses due to suspension of compensation of losses arising from government-ordered loans (¥5 bn), the total losses were estimated to be ¥91.8 billion yen: almost one-fifth of gross national expenditure (GNE) in the fiscal year 1946 (¥474 bn).[12]

The balance sheets of financial institutions and industrial firms were cleaned up in two steps. First, the Financial Institutions Accounting Temporary Measures Act (FIATMA) and the Corporations Accounting Temporary Measures Act (COATMA) came into force in August 1946 in order to prevent the suspension of wartime compensation from seriously damaging the current operations of the firms. Subsequently, in October 1946, the Financial Institutions Reconstruction and Reorganization Act (FIRRA) and the Corporations Reconstruction and Reorganization Act (CORRA) were implemented as more permanent measures to deal with the suspension of wartime compensation.[13]

The restructuring of financial institutions preceded the restructuring of industrial firms. Under FIATMA, the balance sheet of each financial institution was separated into new and old accounts as of 11 August 1946. Those assets that were expected to be uncollectable because of the suspension of wartime compensation were assigned to the old account, and this account later went through a reorganization. The banks were allowed to continue operations in the meantime using the new accounts. In March 1948, the assets in the old accounts were re-evaluated using current prices, and the losses due to suspension of wartime compensation were cancelled out. The following prioritization was used in the cancellation process: first, capital gains on assets were used, next came retained earnings, then up to 90 per cent of the bank's capital would be used, then 70 per cent of the unprotected deposits would be written off, followed by the remaining 10 per cent of the capital, and finally the remaining 30 per cent of the deposits. The reorganization of the old accounts was completed by May 1948, and the new and old accounts were merged.

It is important to note that the banks finished cleaning up their balance sheets relatively quickly. As discussed below, the restructuring of corporations took a much longer time. The swift reorganization of financial institutions reflected the ideas of the Japanese government and Allied Forces that they should first make the banks solvent so that they could lead the post-war reconstruction. As the Ministry of Finance (1983b, p. 300) argues, 'both the General Headquarters and the Ministry of Finance intended to finish the restructuring of financial institutions before that of corporations and rebuild the Japanese economy on the basis of funds of financial institutions'. Indeed, banks played an important role in the restructuring of industrial companies, which is now described.

The restructuring of the non-financial corporations was guided by COATMA and CORRA. The companies that were expected to be damaged by suspension of wartime compensation were declared 'special account companies' (*tokubetsu keiri gaisha*) and covered by COATMA. The balance sheets of these special account companies were separated into new and old accounts on 11 August 1946, and companies were allowed to operate using new accounts. The assets of new accounts included only those assets that were deemed necessary to 'continue the current business and promote post-war development' (Ministry of Finance, 1983b, p. 734).

The new and old accounts were expected to be merged later under the guidance of CORRA, but the restructuring of non-financial companies took much longer than the restructuring of financial institutions. It was not until four years after the process began (in late 1950) that all the special account companies had submitted their restructuring plans. The implementation of the plans took even longer, and the proportion of special account companies that completed restructuring exceeded 80 per cent only in 1953. About 12 per cent of these companies seem to have disappeared without ever completing the restructuring (Ministry of Finance, 1983b, pp. 899–900).

In the process of restructuring the non-financial firms, each firm had to select a set of 'special managers' (*tokubetsu kanrinin*). As a rule, special managers consisted of two representatives from company executives and two representatives of the firm's creditors. Thus, in almost all cases, former munitions companies had representatives from their designated financial institutions as their special managers. For example, as pointed out earlier, Mitsuo Ogasawara of the Mitsubishi

Bank became a special manager of Ajinomoto. At Daihatsu Kogyo (formerly Hatsudoki Seizo), Tadao Watanabe of the Sanwa Bank, which was its designated financial institution, served as a special manager (Daihatsu Kōgyō, 1957, p. 85).

The special managers played a central role in the restructuring process. For instance, it was their responsibility to determine which assets should be included in the new account. They were also required to draw up a restructuring plan, submit it to the Finance Minister, and have it approved. Miyajima (1992, pp. 229–30) reports that in constructing the restructuring plan, the special managers had to assess the value of their remaining assets, make plans for future production and finance, and create forecasts of balance sheets and income statements. Accordingly, the restructuring of special account companies gave the special managers (and therefore the banks) an excellent opportunity to acquire information about the companies. Miyajima (1992) argues that the 'banks accumulated information about borrowers during this period rather more intensively than the period of the Designated Financial Institutions System, when the government legally forced loan contracts and basically guaranteed against the risk'. Ultimately, the accumulation of information and the responsibility associated with the restructuring process have significantly enhanced the monitoring capabilities of the banks. This process served to reverse the deterioration of bank monitoring activities that had been brought on by the wartime forced lending arrangements.

11.3.2 The post-war 'credit crunch'

The second factor that contributed to an increase of bank monitoring was the acute 'credit crunch' during this period. The credit situation became especially serious after the implementation of the Dodge stabilization plan in 1949, which cut off credit expansion through Reconstruction Bank loans. There is abundant anecdotal evidence suggesting that credit in this period were quite tight. For example, Toshio Nakamura of Mitsubishi Bank recalled 'shortage of funds made it difficult to lend even to *keiretsu* firms' during this period (Ohtsuki, 1987, p. 77).

Research reports by the Bank of Japan frequently discussed the credit crunch during this period. The Bank of Japan Research Bureau (1980) contains eight reports that address the problem of the credit crunch, which range over the period December 1947 to December 1951. One of them, entitled 'On the Funds Shortage in the Machinery Industry' and dated 20 July 1949, argues that the credit crunch, which started as a result of increasing trade credits to the government and mining companies, became more serious and permanent as the economy fell into a recession following the Dodge stabilization. The report concludes by stressing the importance of reducing the work force to aid recovery from recession.

Many companies tried to reduce their labour force, and such attempts often lead to labour conflicts. In fact, labour conflicts happened often, even before the Dodge stabilization. One can interpret the frequent labour conflicts during this period as a battle between managers and workers over corporate control, as Teranishi (1993a, 1993b) does. The recession under the Dodge stabilization plan fuelled the conflict between managers and workers, and labour conflicts in turn made the liquidity problems more serious. Eventually, managers prevailed in this battle over corporate control, but they had to turn to banks for help. Thus, by helping companies through their financing problems, banks increased their power over industrial firms.

Banks rescued many companies from liquidity crises, and sometimes directly intervened in their management. In his memoirs, Eiji Toyoda, who was the president of Toyota Auto from 1967 to 1982, looks back on the Dodge Line days as the period when Toyota Auto reluctantly started to depend on banks, especially the Mitsui Bank, and was forced to accept bank intervention in management (Nihon Keizai Shimbunsha, 1987). The Mitsui Bank and other banks helped Toyota through its liquidity crisis in 1950, but required substantial lay-offs and a spin-off of the sales department as conditions of the rescue. The Mitsui Bank also sent in a director, Fukio Nakagawa, who later served as the president of Toyota.

The case of Toyota was by no means an exception. Indeed, Miyajima (1992, pp. 233–5) argues that between 1949 and 1952 many banks began sending their employees in regularly as directors to the companies to which they made loans. Thus the credit crunch seems to have increased the role of banks in corporate governance.

During this period, however, the banks also suffered from a shortage of funds. For instance, Makoto Usami of the Mitsubishi Bank recalls that 'the demand for funds came in continuously, but not the deposits' (Nihon Keizai Shimbun-sha, 1980). Recent memories of high inflation and the deposit freeze undermined the public's trust and reduced their willingness to let the banks manage their money. The situation was especially serious for large *zaibatsu* banks, which were heavily dependent on deposits by large *zaibatsu* companies, because those companies were in the process of restructuring and did not have much money available to deposit.[14] Thus the large banks had to compete for inter-bank loans and Bank of Japan lending to make up for the shortage of deposits.

This competition among large banks seems to have further helped in giving them proper incentives to monitor firms. Since the banks had their balance sheets cleaned up and were now solvent, they were not inclined to waste money on loans to friendly but unworthy companies. The case of Mitsui Seiki given by Goro Koyama of the Mitsui Bank gives a support to this argument (Edo, 1986, p. 129). Although Mitsui Seiki was *chokkei* (of direct lineage) of Mitsui, and therefore considered to be a central Mitsui company, it got into trouble after the war because of poor management. Koyama argued that the Mitsui Bank should help other firms that were trying hard rather than helping Mitsui Seiki merely because it had the 'Mitsui' name. This argument persuaded President Sato of the Mitsui Bank to let Mitsui Seiki go through restructuring under *Kaisha Kosei Ho* (Restructuring Law). Consequently, Mitsui Seiki became the first company to be restructured under the newly-passed Restructuring Law.[15]

11.3.3 Zaibatsu dissolution

By adding the monitoring activities of the banks to a banking system that was already characterized by close bank–firm ties, the main bank system started its development. This sub-section and the next study why the ties between banks and firms were not broken during the post-war period enabling the wartime and post-war banking systems to show remarkable continuity.

One can identify two aspects of the policies implemented by the Japanese government and the Allied Forces that were responsible for this continuity. First, they failed to break up fully the *zaibatsu*, and the bank–firm ties in *zaibatsu* re-emerged when the former *zaibatsu* firms were regrouped as *keiretsu*, or corporate groups. Second, the banks did not suffer much from the post-war reforms, such as the *Zaibatsu* Dissolution and Deconcentration Law, and were therefore well positioned to play a central role in starting up corporate groups and developing the main bank system.

The *zaibatsu* were supposed to be dissolved by the Holding Company Liquidation Commission (HCLC) in consultation with the Allied Occupational Forces. When HCLC designated 83 companies in 14 *zaibatsu* as the holding companies to be dissolved, the total assets (measured in paid-in-capital) for these *zaibatsu* consisted of 43 per cent of the assets of all the companies in Japan (Yamazaki, 1976, pp. 236–7). As discussed by Hadley (1970) in detail, two measures were taken to break up the *zaibatsu*. First, shares held by the designated holding companies were transferred to HCLC, which then sold them to new owners. Second, *zaibatsu* family members, who were influential in the control of *zaibatsu* companies, were purged from top positions in these companies.

Following the *zaibatsu* dissolution by HCLC, however, many of the former *zaibatsu* companies gradually reunited as *keiretsu*. Hadley (1970, ch. 11) compares the core companies of the three largest *keiretsu* (Mitsubishi, Sumitomo and Mitsui) as of 1966 to their *zaibatsu* ancestors, and finds that most core companies in *keiretsu* in fact belonged to pre-war *zaibatsu*. Of 25 members of *Kin'yo-kai* (a group of Mitsubishi core companies) in 1966, 20 were *zaibatsu* subsidiaries. Four were newly-established companies after the war. There was only one old company which was not a subsidiary in the Mitsubishi *zaibatsu* (Kirin Beer). All 17 members of Mitsui's *Ni-moku-kai* were *zaibatsu* subsidiaries. Sumitomo's *Hakusui-kai* included 14 *zaibatsu* subsidiaries in its 17 members. Another one (Sumitomo *shoji*) was a part of Sumitomo *honsha* before the war. The other two are new members. Thus 52 out of 59 core companies of the three largest *keiretsu* in 1966 were former *zaibatsu* companies.

The personal ties among the managers of the former *zaibatsu* were obviously important in the process of the reaffiliation. Personal ties within *zaibatsu* was very strong because, according to some observers, 'the *zaibatsu* organizations combined the modern holding company with feudal loyalty' (Hadley, 1970, p. 78). Thus one would expect the managers of the various *zaibatsu* subsidiaries to feel a certain amount of kinship. This is perhaps best demonstrated by the farewell address to the employees given at the time of the break-up of Sumitomo *honsha*, by the General Director of the *honsha*, Mr Furuta. He said 'Now the *honsha* will disappear and the subsidiaries will be left on their own, but never forget that all the Sumitomo companies share the same history and roots and are brothers. Of course, we cannot offend the GHQ by holding meetings these days, but keep the spiritual ties, keep in touch with each other and co-ordinate your efforts to rebuild Japan' (Tsuda, 1988, pp. 91–2). Shortly, after the resistance to the *zaibatsu* died down, the former employees of the *zaibatsu* began to meet again. Ohtsuki (1987, p. 72) reports that former Mitsubishi managers began to infrequently convene for group lunches and eventually (by 1952) these lunches had evolved into the Kin'yo-kai – the Presidents' Council gathering for Mitsubishi. Tsuda (1988, pp. 91–5) and Edo (1986, pp. 91–4) also suggest personal ties played an important role in the formation of the Presidents' Council meetings for Sumitomo and Mitsui. Thus, while the paper ties between many of the large companies were severed, the *de facto* ties were left largely intact.

11.3.4 The anti-trust and banking sector

While the efforts of the Allied Forces to break up *zaibatsu* was incomplete, the attempt to break up large financial institutions never materialized. Although many Japanese banks expected the Allied Forces to apply anti-trust to them and prepared some plans for break-ups (Matsuzawa, 1985, pp. 25–7), it never happened. The regulations that resulted from the Occupation did not lead to any spin-offs or break-ups for financial institutions and allowed them to play leading roles in post-war corporate finance.

There were discussions between the Allied Forces and the Ministry of Finance on whether the Deconcentration Law should also be applied to financial institutions, but by the time the old and new accounts of banks were merged, they reached the conclusion that anti-trust measures would not be taken against financial institutions and that these institutions would lead the post-war reconstruction of the economy (Ministry of Finance, 1983b, pp. 300–5).

There were also bureaucratic and political factors that helped to prevent the reorganization of the banking sector. First, the administrative body that was charged with carrying out the programme of breaking up *zaibatsu*, the Economic and Scientific Section of the General Headquarters of the Supreme Commander of Allied Powers, consisted of two distinct divisions. One division was entitled the Antitrust and Cartel Division, while the other was designated the Finance Division. According to Hadley (1970), a bureaucratic war broke out. On the one hand, the Antitrust and Cartel Division claimed responsibility over all anti-trust matters, including any issues relating to banking anti-trust. On the other, the Finance Division saw itself as having full jurisdiction over financial institutions. This dispute seems to have led to an administrative deadlock.

The second critical factor was the combination of a lack of co-operation from the Japanese government and a lack of commitment from the US government. For instance, on 4 November 1945, General MacArthur was presented with a plan by the Japanese government on how they would proceed with the dissolution of *zaibatsu*. MacArthur accepted the plan two days later, but it took over nine months before any action was taken. Eventually, by September 1946, the Japanese began to draw up a list of companies targeted for disbandment. The first list proposed by the Japanese was rejected by the Allies as being too limited. Over the course of the next twelve months, the two sides agreed to expand the list to include 83 companies, but the expanded list still did not include any financial institutions. Finally, by December 1947, a significant piece of anti-trust legislation, the Deconcentration Law (FEC 230), was passed and it appeared that banking reform was also inevitable.

However, the law was immediately the subject of sharp attacks from conservatives in the USA. For example, in the Senate debate, Senator Knowland from California, outraged by the intrusive nature of the US policy that would among other things automatically remove from authority any businessmen that had previously been involved in the control of large business organizations, stated that, 'While I am in complete accord with the policy of breaking up cartels and trusts in Germany and Japan, I believe FEC 230 goes far beyond this . . . If the some of the doctrine set forth in FEC 230 had been proposed by the government of the U.S.S.R. or even the labor government of Great Britain, I could have understood it. As a statement of U.S. policy being urged by the government of the United States, I find a number of proposals so shocking that I have today written a letter to the Secretary of State' (Congressional Record, 1948 January, p. 298). Within months, and before any action regarding banks had been taken, the USA had reversed its position, and allowed the banks to lead the reconstruction efforts.

11.4 CONCLUDING REMARKS

Institutional inertia combined with the increase of monitoring ability by banks let the main bank system start to develop. By the early 1960s, when *Keiretsu no Kenkyu* was first published, many of the features of the main bank system were in place. Banks were firmly established as the primary providers of external financing for firms. Banks had also been permitted to hold equity (as well as debt) claims of their clients and were regularly taking an active role in corporate governance (for instance, by serving on boards of directors). Firms and banks were continuing to pair off, so that everyone could identify clearly the main bank of a particular firm.

This chapter has studied how an institution called the main bank system developed in Japan. The four changes during the war, (i) a concentration of the banking industry; (ii) a higher dependence on bank borrowing; (iii) the development and affirmation of close bank-firm ties; and (iv) the decline in shareholders' power, led to the creation of the prototype of the main bank system. The lack of commitment by the Japanese government and the Allied Forces to break up the close bank–firm ties insured that many aspects of wartime corporate finance were carried over to the post-war period. Then the banks gained substantial power to monitor the firms, through their experience in the restructuring of industrial firms and in the period of severe credit crunch, and the main bank system started to develop.

One can make several interesting observations in this evolutionary process of the main bank system. First, the events that laid the foundations for the development of the main bank system are those that could have happened (and can happen) in an economy other than Japan. In this sense, it is possible for a financial system such as the main bank system to develop outside Japan. Second, the Japanese government's policies, especially its wartime controls, played an important role. This suggests that a government, if it wishes, may be able to 'nurture' the development of the main bank system to some extent. Finally, the monitoring role of the banks, which is often considered to be central to the main bank system, became apparent only in the post-war period. The prototype of the main bank system looked quite different from the modern main bank system in this respect. This experience shows that a banking system with fairly efficient monitoring can emerge from an apparently chaotic banking system that does not monitor firms.

All three observations are good news for policy-makers in developing countries or former socialist economies that are trying to learn some lessons from Japanese experience.[16] If the policy-makers find a banking system like the main bank system desirable for the current situation in their economy, then they can help the development of such a system. The main bank system does not have to be unique to Japan; and it could grow out of a totally inefficient banking system.

NOTES

1. For a survey of the research on the main bank system, see Aoki *et al.* (1994).
2. The total number of banks in 1925 was 1537, but the data used for the analysis were not available for 22 banks (Teranishi 1982, pp. 314–15). The general price level almost tripled between 1904 and 1925. According to the estimates of Ohkawa *et al.* (1967), the CPI inflation rate during

these 20 years was 149 per cent. Thus ¥1 million in 1904 corresponds to about ¥2.5 million in 1925.

3. The following information is taken from Asajima (1983, 1987b).

4. Clause 11 of the Total National Mobilization Law states, 'When it is necessary for wartime total national mobilization, the government, under the guidance of an Imperial Order, can limit or prohibit establishment of a company, new share issues, merger, change of business, new bond issues, and payment of un-paid-in capital, can give necessary orders regarding accounting of companies such as use of profits or depreciation, and can give necessary orders regarding use of funds to banks, trust companies, insurance companies and others designated by an Imperial Order.' (Bank of Japan Research Bureau, 1973, pp. 612–13).

5. Large firms sometimes had more than one bank assigned to help them.

6. See Bank of Japan Research Bureau (1973, p. 397) for the text of the Selection Policy. See also Mitsubishi Bank (1954, pp. 348–50).

7. Another case that suggests a lack of close ties between Ajinomoto and Mitsubishi is that another munitions company, Showa Nosan Kako, which was established by Ajinomoto to deal with the sale of alcohol in 1934, was assigned Teikoku and Yasuda Banks as its designated institutions. Interestingly, Showa Nosan Kako, which changed its name to Sanraku Ocean after the war, had Mitsubishi Trust as its largest lender and third largest shareholder in 1962 (and also in 1974). This suggests that the ties established through government assignments were not as strong as the ties between a company and its former subsidiaries.

8. The data are from Keizai Chosa Kyokai's *Keiretsu no Kenkyu*.

9. A pay-out ratio is the proportion of the dividend payments per share to the par value of the share.

10. For a detailed description of negotiations between the Japanese government and the Allies, see Ministry of Finance, 1983a, pp. 183–347.

11. The estimate was published on 2 October 1946. See Ministry of Finance, 1983b, p. 699.

12. The GNE data is from Ministry of Finance, 1978, pp. 26–7.

13. For a more detailed discussion of restructuring process, see Hoshi *et al.* (1994).

14. Sumitomo Ginko, 1979, pp. 400–1. Also see Miyajima, 1992, table 5–6, p. 229.

15. Mitsui Seiki later came out of bankruptcy to become a healthy company once again. As Hoshi (1993) shows, close ties with the Mitsui Bank were not severed even after the restructuring. In 1974, the Mitsui Bank was the largest lender and the third largest shareholder of Mitsui Seiki. Today, Mitsui Seiki still keeps its close ties to the Mitsui Bank. As of 1989, the Mitsui is still the largest lender and the fourth largest shareholder (*Keiretsu no Kenkyu, 1991*).

16. There are some studies that examine the relevance of the main bank system for financial system reform in transforming socialist economies. See Hoshi *et al.* (1994), Qian (1994) and Patrick (1994).

REFERENCES

Ajinomoto 1971. *Ajinomoto Kabushiki Gaisha Sha-shi* (Ajinomoto's Company History), 2 vols, Tōkyō: Ajinomoto.

Ajinomoto 1989. *Aji o Tagayasu: Ajinomoto Hachijunen-shi* (Cultivating Tastes: Eighty Year History of Ajinomoto), Tōkyō: Ajinomoto.

Ando, Yoshio 1979. *Kindai Nihon Keizaishi Yoran*, 2nd edn, Tōkyō: University of Tōkyō Press.

Aoki, Masahiko, Hugh Patrick and Paul Sheard 1994. 'The Japanese Main Bank System; An Introductory Overview', in Masahiko Aoki and Hugh Patrick (eds), *The Japanese Main Bank System: Its Relevancy for Developing and Transforming Economies*, Oxford University Press.

Asajima, Shoichi 1983. *Senkan-ki Sumitomo Zaibatsu Keiei-shi* (Business History of the Sumitomo Zaibatsu in the Inter-war Period), Tōkyō: University of Tōkyō Press.

Asajima, Shoichi 1986. *Mitsubishi Zaibatsu no Kin'yu Kozo* (Financial Structure of the Mitsubishi Zaibatsu), Tōkyō: Ochanomizu Shobo.

Asajima, Shoichi 1987a. 'Mitsubishi Zaibatsu', in Shoichi Asajima (ed.), *Zaibatsu Kin'yu Kozo no Hikaku Kenkyu*. (A Comparative Study of the Financial Structure of Zaibatsu), Tōkyō: Ochanomizu Shobo, pp. 95–157.

Asajima, Shoichi 1987b. 'Sumitomo Zaibatsu', in Shoichi Asajima (ed.), *Zaibatsu Kin'yu Kozo no Hikaku Kenkyu*. (A Comparative Study of the Financial Structure of Zaibatsu), Tōkyō: Ochanomizu Shobo, pp. 159–213.

Bank of Japan Research Bureau 1973. *Nihon Kin'yu-shi Shiryo: Showa Hen, Vol. 34* (Data for Japanese Financial History: Showa Volumes. Vol. 34) Tōkyō: Ministry of Finance Printing Bureau.

Bank of Japan Research Bureau 1980. *Nihon Kin'yu-shi Shiryo: Showa Zoku-hen, Vol. 8* (Data for Japanese Financial History: More Showa Volumes, Vol. 8) Tōkyō: Ministry of Finance Printing Bureau.

Bank of Japan Statistics Bureau 1966. *Hundred-Year Statistics of the Japanese Economy*, Tōkyō: Bank of Japan.

Daihatsu Kōgyō 1957. *Go-Ju-nen-shi* (Fifty-Year History), Tōkyō: Daihatsu Kōgyō.

Edo, Hideo, 1986. *Watashi no Mitsui Showa-shi* (My Showa History in Mitsui) Tōkyō, Japan: Toyo Keizai Shimpo-sha.

Fujino, Shozaburo 1965. *Nihon no Keiki Junkan* (Japanese Business Cycles) Tōkyō, Japan: Keiso Shobo.

Goto, Shin'ichi 1991. *Ginko Godo no Jissho-teki Kenkyu* (An Empirical Investigation of Bank Mergers) Tōkyō, Japan: Nihon Keizai Hyoron-sha.

Hadley, Eleanor M. 1970. *Antitrust in Japan*, Princeton, NJ: Princeton University Press.

Hashimoto, Juro 1992. 'Zaibatsu no Kontserun-ka', in Juro Hashimoto and Haruto Takeda (eds), *Nihon Keizai no Hatten to Keiretsu* (The Development of Japanese Economy and Industrial Groups), Tōkyō: University of Tōkyō Press, pp. 91–148.

Hirota, Shin'ichi 1990. 'Nihon ni okeru Mein Banku no Hoken Teikyo Kino ni tsuite', (On the Insurance Provision Mechanism of Main Banks in Japan), *Doshisha Daigaku Keizai Ronso*, 41, pp. 329–52.

Horiuchi, Akiyoshi 1989. 'Informational Properties of the Japanese Financial

System', *Japan and the World Economy*, 1, pp. 255–78.

Horiuchi, Akiyoshi, Frank Packer and Shin'ichi Fukuda 1988. 'What Role Has the "Main Bank" Played in Japan?', *Journal of the Japanese and International Economies*, 2, pp. 159–80.

Hoshi, Takeo 1993. 'Evolution of the Main Bank System in Japan'. University of California, San Diego, IR/PS Research Report #93–04.

Hoshi, Takeo, Anil Kashyap and Gary Loveman 1994. 'Lessons from the Japanese Main Bank System for Financial System Reform in Poland', in Masahiko Aoki and Hugh Patrick (eds), *The Japanese Main Bank System: Its Relevancy for Developing and Transforming Economies*, Oxford University Press.

Hoshi, Takeo, Anil Kashyap and David Scharfstein 1990. 'The Role of Banks in Reducing the Costs of Financial Distress in Japan', *Journal of Financial Economics*, 27, pp. 67–88.

Hoshi, Takeo, Anil Kashyap and David Scharfstein 1991. 'Corporate Structure, Liquidity, and Investment: Evidence from Japanese Industrial Groups', *Quarterly Journal of Economics*, 106, pp. 33–60.

Kaplan, Steven and Bernadette Minton 1993. '"Outside" Intervention in Japanese Companies: Its Determinants and Its Implications for Managers'. manuscript, Graduate School of Business, University of Chicago.

Kasuga, Yutaka 1987. 'Mitsui Zaibatsu,' in Shoichi Asajima (ed.) *Zaibatsu Kin'yu Kozo no Hikaku Kenkyu*. (A Comparative Study of the Financial Structure of Zaibatsu), Tōkyō: Ochanomizu Shobō, pp. 15–93.

Keiretsu no Kenkyu (A Study of Keiretsu) various issues, Tōkyō, Japan: Keizai Chosa Kyokai.

Kobe University Research Institute of Economics and Management 1986. *Shuyo Kigyo no Keifuzu*, (Genealogical Chart of Japanese Major Corporations), Tōkyō: Yushodo Press.

Matsuzawa, Takuji 1985. *Watashi no Ginko Showa-shi* (My Showa Banking History), Tōkyō: Toyo Keizai Shinpo-sha.

Ministry of Finance 1976. *Showa Zaisei-shi: Shusen kara Kowa made. Vol. 12: Kin'yu (1)* (Financial History of Showa: War's End to Peace Treaty. Vol. 12: Finance (1)) (written by Takafusa Nakamura, Kaichi Shimura and Shiro Hara), Tōkyō: Toyo Keizai Shimpo-sha.

Ministry of Finance 1978. *Showa Zaisei-shi: Shusen kara Kowa made. Vol. 19: Tokei* (Financial History of Showa: War's End to Peace Treaty. Vol. 19: Statistical Data), Tōkyō: Toyo Keizai Shimpo-sha.

Ministry of Finance 1983a. *Showa Zaisei-shi: Shusen kara Kowa made. Vol. 11: Seifu Saimu* (Financial History of Showa: War's End to Peace Treaty. Vol. 11: Government Debt) (written by Saburo Kato), Tōkyō: Toyo Keizai Shimpo-sha.

Ministry of Finance 1983b. *Showa Zaisei-shi: Shusen kara Kowa made. Vol. 13: Kin'yu (2), Kigyo Zaimu, Mikaeri Shikin* (Financial History of Showa: War's End to Peace Treaty. Vol. 13: Finance (2), Corporate Finance, and Assistance Funds) (written by Toshimitsu Imuta, Osamu Ito, Shiro Hara, Masayasu Miyazaki and Yoshimasa Shibata), Tōkyō: Toyo Keizai Shimpo-sha.

Mitsubishi Bank 1954. *Mitsubishi Ginko-shi* (History of the Mitsubishi Bank) Tōkyō.

Miyajima, Hideaki 1992. 'Zaibatsu Kaitai' (*Zaibatsu* Dissolution) in Juro Hashimoto and Haruto Takeda (eds), *Nihon Keizai no Hatten to Keiretsu*

(The Development of Japanese Economy and Industrial Groups), Tōkyō: University of Tōkyō Press, pp. 203–54.

Miyazaki, Masayasu and Osamu Ito 1989. 'Senji Sengo no Sangyo to Kigyo' (Industries and Corporations during and after the War), in Takafusa Nakamura (ed.), *Nihon Keizaishi 7: 'Keikaku-ka' to 'Minshu-ka'*, (Japanese Economic History 7: 'Planning' and 'Democratizing') Tōkyō: Iwanami Shoten, pp. 165–235.

Nakamura, Takafusa 1971. *Economics Growth in Prewar Japan* (translated by Robert A. Feldman) New Haven, Conn.: Yale University Press.

Nakamura, Takafusa 1989. 'Gaisetsu 1937–54 nen' (Introduction 1937–54), in Takafusa Nakamura (ed.), *Nihon Keizaishi 7: 'Keikaku-ka' to 'Minshuka'*, (Japanese Economic History 7: 'Planning' and 'Democratizing') Tōkyō: Iwanami Shoten, pp. 1–68.

Nakatani, Iwao 1984. 'The Economic Role of Financial Corporate Grouping', in Masahiko Aoki (ed.), *The Economic Analysis of the Japanese Firm*, Amsterdam: North-Holland Elsevier, pp. 227–58.

Nihon Keizai Shimbun-sha 1980. *Watashi no Rirekisho: Keizai-jin. Vol. 14* (My Personal History: Business People. Vol. 14) Tōkyō: Nihon Keizai Shimbun-sha.

Nihon Keizai Shimbun-sha 1987. *Watashi no Rirekisho: Keizai-jin. Vol. 22* (My Personal History: Business People. Vol. 22) Tōkyō: Nihon Keizai Shimbun-sha.

Ohkawa, Kazushi, Miyohei Shinohara and Mataji Umemura (eds) 1967. *Estimates of Long-term Economic Statistics of Japan since 1868. Vol. 8 Prices*, Tōkyō: Toyo Keizai Shinpo-sha.

Ohtsuki, Bunpei 1987. *Watashi no Mitsubishi Showa-shi.* (My Showa History in Mitsubishi) Tokyo: Toyo Keizai Shimpo-sha.

Okazaki, Tetsuji 1991. 'Senji Keikaku Keizai to Kigyo' (War-Time Planned Economy and Firms), in University of Tōkyō, Social Science Research Institute (ed.), *Gendai Nihon Shakai. 4: Rekishi-teki Zentei* (Contemporary Japanese Society. 4: Historical Presumptions) Tōkyō: University of Tōkyō Press, pp. 363–98.

Okazaki, Tetsuji 1993a. 'The Japanese Firm under the Wartime Planned Economy', *Journal of the Japanese and International Economies*, 7, pp. 175–203.

Okazaki, Tetsuji 1993b. 'Kigyo System' (Enterprise System), in Tetsuji Okazaki and Masahiro Okuno (eds), *Gendai Nihon Keizai System no Genryu* (The Origin of the Contemporary Japanese Economic System), Tōkyō: Nihon Keizai Shimbun-sha, pp. 97–44.

Pascale, Richard and Thomas Rohlen 1983. 'The Mazda Turnaround', *Journal of Japanese Studies*, 9, pp. 219–63.

Patrick, Hugh 1981. 'Senkan-ki ni okeru Nihon Kin'yu Seido no Seisei' (Evolution of the Japanese Financial System during the Inter-War Period), in Takafusa Nakamura (ed.), *Senkan-ki no Nihon Keizai Bunseki* (An Analysis of the Japanese Economy during the Inter-War Period) Tōkyō: Yamakawa Shuppan-sha, pp. 135–64.

Patrick, Hugh 1994. 'The Relevance of Japanese Finance and its Main Bank System' in Masahiko Aoki and Hugh Patrick (eds), *The Japanese Main Bank System: Its Relevancy for Developing and Transforming Economies*, Oxford University Press.

Qian, Yingyi 1994. 'Lessons and Relevance of the Japanese Main-Bank System for Financial Reform in China' in Masahiko Aoki and Hugh Patrick (eds.), *The Japanese Main Bank System: Its Relevancy for Developing and Transforming Economies*, Oxford University Press.

Sawai, Minoru 1992. 'Senji Keizai to Zaibatsu' (War Economy and *Zaibatsu*), in Juro Hashimoto and Haruto Takeda (eds), *Nihon Keizai no Hatten to Keiretsu* (The Development of Japanese Economy and Industrial Groups), Tōkyō: University of Tōkyō Press, pp. 149–202.

Schoenholtz, Kermit and Masahiko Takeda 1985. 'Joho Katsudo to Mein Banku sei', (Informational Activities and the Main Bank System), *Kin'yu Kenkyu*, 4, pp. 1–24.

Sheard, Paul 1989. 'The Main Bank System and Corporate Monitoring and Control in Japan', *Journal of Economic Behavior and Organization*, 11, pp. 399–422.

Sheard, Paul 1991. 'Reciprocal Delegated Monitoring in the Japanese Main Bank System', *Journal of the Japanese and International Economies*, 8, pp. 1–21.

Sheard, Paul 1992. 'The Role of the Japanese Main Bank when Borrowing Firms are in Financial Distress'. Stanford University, CEPR Working Paper No. 330.

Shibagaki, Kazuo 1974. 'Zaibatsu Kaitai to Shuchu Haijo' (Zaibatsu Dissolution and Elimination of Concentration), in University of Tōkyō, Social Science Research Institute (ed.), *Sengo Kaikaku. 7: Keizai Kaikaku* (Post-War Reforms. 7: Economic Reforms) Tōkyō, Japan: University of Tōkyō Press, pp. 33–107.

Sumitomo Ginko 1979. *Sumitomo Ginko Hachi-Ju-nen-shi* (Eighty Years' History of Sumitomo Bank), Tōkyō: Sumitomo Bank.

Teranishi, Juro 1982. *Nihon no Keizai Hatten to Kin'yu* (Japanese Economic Development and Financial System), Tōkyō: Iwanami Shoten.

Teranishi, Juro 1993a. 'Mein Banku Sisutemu' (Main Bank System), in Tetsuji Okazaki and Masahiro Okuno (eds), *Gendai Nihon Keizai System no Genryu* (The Origin of the Contemporary Japanese Economic System), Tōkyō: Nihon Keizai Shimbun-sha, pp. 61–95.

Teranishi, Juro 1993b. 'Emergence and Establishment of the Financial System in Postwar Japan – Government Intervention, Indirect Financing and the Corporate Monitoring System', paper prepared for the World Bank project 'Strategies for Rapid Growth: Public Policy and the Asian Miracle'.

Teranishi, Juro 1994. 'Emergence of Loan Syndication in Wartime Japan: An Investigation into the Historical Origins of the Main Bank System', in Masahiko Aoki and Hugh Patrick (eds), *The Japanese Main Bank System: Its Relevancy for Developing and Transforming Economies*, Oxford University Press.

Tsuda, Hisashi 1988. *Watashi no Sumitomo Showa-shi* (My Showa History in Sumitomo) Tōkyō: Toyo Keizai Shimpo-sha.

Yamazaki, Hiroaki 1979. 'Senji-ka no Sangyo Kozo to Dokusen Soshiki' (Industrial Structure and Monopolistic Organization during the War) in University of Tōkyō, Social Science Research Institute (ed.), *Fascism-ki no Kokka to Shakai. 2: Sen-ji Nihon Keizai* (State and Society under Fascism. 2: War-Time Japanese Economy) Tōkyō: University of Tōkyō Press, pp. 217–89.

12 Monetary Policy in Japan: A Perspective on Tools, Transmission Channels and Outcomes

Mitsuaki Okabe*

12.1 INTRODUCTION

In Japan, as in many other countries, monetary policy has been substantially responsible for the nation's macroeconomic performance, for good or ill. When changes occur in the economic structure, in the regulatory framework or in the international environment, it is inevitable that changes take place in the conduct of policy and in the process of transmission of policy effects.

There is abundant documentation to explain the changes in Japanese financial markets, and many specific aspects of Japanese monetary policy have been scrutinized in recent years.[1] But at present there appears to be no comprehensive paper, at least not published in English, that deals simultaneously with the structural changes of the financial markets and economy and their relationship to policy conduct and policy transmission channels. This chapter intends to fill that gap. By surveying the existing literature on the subject extensively, it aims to provide a perspective on the transmission channels of Japanese monetary policy since 1975. In particular, it discusses the changes to this mechanism brought about by the structural, regulatory and environmental changes in the Japanese financial markets and the economy.[2]

* An earlier version of this paper was presented at the First Conference on the Contemporary Japanese Economy at Macquarie University, Sydney, 25–26 March, 1993 and seminars at the Australian National University and the Reserve Bank of Australia. The author is grateful to Bill Norton, Paul Sheard, Peter Drysdale, Wataru Takahashi, Hiroshi Yoshikawa, Thomas Cargill and the conference and seminar participants for their comments, and to Helen Smith for editorial assistance. Views expressed herein and any remaining errors are strictly of the author and not of the Bank of Japan nor any of the above individuals.

In Section 12.2, the transmission of the effects of Japanese monetary policy is classified into four channels and the characteristics of each channel is explained. Section 12.3 highlights key structural changes made to the Japanese economy over the last twenty years and explains their effects on policy tools and policy transmission processes using the four-channel classification described in Section 12.2. Section 12.4 deals with the conduct of monetary policy of the Bank of Japan and presents a systematic summary as well as a brief econometric analysis by estimating policy reaction functions. Finally, Section 12.5 gives a general summary of the chapter, together with some implications for desirable monetary policy.

12.2 MAIN TRANSMISSION CHANNELS OF JAPANESE MONETARY POLICY

The effects of monetary policy are transmitted to the entire economy through various channels and they appear in many aspects of it. The character of the process and the effects naturally vary, depending on many factors; in particular, depending on the structure of the economy at a given period of time, the degree of financial deregulation, the international environment, and the stage of the business cycle during which the policy is implemented. In the case of Japanese monetary policy and its effects, there are, of course, similarities to other developed market economies, as well as subtle differences. However, the transmission channels of Japanese monetary policy may be schematically and broadly understood as in Figure 12.1,[3] as will be explained in detail later.

If we take the example of a tightening policy, that is, a policy to raise interest rates in an attempt to restrain inflation, the policy and its effects may be described as follows. The Bank of Japan (BOJ), the Japanese central bank, usually raises the official discount rate first and tries to reduce the supply of reserves (base money or high-powered money) by using various instruments of market control. These actions tighten the demand–supply condition in the inter-bank, short-term money market, and generate the expectation among the market participants of a higher short-term interest rate in future. That is, the signalling by the Bank of Japan to raise interest rates is thus effectively transmitted, in the first instance, to this market.[4] An initial rise of interest rates (call-loan rates and bill rates) in the inter-bank market raises, by arbitrage

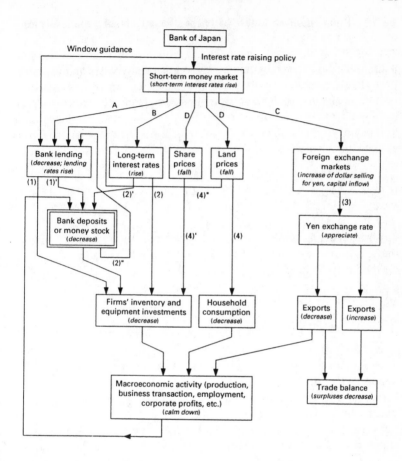

Source: Okabe (1991), figure 2.

FIGURE 12.1   Transmission mechanism of monetary policy in Japan: diversification of its channels

transactions, the interest rates in other short-term markets, called open markets, in which non-banks are also allowed to participate.[5] Therefore the interest rate level in the whole short-term market rises. Moreover, in implementing a tightening policy, the Bank of Japan also used to resort to 'window guidance', a moral persuasion or credit control on increases in the total amount of loans by city banks, as a supplementary measure.

12.2.1   Four main channels of transmission of the policy effects

The effects of the above-mentioned interest rate control and window guidance on the whole economy can be summarized in terms of the four channels of Figure 12.1 which also shows the effect on money supply (monetary aggregates), an intermediate target of monetary policy in Japan.

1.   Effects on lending

The first channel in which the influence of tightening policy appears is in the change of attitude of lending by financial institutions (hereafter called simply 'banks'), shown as Channel A in the diagram. This may be called the *lending effect*.

When interest rate levels rise as a result of a tight monetary policy, the speed of the interest rate rises can vary substantially, depending on the kinds of interest rates. Interest rates in short-term money markets, which indicates the marginal funding costs for banks, rise immediately and more flexibly in their magnitude, while the lending rates of banks usually tend to be staggered or sticky and do not rise as quickly or to such an extent as short-term money market rates. This is because, first, banks do not pass on the increase in funding costs to their clients immediately, especially in Japan, since they place a greater importance on long-term customer relationships, particularly with their corporate clients, rather than maintain a distant relationship and pursue the immediate gain in profit.[6] And second, lending rates in Japan (in particular, long-term rates) once were more or less regulated so that a rise in short-term money market rates would not bring an immediate rise in lending rates. Lending rates do eventually rise but they are staggered because they are paired with bank deposit rates which have been regulated substantially. Under these circumstances, where the cost of funding rises in comparison with the cost of lending, the marginal revenue of bank lending deteriorates, thus generating pressure on banks to reduce lending. This leads to a decline in money supply (bank deposits), on the one hand, and on the other it puts a brake on investment and production activities of non-bank firms because of the decline in the availability of funds. These effects are shown as 1 and 1' in Figure 12.1.

The rise of short-term rates has one more channel to reduce bank lending. After a rise in interest rates, firms find it more profitable to hold various financial assets with market-determined rates, such as CDs or freely-traded government bonds, than to hold bank deposits whose interest rates are regulated and are less flexible in their movement. The resulting interest rate gap between two kinds of financial assets reduces bank deposits in favour of market-rate assets, so that banks are now compelled to reduce the lending (financial disintermediation) due to the decline of the deposits which are the source of funds for its lending. This is shown by 2' and 2" in Figure 12.1. Therefore, the business activity of firms also suffers from this channel of reduced availability of credit.

If a firm's investment and production activities are restrained by the reduction in bank lending as above, it eases the demand-and-supply situation of goods and services in the macroeconomy and works to fulfil the policy goal of achieving price stability. When we look at the effects of these two channels on money supply or monetary aggregates, both channels may be said to be affecting money stock from the supply side, rather than from the demand side, of money. It should be noted also that the effects on the economy and money supply are generated because of the coexistence of market-determined interest rates, and regulated or sticky interest rates.

Window guidance, which complements the effects of interest rate policy, also reduces money supply by directly reducing bank lending (see 'window guidance' and the channel 1' in Figure 12.1), and restrain business activity by limiting the availability of funds (channel 1 in the same figure).

2. *Effects on expenditure*

The second effect of a tightening policy is the direct restraint of the expenditure of firms and households because of the general rise of interest rates, including long-term interest rates. This is shown as Channel B in Figure 12.1, and can be called the *expenditure effect*.

When short-term interest rates rise, long-term interest rates (yields of long-term bonds) usually also rise, because of arbitrage transactions taking place between these markets.[7] The rise of long-term interest rates or the yield of corporate bonds means for a firm an increase in the cost of financing for investment, regardless of whether the financing is by borrowing from banks or by issuing corporate bonds. Therefore, with given expected profit rates, firms become more restrictive in inventory and equipment investment because of cost–profit considerations, when contrasted with a consideration of the availability of funds. This is shown as 2 in Figure 12.1. Also, the rise of deposit interest rates, although the degree of the rise is somewhat limited, gives households more incentive to save and restrain consumption. These effects on firms and households to restrain expenditure help to check inflation and stabilize prices.

In terms of the effects on money supply (money stock), all these restraining effects on expenditure imply a decrease in the demand for money. Therefore money stock is subdued, in this case, from the demand side rather than from supply side. Moreover, there is another aspect which reduces money stock from the demand side: since firms face the increased cost of financing, or an increase in the opportunity cost of holding bank deposits, they restrict the issuing of corporate bonds or borrowing from banks, or they convert existing bank deposits into various long-term bonds. All these actions by firms mean a decrease in the demand for money, as shown in 2' in Figure 12.1. Therefore tight monetary policy works to reduce money stock.

3. *Effects associated with exchange rate changes*

The third effect of a tightening policy is the restraining effect on the aggregate demand associated with appreciation of the yen exchange rate. This effect takes place because a rise in Japanese interest rates, in comparison with the interest rates of other counties, tends to appreciate the Japanese yen, thus depressing foreign demand for Japanese products and increasing Japanese demand for foreign products, hence the decline of aggregate demand for the Japanese economy. This channel is shown as Channel C in Figure 12.1, and may be called the *exchange rate effect*.

If the Japanese interest rate becomes comparatively higher than overseas interest rates, the holding of yen-denominated assets becomes more profitable than holding assets denominated in a foreign currency; for example, assets denominated in US dollars. This generates pressure to buy yen and sell dollars in the foreign exchange market, thus appreciating the yen *vis-à-vis* the dollar, as shown in 3 in Figure 12.1. With the higher value of the yen, the overseas demand for Japanese products, or Japanese exports, declines and the domestic demand for foreign products, or Japanese imports, increases. Thus the decline of net exports (usually a decrease in trade balance surplus) is expected in the long run, since the required elasticity conditions (generalized Marshall–Lerner condition) are met in the long run regardless of whether the trade balance is measured in dollars or yen (see Table 12.1).[8] In terms of aggregate demand, appreciation of the yen initiated by the rise of

TABLE 12.1 Price elasticities of Japanese imports and exports and conditions for the decrease of trade surplus as a result of the yen appreciation

		Bank of Japan	White Paper on the Economy	Economic Planning Agency (world econometric model)	White Paper on Trade and Industry	K. Ueda (University of Tokyo)
Short-term elasticity:	Exports (a)	0.3	0.2	0.3	0.3	0.7
	Imports (b)	0.1	0.1	0.2	0.2	0.3
Trade balance in yen:	$(1.4 \times a + b)$	0.5	0.3	0.7	0.6	1.2
Trade balance in dollars:	$(a + 0.7 \times b)$	0.4	0.2	0.5	0.4	0.9
Long-term elasticity:	Exports (a)	1.1	0.8	1.2	1.1	1.8
	Imports (b)	0.2	0.2	0.5	0.6	0.5
Trade balance in yen:	$(1.4 \times a + b)$	1.7	1.2	2.2	2.2	3.0
Trade balance in dollars:	$(a + 0.7 \times b)$	1.2	0.9	1.6	1.5	2.1

Notes: 1. Short-term elasticity refers to a half-year elasticity; long-term elasticity refers to the terminal elasticity.
2. See Note 8 in the text.

Source: Okabe (1989) table 1.

interest rates has a deflationary impact, at least in the short run, because it has a negative effect on Japanese exports. Therefore, the policy
of raising interest rates contributes to restraining inflationary pressure
in the economy.

As to money supply, it also declines because of the decrease in the
demand for money, reflecting the reduced aggregate demand.

4. Effects associated with the change in the value of assets

The fourth effect of a rise in interest rates is the restraining effect on
expenditure stemming from the decrease in the value of various stocks
or wealth, such as land and corporate shares, brought about by higher
interest rates. This effect is shown as Channel D in Figure 12.1, and
may be called the (negative) *wealth effect* or *stock effect*.

Generally speaking, the asset price or the price of stock is the discounted present value of a stream of future earnings which are expected to be generated by the asset (in the case of corporate shares,
the asset which ultimately matters is the total asset, especially the capital
stock and land, which the corporation possesses), so a rise in the interest
rate or the rate of discount[9] reduces the current price of various assets
(land and corporate shares).

The decline in the value of these assets decreases expenditures of
both firms and households. In the case of households, the diminished
value of the assets precipitates the household to increase saving and
reduce consumption, because it tries to restore the original value of
the assets by supplementing the lost value out of current income. This
is the (negative) wealth effect, and is shown as 4 in Figure 12.1. Moreover, in Japan, the decline of land value means a reduction in the
value of collateral for bank borrowing, as shown as channel 4", so
housing investment tends to decline.[10] For firms, the decline in the
value of land and share prices also restricts their expenditure by limiting the availability of funds. There are two reasons for this: first, as
in the case of households, the diminishing value of assets leads to a
reduction in the value of potential collateral for loans, thus reducing
the ability of firms to borrow from banks; second, the decline of share
prices makes equity financing (such as issuing new shares or bonds
with warrants) more costly and difficult, and thus renders the financing
of investment activities more restrictive. One may give a macroeconomic
interpretation to the latter effect: the decline of the share price means
that the market lowers its valuation of the capital stock of the firm,
thus impairing the incentive of the firm to invest in capital stock (Tobin's

q effect). Raising interest rates thus has a restraining effect on expenditure of both households and firms, and decreases money stock from the demand side accordingly.

To sum up, tightening monetary policy by raising interest rates causes banks to restrain lending, depresses equipment and housing investments and personal consumption, and reduces net foreign demand for Japanese products. All these effects contribute to ease demand and supply situation in domestic goods and services markets, and thus reduce inflationary pressure, stabilize prices, and achieve the policy objective. On the other hand, tight monetary policy reduces the surplus in the trade balance, and decreases money supply.

12.2.2. Empirical studies of the policy effects

These effects and the transmission mechanism of monetary policy in Japan have been documented widely in various empirical studies. First of all, unidirectional causality (in the sense of Granger) from policy-determined interest rates, that is, call-loan and bill rates, to money supply has been observed by using various statistical methods.[11] This indicates empirically that in Japan the control of money supply is initiated by controlling market interest rates, as seen above. Moreover, the relationship of money supply to key macroeconomic variables, as explained above, is widely confirmed by using recently developed statistical techniques, such as vector autoregressive (VAR) models and calculating the impulse-response functions to study the dynamic effects of various policy shocks. In particular, it has been shown that (a) changes in interest rates, as well as changes in money supply, play a role in the policy transmission process in affecting real variables.[12] It is also shown that when money supply increases, (b) it raises domestic prices in generally stable manner, though the relationship has substantially been blurred in recent years;[13] (c) it raises real GNP initially but in the long run the rise disappears and only the rise in the inflation rate remains;[14] and (d) it depreciates the yen exchange rate in the long run.[15]

Whether monetary policy works through credit or money is hotly debated in some other countries, particularly in the USA,[16] but in Japan the issue has not been debated so keenly. Rather, much evidence has been presented in Japan for both cases.[17] The lack of debate on this issue is presumably due to the fact that, when looked at statistically, in Japan the importance of lending has been far greater as a counterbalance of money in the balance sheet of financial institutions[18] and, accordingly, movements of money and credit have not diverged as widely as in the USA. In future, however, the debate will become keener because monetary aggregates have been losing their importance as an indicator of monetary policy.

12.3 CHANGES IN THE RELATIVE IMPORTANCE OF POLICY TOOLS AND TRANSMISSION CHANNELS

Which tool and channel of transmission of monetary policy should be said to be more important in Japan? It depends on the phase of the business cycle .in the economy and, more importantly, on the basic structure of the economy at any given time, such as the degree of direct control or deregulation concerning interest rates and other financial transactions, the degree of international integration of Japanese financial markets into the overseas markets, and the degree of financial and other asset accumulation.

In this section, changes in the importance of one of the traditional policy tools, namely window guidance, will be discussed, and then changes in the transmission channels of policy effects will be analyzed.

12.3.1 Declined effectiveness of window guidance and its abolition

One of the most conspicuous changes over the past twenty years in realizing the expected policy effects of monetary policy is the decline of the effectiveness of window guidance.

Since the 1970s, some economists have been arguing that window guidance could not be an effective means of macroeconomic policy to control money supply or aggregate demand.[19] This view was asserted for two reasons. First, even if the BOJ could curb the lending of those banks subject to its direct control (primarily the city banks) and could restrict the kind of lending that was subject to guidance (yen-denominated domestic lending), other lending could increase, such as the lending by other banks and financial institutions which were not subject to guidance (such as regional banks), and lending which was not subject to guidance (such as dollar-denominated lending). Second, even if bank lending is directly controlled by the BOJ bank deposits or money supply need not be reduced, as the banks could change the structure of their asset holdings by shifting away from lending to bond holding (substitutability of bond holding and lending); thereby the size of deposits may remain unchanged.

Contrary to this view, some economists have argued that even if the regulation affected only bank lending it was an effective means of macroeconomic policy, as long as there existed insufficient linkage (incomplete integration) of various financial markets, or as long as bank borrowing and bond issuing were deemed to be an incomplete substitute as a means of finance for firms (especially in the case of small firms, which are excluded from the bond-issuing market). In particular, it was asserted that, if one of these conditions was satisfied, credit rationing in bank lending markets could take place effectively, and window guidance could exert influence on the total amount of credit available. Therefore, it is argued, the influence of window guidance on business investment activities had not been negligible.[20]

The debate does not seem to have been settled. However, it is important to note that when the BOJ uses window guidance it is always as a way to supplement other orthodox means (of controlling interest rates) and never as a means in its own right. Thus the effectiveness of this policy tool should be evaluated only in this context.[21]

In any case, Japanese financial markets have recently undergone substantial structural changes. The linkage of various domestic financial markets has increased constantly because of deregulation measures in interest rates and transactions, and also the integration of domestic and overseas markets has taken place. Moreover, the instruments of funding for Japanese corporations have been diversified, in both domestic and international markets. Thus the deregulation and internationalization of the Japanese financial markets, as well as diversification of funding instruments of Japanese corporations, have reduced the role of window guidance substantially as a means of controlling monetary aggregates and eventually macroeconomic activity. Given these developments, in July 1991 the BOJ announced it would abolish this measure as part of the ordinary instruments of monetary policy. Therefore the importance of this policy instrument in Figure 12.1 is now only historical.

12.3.2 Increased importance of the channels through interest rate changes

Since the late 1970s, an important change in the transmission of monetary policy effects has been taking place. The effectiveness of direct, quantitative measures, such as window guidance, has been declining, while the effectiveness of policy through various channels associated with interest rate changes has been expanding and strengthening. If we utilize the classification of the four channels of A, B, C and D, as explained earlier, it is roughly in this order that the policy has chronologically and continuously added transmission channels, thus diversifying the channels and making the overall policy effect more forceful.[22] This change in the channels is explained in detail below.

1. *Effects of deregulation*

Up to the latter half of the 1970s, which for Japan was the initial period of the financial deregulation, Channel A was a dominant mechanism. This is because that channel relies, as explained above, on the relative rigidity of bank lending rates and deposit rates compared with some market interest rates. But, as many forms of financial deregulation progressed, such as the introduction of instruments with market-determined interest rates (certificates of deposit, large-denomination deposits and money-market certificates) and relaxation of the restrictions on various transactions,[23] the channel of controlling money stock from the supply side gradually lost its effectiveness.

In accordance with the implementation of various measures of deregulation, Channel B gradually gained in importance. This is because interest rates (especially long-term government bond yield) became increasingly market-determined and, with the integration of various domestic markets, responded more quickly and more fluidly to interest rate changes initiated by the Bank of Japan. For example, the introduction of the market-rate certificates of deposit (CDs) in 1979 effectively linked various short-term money markets by increasing arbitrage transactions, thus making interest rate differentials between markets, such as bill markets and the *gensaki* (repo) markets, smaller after the early 1980s. Similarly, increased linkage in interest rates between some other markets also began to be observed, such as between the *gensaki* market and the long-term government bond market.[24]

The best example illustrating the varied response of market rates to policy action is the sharp contrast between the outcomes of policies in 1982 and in 1985, where in both cases the BOJ attempted to raise market interest rates without changing the official discount rate. Both these policies aimed at preventing the yen from depreciating further, which would have increased the Japanese trade balance surplus and intensified the trade friction with the USA. In 1985, the restrictions on transactions in interbank funds markets had become far less than in 1982 and the banks began to rely more on funding at market rates rather than taking deposits at regulated rates. Under these circumstances in 1985, (a) inter-bank rates rose more quickly and by a larger magnitude in response to the policy of the BOJ; (b) interest rates in the open (non-banks participating), short-term markets rose more smoothly; and (c) long-term interest rates (yield of long-term government bonds) were more sensitive to the rise of short-term interest rates, and rose much faster and by a larger magnitude.[25] This meant that, for both firms and individuals, the cost of finance for investment or consumption (or the opportunity cost of holding deposits) could be perceived more accurately and was affected more quickly in accordance with interest-rate policy, so that it became more rational for them to behave in accordance with the movement of interest rates. Therefore the policy effects of interest rate changes on the real side of the economy are strengthened (interest-rate elasticities of investment and consumption may be thought to have become larger).[26]

Another important aspect of deregulation is that it provides a condition for faster transmission of the interest rate policy effects resulting from a change in the behaviour of financial institutions. For financial institutions, the ratio of the amount of funding by instruments with market-determined interest rates, to the total amount of funding has risen sharply in recent years. When looking at the composition of deposits (the most important source of funds for banks) at the end of 1989, more than 70 per cent of deposits held by corporate businesses were those with market interest rates, while the ratio of deposits held by individuals was relatively low, at about 20 per cent (see Figure 12.2). These ratio rose rapidly thereafter, and by March 1993 had grown to 98.6 per cent and 70.1 per cent, respectively.[27] Reflecting these changes in the funding structure, banks have shown an increasing tendency to adopt a flexible lending rate and to widen the spectrum of lending in accordance with changes in funding rates, so that lending rates now move more closely with short-term money market rates. This means that interest rate changes by the BOJ now have a stronger influence on the supply of money and credit, and accordingly on the behaviour of firms and households.

2. Effects of internationalization of Japanese financial markets

Following the deregulation of domestic financial markets, similar deregulation measures were also carried out in international financial transactions, which culminated in 1980 in the full-scale liberalization of international financial transactions.[28] The integration of domestic and overseas financial markets has made Channel C play an important role in Japanese monetary policy.

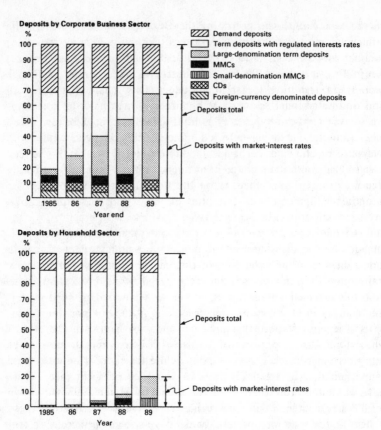

Source: 'Flow of Funds in Japan in 1989'. Special Paper, no. 191, Bank of Japan Research and Statistics Department, August 1990.

FIGURE 12.2 Ratios of deposits with market-determined interest rates, all financial institutions, at the year end

The internationalization of financial markets has meant in general an increase in financial transactions between residents and non-residents of a country. Included are the transactions by both banks and non-bank firms, and the assets transacted include both yen-denominated and foreign-currency-denominated assets. Therefore internationalization can be regarded as an integration of domestic and overseas financial markets. Since it expands the holding of yen-denominated assets by overseas residents, whose financial behaviour depends particularly on overseas factors (for example, the US interest rates) and on the yen exchange rate, domestic (yen) interest rates tend to be influenced more by these factors than previously. Therefore, policy conduct as well as the effects of interest rate policy has changed.

Increased international linkage of interest rates Since the liberalization of international financial transactions, which actively encourage cross-border and cross-currency arbitrage transactions, Japanese interest rates, in particular longer-term interest rates, have shown linkages with overseas interest rates (especially US interest rates).

In internationally integrated financial markets, where active arbitrage transactions can take place, a domestic (yen) interest rate of a given period should theoretically become the sum of two factors: (a) the overseas (US dollar) interest rate of the corresponding maturity period; and (b) the expected rate of loss or gain arising from exchange rate changes during the same period. Since the market treatment and the nature of factor (b) varies depending on the length of the period of transaction, it is mainly the Japanese long-term interest rates, rather than the Japanese short-term interest rates, that are more affected by the changes in US interest rates.[29]

In fact, various studies have shown that the movement of short-term interest rates in Japan, as well as those in other major countries, are relatively independent of each other in comparison with long-term interest rates, and that long-term interest rates, particularly after the 1980s, have exhibited more international linkages in comparison with short-term interest rates, when compared with the 1970s.[30]

The first reason for this linkage of long-term interest rates is probably the increased international integration of financial markets. In many countries, exchange control was abolished or restrictions on international financial transactions were relaxed in the late 1970s, and many new financial markets or financial instruments which began to link various markets were introduced, thus integrating financial markets internationally.[31] In the case of Japan, increased international investment by private investors, particularly by institutional investors such as life-insurance companies, played an important role in integrating domestic and overseas markets. Second, the conduct of interest rate policies themselves in various countries in effect increased the international linkage of long-term interest rates.[32] When the foreign long-term interest rate rises, pressure is generated for the domestic currency to depreciate, thereby putting upward pressure on import prices, and hence domestic prices overall. Faced with this situation, monetary authorities often try to raise domestic short-term interest rates to protect the currency from depreciating, as was done in Germany in 1981–82, and Japan in 1982. This kind of policy response raises domestic long-term rates when foreign long-term rates rise, thus in effect creating interest rate linkages internationally.

Although the BOJ has been able to control short-term interest rates, the tendency of international linkages in long-term interest rates have thus been observed, particularly after the 1980s. This has caused a change in policy conduct and policy transmission processes, to which we now turn.

Increased importance of the role of the yen exchange rate   The internationalization of Japanese financial markets has changed the relationship between trade imbalance and international capital flow, since increased opportunity of arbitrage transaction and the resulting increased international linkage of long-term interest rates makes the capital outflow (inflow) more sensitive to an interest rate change than before for a given size of trade surplus (deficit). In other words, a larger trade surplus (deficit) of a country can remain than previously for a given size of international interest rate differential.[33] Therefore, when Japanese financial markets are internationalized, monetary policy effects also change, in the following way (for a diagrammatical demonstration of these propositions, see the Appendix to this chapter on p. 347): (a) the effectiveness of monetary policy on the domestic interest rate declines, as already discussed; (b) although the direct effect of interest rate change on domestic demand (private investment) declines as a result of (a), the effect of interest rate change on aggregate demand increases, because it exerts a strong influence on net exports owing to the policy's increased influence on the yen exchange rate; and accordingly, (c) effectiveness of monetary policy on domestic economic activity increases (interest rate policy may become even more effective on domestic demand if changes in net exports subsequently exert strong influence on such domestic expenditure as corporate investment). These changes broadly suggest that fluctuations in the yen exchange rate, whether caused by interest rate changes or by other factors, have more implications for the economy than before,[34] and conversely, exchange rate changes become more important in conducting monetary policy (as discussed in Section 12.4 below).

The internationalization of the Japanese financial markets therefore has strengthened the Channel C of the effect of interest rate policy on the Japanese economy.

3. Effects of accumulation of financial and other assets

Another structural change of the Japanese economy is the accumulation of financial and other tangible assets relative to the size of the economic activity. As shown in Table 12.2, the total assets of Japan at the end of 1990 were ¥7106 trillion, consisting roughly equally of tangible assets (land and fixed assets) and financial assets. The amount in 1990 became 12 times larger than in 1970, and 2.7 times larger than in 1980. The size has increased not only in absolute terms but also when measured in relation to GNP: total assets as a percentage of GNP were 8.1 per cent in 1970, 11.0 per cent in 1980 and 16.6 per cent in 1990.[35]

The accumulation of assets has made firms and households more sensitive to interest rate changes than before, because the values of these assets, which are in principle the discounted sum of streams of revenues generated by assets, change directly according to movement in interest rates. Moreover, continuous liberalization of interest rates has provided a condition for this effect to take place more effectively than before. Accordingly, the effect (the wealth effect) on personal consumption arising from the change in value of financial assets, including corporate shares, has been widely recognized and played an important role in business fluctuations in the late 1980s and early 1990s.[36] For Japanese firms, changes in the value of land are presumed to have had larger effects on their investment behaviour than in other countries, for two reasons. First, when land prices increase, firms have, in effect, a larger value of collateral for bank borrowing, because in Japan land is a typical form of collateral for bank borrowing. This enables a firm to borrow more and relaxes the availability constraint of funds in investment. Second, as the land price increases, the share price of firms holding land also rises, with investors realizing that the total value of a firm includes the implicit value of the land that is on the firm's balance sheet. In fact, when the mutual relationships of long-term interest rates, land values and share prices are analyzed (see Table 12.3), the increasing tendency for mutual dependence of land and share prices can clearly be observed over recent years (in particular, the reliance of share price on land value). Accordingly, the increase in land prices pushes up share prices making equity finance easier and at lower cost, and thus stimulating investment.[37]

Various asset prices, especially land and share prices, rose rapidly in the late 1980s and declined after 1990, owing to many factors, including, most importantly, monetary policy.[38] The effects of the price

TABLE 12.2   Assets of Japan as percentage of the GNP

	1970	*1980*	*1990*
Tangible assets	4.0	5.6	8.0
Non-reproducible tangible assets	2.4	3.1	5.6
Net fixed assets	1.3	2.2	2.3
Financial assets	4.1	5.4	8.6
Total assets	8.1	11.0	16.6
(In ¥ trillions)	(590)	(2 642)	(7 106)

Source: Economic Planning Agency, *Annual Report on National Accounts 1992*, and *Report on National Accounts from 1955 to 1989*.

TABLE 12.3   Mutual relationships of assets markets in Japan

	Explanatory variables		
	Long-term interest rate	*Land values*	*Share prices*
Earlier period: 1975–81			
Explained variables			
Long-term interest rate	93.2	0.1	6.7
Land values	20.0	75.4	4.5
Share prices	3.3	0.3	96.4
Later period: 1982–8			
Explained variables			
Long-term interest rate	59.4	30.0	10.6
Land values	12.0	71.5	16.5
Share prices	6.0	61.4	32.6

Notes: 1. Analysis of variance is accomplished by a multivariate auto-regression model. Values in the table show the degree of influence of each of the explanatory variables (including the relevant explained variables themselves) on variations in given explained variables. (The degree of influence of each explanatory variable is shown as a percentage at the end of the 30th quarter.)
2. The data used are as follows. Long-term interest rate: the yield of government bond with longest maturity; Land values: urban land price index; Share price: Tōkyō stock exchange price index. The percentage increase over the previous year is used for land values and share prices.

Source: Economic Planning Agency, *Annual Report of the Japanese Economy 1988–89*, August 1989, table 4–2–8.

TABLE 12.4   Monetary policy and some related economic variables in Japan, 1984–92

	Official discount rate*	Money supply M2 + CDs)**	Share prices (Nikkei Index)**	Land price (Officially published residential land price)**	Private capital investment***	Personal consumption***
1984	5.0	7.8	16.7	2.2	11.7	2.7
1985	5.0	8.4	13.6	2.2	12.1	3.4
1986	3.0	8.7	42.6	7.6	4.4	3.4
1987	2.5	10.4	15.3	25.0	6.7	4.2
1988	2.5	11.2	39.9	7.9	14.8	5.2
1989	4.25	9.9	29.0	17.0	16.5	4.4
1990	6.0	11.7	−38.1	10.7	11.4	7.7
1991	4.5	3.6	−4.6	−5.6	5.7	2.1
1992	3.25	0.6	−26.4	−8.7	−4.1	1.8

Notes: * At the end of the year
            ** Percentage change at the end of the year over the previous year.
           *** Percentage change of the average over the previous year (real value at 1985 prices).

Source: Bank of Japan, *Economic Statistics Annual 1992*; Economic Planning Agency, *Annual Report on National Accounts 1992*.

fluctuation of these assets on the aggregate demand and on the behaviour of financial institutions are shown in terms of crude statistics in Table 12.4 (figures in bold characters indicate the effect associated with lowering the official discount rate). The importance of this channel for the economy has been recognized and documented widely, including in various government documents.[39] This suggests that Channel D, as seen above, seems to be playing an increasingly important role in the transmission process of monetary policy effects.

To sum up, three of the four channels of policy transmission (B, C and D) exert their effects on expenditure via interest rate changes, rather than via direct and quantitative control of bank lending. Therefore, from the viewpoint of controlling monetary aggregates, it can be said that money supply (monetary aggregates) is increasingly controlled from the demand side, rather than the supply side. This means that monetary aggregates have developed the character of more or less *coincident* indicators, rather than being *leading* indicators, of macroeconomic activity.

These changes in circumstances have important implications for the implementation of monetary policy: the effective controlling of market interest rates has become more important, on the one hand, and the significance of money supply or monetary aggregates, as indicators of monetary policy, has changed, on the other.[40] Under these circumstances, various kinds of indicators (information variables) to complement monetary aggregates have been investigated by the BOJ, such as *P*-star, commodity prices, land prices and the slope of the yield curve of interest rates, but it seems that there is no indicator that totally replaces monetary aggregates, although some of these indicators provide additional information on future price movements.[41]

12.4   CONDUCT OF THE BANK OF JAPAN'S MONETARY POLICY AND ITS CHANGES

The BOJ monetary policy has been inescapably influenced by changes in the structure and the environment of the Japanese economy. As already discussed, window guidance, once an important policy tool to control directly total bank lending, was abandoned recently. It had became increasingly impotent as a policy tool as deregulation proceeded on both domestic and international fronts. Instead, effective control of market interest rates has become a main means of monetary policy implementation.

Depending on the situation, policy goals of the BOJ and the policy-inducing economic variables seem to have changed from time to time, though in a subtle way. Table 12.5 summarizes these changes since 1975 by depicting important variables mentioned in the official statement by the Bank when the official discount rate was changed. From this table, one can conclude the following: (a) effective demand (general business condition) and prices (inflation rate) have always been important policy objectives, or the background of policy change, or both; (b) in recent years, especially after the Plaza Accord (the agreement in 1985 of the Group of Five countries to take concerted action to rectify the overvaluation of the US dollar) and until 1990, the balance of payments and the yen exchange rate have become important goals of the policy; (c) money supply had not been referred to very frequently, except in recent years; and (d) since 1989, the actual movement of market interest rate has become an important factor in formulating the policy.

Point (a) implies that the main objective of the policy has been to stabilize prices by controlling aggregate demand: the most conventional role of any central bank. Point (b) is certainly a result of the internationalization of Japanese financial and other markets. Since the exchange

TABLE 12.5 Factors stated by the Bank of Japan in announcing changes in the official discount rate

Date		Discount rate after change (size of change) (%)		Factors cited in explanation						
				Effective demand	Prices	Balance of payments	Exchange rate of the yen	Money supply	Market interest rates	Money market stability
1975	4	8.5	(−0.5)	O	¶	−	−	−	−	−
	6	8.0	(−0.5)	O	O∆	−	−	−	−	−
	8	7.5	(−0.5)	¶	O∆	−	−	−	−	−
	10	6.5	(−1.0)	¶	O∆	−	−	−	−	−
1977	3	6.0	(−0.5)	¶	O∆	O	−	−	−	−
	4	5.0	(−1.0)	¶	O∆	−	−	−	−	−
	9	4.25	(−0.75)	¶	O∆	−	−	−	−	−
1978	3	3.5	(−0.75)	¶	−	¶	¶	−	−	−
1979	4	4.25	(+0.75)	¶	¶	O	¶	−	−	−
	7	5.25	(+1.0)	O	¶	−	−	O	−	−
	11	6.25	(+1.0)	O	¶	−	¶	O	−	−
1980	2	7.25	(+1.0)	O	¶	O	¶	−	−	−
	3	9.0	(+1.75)	O	¶	−	¶	−	−	−
	8	8.25	(−0.75)	¶	¶	−	O	−	−	−
	11	7.25	(−1.0)	O	O∆	−	O	−	−	−
1981	3	6.25	(−1.0)	O	O∆	−	O	−	−	−
	12	5.5	(−0.75)	O	O∆	O	O	O∆	−	−
1983	10	5.0	(−0.5)	¶	O∆	−	O∆	−	−	−
1986	1	4.5	(−0.5)	¶	O∆	¶	O∆	−	−	−
	3	4.0	(−0.5)	¶	O∆	¶	¶	−	−	−
	4	3.5	(−0.5)	¶	−	¶	¶	−	−	−
	11	3.0	(−0.5)	¶	O∆	−	¶	O∆	−	−
1987	2	2.5	(−0.5)	¶	−	−	¶	O∆	−	−
1989	5	3.25	(+0.75)	¶	¶	¶	O	−	O	−
	10	3.75	(+0.5)	¶	¶	−	O	O	O	−
	12	4.25	(+0.5)	¶	¶	−	O	O	O	−
1990	3	5.25	(+1.0)	¶	¶	−	O	O	O	¶
	8	6.0	(+0.75)	¶	¶	−	−	O	O	¶
1991	7	5.5	(−0.5)	¶	O∆	−	−	O	O	−
	11	5.0	(−0.5)	¶	O∆	−	O	O	O	−
	12	4.5	(−0.5)	¶	O	−	−	O	O	−
1992	4	3.75	(−0.75)	¶	O	−	−	O	O	−
	7	3.25	(−0.5)	¶	O	−	O	O	O	−
1993	2	2.5	(−0.75)	¶	O	O	O	O	O	−
	9	1.75	(−0.75)	¶	O	O	O	O	O	−

Notes: ¶ indicates a factor identified as a policy objective.
O indicates a factor mentioned in the assessment of the current economic and financial situation.
∆ indicates a factor mentioned with a proviso.

Source: Okabe (1992), with updates for the period after July 1991.

rate definitely influences the balance of payments in Japan (see Table 12.1 on p. 329), influencing the yen exchange rate by interest rate policy can claim some validity, as long as controlling (reducing) the balance of payments (surplus) can be deemed to be a policy objective. Point (c) implies that the BOJ was not a rigid monetarist, although it looked at money supply as an important index. Some observers regard the BOJ as being monetarist in deed,[42] while others do not,[43] but the approach might well in fact have been more pragmatic: as an insider once called it, 'eclectic gradualism'.[44] Point (d) is a natural outcome of extensive liberalization of interest rates. Market interest rates, when fully liberalized and moving flexibly, reflect not only the BOJ's interest rate policy but also various factors of the economy, such as the expected inflation rate of market participants. Accordingly, this movement provides the Bank with valuable information and there is good reason for the Bank to include the movement of market interest rates in its assessment of the economic situation.

Table 12.5 can be treated somewhat quantitatively by estimating the policy response function of the BOJ. By correcting flaws in earlier studies of this type, the estimated result is shown in Table 12.6.[45] The result is consistent with those of points (a) and (b) above, both of which were also obtained in earlier studies. Moreover, it is shown here that it is not the price level nor the rate of inflation, but the rate of acceleration of the inflation rate that seems to have been important in the policy formulation of the Bank. Also shown is that, following the Plaza Accord, the yen exchange rate, along with the balance of payments, has become an important policy goal.

12.5 CONCLUSIONS

The structure, regulatory framework and international environment of the Japanese economy have changed significantly over the past 10–15 years. The deregulation of interest rates and various transactions has proceeded continuously, the international integration of financial markets is by now virtually completed, and the economy has accumulated financial and other assets rapidly. A brief assessment of these changes is made and some implications are derived below.

First, the liberalization of interest rates and the internationalization of financial markets have compelled the BOJ to reassess the effectiveness of the policy tools in its arsenal. Accordingly, the Bank has abandoned direct, quantitative controls in favour of a policy to control market

TABLE 12.6   An estimation of the policy reaction function of the Bank of Japan's interest rate policy, quarterly estimation

Variable to be explained	Explanatory variables					Relevant statistics		
Call-loan rate	Effective demand	Acceleration of inflation rate	Balance of payments	Exchange rate	Constant term			
Prior to the Plaza Accord (1975/I–85/II)	−0.105 (−0.99)	0.065 (4.69) **	−0.078 (−3.05) **	0.051 (2.26) *	0.488 (1.08)	R^2 SE D.W.	= = =	0.560 0.677 1.78
Total period (1975/I–90/VI)	−0.016 (−0.23)	0.057 (5.06) **	−0.056 (−2.94) **	0.046 (3.09) **	0.146 (0.46)	R^2 SE D.W.	= = =	0.515 0.628 1.72

Notes: 1. Explained variable: Difference from the previous quarter of call-loan rates (collateralized, seasonally adjusted).
Explanatory variables:
Effective demand: rate of change in the previous quarter of real GNP (seasonally adjusted) from the previous quarter.
Acceleration of inflation rate: over-the-year rate of change of the wholesale price in the current quarter *minus* over-the-year rate of change of the wholesale price of the corresponding quarter of a year before.
Balance of payments: difference of the current account surplus (measured as a ratio to export) of the current period from that of the previous quarter.
Exchange rate: rate of change of the exchange rate (yen/dollar) in the previous quarter from the preceding quarter.
2. Figures in parentheses are standard errors of parameters. An asterisk (*) means that the parameter is significant at 5% level, and two asterisks (**) at 1% level.

Source: Okabe (1992).

interest rates. This change should be regarded as being appropriate and in fact more or less unavoidable to enable the Bank to maintain the effectiveness of the policy in a changing environment. This is because direct control of bank lending has lost its effectiveness, and both banks and the economy have become sensitive to market signals. The change in the policy tool coincided favourably with the emerging situation where the accumulation of various assets in the Japanese economy has taken place, because changes in interest rates exert larger effects on the overall economy in the policy transmission processes than in an economy with less asset accumulation.

Second, in terms of the internationalization of Japanese financial markets, a few policy implications can be obtained from the above survey. The first implication is on so-called international policy co-ordination, whereby some kind of manipulation of exchange rates by macroeconomic policy is usually intended, among other objectives. When a country's financial market is internationalized, the degree of international linkage of interest rates increases, especially in long-term interest rates, because of increased cross-border capital transactions by private investors. Therefore, one country's macroeconomic disturbance is easily transmitted to another. This means that, for any large country, keeping its own economy stable is important, not only in its own right but also from the viewpoint of the international economy. In fact, any policy action based on that understanding, rather than on an attempt to co-ordinate policies internationally, is more likely to stabilize the exchange rate and, in a sense, may be regarded as the essence of international policy co-ordination.[46]

The second implication is on targeting the balance of payments or exchange rate by monetary policy. For certain interest rate changes in the past, the BOJ regarded (as has been seen previously) the balance of payments or yen exchange rate more or less as a policy objective depending on the prevailing domestic and international circumstances at the time of the policy. For example, the lowering of the discount rate in February 1987, from 3.25 per cent to 2.5 per cent, at that time the lowest level since the Second World War, was intended to be in line with the so-called Louvre Accord (the agreement by the Group of Five countries to co-ordinate policies to stabilize exchange rates) and was strongly motivated to prevent the US dollar from depreciating further.[47] If this policy was a major reason for the subsequent, unusual rises in money supply, rises in asset prices and the heightened level of macroeconomic activity, and that it subsequently needed to reverse these movements by raising interest rates to bring the economy back to a sustainable path of expansion (see Table 12.4 on p. 341), then monetary policy assigned to the exchange rate would be said to have had an element of error in maintaining the stability of the domestic economy. A similar international environment and policy response was also observed in 1971–2, at the end of the Bretton Woods system of fixed exchange rates. The BOJ's policy in this period has been understood, even by the BOJ itself, to have been inappropriately conducted, as it used interest rate policy for exchange rate objectives (the Bank lowered the interest rate to prevent the yen from appreciating for fear of the damaging effect on export industries as a result of currency appreciation), thereby creating 'excess liquidity' in the economy, generating rampant inflation and subsequently necessitating severe adjustment via a deep recession.[48] These two bitter historical episodes in Japan seem strongly to suggest the danger of assigning interest policy to control the exchange rate.

Moreover, utilizing one policy instrument (interest rates) not only for stabilizing domestic prices but also for multiple objectives, such as foreign exchange rate stabilization, violates the basic principle of policy assignment, which stipulates that in order to achieve multiple policy objectives successfully the same number of policy tools must be available. In some empirical studies on the Japanese economy, the effectiveness of exchange rate targeting by using interest rates is also strongly questioned, and targeting domestic price stability is shown to be superior to exchange rate targeting even for achieving a stable balance of payments.[49] In the management of the balance of payments and the exchange rate, co-ordination with another macro-policy instrument, that is, fiscal policy, or the issue of a macro-policy mix, need to be addressed.

Third, the accumulation of financial and other assets implies that the BOJ should monitor the movement of asset prices more carefully than before, especially in the situation where interest rates have been fully deregulated. This is, first, because the magnitude of the policy effects through this channel has become greater as the result of the accumulation and increased flexibility of these prices, and, second, because asset prices are deeply related to the stability of the financial system. Since assets are extensively utilized as collateral for bank loans, especially in Japan, and the sharp decline of asset prices means large potential losses for financial institutions, so risking the soundness and stability of the financial system as a whole. An unstable financial system would prevent the economy from achieving a stable growth by depriving it of both efficient intermediation of financial resources and an efficient payment and settlement system.

All these considerations serve to remind us of the basic proposition that a country's monetary policy should aim consistently and ultimately at stabilizing domestic prices[50] and at achieving the stability of the financial system, even when external economic situations may sometimes seem to warrant considerations, particularly in an environment where financial markets are internationalized and integrated into the world market.

APPENDIX

Internationalization of financial markets and the effectiveness of monetary policy: an exposition

When internationalization of a country's financial markets takes place, the international linkage of interest rates increases (particularly long-term interest rates; but in this Appendix, short-term and long-term rates are not differentiated). The resulting change in the outcome of interest rate policy can be analyzed by using a simple Mundell–Fleming-type

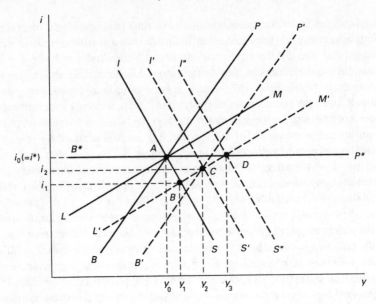

FIGURE 12.A3   International integration of financial markets and its effect
on monetary policy

macro model, an open-economy version of the *IS–LM* model, or a flow-
model of an open economy with capital flows, as shown in Figure 12.A3.[51]

In this diagram, not only are the standard *IS* and *LM* curves depicted
but also the *BP* curve, which is a whole set of income and domestic
interest rates that equilibrates the balance of payments of Japan. The
semi-plane to the right and below the *BP* curve is the area where the
balance of payments is in deficit. When the financial market is not
internationalized, the equilibrium of the economy is shown at point *A*,
an intersection of three curves, where three sectors of the economy are
simultaneously in equilibrium with income y_0 and domestic interest
rate i_0. Suppose that monetary policy was eased by lowering interest
rate, thereby increasing the money stock, shifting the *LM* curve to
L'M'. Then the economy starts to move to point *B*, increasing income
to y_1 and lowering domestic interest rate to i_1. At this point, both the
goods and services market and the money market are in equilibrium,
but domestic interest rates have become lower than overseas interest
rates (i^*), and the current account balance is in deficit. Therefore capital
begins to flow out from Japan by selling the yen for the dollar, and
the exchange rate of the yen depreciates. This makes Japanese prod-

ucts cheaper in international markets, and exports from Japan increase, thereby generating pressure to shift the *IS* curve to the right and upwards and the *BP* curve to the right and downwards. This process continues until domestic interest rates rise substantially, although not completely to the level of overseas interest rate levels (since international financial transactions are regulated, the domestic interest rate does not converge to the international level). The economy finally reaches equilibrium at point *C*, where income has risen further from y_1 to y_2 and the interest rate from i_1 to i_2.

How does the effect of monetary policy change when restrictions on international financial transactions are removed and the Japanese financial market is internationalized? The most important effect is that capital can flow freely across borders, reflecting interest differentials and exchange rate expectations, thus increasing international interest rate linkages, as discussed in the main text. Therefore, when the trade balance becomes a deficit (surplus), foreign capital can be imported (exported) by a smaller rise in domestic interest rate than previously. In terms of the diagram, it means that the *BP* curve becomes more interest-rate sensitive, making the upward slope less steep.[52] Suppose here, for simplicity's sake, that the international capital flow is perfect (and that the current level of the yen exchange rate is expected to continue) so that the *BP* curve becomes horizontal, as shown by the *B*P** curve.

The easing of monetary policy brings the economy from *A* to *B*, and then from *B* to *C*, as in the pre-internationalization case. However, under perfect capital mobility, point *C* cannot be an equilibrium point. This is because at point *C* the balance of payments is still in deficit, while overseas interest rates are still higher than Japanese interest rates. Therefore capital outflow continues, thereby further depreciating the yen and increasing Japanese exports. This process continues until income increases to y_3 and domestic interest rate rises to the international level i^*, thus reaching equilibrium at point *D*.

As is clear by contrasting the above two cases, changes in the effect of monetary policy as a result of the internationalization of Japanese financial markets can be summarized as follows: (i) the effectiveness of monetary policy on the domestic interest rate itself declines; (ii) the direct effect of interest rate change on domestic demand (private investment) declines as a result of (i), but the effect of interest rate change on aggregate demand (through the changes in net exports) is amplified because of its increased influence on the yen exchange rate; and therefore (iii) the effectiveness of monetary policy on domestic economic activity increases.

NOTES

1. Changes in the financial structure are discussed, for instance, in Cargill and Royama (1988) and Hamada and Horiuchi (1987); while various monetary mechanisms are analyzed by papers included in Singleton (1993).
2. This chapter draws substantially from this author's earlier papers in Japanese, in particular Okabe (1991, 1992).
3. This diagram is constructed by the author by arranging, integrating and expanding various issues raised in preceding studies by various researchers, such as Bank of Japan (1985a), Suzuki (1987a, 1987b). Although the diagram shows, for the sake of simplicity, that causality runs as if unidirectionally, it should be noted that most of the economic and financial variables depend on each other and are determined simultaneously.
4. For a detailed explanation of the technique used by the Bank of Japan, see Okina (1993), Nakao and Horii (1991) and Fukui (1986).
5. At present, important short-term, open markets are the markets for certificate of deposits (CDs), commercial papers (CPs), government finance bills (FBs) and treasury bills (TBs), and *gensaki* or repurchase bonds markets.
6. This may be interpreted, as pointed out by Wakita (1983), as keeping an implicit contract between banks and customers to reduce the variability of profits of both parties over business cycles. Prevalence of the so-called main bank system is a typical phenomenon in this regard. For the main bank system, see, for instance, Hoshi (1993).
7. According to the expectation theory of the term structure of interest rates, long-term interest rates are generally understood to be determined as an average of expected short-term interest rates at each given future period of time (plus some kind of risk premium). Kuroda (1983) demonstrated empirically that for the secondary market of the Japanese government bonds the validity of this theory had been greater than generally thought: as early as in the late 1970s, when deregulation of the government bond transaction began. It is worthwhile to note, however, that there may exist such instances where raising short-term interest rates leads to the lowering, rather than raising, of long-term nominal interest rates owing to the decline of the expected rate of future inflation brought about by the former policy action (Bank of Japan, 1985b).
8. In the short run, say, for six months, net exports do not decrease (rather, an increase of net exports is observed due to the J-curve effect); but in the long run, various studies have shown that in Japan it decreases, as shown in Table 12.1. Conditions for a decreasing trade balance as a result of yen appreciation can be shown as follows (proof omitted here):

Trade balance in yen: $me_x + e_m > 1$
Trade balance in dollar: $e_x + (1/m) e_m > 1$

where m is the export-to-import ratio (about 1.4 for Japan for 1981–90), e_x is price (dollar-base)–elasticity of foreign demand for Japanese products, and e_m is price (yen-base)–elasticity of domestic demand for overseas products. If trade is balanced initially, the two conditions reduce to one condition, requiring the sum of export and import elasticities to be greater than unity (Marshall–Lerner condition).

9. The rate for discounting a flow of earnings is usually considered to consist of two parts: the interest rate of a risk-free asset, and the risk premium. Therefore, the policy to raise interest rate levels raise primarily the former component of the interest rate level, thus raising the rate of discount.

10. It should be noted that the decline of land prices has, on the other hand, a positive effect on housing investment, since it makes the cost of acquiring land (an important factor in Japan to initiate housing investment) easier.

11. Okubo (1983), Bank of Japan (1985a), and Suzuki *et al.* (1988).

12. Economic Planning Agency (1982), Yoshikawa (1993). The latter regards the interest rate as playing a key role and the movement of money supply only as responding endogenously to real output changes, and does not find an intrinsic role for money in influencing real variables.

13. Okubo (1983), Economic Planning Agency (1988, 1989). According to Bank of Japan (1988a), domestic prices begin to rise with a time lag of one and a half years after the increase in money supply, and the inflation rate becomes about the same as the rate of initial increase of money supply, particularly in the 1970s. But after the 1980s, the time lag and the relationship itself seem to have been blurred substantially due to the introduction of various new financial assets (Bank of Japan, 1992).

14. Economic Planning Agency (1984), Bank of Japan (1988).

15. Economic Planning Agency (1984).

16. For the recent arguments, see Bernanke and Blinder (1992), Morgan (1992).

17. Statistical analyses of Bank of Japan (1988b) and Iwabuchi (1990) show the importance of money over credit in influencing real variables and prices, while Ueda (1993) and Hideshima and Ishida (1993) emphasize the importance of credit (lending) in the transmission process of the policy.

18. On the balance sheet of commercial banks in 1982, lending had a share of 61.6 per cent of the total assets in Japan, while 53.5 per cent in the USA, the ratio of lending to total deposits was 0.932 in Japan, and 0.748 in the USA (Bank of Japan, *Comparative Economic and Financial Statistics 1990.*)

19. For example, Horiuchi (1980).

20. For example, Ueda (1984, 1993). An empirical study by Hoshi *et al.* (1993) find that this effect appeared primarily in inventory investment.

21. Kuroda (1979).

22. Bank of Japan (1985a), Suzuki (1989).

23. For a survey of deregulation, see Shigehara (1991).

24. Bank of Japan (1986a).

25. Bank of Japan (1986a).

26. By using VAR models, Horie *et al.* (1987) showed that the influence of long-term real interest rates on domestic private demand had become stronger for the period after 1976.

27. *Bank of Japan Monthly Bulletin*, June 1993, p. 72.

28. Full liberalization of international financial transactions took place in 1980 when the New Foreign Exchange and Foreign Trade Control Law came into effect, liberalizing, in principle, all cross-border capital transactions.

29. In an open economy, domestic short-term and long-term interest rates satisfy the following relationship with regard to foreign interest rates and the exchange rate (Bank of Japan, 1984; Kool and Tatom, 1988):

$$i_s = i_s^* + [(f - e) / e]n \qquad (1)$$
$$i_L = i_L^* + [(\hat{e} - e) / e]m \qquad (2)$$

where i_s and i_s^* are domestic and foreign short-term interest rates, respectively, of the same maturity and risk; i_L and i_L^* are domestic and foreign long-term interest rates, respectively, of the same maturity and risk; e is the spot foreign exchange rate (yen/dollar); f is the forward exchange rate; $\hat{e}$ is the long-term expected foreign exchange rate; and n and m are annualizing factors ($n = 12 \div$ number of months to maturity, $m =$ reciprocal of the number of years to maturity). Equation (1) shows that the yen short-term interest rate is equal to the sum of the dollar short-term interest rate and the rate of discount or premium of the yen (covered interest rate parity). Since short-term international financial transactions are conducted on a covered basis utilizing forward exchange market, changes in the short-term dollar interest rate is reflected mainly in the forward premium or discount, without much affecting the yen short-term interest rate. On the other hand, long-term transactions usually take place on an uncovered basis, and the expected yen exchange rate for the investment period remains unchanged in the short run. Therefore changes in the long-term dollar interest rate, at least a part thereof, affect the long-term yen interest rate. It should be noted, however, that short-term and long-term domestic interests are closely linked by the term structure and that all the variables in the two equations should be regarded as being determined simultaneously, though there are differences in the degree of exogeneity.

30. Fukao and Okubo (1982), Economic Planning Agency (1984, 1988). Hutchison and Singh (1993) found a very high degree of real interest rate linkage since the early 1980s between the USA and Japan in an equilibrium setting, and they argue, by using a vector error correction model and the response functions, that international arbitrage puts pressure on the interest rate differentials to go to zero within 1–2 years.

31. Economic Planning Agency (1984, 1985), Singleton (1989).

32. Economic Planning Agency (1984); Bank of Japan (1986b); Kool and Tatom (1988).

33. Fukao (1989).

34. For instance, Nambara and Fukao (1989) show, by constructing a three-variable VAR model (money supply, yen exchange rate and nominal GNP), that the yen exchange rate, along with money supply, has strong unidirectional influence on nominal GNP.

35. Since domestic financial assets are matched by domestic financial liabilities, they cancel each other out; land prices are generally deemed to have been overvalued (in the sense that land prices are difficult to explain rationally by using a relatively low level of current rent and estimated future rent). The figures may therefore overstate the trend of accumulation. However, when taking account of the increase of net fixed assets as well,

the trend increase of total assets relative to GNP is certainly undeniable.

36. Economic Planning Agency (1989, 1991, 1992).
37. Economic Planning Agency (1989, 1991).
38. For the analysis of land price movements, see Bank of Japan (1990b).
39. Economic Planning Agency (1989, 1990, 1991, 1992).
40. The time lag between money supply and the price level, for instance, becomes shorter or nil, and the demand for money function is likely to become unstable. For these issues for Japan, see Suzuki (1989), Yoshida and Rasche (1990) and Bank of Japan (1992).
41. For *P*-star and other variables, see Bank of Japan (1990a) and Kato (1991), respectively.
42. Friedman (1983), Meltzer (1986)
43. Ito (1989).
44. Suzuki (1985).
45. Similar estimations of the policy reaction function have been conducted by the Economic Planning Agency (1984, 1985), Asako and Kano (1989), Hutchison (1988) and Bryant (1991). In many of these studies, however, the choice of variables does not seem appropriate and changes in the response of the Bank over time is not allowed for.
46. For this purpose, Meltzer (1990) strongly proposes common international rules. It should be noted, however, that the long-run equilibrium exchange rate should be regarded as being determined not simply by macroeconomic policies but also by many other factors that influence Japanese labour productivity in comparison with other countries (Yoshikawa, 1990).
47. Bank of Japan (1987). In a sense, in Japan, monetary policy was over-burdened for the purpose of stabilizing the yen–dollar exchange rate, since fiscal policy, which had maintained an austere policy stance under the medium-term fiscal reconstruction program of 1983–90, was not utilized effectively. In retrospect, fiscal policy should have been more expansionary, to reduce the Japanese current account surplus, and thus preventing the yen's further appreciation – and also preventing the excessive burden on monetary policy.
48. Bank of Japan (1983), Komiya (1976).
49. Meltzer (1985) shows empirically that the financial system dampens the influence of changes in exchange rates on output and prices. Taylor (1989) found, in his simulation analysis of major countries by utilizing a macroeconometric model, that the policy of targeting domestic price stability is superior to the policy of targeing the exchange rate, not only in achieving domestic price stability and domestic aggregate demand effectively but also in achieving balance of payments stability.
50. Precise measurement of the price level involves many conceptual and technical problems, and conventional indexes need to be improved in many ways: as argued, for instance, by Gordon (1993). As Shibuya (1992) attempted, integrating asset prices to derive a measure of intertemporal cost of living is an interesting and promising direction for research. For the Bank of Japan, as for any other central bank, price stabilization is not the sole policy objective: the other major objective being the maintenance of a stable and efficient financial system (Kuroda and Kinoshita, 1993).

51. This diagram is developed from those in Dornbusch and Fischer (1987), and Frenkel and Mussa (1985). Although this is a flow-model, similar results may be obtained by using a more general stock-model (Nambara and Fukao, 1989).
52. This flattening of the *BP* curve of the Japanese economy is shown by using a government (Economic Planning Agency) econometric macro-model of the economy (Sadahiro *et al.*, 1987).

REFERENCES

Asako, K., and S. Kano 1989. 'Objectives and Controllability of Fiscal and Monetary Policies in Japan: 1968–86' (in Japanese), *Financial Review*, no. 11, Tōkyō: Institute for Fiscal and Monetary Studies, Ministry of Finance.
Bank of Japan 1983. *A One Hundred Year History of the Bank of Japan*, Vol. 6, (in Japanese) Tōkyō: Bank of Japan.
Bank of Japan 1984. 'Stepped-up Capital Movements In and Out of Japan and Their Effect on the Japanese Financial Market', Research and Statistics Department Special Paper no. 112, March.
Bank of Japan 1985a. 'Recent Developments in the Money Supply', Research and Statistics Department Special Paper no. 120, June.
Bank of Japan 1985b. 'Characteristics of Intest Rate Fluctuations Amidst Deregulation and Internationalization of Financing', Research and Statistics Department Special Paper no. 126, October.
Bank of Japan 1986a. 'On the Recent Developments of Short-Term Money Markets' (in Japanese), *Bank of Japan Research Monthly*, February.
Bank of Japan 1986b. 'The Recent Development in the Japanese Economy and Macroeconomic Policy Objectives, Research and Statistics Department Special Paper no. 137, May.
Bank of Japan 1987. 'Economic and Monetary Developments in 1986' (in Japanese), *Bank of Japan Research Monthly*, May (also published in English as *Annual Review of Monetary and Economic Developments in Fiscal 1986*, Tōkyō: Bank of Japan).
Bank of Japan 1988a. 'Recent Growth of Money Stock', Research and Statistics Department Special Paper no. 162, March.
Bank of Japan 1988b. 'On Credit Aggregates' (in Japanese), *Bank of Japan Research Monthly*, November.
Bank of Japan 1990a. 'A Study of Potential Pressure on Prices: Application of *P** to the Japanese Economy', Research and Statistics Department Special Paper no. 186, February.
Bank of Japan 1990b. 'The Recent Rise in Japan's Land Prices: Its Background and Implications', Research and Statistics Department Special Paper no. 193, December.
Bank of Japan 1992. 'Recent Developments in Monetary Aggregates: Analysis and Evaluation', Research and Statistics Department Special Paper no. 221, September.
Bernanke, B. and A. S. Blinder 1992. 'The Federal Funds Rate and the Channels of Monetary Transmission', *American Economic Review*, 82, 4, September.
Bryant, R. C. 1991. 'Model Representations of Japanese Monetary Policy',

Bank of Japan Monetary and Economic Studies, 9, 2, September.

Cargill, T. F. and S. Royama 1988. *The Transition of Finance in Japan and the United States: A Comparative Perspective*, Stanford, California: Hoover Institution Press.

Dornbusch, R. and S. Fischer 1987. *Macroeconomics*, 4th edn, New York: McGraw-Hill.

Economic Planning Agency, *Annual Report of the Japanese Economy*, yearly.

Frenkel, J. A. and M. Mussa 1985. 'Asset Markets, Exchange Rates and the Balance of Payments', *Handbook of International Economics*, Amsterdam: Elsevier Science.

Friedman, M. 1983. 'Monetarism in Rhetoric and Practice', *Bank of Japan Monetary and Economic Studies*, 1, 2, October.

Fukao, M. 1989. 'Exchange Rate Fluctuations, Balance of Payments Imbalances and Internationalization of Financial Markets', *Bank of Japan Monetary and Economic Studies*, 7, 2, August.

Fukao, M. and T. Okubo 1982. 'International Linkage of Interest Rates: The Case of Japan and the United States', Discussion Paper Series no. 13, Institute for Monetary and Economic Studies, Bank of Japan, June.

Fukui, T. 1986. 'Recent Developments of the Short-term Money Market in Japan and Changes in Monetary Control Techniques and Procedures by the Bank of Japan', Bank of Japan Research and Statistics Department Special Paper no. 130, January.

Gordon, R. 1993. 'Measuring the Aggregate Price Level: Implications for Economic Performance and Policy', in K. Shigehara (ed.), *Price Stabilization in the 1990s*, London: Macmillan.

Hamada, K. and A. Horiuchi 1987. 'The Political Economy of the Financial Market', in K. Yamamura and Y. Yasuba (eds), *The Political Economy of Japan, Vol. 1: The Domestic Transformation*, Palo Alto, Calif.: Stanford University Press.

Hideshima, H. and K. Ishida 1993. 'Bank Lending and Effects of Monetary Policy' (in Japanese), Research Paper (5)1–2, Institute for Monetary and Economic Studies, Bank of Japan.

Horie, Y., S. Naniwa and S. Ishihara 1987. 'The Changes of Japanese Business Cycles', *Bank of Japan Monetary and Economic Studies*, 5, 3, December.

Horiuchi, A. 1980. *Monetary Policy in Japan: An Empirical Analysis of Monetary and Banking Mechanism* (in Japanese), Tōkyō: Toyo Keizai.

Hoshi, T. 1993. 'The Economic Role of Corporate Grouping and the Main Bank System', in M. Aoki and R. Dore (eds), *The Japanese Firm: The Sources of Competitive Strength*, Oxford University Press.

Hoshi, T., D. Scharfstein and K. J. Singleton 1993. 'Japanese Corporate Investment and Bank of Japan Guidance of Commercial Bank Lending', in K. Singleton (ed.), *Japanese Monetary Policy*, University of Chicago Press.

Hutchison, M. M. 1988. 'Monetary Control with an Exchange Rate Objective: The Bank of Japan, 1973–86', *Journal of International Money and Finance*, 7.

Hutchison, M. M. and N. Singh 1993. 'How Open are Japanese Financial Markets? Evidence from Equilibrium Real Interest Rate Linkages,' mimeo University of California, Santa Cruz.

Ito, T. 1989. 'Is Bank of Japan a Closet Monetarist? Monetary Targeting in Japan', NBER Working Paper no. 2874.

Iwabuchi, J. 1990. 'On the Effects of Financial Variables on Real Variables: A Re-examination Using "Structural" VAR Models' (in Japanese), *Kinyuu Kenkyuu* (Monetary Studies), Bank of Japan, 9, 3, October.

Kato, K. 1991. 'The Information Content of Financial and Economic Variables: Empirical Tests of Information Variables in Japan', *Bank of Japan Monetary and Economic Studies*, 9, 1, March.

Komiya, R. 1976. 'Causes of the Inflation of 1973–74' (in Japanese) *Economic Study Papers*, 41, 1, University of Tōkyō, April.

Kool, C. and J. A. Tatom 1988. 'International Linkages in the Term Structure of Interest Rates', *Federal Reserve Bank of St. Louis Review*, 70, 4, July–August.

Kuroda, A. 1983. 'Expected Inflation Rates and the Term Structure of Interest Rates', *Bank of Japan Monetary and Economic Studies*, 1, 1, June.

Kuroda, A. and T. Kinoshita 1993. 'Central Banking in Japan: An Overview', Working Paper 93–1, Centre for Japanese Economic Studies, Macquarie University, Sydney.

Kuroda, I. 1979. 'Re-examiantion of Analyses on the Window Guidance (in Japanese), *Contemporary Economy Quarterly*, Winter.

Meltzer, A. 1985. 'Variability of Prices, Output and Money under Fixed and Fluctuating Exchange Rates: An Empirical Study of Monetary Regimes in Japan and the United States', *Bank of Japan Monetary and Economic Studies*, 3, 3, December.

Meltzer, A. 1986. 'Lessons from the Experience of Japan and the United States under Fixed and Fluctuating Exchange Rates', *Bank of Japan Monetary and Economic Studies*, 4, 2, October.

Meltzer, A. 1990. 'Efficiency and Stability in World Finance', in Y. Suzuki, J. Miyake and M. Okabe (eds), *The Evolution of the International Monetary System: How Can Efficiency and Stability be Attained?*, Tōkyō: University of Tōkyō Press.

Morgan, D. P. 1992. 'Are Bank Loans a Force in Monetary Policy?, *Federal Reserve Bank of Kansas City Review*, second quarter.

Nakao, M. and A. Horii 1991. 'The Process of Decision-making and Implementation of Monetary Policy in Japan', Research and Statistics Department Special Paper no. 198, March.

Nambara, A. and M. Fukao 1989. 'International Interest Rate Linkages and Monetary Policy: A Japanese Perspective', *International Interest Rate Linkages and Monetary Policy*, Bank for International Settlements, Basle, March.

Okabe, M. 1989. 'Monetary Policy under the Appreciating Yen' (in Japanese), *Transactions of Japan Society of Monetary Economics*, January.

Okabe, M. 1991. 'Monetary Policy in Japan: Policy Implementation and the Transmission Processes of the Effects, 1975–1989 (A Literature Survey)' (in Japanese), *Transactions of Japan Society of Monetary Economics*, January.

Okabe, M. 1992. 'New Developments in Monetary Policy in Japan' (in Japanese), in K. Shigehara (ed.), *New Developments in Monetary Theory and Monetary Policy*, Tōkyō: Yuhikaku.

Okina, K. 1993. 'Market Operations in Japan: Theory and Practice', in K. Singleton (ed.), *Japanese Monetary Policy*, University of Chicago Press.

Okubo, T. 1983. 'Money, Interest, Income and Prices', *Bank of Japan Monetary and Economic Studies*, 1, 2, October.

Sadahiro, A. et al. 1987. 'An Econometric Model of the Japanese Economy in the EPA World Economy Model' (in Japanese) *Economic Analysis*, no. 110, July.

Shibuya, H. 1992. 'Dynamic Equilibrium Price Index: Asset Price and Inflation', *Bank of Japan Monetary and Economic Studies*, 10, 1, February.

Shigehara, K. 1991. 'Japan's Experience with Use of Monetary Policy and the Process of Liberalization', *Bank of Japan Monetary and Economic Studies*, 9, 1, March.

Singleton, K. J. 1989. 'Interpreting Changes in the Volatility of Yields on Japanese Long-term Bonds', *Bank of Japan Monetary and Economic Studies*, 7, 3, December.

Singleton, K. J. (ed.) 1993. *Japanese Monetary Policy*, University of Chicago Press.

Suzuki, Y. 1985. 'Japan's Monetary Policy over the Past Ten Years', *Bank of Japan Monetary and Economic Studies*, 3, 2, September.

Suzuki, Y. (ed.) 1987a. *The Japanese Financial System*, Oxford University Press.

Suzuki, Y. 1987b. *Money, Finance and Macroeconomic Performance in Japan*, New Haven, Conn., Yale University Press.

Suzuki, Y. 1989. 'Targets and Operating Procedures of Japanese Monetary Policy in the 1990s', *Monetary Policy Issues in the 1990s*, Kansas City, Missouri: Federal Reserve Bank of Kansas City.

Suzuki, Y., A. Kuroda and H. Shirakawa 1988. 'Monetary Control in Japan', *Bank of Japan Monetary and Economic Studies*, 6, 2, November.

Taylor, J. B. 1989. 'Policy Analysis with a Multicountry Model', in R. C. Bryant G. Holtham and P. Hooper (eds), *Macroeconomic Policies in an Interdependent World*, Washington, D.C.: Brookings Institution.

Ueda, K. 1984. 'Credit Market and Monetary Policy' (in Japanese), *Ōsaka University Economic Studies*, 34, 2–3, December.

Ueda, K. 1993. 'A Comparative Perspective on Japanese Monetary Policy: The Short-run Monetary Control and the Transmission Mechanism', in K. Singleton (ed.), *Japanese Monetary Policy*, University of Chicago Press.

Wakita, Y. 1983. 'Bank Lending Markets and Contracted Transactions: An Interpretation of the Rigidity of Bank Lending Rates' (in Japanese), *Kinyū Kenkyū*, 2, 1, Institute for Monetary and Economic Studies, Bank of Japan, March.

Yoshida, T. and R. Rasche 1990. 'The M2 Demand in Japan: Shifted and Unstable?', *Bank of Japan Monetary and Economic Studies*, 8, 2, August.

Yoshikawa, H. 1990. 'On the Equilibrium Yen–Dollar Rate', *American Economic Review*, 80, 3, June.

Yoshikawa, H. 1993. 'Monetary Policy and the Real Economy', in K. Singleton (ed.), *Japanese Monetary Policy*, University of Chicago Press.

13 The Bank of Japan and the Federal Reserve: Financial Liberalization, Independence, and Regulatory Responsibility

Thomas F. Cargill*

13.1 INTRODUCTION

Few disagree government has the responsibility to provide a stable financial and monetary environment, though considerable debate exists over how this responsibility should be carried out and what type of institutions should be assigned the responsibility. Prior to the advent of Keynesian demand management after the Second World War, central banks carried out this objective in three ways: (i) by providing monetary growth to match the needs of trade so as to stabilize the price level; (ii) by providing lender-of-last-resort services to limit contagion and runs on depository institutions; and (iii) by providing financial regulation and supervision to limit risk-taking by depository institutions.[1]

The Keynesian model rationalized the activist approach to government stabilization and thus established an additional method by which central bank policy contributed to a stable financial and monetary environment. Central banks became active agents of counter-cyclical demand management designed to smooth out economic fluctuations[2] and to stimulate economic growth. By the 1960s central banks were expected to contribute effectively to a wide range of goals, from balance of payments equilibrium to full employment, as well as the more traditional goals of price stability and sound banking.

* This chapter was prepared while the author was a Visiting Scholar at the Centre for Japanese Economic Studies, Macquarie University, Sydney, Australia, in August 1993.

Events during the past two decades have altered fundamentally views about central bank policy and how it can contribute effectively to a stable financial and monetary environment. Four events are particularly significant.

First, the relationship between central bank policy and economic activity is more clearly understood. The short-run relationship between central bank policy and real variables cannot usefully be exploited to achieve lasting results and is likely to divert the central bank from achieving long-run price stability. Second, the transition toward open and competitive financial markets during the past two decades raised new issues for central bank policy, ranging from operating procedures to prudential (lender-of-last-resort) policies. In addition, the transition highlighted the critical importance of price stability. Countries experiencing lower and more stable inflation rates experienced a smoother financial transition than countries whose central bank failed to achieve price stability.

Third, rejection of the market-failure rationale of government regulation in favour of public-choice and bureaucracy-based models provided insights into why disruptive financial regulations were permitted to remain in place and why central banks often failed to achieve price stability. These models in turn generated interest in the political business cycle hypothesis which posits a relationship between macroeconomic performance and political institutions, with central bank policy providing the primary linking mechanism. Fourth, financial liberalization, efforts to establish a European monetary union, and political changes in Western and Eastern Europe provided an unequalled opportunity to reconsider the institutional structure and role of central banking.

These events have altered views about central bank policy, especially the view that central bank policy could achieve a lasting and positive impact on real economic performance beyond maintaining long-run price stability and offering lender-of-last-resort services on occasion. Current debate focuses on how to provide central banks with the flexibility to achieve price stability. Of the many issues raised in the discussion, three are particularly significant.

First, what role should central bank policy play in the financial liberalization process? Second, what is the proper institutional relationship between the central bank and government? Third, what formal regulatory role should be assigned to central banks? These issues are considered in comparative perspective between the Bank of Japan (BOJ) and the Federal Reserve (FR). Aside from being among the most important central banks, representing the two largest economies in the world, the BOJ and the FR offer meaningful insights into these issues because of their differing institutional structure and performance.

13.2   BANK OF JAPAN AND FEDERAL RESERVE

The BOJ and the FR have similar origins in that each was established in response to the failure of a national banking system originally designed to provide a unified currency. The United States and Japan established national banking systems in 1863 and 1872, respectively. Each system, for different reasons, was a failure, and each country established central banks in response, but with two notable differences. First, Japan established a central bank in 1882 after ten years of adverse experience, whereas the FR was not established until 1913, after fifty years of adverse experience. Second, inflation and over-issuance of currency were prominent problems with Japan's national banking system and thus the BOJ was established in the context of efforts to achieve price stability. The US failures were related more to inefficiencies in cheque clearing and an unstable reserve requirement structure responsible for several financial panics; thus, the FR was established without a specific mandate to control inflation.

Government mandate to the central bank

The Bank of Japan Law enacted in October 1882 was the original legal basis and mandate to the BOJ; however, the law was revised in 1942 to reflect wartime conditions. The 1942 version of the law has remained essentially unchanged despite efforts by the BOJ to have the law revised.

Article 1 provides the following mandate to the BOJ:

> The Bank of Japan has for its object the regulation of the currency, the control and facilitation of credit and finance, and the maintenance and fostering of the credit system, pursuant to the national policy, in order that the general economic activities of the nation might adequately be enhanced.

The mandate is consistent with central bank responsibilities, ranging from financial regulation to stabilization policy; for example, Suzuki (1987, p. 305) suggests that the last part of Article 1 can be read as 'to foster the stable development of the Japanese economy'. In practice, the BOJ's responsibilities have evolved to focus on price stability and, more recently, prudential considerations. For example, a recent BOJ report (1993, p. 1) states: 'The Bank of Japan has two missions: stabilizing the value of money and fostering a sound and safe financial system – both of which contribute to the stability of the Japanese economy.'

The Federal Reserve Act of 1913 is the legal basis and mandate for the FR. The original act sets out the FR's responsibilities:

> To provide for the establishment of Federal Reserve Banks, to furnish an elastic currency, to afford means of rediscounting commercial paper, to establish a more effective supervision of banking in the United States, and for other purposes.

The mandate is more specific than the Bank of Japan Law, and at the same time appears specifically to exclude stabilization responsibilities. While this may have been the intent of the original 1913 legislation, the mandate to pursue stabilization objectives was expressed by Congress in the 1946 Employment Act, Concurrent Resolution 133 in 1975, and the Humphrey–Hawkins Act of 1978. The 1977 amendment to the Federal Reserve Act formally adopted a stabilization objective:

> The Board of Governors of the Federal Reserve System and the Federal Open Market Committee shall maintain long run growth of the monetary and credit aggregate commensurate with the economy's long run potential to increase production, so as to promote the goals of maximum employment, stable prices, and moderate long-term interest rates.

This amendment was the outcome of a series of discussions between the Federal Reserve and Congress over reporting requirements, monetary aggregate targeting, and monetary policy objectives.

Two general considerations can be drawn from the actual conduct of central bank policy in Japan and the United States. First, while the Bank of Japan Law is consistent with assigning a formal regulatory role to the BOJ, the Ministry of Finance has assumed the major responsibility for financial regulation. In contrast, the FR from the beginning was assigned a formal regulatory role, which has increased over time. Second, the objectives of the BOJ have been more narrowly defined in terms of price stability than in the case of the FR. The FR, as evident from the 1977 amendments to the 1913 Act, possesses a variety of objectives that are frequently in conflict.

Structure

The BOJ is organized as a special government corporation, with 55 per cent of the shares held by the government and the remaining 45 per cent held by private individuals (36.7 per cent of the total shares in 1992), private institutions (7.9 per cent of the total), and local governments (0.4 per cent of the total). Trading is permitted. The FR is organized as a government institution with all outstanding shares held by member banks. Trading is not permitted. Member banks consist of all nationally chartered banks and state chartered banks that have successfully applied for FR membership status.

The revenue of both central banks comes from loans to depository institutions through the discount window, interest on government securities, and fees for various services provided to depository institutions. Interest on government securities is a relatively larger percentage of revenue for the FR because of greater reliance on open market operations as an instrument of policy (96 per cent, against 38 per cent in 1986). In contrast, interest on loans to depository institutions is a relatively larger percentage of revenue for the BOJ because of greater reliance on the discount window as a policy instrument (3.9 versus 1.7 per cent in 1986). In both cases the majority (85 to 95 per cent) of net income is transferred to the government, with the remainder added to surplus and paid out as dividends (5 per cent on BOJ shares and 6 per cent on FR shares).

The major structural difference between the BOJ and the FR resides in the role of regionalism in the latter and the lack of regionalism in the former. The FR is a decentralized central bank consisting of a dominant Board of Governors located in Washington, D.C. and 12 Federal Reserve District Banks. The Federal Open Market Committee, responsible for open market operations, is the connecting link between the district banks and the Board. The 12-member Open Market Committee consists of the 7 members of the Board of Governors, the president of the New York Federal Reserve Bank, and 4 other district bank presidents chosen from the 11 remaining district banks on a rotating basis. The Governor is the chair of the Open Market Committee. The non-voting presidents of the district banks participate in the Open Market Committee meetings. The Federal Reserve Act confers responsibility for administering the discount window to the 12 district banks.

The role of regionalism in US central bank policy has steadily declined since the FR was first established; however, regionalism remains an important and controversial component of US monetary policy. The district presidents tend to support more restrictive monetary policy than does the Board of Governors (Belden, 1991) and at the same time are not subject to a political appointment process; rather, they are appointed by each District Bank's Board of Directors, subject to approval by the Board of Governors. The appointment process is a controversial feature of the FR and has come increasingly under attack.

The main office of the BOJ is located in Tōkyō, where the two major decision-making bodies are located. The Policy Board is formally the highest decision-making body of the BOJ and consists of 7 members, 5 of whom are voting members. The voting members include the Governor of the BOJ and 4 Cabinet-appointed and Diet-confirmed members representing banking, industry and agriculture. The 2 non-voting members represent the Economic Planning Agency and the Ministry of Finance.

A number of commentators regard the Policy Board as the main decision-making body in the BOJ and often compare it to the Board of Governors; however, this is incorrect. The major responsibility for formulating monetary policy resides with the Executive Committee, which consists of the Governor (who chairs the Executive Committee), two Deputy Governors, and several administrators from various departments within the BOJ. The Policy Board formally accepts the decisions of the Executive Committee.

Regionalism plays no meaningful role in the selection of members of either the Policy Board or the Executive Committee, despite the fact that BOJ district banks are located throughout in Japan.

Aside from the relative roles of regionalism there are two other differences between the BOJ and the FR. First, monetary policy in the United States is frequently identified with the Chair of the Board of Governors, who in turn has considerable influence over the Board and the Open Market Committee (Maisel, 1973). In contrast, it would be unusual for Japanese monetary policy to be identified with the Governor of the BOJ although he is the official spokesperson for the Bank. Second, the Board of Governors of the FR often makes decisions independently of the research staff and, in fact, Governor Arthur Burns on occasion in the 1970s emphasized in congressional hearings that he paid little attention to some of the research conducted by the Board staff. In contrast, it would be most unusual for the Executive Committee, given its composition, to make decisions independently of the Bank's research staff, especially the Research and Statistics Department and the International Department. In this respect it would not be inaccurate to characterize US monetary policy decision-making as 'top down' in contrast to Japanese decision-making as 'bottom up'.

Central bank independence

The formal relationship between the central bank and the government defines the degree of 'central bank independence'. No central bank is independent of the influence of government, since the central bank's legal existence and mandate come from the government. It is even questionable as to whether formal independence can be equated with substantive independence. Substantive independence means that central banks have the institutional structure and incentives to carry out those policies for which they are designed and for which they are capable of achieving; specifically, price stability, and lender-of-last-resort services on occasion.

The BOJ is a formally *dependent* central bank, whereas the FR is a formally *independent* central bank. This view is supported by virtually all aspects of the formal structure and the enacting legislation of the two central banks. The Federal Reserve Act clearly intends the FR to be formally independent of government, whereas the Bank of Japan Law clearly intends the BOJ to be under the supervision of the Ministry of Finance. A close review of the appointment process to important decision-making bodies, reporting requirements to government, internal budget decisions, exposure to external auditing, and implementation of monetary policy instruments all suggest that the BOJ is formally a dependent central bank, and the FR is a formally independent central bank (Cargill, 1989).

This assessment is consistent with most efforts to construct indexes of central bank independence, with two notable exceptions. Bade and Parkin (1985) made the first attempt to index central bank independence, and their methodology has served as the basis for more recent efforts at indexation. Based on their analysis they assigned the same index value to the BOJ and the FR.[3] Alesina (1988) extended the Bade and Parkin rankings, but accepted the equal ranking estimated for the BOJ and the FR.

Bade, Parkin and Alesina are incorrect on the relative ranking of the two central banks, and the error persists even in the most recent studies using the Bade–Parkin–Alesina rankings (Alesina and Summers, 1993; Havrilesky and Granato, 1993).

Burdekin and Willett (1991) and Eijffinger and Schaling (1993) explicitly reject the Bade–Parkin–Alesina ranking and both assign a lower independence index value to the Bank of Japan (BOJ). Grilli *et al.* (1991) and Cukierman *et al.* (1993) also propose rankings that assign a much lower independence index to the BOJ. Cukierman, Webb and Neyapti (CWN) (1993) offer the most extensive effort to index independence, and in their view, on a scale of 1.0 (maximum independence) to 0.0 (minimum independence), the BOJ is assigned a value of 0.18, compared to a value of 0.48 for the FR. The FR is at least twice as independent as the BOJ. Grilli *et al.* offer a similar cardinal ranking, as do Eijffinger and Schaling. Four indexes for 21 industrial countries are reported in Table 13.1

Operating procedures The money supply process in Japan and the United States is fundamentally the same, although each central bank has developed a different set of policy instruments to influence the monetary aggregates. Differences between central bank policy and macroeconomic performance cannot be explained by differences in technical operating procedures (Dotsey, 1986; Cargill and Hutchison, 1990).

BOJ operating procedures have changed significantly during the past twenty years in response to financial liberalization (Cargill and Hutchison, 1988; Suzuki, 1986). The operating environment from the 1950s to the early 1970s, prior to liberalization, possessed three distinct features: (i) a simple flow-of-funds structure in which the large surplus of the household sector was transferred via indirect finance (primarily bank finance) to the corporate sector; (ii) a rigid and administratively controlled interest rate structure for indirect finance; and (iii) an internationally isolated financial environment with binding restrictions on the inflow and outflow of capital. In this environment the BOJ pursued an 'interest-rate-focused' policy intended to influence the allocation of credit (Suzuki, 1980). The BOJ employed the discount rate and window guidance to influence the interbank rate, one of only two market-determined interest rates,[4] which in turn influenced bank portfolio decisions to alter the availability of credit.

Liberalization brought many changes to the BOJ's operating environment. These changes are expected to continue in the 1990s as the Ministry of Finance continues to implement liberalization policies (Choy, 1993b).

The flow-of-funds structure has become more complex. The household sector remains a large surplus unit, but consumer credit has grown rapidly in the past decade and the central government has become a major borrower of funds. Domestic and international money and capital markets now provide a significant financing channel for the corporate

TABLE 13.1 Central bank independence index values: industrial economies (higher values of the index indicate greater formal independence: countries ranked according to CWN index)

Country	CWN	BPA	GMT	BWW
Germany	0.69	4	13	3
Switzerland	0.64	4	12	3
Austria	0.61	n.a.	n.a.	2
Denmark	0.50	2	8	n.a.
United States	0.48	3	12	2
Canada	0.45	2	11	1
Ireland	0.44	n.a.	n.a.	n.a.
The Netherlands	0.42	2	10	1
Australia	0.36	1	9	1
Iceland	0.34	n.a.	n.a.	n.a.
Luxemburg	0.33	n.a.	n.a.	n.a.
Sweden	0.29	2	n.a.	1
Finland	0.28	n.a.	n.a.	n.a.
United Kingdom	0.27	2	6	1
Italy	0.25	1.5	5	1
New Zealand	0.24	1	3	1
France	0.24	2	7	1
Spain	0.23	1	5	n.a.
Japan	0.18	3	6	1
Norway	0.17	2	n.a.	n.a.
Belgium	0.17	2	7	1

Notes:

CWN   Cukierman, Webb, and Neyapti (1993, p. 362): 1980–9 period, 1 . 0 to 0.0 scale.
BPA   Bade–Parkin–Alesina reported in Alesina and Summers (1993, p. 154): 1973–88 period, 4-point scale.
GMT   Grilli, Masciandaro and Tabellini index reported in Alesina and Summers (1993, p. 154): 1973–88 period, 12-point scale.
BWW   Burdekin, Wihlborg and Willett (1992, p. 235): 1960–89 period, 3-point scale.
n.a.   Not assigned an independence index.

sector. The regulatory wall between securities and banking markets has been relaxed (Cargill and Todd, 1993). The rigid interest-rate structure has been replaced by market-determined interest rates. At present, interest rates are liberalized, with the exception of rates on small deposits and postal savings rates. Japan's financial system has become internationalized to a high degree, with further liberalization planned in the future.

The BOJ has adapted its policy procedures and instruments to the more liberated financial environment. Window guidance has officially been abandoned, while open market operations have become an important policy instrument. The BOJ continues to operate with an 'interest-rate-focused' policy, but now its operating procedures are designed to influence interest rates as well as the availability of credit (Fukui, 1986) with the money supply, defined as M2+CDs, as the ultimate intermediate target. The BOJ publishes quarterly 'forecasts' or 'projections' of the M2+CD money supply; however, these are not regarded as targets but merely the Bank's projection of the quarterly growth rate of the money supply.

The FR has long employed an 'interest-rate-focused' policy. By the early 1970s the FR had developed a federal funds (interbank market in Japan) operating procedure that relied almost exclusively on open market operations. The only significant departure from this procedure occurred from 1980 to 1982, when the FR adopted a 'reserve-focused' operating procedure as part of a monetarist experiment. The FR has been less consistent than the BOJ regarding intermediate targets. During the past twenty years the FR's intermediate targets have included long-term interest rates, credit aggregates and monetary aggregates. Since 1975 the FR has announced annual monetary aggregate target ranges. The ranges have been set fairly wide, and even with wide ranges, it does not always achieve the official targets. At present the monetary aggregate targets for all practical purposes are ignored.

Like the BOJ the FR has experienced significant changes in its operating environment because of financial liberalization. FR policy has also had to adapt to a new environment: for example, reserve requirements were extended to non-bank depository institutions in 1980. On balance however, the BOJ has been required to make more significant changes in its operating procedures in response to financial liberalization compared to the FR.

13.3   CENTRAL BANK POLICY AND FINANCIAL LIBERALIZATION

The transition of domestic financial systems towards open and competitive structures has been in progress for over two decades in a number of developed and developing economies. The transition is referred to as 'deregulation' in the United States and 'financial liberalization' in Japan. The process emerged from conflicts between a new economic, technological or political environment and an existing financial and monetary structure. The conflict generated a series of market and regulatory innovations designed to circumvent and relax the binding constraints. The process is often disruptive, and characterized by regulatory-market conflicts; however, the end result is a financial and monetary structure distinctly different from the previous structure. This can be seen clearly by comparing the structure of finance in Japan and the United States both before and after the mid-1970s, when financial liberalization became an ongoing process in each country (Cargill and Royama, 1988).

Central bank policy has played an important role in the financial transition of both Japan and the USA. Failure of the FR to maintain price stability in the late 1960s and the 1970s was responsible for some of the most serious failures of the United States transition, one of which was the collapse of the savings and loan (S&L) industry in the second half of the 1980s. Inflationary monetary policy was directly responsible for the wide gap between deposit ceilings (Regulation Q) and money market interest rates which, in turn, weakened the S&L industry, for two reasons: (i) The Regulation Q-money market interest rate gap induced significant disintermediation of funds from S&Ls to money markets. Financial innovations such as money market mutual funds made it increasingly easy for even small depositors to take advantage of market rates of interest; and (ii) S&Ls were eventually permitted to offer market-determined deposit rates such as in 1978 when they were authorized to issue an unregulated six-month time certificate; however, this merely shifted the problem from one of disintermediation risk to interest rate risk. S&Ls allocated virtually all their funds to long-term fixed-rate mortgages and thus experienced significant interest rate risk by the end of the 1970s.

Estimates by Kane (1985) and others suggest the S&L industry was already insolvent in a market-value accounting sense by 1980. The policy failures made after 1980 by the S&L regulatory authorities, Congress, and the Reagan and Bush administrations merely compounded an already existing problem created by inflationary monetary policy.

BOJ policy, in contrast, provided a more stable environment for financial transition, at least up to 1985, by achieving a successful price stabilization record. The stable price environment permitted the Ministry of Finance to pursue a more gradual and less disruptive transition than was possible in the United States because the gap between regulated and unregulated interest rates was kept smaller. In turn, this permitted financial institutions to adapt to the new environment with fewer disruptions. There is no counterpart to the financial disruptions in the United States caused by inflationary monetary policy from the late 1960s to the early 1980s. This inflationary period can, without exaggeration, be called the Great Inflation in terms of the disruptions it caused. It should be regarded as the second most serious FR policy failure since its establishment, the first being the failure to provide adequate lender-of-last-resort services during the Great Depression.

The second half of the 1980s, however, witnessed a reversal of stable monetary policy in Japan and tarnished the BOJ's record. During this period the BOJ adopted an easy monetary policy stance, with unfortunate results. While the overall inflation rate remained low, equity asset and land prices rose significantly. The BOJ reversed the error in 1989 and initiated a tighter policy that burst the 'bubble economy'; however, the effects continue to linger in the form of a serious non-performing loan problem estimated to be anywhere from ¥40–¥60 trillion ($400–$600 bn at ¥100 = $1.00).

The large banks have received the greatest amount of attention in Japan because of the Bank for International Settlements (BIS) capital requirements; however, there is also a serious non-performing loan problem with Japan's 3500 or so agricultural credit co-operatives. Ostrom (1992) draws several parallels between the credit co-operatives and the S&Ls in the United States: (i) credit co-operatives have diversified significantly away from their traditional specialization on loans to farmers, related to agricultural operations; (ii) credit co-operatives have strong ties to the local community and politicians; and (iii) credit co-operatives hold significant amounts of real-estate-related loans in the form of loans to eight major housing loan companies.

In addition, there are other parallels. Credit co-operatives are not regulated and supervised by the Ministry of Finance, and the extent and sophistication of local regulation and supervision is likely to be uneven; thus, credit co-operatives have diversified without central supervision.

The regulatory response to these problems has been disappointing when viewed in the context of the policy failures in the United States. On 18 August 1992 the Japanese government announced a temporary rule change to allow corporations to defer reporting stock portfolio losses until the end of the fiscal year in March 1993; permitted other accounting innovations that delay or conceal the impact of stock and land price declines on assets; permitted Postal Life Insurance System support of the stock market via funds provided to trust banks; postponed sales of government-held shares of Nippon Telegraph and Telephone

(NTT) and Japan National Railways (JNR); provided less than candid estimates on the magnitude of the non-performing loan problem; and encouraged the establishment of a private Resolution Trust Corporation-type institution[5] to purchase assets from troubled depositories that at least with the initial funding levels provided will have no meaningful impact on the non-performing loan problem (Choy, 1993a; Salomon Brothers, 1992).

The outcome of the current problem is uncertain. The Japanese economy may very well ride out the temporary disruptions and slowly absorb the non-performing loans. Even if the economy improves over the next few years however, taxpayer-supplied funding will be required to deal with the non-performing loan problem.

Irrespective of the outcome of the non-performing loan problem in Japan however, the BOJ's record has been tarnished. The BOJ realized the error and reversed itself sharply in 1989, much to the displeasure of the Ministry of Finance, and has slowly began to re-establish some of its lost credibility.

The experiences of Japan and the United States during the past two decades as each country's financial system has evolved towards open and competitive markets suggests two roles for central bank policy.

First, price stability is critically important as a pre-condition for a smooth financial transition. The inflation of the 1970s in the United States bears considerable responsibility for the financial disruptions of the past two decades, including the ultimate collapse of the S&L industry and the resulting taxpayer bail-out effort. BOJ policy was far more successful in providing a conducive background for financial reform to occur, at least up to 1985. Second, price stability in the broad sense is not the sole criterion for a stable financial and monetary environment. The BOJ's inflation record was impressive even in the second half of the 1980s, with the lowest inflation rate among the industrial countries. It is understandable why the BOJ was willing to permit higher monetary growth for other objectives,[6] given the economy's inflation performance. At the same time, easy monetary policy provided the foundation for a speculative 'bubble', with subsequent adverse impacts on the economy. Once the 'bubble' had become apparent the BOJ should have reacted. Whether the bubble would have occurred to some degree if the BOJ had not opted for an expansionary policy in 1985 is an open question; however, BOJ policy did not help matters by waiting for over three years to react.

13.4 CENTRAL BANK INDEPENDENCE

The issue of independence has been a focal point of recent discussion over central bank policy. This is an old topic, but renewed interest in the topic has come from several sources. The adverse effects of inflation in the United States and elsewhere in the 1970s and the painful dis-inflation processes experienced in the early 1980s highlighted the importance of price stability. Combined with the widespread acceptance of inflation as a monetary process that could only be brought under control by non-inflationary monetary growth raised the question of how best to achieve price stability. The question focused on new central bank operating procedures; difficulties created by money supply and demand function shifts due to financial liberalization; difficulties created by increased capital mobility between countries; and the degree to which central bank policy was influenced by government policies in conflict with price stability. The latter issue was elevated in importance because the financial transition process in many countries provided an opportunity to re-examine their financial and monetary institutions. In addition, the attempt to establish a monetary union in Europe and the need to establish central banking institutions from scratch in the former USSR brought the independence question to the forefront.

The advocates of formal independence have accepted uncritically the view that formally independent central banks are likely to generate better monetary policy outcomes. This view is supported by a growing body of empirical research suggesting a statistical relationship between central bank independence and inflation performance across a variety of industrial countries. These studies interpret independence to mean 'autonomy from government', and they draw strong implications from the empirical evidence. According to Alesina and Summers (1993, p. 154) their work 'verifies what previous work has highlighted – a near perfect negative correlation between inflation and central bank independence'. The policy implications are stated in equally strong terms; for example, according to Havrilesky and Granato (1993, p. 258) 'reforms which would increase central bank autonomy will reduce long term inflation'.

The results of the empirical studies have even appeared in the popular financial news, especially in the USA. John Berry (1993) recently wrote in the *Washington Post* that the correlation between central bank independence and inflation is a warning to politicians to leave the central bank alone if they are interested in long-term price stability.

These studies have influenced policy in two ways. First, they have formed the basis of actual policy recommendations for the design of the European Central Bank (Burdekin et al. 1992); and, second, they have been used to argue against current efforts by Congress to reduce the FR's formal independence. It will also be no surprise if they are used by the BOJ to secure revision of the 1942 Bank of Japan Law.

The relationship between central bank independence and inflation performance, however, is far more complicated than suggested by these studies, and on close examination the empirical literature is not nearly as robust as has been claimed. There are at least four reasons for doubting the usefulness of these studies on the question of central bank independence.

First, the studies are clearly contradicted by the inflation records of the BOJ and the FR (Cargill, 1993, 1994). Comparison of inflation rates during the past twenty years shows the BOJ with a better inflation record than the FR despite being a more formally dependent central bank. The differing performance cannot be explained by technical considerations such as differences in operating procedures, differences in the stability of demand and supply functions for money, or differences in the degree of financial liberalization. Only in the 1950s and early 1960s did Japan exhibit a consistently higher inflation rate, but given Japan's rapid rate of real economic growth during this period, it is unclear what implications can be drawn between the two inflation records through the early 1960s.

CWN and other studies note Japan's superior inflation record during the past two decades, but make no serious effort to rationalize the difference between the predictions of the general statistical relationship between formal independence and inflation performance and the two inflation records of the BOJ and the FR. Perhaps these studies regard the comparative results for Japan and the USA as a special case; however, it is difficult to argue that Japan and the USA are special cases, while at the same time using the statistical relationships to help decide a specific structural policy question for a specific central bank.

Second, the indexation of central bank independence is predicated on the view that researchers will come up with the same or similar cardinal ranking by studying the laws that define the relationship between the central bank and the government. At a minimum, the indexes possess measurement errors, since a major element of subjective evaluation is involved in the transfer function between central bank laws and a numerical index. The fact that measurement error would lower the size of the coefficient on the independence variable should be of little comfort because measurement error also biases the standard error of the coefficient downwards. There are substantial differences of opinion about the ranking for specific countries,[7] the degree to which independence can be differentiated between countries, and the time period for which the indexes are applicable. Combined with overly simplistic regression models, the data are a weak reed upon which to base policy recommendations for the structure of a specific central bank.

The two central banks can be used to illustrate the strong assumptions underlying indexation efforts. Cukierman *et al.* (1993) calculate the BOJ and the FR index at 0.48 and 0.18 respectively over the period 1950–89. They thus ignore the impact of Concurrent Resolution 133 in 1975 and the Humphrey–Hawkins Act of 1978 on the FR's independence. These two political events required the FR to report to Congress and announce monetary aggregate targets. They represented a significant change in the relationship between the FR and Congress. Similarly the fact that President Reagan had had the unprecedented opportunity of appointing all the members to the Board of Governors by the time he left office in 1988 is ignored. Nor is the effort on the part of Governor Burns in 1976 and 1977 to ingratiate himself with the Carter Administration by expansionary monetary policy acknowledged as an indication of declining independence. These are significant events in the history of the FR and it seems odd that these are regarded as being consistent with a time-invariant index of independence.

CWN also calculate a constant index for the BOJ over the 1950–89 period. Time constancy in this case is an even stronger assumption than in the case of the FR. The BOJ has clearly become more 'independent' since the inflation of 1970–3 and continued financial liberalization has enhanced its independence.

The basic problem with indexes is that they ultimately rely on a researcher's interpretation of central bank laws and, as such, immediately expose the ranking to two problems. First, reliance on laws can be misleading even if all researchers agree on the same transfer function from laws to numerical index. The FR is a formally independent central bank but has a poor inflation record, especially considering the damage inflation did to the economy between 1965 and the early 1980s. Japan, a formally dependent central bank, has one of the better inflation records, especially if one begins the comparison after 1973. Second, reliance on laws to construct indexes for many countries almost insures important historical, institutional and structural changes occurring in a given country will be overlooked in the effort to construct a simple ranking. This leads one to regard the index as constant during periods of time for which events suggest the degree of central bank independence is changing.

Third, the statistical relationship is not as strong as researchers claim. The Burdekin *et al.* (1991) index lacks sufficient differentiation between countries to serve as a database for regression analysis; however, other indexes have sufficient variation across countries to estimate simple regression equations. The Bade–Parkin–Alesina index, however, has at least one error with respect to Japan and, according to Eijffinger and Schaling, contains other errors. Eijffinger and Schaling are also critical of the Grilli, Masciandaro and Tabellini index.[8]

The CWN index effort is the most impressive attempt to index central bank independence in terms of the degree of differentiation between countries (21 industrial and 51 developing countries), extent of information used to calculate each country's index value, and period of time covered. Their regression results are based on decade averages for four periods: 1950–9, 1960–71, 1972–9 and 1980–9. That is, there are four observations for each country for the inflation rate, index of independence and the turnover rate. Their most impressive results are for the 21 industrialized countries over the 1950–89 period. The coefficient on the index variable is negative and significant at the 5 per cent level; however, the turnover coefficient is significant at the 10 per cent level but yields an incorrect sign. In addition, the regression equation explains only 34 per cent of the variation of a smoothed inflation rate dependent variable.

Considering the simple regression model estimated over such a long time period in which major structural changes have taken place, and the fact none of the claimed statistical relationships can explain more than 50 per cent of the variation in the inflation rate, it is difficult to attribute the degree of importance to the relationship between central bank independence and inflation performance claimed in these studies.

The comments on the statistical evidence are not meant to deny a statistical relationship between the indexes of independence and the average inflation rates posited in these studies. What they do show, however, is the lack of robustness of the statistical association between central bank independence and inflation performance. The data and econometric problems alone should suggest caution but, more importantly, the failure of these correlations to account for the inflation records of the BOJ and the FR suggest that the hypothesis needs additional work. There is a heavy burden of proof on those who use these results to argue for more formal independence to account for the relative performance of the BOJ.

Current status of the debate over formal independence in Japan and the United States

The BOJ and the FR are both involved in ongoing discussions with their respective governments: to gain more formal independence in the case of the BOJ; and to maintain existing formal independence in the case of the FR.

The BOJ has been unsuccessful in obtaining a revision of the 1942 Bank of Japan Act which explicitly places the Ministry of Finance over the Bank. The issue was discussed in the late 1950s (Shionoya, 1962) and raised again publicly in 1987 by Suzuki (1987). While there are no immediate plans to revise the Bank of Japan Law, it is only a matter of time before the law is revised since it is an anachronism and increasingly out of step with Japan's financial system. It seems only reasonable that the Ministry of Finance will at some point in the near future revise the wartime version of the Bank of Japan Law, if for no other reason than to further dissociate Japan from the war. However, it is unlikely that the BOJ will receive the type of formal independence afforded to the FR. The BOJ was never intended to be a separate entity within the Japanese system of financial and monetary regulation. Government institutions reflect the historical and political evolution of their country, and Japan relative to the United States has lacked an emphasis on decentralized decision-making, democratic-type institutions, and openness to political and economic markets. As a result, Japan's government institutions are far more centralized than their counterparts would be in the United States.

The BOJ, has however, achieved a significant position of substantive independence over the past two decades; that is, the BOJ now has considerable flexibility to formulate and execute monetary policy without constraints from the Ministry of Finance. However, the BOJ has not been entirely successful on the substantive independence front. The Ministry of Finance has resisted efforts to develop a viable Treasury bill market, which would not only improve the efficiency of the Japanese financial system, but also give the BOJ the ability to conduct flexible open market operations. The Ministry of Finance has also resisted efforts to deal with the Postal Savings System, which presently accounts for about 30 per cent of household deposits in Japan. The BOJ has repeatedly argued that the Postal Savings System interferes with monetary policy by adjusting interest rates and types of deposit to attract funds whenever monetary policy is changed.

The FR has always possessed a high degree of formal independence, and hence the potential to pursue substantive independent monetary policy. The record of FR policy, however, is not impressive. The two major financial debacles in the United States – the Great Depression and the Great Inflation – are the direct result of FR policy failure despite a high degree of formal independence. These were the failures of a government agency without a clear mandate to judge performance, and, in fact, some economists (Kane, 1990) have argued that the formal independence of the FR makes it susceptible to as much political influence as if it were formally dependent. Formal independence in the US government is a valued commodity which the FR is willing to maintain in the form of reduced substantive independence. Finally, formal independence is no safeguard against misguided or plainly incompetent decision-making by the central bank.

The past two decades have witnessed several efforts to reduce the formal independence of the FR, but without much success. In the 1970s Congress reduced the FR's formal independence by requiring it to announce annual monetary aggregate targets and to confer with Congress biannually. Many regard these Congressional supervision efforts, however, as a failure (Weintraub, 1975). More recently, the FR's independence has come under attack from Representative Gonzales, Chairman of the House Banking, Finance and Urban Affairs Committee. His proposed Federal Reserve System Accountability Act of 1993 would have significantly reduced the formal independence of the Federal Reserve by requiring that presidents of each of the 12 District Banks be subject to presidential appointment and Senate confirmation, and require full Government Accounting Office audits. There was considerable concern among FR officials that this type of legislation had a reasonable chance of passage, given the Democrat-controlled Congress and a Democratic President. However, the issue has recently been put to rest; in a letter to Representative Gonzales released on 24 September 1993, President Clinton indicated that he was 'disinclined' to seek major structural changes in the FR at this time since he was satisfied with current monetary policy. Should the FR, however, move towards higher interest rates to combat inflation, the Gonzales proposals are likely to re-emerge.

What implications can be drawn from the BOJ and FR regarding formal independence? Formal independence is no guarantee of a stable financial and monetary framework, any more than is formal dependence a guarantee. The BOJ has had two serious policy failures in the past twenty years: the inflation of the early 1970s, and the land and stock market bubble of the second half of the 1980s. Overall, however, the BOJ has a better record than the FR.

A close study of the BOJ and the FR suggest factors other than technical considerations and degrees of formal relationship between the central bank and the government are more important for understanding relative macroeconomic performance. Cargill and Hutchison (1990), for example, review a variety of factors ranging from political structure to the short-run trade-off between employment and inflation as contributing to the relative difference in macroeconomic performance and central bank policy. The formal independence of the central bank, based on a comparative analysis of the BOJ and the FR, may very well be one of the least important elements of the ability of a central bank to achieve a stable financial and monetary environment.

The question remains: what is the proper relationship between the central bank and the government? There are two elements to a response. First, there is probably something to be said for some degree of formal independence to guard against the possibility of an irresponsible government attempting to solve problems by inflationary monetary policy. Unfortunately, the record is clear, at least from the comparative analysis of the BOJ and the FR, that formal independence is no guarantee of price stability, nor is it a guarantee of political pressure. Second, the issue should focus on central bank accountability for low and steady inflation rather than formal relationships between the central bank and the government. Too much attention is devoted to formal independence and not enough attention to setting up a system of incentives that will maximize the probability that the central bank will achieve long-run price stability. Once its accepted that central banks cannot change the real performance of the economy permanently but can only determine the value of money, the central bank needs a set of incentives to insure price stabilization. It is naïve to argue that mere formal independence will assure an optimal monetary policy. Mandates to the central bank in the form of a contract such as described in Walsh (1993) offer a much more meaningful focal point for discussion rather than insistence on formal independence. In the contract approach, the inflation performance standard is specified and the contract provides the bank with complete flexibility to achieve the standard. The central bank is penalized or rewarded on the basis of whether a simple target rule is missed or achieved. The most interesting application of the contract approach is currently under way in New Zealand.

13.6   CENTRAL BANKS AND FINANCIAL REGULATORY RESPONSIBILITIES

Central banks assume varying degrees of regulatory responsibility over the financial system, consistent with their role as a lender of last resort. The BOJ and the FR represent contrasting approaches.

The BOJ has not played a major role in financial regulation, and what formal roles it has played are declining in importance. The BOJ played a formal role in setting deposit rate ceilings (Suzuki, 1987, p. 148); however, with continued deposit-rate liberalization this is becoming less important over time. The BOJ also played a formal role by deciding 'window guidance' or loan expansion limits for private financial institutions; however, with the advent of liberalization and greater reliance on open-market operations, window guidance has been abandoned. While the BOJ does not formally establish regulatory parameters, the Bank does play a role in bank supervision.

The primary regulatory parameters of the Japanese financial system are set by the Ministry of Finance, who combines into one administrative entity almost all aspects of regulation over financial institutions and markets, with one major exception. The Ministry of Posts and Telecommunications has regulatory responsibility over the Postal Savings System, a major component of the Japanese financial system.

There are no efforts currently to restructure the relationship between the BOJ and the Ministry of Finance with regard to regulatory responsibilities; however, the BOJ has raised two issues with the Ministry over regulatory issues. First, the Bank has repeatedly pressured the Ministry of Finance to remove regulatory advantages provided to the Postal Savings System. Ultimately, this will require privatization of the System which, to say the least, would be economically and politically difficult. Second, the Bank has argued for a more independent role in the bank deposit insurance system. At present the Ministry of Finance dominates the Deposit Insurance Corporation established in 1971, with no plans to broaden the role of the BOJ.

The lack of formal regulatory responsibilities of the BOJ, however, does not mean that the Bank has no influence. In fact, the BOJ has had considerable influence on the Ministry of Finance in shaping financial regulations during the past two decades. Despite the Bank's inability to achieve a resolution of the Postal Savings problem, the progress of financial liberalization in Japan is due in a major way to the BOJ's support for liberalization.

The financial regulatory structure in the United States differs in three important respects from that of Japan. First, the FR has considerable regulatory responsibility over financial institutions and markets, and the trend has been to increase the regulatory responsibilities of the FR, in contrast to the trend in Japan. The FR's responsibilities have grown significantly during the past decade because of merger and acquisition activity, and via legislation that has extended its influence to non-bank depository institutions. Second, the FR is only one of many regulatory authorities. The United States possesses a multiplicity of regulatory authorities at both federal and state level. Third, regulatory authorities in the United States lack the type of administrative-guidance powers of the Ministry of Finance; rather, the regulatory structure emphasizes legislation and court-determined interpretations to settle conflicts over how the legislation is to be applied in practice.

There have been a number of efforts to revise the regulatory structure and the regulatory role of the FR. The multiplicity of regulatory authorities is inefficient and several attempts have been made to reduce the regulatory authorities to a smaller number, the most recent attempt occurring in 1993. There is a general consensus that the USA possesses too many regulators; however, the political cost of reducing the number of regulatory authorities is regarded as being far in excess of any gains in efficiency. There have even been some efforts to remove the regulatory powers of the FR, but this has been met with even less support than the suggestion to reduce the number of regulatory authorities in the USA. The FR is far too entrenched in the politics of regulatory policy to fear much from efforts to reduce its formal role.

There appear to be at least two arguments in support of a major regulatory role for central banks. One argument can be drawn from the central bank independence literature. If one can make an argument that formally independent central banks are more likely to achieve price stability, then this argument can be extended to assigning a major regulatory responsibility to the central bank so that regulation is less susceptible to political considerations. The other and more frequently expressed argument relies on the lender-of-last-resort function of the central bank: central banks as creators of a high-powered money function as lenders of last resort on occasion to prevent disruptive runs on the banking system. Many argue this role requires a major regulatory and supervisory role for the central bank (Goodhart, 1988, p. 8).

The BOJ and the FR offer two models of regulatory responsibility; however, implications that can be drawn from the two central banks are limited because of the multiplicity of regulators in the United States and the more unified regulatory structure in Japan. One might be tempted to argue that Japan's more consistent and successful monetary policy, at least up to 1985, was made easier because there were fewer conflicts between policy and regulatory goals, but other factors are likely to have been more important.

The issue is therefore approached in general terms. Two questions seem important. Does the lender-of-last-resort role of the central bank require it to assume major regulatory responsibility? If the answer is 'no', are there other reasons to assign regulatory responsibility to the central bank?

There is nothing inherent in administering the discount window that requires a formal regulatory role for the central bank. Financial regulation is an ongoing process that involves all regulated institutions, whereas lender of last resort is directed to a small number of institutions, and short-run orientated. While the central bank needs detailed information about the financial condition of a borrowing institution, this information would be readily available from the bank in question and the regulatory authority. The central bank would assume an informal role in assisting the regulatory agency regarding what type of information would be required to make lender-of-last-resort decisions, but there is no reason why it should be the responsibility of the central bank to collect the information and monitor the activities of banks, as is now done by the FR.

The only argument for a formal regulatory responsibility is that the central bank stands at the centre of the financial system and has a comparative advantage in gathering and analyzing financial information. This is a weak argument to assign regulatory responsibilities to the central bank, especially when one considers the potential problems when central banks become involved in financial regulation.

There are a number of reasons why conflicts can arise between the basic responsibilities of the central bank and regulation. The more the central bank distances itself from the regulated entity the more likely it will more effectively pursue long-run objectives. The special interest and public choice approaches to regulation argue that the regulatory authority and the regulated entity form relationships which are ultimately harmful to the economy.[9] The FR in the 1960s permitted the extension of Regulation Q deposit rate ceilings to thrift institutions and thus became less inclined to pursue tight monetary policy in the 1970s for fear that it would increase the gap between Regulation Q ceilings on money market interest rates. The FR in the late 1970s was constrained by the declining membership problem from pursuing a more aggressive anti-inflation policy. The FR was a major advocate of the 'too big to fail' policy of the 1980s. All these examples represent a conflict between the ultimate price stabilization goal of monetary policy and the formal regulatory responsibilities of the FR. Basically, they divert attention and resources from the long-run goal of price stability to short-run issues that could have just as easily been handled by other regulatory authorities.

13.7 CONCLUDING COMMENTS

A comparative review of the BOJ and the FR offers far more than merely understanding more about two major central banks representing the two largest economies in the world. The comparative perspective offers meaningful insights into how central bank policy can either be a disruptive or a stabilizing influence to the financial liberalization process; the complexity of the relationship between formal central bank independence and the outcomes of central bank policy; and the problems that emerge when central banks become too involved in financial regulation.

The main points of the chapter can be stated briefly. The most meaningful contribution the central bank can make to financial liberalization is to maintain price stability and thereby narrow the gap between regulated and unregulated interest rates. Price stability, however, is only necessary, not sufficient, for a stable financial environment. Central banks need to consider asset prices in specific markets.

The formal relationship between the central bank and the government may be one of the least important considerations for optimal monetary policy. Incentives to pursue price stability are far more important, and much of the current discussion focused on central bank independence is misplaced. There is only one sound argument for some degree of formal independence. The central bank then has the legal authority to refuse to accommodate an irresponsible government.

Central banks should focus on what they and no other government entity can accomplishment: price stability and lender-of-last-resort services. Neither of these requires the central bank to play a major regulatory role in the financial system.

NOTES

1. M. Friedman (1959) offers a concise rationalization of central banking in a market economy.
2. In the early years of the Keynesian revolution central bank policy was regarded as an ineffective instrument of economic stabilization relative to fiscal policy; however, by the 1970s, the tables were turned, and central bank policy came to be regarded as the superior stabilization instrument.
3. The Bade and Parkin rankings are reproduced in Eijffinger and Schaling (1993, p. 63).
4. The *gensaki* rate for repurchase agreements secured by government securities was also competitively determined. Prior to 1976 the *gensaki* market was not officially recognized, although the Ministry of Finance did not interfere with the market.
5. The Resolution Trust Corporation was established by the Financial Institutions Reform, Recovery and Enforcement Act of 1989 to liquidate insolvent S&Ls.
6. The BOJ permitted faster monetary and credit growth to support the dollar; for example, see Ito, 1993, p. 133.
7. Some of these differences are discussed in Burdekin *et al.*, (1991, pp. 235–7) and Eijffinger and Schaling, 1993.
8. The statistical significance between the index values and inflation is not influenced by the Japan versus United States error, however. Changing the Japan index in Alesina and Summers (1993, p. 154) from 3 to 1 and regressing the 1973–88 average inflation rates against the country independence indexes yields the following results: Inflation = 13.2 + (−2.4) Index, with a t value of −3.6 for the coefficient on the index variable, and an $R^2 = 0.44$. While the index coefficient is significant, the correlation is considerably less than 'perfectly negative', as alleged in Alesina and Summers.
9. See Kane (1988), for example.

REFERENCES

Alesina, Alberto 1988, 'Macroeconomics and Politics', in Stanley Fischer (ed.), *NBER Macroeconomic Annual*, Cambridge, Mass.: MIT Press.

Alesina, Alberto and Lawrence H. Summers 1993. 'Central Bank Independence and Macroeconomic Performance', *Journal of Money, Credit and Banking*, 25 (May) pp. 151–62.

Bade, Robin and Michael Parkin 1985. 'Central Bank Laws and Monetary Policy', unpublished, University of Western Ontario.

Bank of Japan 1993. 'Treasury Business of the Bank of Japan'. Special Paper No. 226, March.

Belden, Susan 1991. 'Rationale for Dissent: The Case of FOMC Members', *Contemporary Policy Issues*, 9 (July) pp. 59–70.

Berry, John M. 1993. 'More Independence Means Lower Inflation, Studies Show', *Washington Post*, 17 February.

Burdekin, C. K. Richard and Thomas D. Willett 1991. 'Central Bank Reform: The Federal Reserve in International Perspective', *Public Budgeting and Financial Management*, 3, pp. 619–49.

Burdekin, C. K. Richard, Clas Wihlborg and Thomas D. Willett 1992. 'A Monetary Constitution Case for an Independent European Central Bank', *The World Economy*, 15 (March) pp. 231–49.

Cargill, Thomas F. 1989. *Central Bank Independence and Regulatory Responsibilities: The Bank of Japan and the Federal Reserve*, Salomon Brothers Center of the Study of Financial Institutions, 2, New York University.

Cargill, Thomas F. 1993. 'The Bank of Japan: A Dependent but Price Stabilizing Central Bank', *Public Budgeting and Financial Management*, 5, pp. 131–9.

Cargill, Thomas F. 1994. 'The Bank of Japan and the Federal Reserve: An Essay on Central Bank Independence', in Kevin D. Hoover and Steven M. Sheffrin (eds.) *Essays in Honor of Thomas Mayer*, London: Edward Elgar (forthcoming).

Cargill, Thomas F. and Michael M. Hutchison 1988. 'The Response of the Bank of Japan to Macroeconomic and Financial Change', in Hang-Sheng Cheng (ed.), *Monetary Policy in Pacific Basin Countries* Boston: Kluwer-Academic Publishers.

Cargill, Thomas F. and Michael M. Hutchison 1990. 'Monetary Policy and Political Economy: The Federal Reserve and the Bank of Japan', in Thomas Mayer (ed.), *The Political Economy of American Monetary Policy*, New York: Cambridge University Press.

Cargill Thomas F. and Shoichi Royama 1988. *The Transition of Finance in Japan and the United States: A Comparative Perspective*, Stanford, Calif.: Hoover Institution Press.

Cargill, Thomas F. and Gregory F. W. Todd 1993. 'Japan's Financial System Reform Law: Progress Toward Financial Liberalization?", *Brooklyn Journal of International Law*, 19, pp. 47–84.

Choy, Jon 1993a. 'Japanese Banks Attack Problem Loans', *Japan Economic Institute Report*, No. 4B 5 February pp. 4–5.

Choy, Jon 1993b. 'Japanese Financial Deregulation on Track for Now', *Japan Economic Institute Report*, Washington, D.C.: Japan Economic Institute, 9 July pp. 1–3.

Cukierman, Alex, Steven B. Webb and Bilin Neyapti 1993. 'Measuring the Independence of Central Banks and Its Effect on Policy Outcomes', *World Bank Economic Review*, 6, pp. 353–98.

Dotsey, Michael 1986. 'Japanese Monetary Policy: A Comparative Analysis', *Monetary and Economic Studies*, Bank of Japan, pp. 105–27.

Eijffinger, Sylvester and Eric Schaling 1993. 'Central Bank Independence in Twelve Industrial Countries', *Banca Nazionale Del Lavoro: Quarterly Review*, March, pp. 49–89.

Friedman, Milton 1959. *A Program for Monetary Stability*, New York: Fordham University Press.

Fukui, Toshihiko 1986. 'Recent Developments of the Short-Term Money Market in Japan and Changes in Monetary Control Technique and Procedures by the Bank of Japan', Bank of Japan, Research and Statistics Department, Special Paper No. 130, January.

Goodhart, Charles 1988. *The Evolution of Central Banks*, Cambridge, Mass.: MIT Press.

Grilli, Vittorio, Donato Masciandaro and Guido Tabellini 1991. 'Political and Monetary Institutions and Public Finance Policies in the Industrial Countries', *Economy Policy*, 13 (October), pp. 341–92.

Havrilesky, Thomas and James Granato 1993. 'Determinants of Inflation Performance: Corporatist Structures vs. Central Bank Autonomy', *Public Choice*, 76, pp. 249–61.

Ito, Takatoshi 1993. *The Japanese Economy*, Cambridge, Mass.: MIT Press.

Kane, Edward J. 1985. *The Gathering Crisis in Federal Deposit Insurance*, Cambridge, Mass.: MIT Press.

Kane, J. Edward 1989. *The S&L Insurance Mess: How Did it Happen?*, Washington, D.C.: Urban Institute Press.

Kane, Edward J. 1990. 'Bureaucratic Self-interest as an Obstacle to Monetary Reform', in Thomas Mayer (ed.), *The Political Economy of American Monetary Policy*, New York: Cambridge University Press.

Maisel, Sherman J. 1973. *Managing the Dollar*, New York: W. W. Norton.

Ostrom, Douglas 1992. 'A Savings and Loan-Style Crisis for Japan?', *Japan Economic Institute*, 2 October.

Salomon Brothers 1992. *Japanese Economic/Market Analysis*. 2 November, Tōkyō.

Shionoya, Tsukumo 1962. *Problems Surrounding the Revision of the Bank of Japan Law*, Nagoya, Japan: The Beckhard Foundation.

Suzuki, Yoshi 1980. *Money and Banking in Contemporary Japan*, New Haven, Conn.: Yale University Press.

Suzuki, Yoshio (ed.) 1987. *The Japanese Financial System*, Oxford: Clarendon Press.

Walsh, Carl 1993. 'Optimal contracts for independent Central Bankers: Private Information, Performance Measures and Reappointment', Working Paper, February.

Weintraub, Robert W. 1978. 'Congressional Supervision of Monetary Policy', *Journal of Monetary Economics*, 4, pp. 341–62.

Part IV

International Economic Relations

14 Is Japan Establishing a Trade Bloc in East Asia and the Pacific?

Jeffrey A. Frankel*

A debate began in 1991 over the advantages and disadvantages of a global trend towards three economic blocs – the Western Hemisphere, centred on the United States; Europe, centred on the European Community; and East Asia, centred on Japan. Krugman (1991a), Bhagwati (1990, 1992) and Bergsten (1991), argue that the trend is, on balance, bad. Krugman (1991b) and Lawrence (1991c) argue that it is, on balance, good.[1] Most appear to agree, however, that a trend towards three blocs is indeed underway.

There is no agreed standard definition of an 'economic bloc'. A useful definition might be 'a group of countries who are concentrating their trade and financial relationships with each other, in preference to the rest of the world'. One might wish to add to the definition the criterion that this concentration is the outcome of government policy, or at least of factors that are non-economic in origin, such as a common language or culture. In two of the three parts of the world mentioned above, there have clearly been recent deliberate political steps towards economic integration. In Europe, the previously-lethargic Economic Community (EC) has burst forth with the programmes of the Single Market, European Monetary Union, and more. In the Western

* This chapter has been abridged and updated from an original paper, which included more on financial links, written for an NBER conference held on 3–5 April 1992 at Del Mar, California. It appears in *Regionalism and Rivalry: Japan and the U.S. in Pacific Asia*, edited by Jeffrey Frankel and Miles Kahler (Chicago: University of Chicago Press) © 1993 by the National Bureau of Economic Research. All rights reserved. An earlier abridged version is also forthcoming in a book to be edited by Dilip Das.

The author would like to thank Benjamin Chui and Shang-Jin Wei for extremely efficient research assistance, and Warwick McKibbin for data. He would also like to thank Miles Kahler, Robert Lawrence and other participants at the Del Mar conference, as well as Tamin Bayoumi, for useful comments. Finally, he would like to thank the Japan–United States Friendship Commission (an agency of the US government) for research support.

Hemisphere, earlier unsuccessful attempts at regional integration have given way to the Canadian–US Free Trade Agreement, followed by the North America Free Trade Area and Enterprise for the Americas Initiative.[2]

In East Asia, by contrast, overt preferential trading arrangements or other political moves to promote regional economic integration are lacking, as has been noted by others.[3] The ASEAN countries (Association of South East Asian Nations), are certainly taking steps in the direction of turning what used to be a regional security group into a free trade area of sorts. But when Americans worry, as they are wont to do, about a trading bloc forming in Asia, it is generally not ASEAN that concerns them. Rather it is the possibility of an East-Asia- or Pacific-wide bloc dominated by Japan.

Japan is, in fact, unusual among major countries in *not* having preferential trading arrangements with smaller neighbouring countries. But the hypothesis that has been put forward is that Japan is forming an economic bloc in the same way as it runs its economy: by means of policies that are implicit, indirect and invisible. Specifically, the hypothesis is that Japan operates, by means of such instruments as flows of aid, foreign direct investment and other forms of finance, to influence its neighbours' trade towards itself.[4] This is a hypothesis that should not be accepted uncritically, but rather needs to be examined empirically.

After examining some of the relevant statistics, this chapter argues that the evidence of an evolving East Asian trade bloc centred on Japan is not as clear as many believe. Trade between Japan and other Asian countries increased substantially in the late 1980s. But *intraregional trade bias did not increase*, as it did, for example, within the EC.

14.1 IS A TRADE BLOC FORMING IN PACIFIC ASIA?

We must begin by acknowledging the obvious: the greatly increased economic weight of East Asian countries in the world. The rapid outward-oriented growth of Japan, followed by the four East Asian newly industrialized countries (NICs) and more recently by some of the other ASEAN countries, is one of the most remarkable and widely-remarked trends in the world economy over the last three decades. But when one asks whether a bloc is forming in East Asia, one is presumably asking something more than whether these economies are getting larger, or even whether economic flows among them are increasing. One must ask whether the share of intraregional trade is higher, or increasing more rapidly, than would be predicted based on such factors as the GNP or growth rates of the countries involved.

14.1.1 Adjusting intraregional trade for growth

Table 14.1 reports three alternative ways of computing intraregional trade bias. The first part of the table is based on a simple breakdown of trade (exports plus imports) undertaken by countries in East Asia into trade with other members of the same regional grouping, versus trade with other parts of the world.[5] For comparison, the analogous statistics are reported for Western Europe (the EC Twelve) and for the Western Hemisphere.

The share of intraregional trade in East Asia increased from 23 per cent in 1980 to 39 per cent in 1990. Pronouncements that a clubbish trade bloc is forming in the region are usually based on figures such as these. But the numbers are deceptive.

All three regions show increasing intragroup trade in the 1980s. The region that has both the highest and the fastest-increasing degree of intraregional trade is not Asia but the EC, reaching 47 per cent in 1990. The share of intraregional trade in East Asia has not even been increasing appreciably faster than that in North America.

Quite aside from the comparison with Europe, it is easy to be misled by intraregional trade shares such as those reported in the first three rows of Table 14.1. If one allows for the phenomenon that most of the East Asian countries in the 1980s experienced rapid growth in *total* output and trade, then it is possible that there has, in fact, been no movement towards intraregional bias in the evolving pattern of trade. The increase in the intraregional share of trade that is observed in Table 14.1 could be entirely due to the increase in the economic size of the countries. To take the simplest case, imagine that there were no intraregional bias in 1980, and that each East Asian country conducted trade with other East Asian countries in the same proportion as the latter's weight in world trade (25 per cent). Total trade undertaken by Asian countries increased rapidly over this ten-year period, while total trade world-wide increased less rapidly. Even if there continued to be no regional bias in 1990, the observed intraregional share of trade would have increased by a third (to 31 per cent) due solely to the greater weight of Asian countries in the world economy.

Consider now the more realistic case where, because of transportation costs if nothing else, countries within each of the three groupings undertake trade that is somewhat biased towards trading partners within their

TABLE 14.1   Summary measures of intraregional trade biases

	Year	East Asia	Western Hemisphere	European Community
(1)				
Intraregional	1980	0.23	0.27	0.42
trade/total trade	1985	0.26	0.31	0.42
	1990	0.29	0.29	0.47
(2)				
Intraregional bias	1980	0.91	0.79	0.72
holding constant	1985	0.84	0.78	0.79
for size of trade	1990	0.93	0.85	0.80
(3)				
Bias, holding constant	1980	0.70	0.53	0.23
for GNP, population,	1985	0.40	0.34	0.44
distance, etc	1990	0.60	0.97	0.46

Sources: (1) Computed from International Monetary Fund Direction of Trade
data; (2) Computed as the ratio of (1) to shares of world trade, as
described in text; (3) Gravity regressions, reported in Tables 2, 3
and 4 respectively. They include also significant coefficients on
the APEC bloc, among other variables.

own group (East Asia, North America, and the EC). Although East Asian
trade with other parts of the world has increased rapidly, trade with
other East Asian countries has increased even more rapidly. Does this
mean that the degree of clubbishness or within-region bias has intensified over this period? No, it does not. *Even if there were no increase
at all in the bias toward intra-East Asian trade*, the more rapid growth
of total trade and output experienced by East Asian countries would
show up as a rate of growth of intra-East Asian trade that was faster
than the rate of growth of East Asian trade with the rest of the world.

Think of each East Asian country in 1980 as conducting trade with
other East Asian firms in the same proportion as their weight in world
trade (25 per cent) *multiplied* by a regional bias term to explain the
actual share reported in Table 14.1 (23 per cent). Then the regional
bias term would have to be 0.91 (= 0.23/0.25). An unchanged regional
bias term multiplied by the East Asians' 1990 weight in world trade
would predict that the 1990 intraregional share of trade would be 28
per cent (0.91 x 0.31 = 0.28). This calculation turns out to explain
almost all the increase in the actual intraregional share (to 0.29). Thus,

even with this very simple method of adjustment, the East Asian bias toward within-region trade did not rise much in the 1980s. The implicit intraregional bias rose only from 0.91 to 0.93 (= 0.29/0.31), as shown in the middle rows of Table 14.1.[6]

14.1.2 A test on bilateral trade flows

The analysis should be elaborated by use of a systematic framework for measuring what patterns of bilateral trade are normal around the world: the so-called 'gravity' model.[7] A dummy variable can then be added to represent when both countries in a given pair belong to the same regional grouping, and one can check whether the level and time trend in the East Asia/Pacific grouping exceeds that in other groupings. We do not currently have measures of historical, political, cultural and linguistic ties. Thus it will be possible to interpret the dummy variables as reflecting these factors, rather than necessarily as reflecting discriminatory trade policies. Perhaps we should not regret the merging of these different factors in one term, because, as noted, there are in any case no overt preferential trading arrangements on which theories of a Japanese trading bloc could rely.[8]

The dependent variable is trade (exports plus imports), in log form, between pairs of countries in a given year. We have 63 countries in our data set, so that there are 1,953 data points (= 63 x 62/2) for a given year in which the data set is complete.[9]

One would expect the two most important factors in explaining bilateral trade flows to be the geographical distance between the two countries, and their economic size. These factors are the essence of the gravity model, by analogy with the law of gravitational attraction between masses.

A large part of the apparent bias toward intraregional trade is certainly due to simple geographical proximity. Indeed, Krugman (1991b) suggests that most of it may be due to proximity, so that the three trading blocs are welfare-improving 'natural' groupings (as distinct from 'unnatural' trading arrangements between distant trading partners such as the United Kingdom and members of the British Commonwealth). Although the importance of distance and transportation costs is clear, there is not a lot of theoretical guidance on precisely how they should enter. We experiment a little with functional forms. We also add a dummy 'Adjacent' variable to indicate when two countries share a common border. The basic equation to be estimated is:

$$\log(T_{ij}) = \alpha + \beta_1 \log (GNP_i GNP_j) + \beta_2 \log (GNP/pop_i GNP/pop_j)$$
$$+ \beta_3 \log (DISTANCE) + \beta_4 (ADJACENT) + \gamma_1 (EC_{ij}) + \gamma_2$$
$$(WH_{ij}) + \gamma_3 (ASIA_{ij}) + u_{ij}.$$

The last four explanatory factors are dummy variables. The goal, again, is to see how much of the high level of trade within the East Asian region can be explained by simple economic factors common to bilateral trade throughout the world, and how much is left over to be attributed to a special regional effect.[10]

The practice of entering GNPs in product form is well-established empirically in bilateral trade regressions. It can easily be justified by the modern theory of trade under imperfect competition.[11] In addition, there is reason to believe that GNP per capita has a positive effect, for a given size: as countries become more developed, they tend to specialize more and to trade more. It is also possible that the infrastructure necessary to conduct trade – ports, airports and so on – becomes better-developed with the level of GNP per capita.

The results are reported in Tables 14.2, 14.3 and 14.4. We found all three variables to be highly significant statistically ($>$ 99 per cent level). The coefficient on the log of distance was about –0.56, when the adjacency variable (which is also highly significant statistically) is included at the same time. This means that when the distance between two non-adjacent countries is higher by 1 per cent, the trade between them falls by about 0.56 per cent.[12]

We tested for possible non-linearity in the log-distance term, as it could conceivably be the cause of any apparent bias toward intraregional trade that is left after controlling linearly for distance. Quadratic and cubic terms turned out to be not at all significant. An alternative specification that fits at least as well as the log is to include the level of distance and its square. The significant positive coefficient on the latter confirms the property of the log that 'trade resistance' increases less-than-linearly with distance. The results for the other coefficients are little affected by the choice of functional form for proximity. We report here only results using the log of distance.

The estimated coefficient on GNP per capita is about 0.29 as of 1980, indicating that richer countries do indeed trade more, though this term declines during the 1980s, reaching 0.08 in 1990. The estimated coefficient for the log of the product of the two countries' GNPs is about 0.75, indicating that, though trade increases with size, it increases less-than-proportionately (holding GNP per capita constant).

TABLE 14.2 Gravity model of bilateral trade: 1980

C	GNPs	Per capita GNPs	Distance	Adjacent	EC	Western Hemisphere	ASEAN	EAEC	Asian Pacific	APEC	Pacific rim	R^2 / $\bar{R}^2$	SEE[a]
-11.36** (0.563)	0.763 (0.018)	0.268** (0.021)	-0.597** (0.041)	0.649** (0.185)	0.092 (0.186)	0.449** (0.157)	2.308** (0.408)					0.68 0.68	1.26
-12.05** (0.552)	0.759** (0.017)	0.283** (0.020)	-0.538** (0.041)	0.775** (0.180)	0.193 (0.181)	0.498** (0.153)		2.363** (0.212)				0.70 0.70	1.23
-12.05** (0.553)	0.759** (0.017)	0.283** (0.020)	-0.538** (0.041)	0.772** (0.181)	0.193** (0.181)	0.499** (0.153)	0.081** (0.462)	2.341** (0.247)				0.70 0.70	1.23
-11.97** (0.542)	0.753** (0.017)	0.287** (0.020)	-0.543** (0.040)	0.764** (0.178)	0.214 (0.179)	0.527** (0.151)			2.066** (0.158)			0.71 0.71	1.21
-12.13** (0.546)	0.753** (0.017)	0.290** (0.020)	-0.532** (0.040)	0.770** (0.179)	0.227 (0.179)	0.535** (0.151)	0.087 (0.455)	0.730* (0.332)	1.650** (0.232)			0.71 0.71	1.21
-11.09** (0.532)	0.733** (0.017)	0.281** (0.020)	-0.586** (0.039)	0.694** (0.177)	0.207 (0.178)	0.503** (0.150)				1.863** (0.133)		0.71 0.71	1.21
-11.58** (0.551)	0.739** (0.017)	0.287** (0.020)	-0.557** (0.040)	0.724** (0.177)	0.234 (0.178)	0.526** (0.150)	0.062 (0.451)	0.704* (0.330)	0.355 (0.335)	1.319** (0.248)		0.71 0.71	1.20
-10.83** (0.564)	0.762** (0.018)	0.259** (0.021)	-0.638** (0.021)	0.701** (0.187)	0.033 (0.184)	0.268 (0.188)					0.018 (0.014)	0.68 0.68	1.27
-11.55** (0.554)	0.739** (0.017)	0.288** (0.020)	-0.563** (0.041)	0.716** (0.178)	0.227 (0.174)	0.474** (0.178)	0.062 (0.452)	0.699* (0.330)	0.350 (0.335)	1.321** (0.248)	0.008 (0.013)	0.71 0.71	1.20

Notes: * Statistically significant at 95 per cent level.
** Statistically significant at 99 per cent level.
[a] Standard errors appear below each coefficient.
LHS variable (bilateral exports & imports) and first three RHS variables are in log form.
All others are dummy variables.

TABLE 14.3 Gravity model of bilateral trade: 1985

C	GNPs	Per capita GNPs	Distance	Adjacent	EC	Western Hemisphere	ASEAN	EAEC	Asian Pacific	APEC	Pacific rim	R^2 / $\bar{R}^2$	SEE
-10.54** (0.527)	0.791** (0.017)	0.242** (0.020)	-0.729** (0.040)	0.708 (0.184)	0.306† (0.179)	0.276† (0.162)	1.735** (0.392)					0.72 0.72	1.21
-10.92** (0.519)	0.784** (0.017)	0.248** (0.020)	-0.683** (0.040)	0.804** (0.181)	0.397* (0.176)	0.312* (0.159)		1.841** (0.205)				0.73 0.73	1.19
-10.92** (0.520)	0.784** (0.017)	0.248** (0.020)	-0.683** (0.040)	0.806** (0.182)	0.397* (0.176)	0.311* (0.159)	-0.046 (0.448)	1.854** (0.239)				0.73 0.73	1.19
-10.85** (0.510)	0.778** (0.017)	0.251** (0.019)	-0.685** (0.039)	0.796** (0.178)	0.424* (0.174)	0.341* (0.157)			1.697** (0.153)			0.73 0.73	1.18
-10.91** (0.514)	0.778** (0.017)	0.252** (0.019)	-0.679** (0.039)	0.802** (0.179)	0.431* (0.174)	0.343* (0.157)	-0.045 (0.442)	0.414 (0.322)	1.474** (0.225)			0.73 0.73	1.18
-10.07** (0.506)	0.761** (0.017)	0.243** (0.019)	-0.720** (0.038)	0.739** (0.178)	0.418** (0.156)	0.323† (0.173)				1.522** (0.130)		0.74 0.74	1.17
-10.42** (0.524)	0.765** (0.017)	0.247** (0.019)	-0.698** (0.039)	0.766** (0.179)	0.439† (0.173)	0.339* (0.156)	-0.071 (0.440)	0.398 (0.321)	0.469 (0.327)	1.029** (0.244)		0.74 0.74	1.17
-10.09** (0.528)	0.791** (0.017)	0.239** (0.020)	-0.778** (0.041)	0.731** (0.185)	0.239 (0.179)	-0.024 (0.183)				0.041** (0.013)		0.72 0.72	1.20
-10.28** (0.527)	0.766** (0.017)	0.250** (0.019)	-0.723** (0.040)	0.738* (0.179)	0.415* (0.173)	0.142 (0.177)	-0.073 (0.439)	0.378 (0.320)	0.450 (0.327)	1.034** (0.244)	0.030* (0.013)	0.74 0.74	1.17

Notes: † Statistically significant at 90 per cent level.
　　　　 * Statistically significant at 95 per cent level.
　　　　 ** Statistically significant at 99 per cent level.
　　　　 Standard errors appear below each coefficient.
LHS variable (bilateral exports & imports) and first three RHS variables are in log form.
All others are dummy variables.

TABLE 14.4 Gravity model of bilateral trade, 1990

C	GNPs	Per capita GNPs	Distance	Adjacent	EC	Western Hemisphere	ASEAN	EAEC	Asian Pacific	APEC	Pacific rim	R^2/$\bar{R}^2$	SEE[a]
2.77** (0.36)	0.787** (0.016)	0.078** (0.017)	-0.589** (0.038)	0.732** (0.166)	0.341* (0.166)	0.934** (0.148)	1.879** (0.378)					0.75 0.75	1.11
2.54** (0.35)	0.779** (0.016)	0.082** (0.017)	-0.559** (0.038)	0.794** (0.162)	0.412* (0.163)	0.957** (0.145)		1.997** (0.215)				0.76 0.76	1.09
2.54** (0.35)	0.779** (0.016)	0.082** (0.017)	-0.559** (0.038)	0.797** (0.163)	0.412* (0.163)	0.955** (0.145)	-0.109 (0.450)	2.032** (0.261)				0.76 0.76	1.09
2.57** (0.35)	0.773** (0.016)	0.86** (0.016)	-0.561** (0.037)	0.790** (0.160)	0.437** (0.160)	0.983** (0.143)			1.746** (0.152)			0.77 0.77	1.08
2.52** (0.35)	0.773** (0.016)	0.087** (0.016)	-0.555** (0.037)	0.794** (0.160)	0.446** (0.160)	0.986** (0.143)	-0.107 (0.443)	0.612†† (0.331)	1.456** (0.213)			0.77 0.77	1.08
3.02** (0.34)	0.756** (0.016)	0.083** (0.016)	-0.597** (0.036)	0.730** (0.158)	0.444** (0.159)	0.984** (0.141)				1.597** (0.128)		0.77 0.77	1.07
2.83** (0.35)	0.760** (0.016)	0.085** (0.016)	-0.579** (0.037)	0.750** (0.159)	0.460** (0.159)	0.967** (0.142)	-0.144 (0.440)	0.604†† (0.328)	0.289 (0.309)	1.194** (0.231)		0.77 0.77	1.07
3.04** (0.37)	0.788** (0.017)	0.073** (0.017)	-0.619** (0.040)	0.780** (0.167)	0.296†† (0.167)	0.789** (0.170)					0.015 (0.013)	0.75 0.75	1.12
2.87** (0.38)	0.760** (0.016)	0.086** (0.016)	-0.584** (0.038)	0.743** (0.160)	0.454** (0.159)	0.925** (0.163)	-0.143 (0.440)	0.600†† (0.328)	0.284 (0.309)	1.196** (0.231)	0.006 (0.012)	0.77 0.77	1.07

Notes: ††, * and ** denote significance at the 90, 95 and 99 per cent level respectively. Standard errors appear in parentheses. LHS variable (bilateral exports and imports) and first three RHS variables are in log form. All others are dummy variables.
[a] Standard error of estimate.

This presumably reflects the widely-known pattern that small economies tend to be more open to international trade than larger, more diversified, economies.

If there were nothing to the notion of trading blocs, then these basic variables would soak up most of the explanatory power. There would be little left to attribute to a dummy variable representing whether two trading partners are located in the same region. In this case, the level and trend in intraregional trade would be due solely to the proximity of the countries, and to their rate of overall economic growth. But we found that dummy variables for intraregional trade *are* statistically significant, both in East Asia and elsewhere in the world. If two countries are both located in the Western Hemisphere, for example, they will trade with each other an estimated 70 per cent more than they would otherwise, even after taking into account distance and the other gravity variables ($\exp(0.53) = 1.70$). Intraregional trade goes beyond what can be explained by proximity.

The empirical equation is too far removed from theoretical foundations to allow conclusions to be drawn regarding economic welfare. But it is possible that the amount of intraregional bias explained by proximity, as compared to explicit or implicit regional trading arrangements, is small enough in our results that those arrangements are welfare-reducing. This could be the case if trade diversion outweighs trade creation. Inspired by Krugman's (1991a, 1991b) 'natural trading bloc' terminology, we might then refer to the observed intraregional trade bias as evidence of 'super-natural' trading blocs. The issue merits future research.

When the boundaries of the East Asian bloc are drawn along the lines of those suggested by Malaysian Prime Minister Mahatir in his proposed East Asian Economic Caucus, which excludes Australia and New Zealand, the coefficient on the East Asian bloc appears to be the strongest and most significant of any in the world. Even when the boundaries are drawn in this way, however, there is no evidence of an *increase* in the intraregional bias of East Asian trade during the 1980s: the estimated coefficient in fact decreases somewhat between 1980 and 1990. Thus the gravity results corroborate the back-of-the-envelope calculations reported in the preceding section. The precise pattern is a decrease in the first half of the decade, followed by a very slight increase in the second half, matching the results of Petri (1991).[13] None of these changes over time is statistically significant.

It is perhaps surprising that the estimated *level* of the intraregional trade bias was higher in East Asia as of 1980 than in the other two regions. One possible explanation is that there has been historically a sort of 'trading culture' in Asia. To the extent that such a culture exists and can be identified with a particular nation or ethnic group, I find the overseas Chinese to be a more plausible factor than the Japanese. But there are other possible regional effects that may be showing up spuriously as an East Asian bloc, to be considered below.

Of the three trading blocs, the EC and the Western Hemisphere are the two that have shown rapid intensification during the course of the 1980s. Both show an approximate doubling of their estimated intraregional bias coefficients. As of 1980, trade within the EC is not strong enough – after holding constant for the close geographical proximity and high incomes per capita of European countries – for the bias coefficient of 0.2 to appear statistically significant. The EC coefficient increased rapidly in level and significance in the first half of the 1980s, reaching about 0.4 by 1985, and continued to increase a little in the second half. The effect of two countries being located in Europe *per se*, when tested, does not show up as being nearly as strong in magnitude or significance as the effect of membership in the EC *per se*.

The Western Hemisphere coefficient experienced all its increase in the second half of the decade, exceeding 0.9 by 1990. The rapid increase in the Western Hemisphere intraregional bias in the second half of the 1980s is in itself an important new finding. The recovery of Latin-American imports from the United States after the compression that followed the 1982 debt crisis must be part of this phenomenon. The Canada–US Free Trade Agreement signed in 1988 may also be part of the explanation.

We consider a sequence of nested candidates for trading blocs in the Pacific. The significance of a given bloc effect turns out to depend on which other blocs are tested at the same time. One logical way to draw the boundaries is to include all the countries with eastern coasts on the Pacific, consistent with the statistics considered in the preceding section. We call this grouping 'Asia-Pacific' in the tables. Its coefficient and significance level are both higher than the EAEC (East Asian Economic Caucus, formerly the East Asian Economic Group) dummy. When we broaden the bloc search wider and test for an effect of Asian Pacific Economic Co-operation (APEC), which also includes the United States and Canada, it is highly significant; and the significance of the Asian Pacific dummy completely disappears. The EAEC dummy remains significant in 1980 and 1990, though at a lower level than the initial results which did not consider any wider Pacific groupings.

APEC appears to be the correct place to draw the boundary. When we test for the broadest definition of a Pacific bloc, including Latin America, it is not at all significant, and the other coefficients do not change (it is called 'Pacific Rim' in the tables). It remains true that the intraregional biases in the EC and Western Hemisphere blocs each roughly doubled between 1980 and 1990, while intraregional biases in the East Asia and Pacific areas did not increase at all. The only surprising new finding is the APEC effect: the USA and Canada appear to be full partners in the Pacific bloc, even while simultaneously belonging to the significant but distinct Western Hemisphere bloc. The APEC coefficient is the strongest of any. Its estimate holds relatively steady at 1.3 (1980), 1.0 (1985) and 1.2 (1990). The implication is that a pair of APEC countries trade three times as much as two otherwise-similar countries [$\exp(1.2) = 3.3$].[14]

One possible explanation for the apparent intraregional trade biases within East Asia and within the APEC grouping is that transportation between Asian Pacific countries is mostly by water, while transportation among European or Western Hemisphere countries is more often overland, and that ocean-shipping is less expensive than shipping by rail or road. This issue bears further investigation. (Wang, 1992, enters land distance and water distance separately in a gravity model. She finds a small, though statistically significant, difference in coefficients.) The issue of water versus land transport should not affect results regarding *changes* in intraregional trade bias in the 1980s, however, given that the nature of shipping costs does not appear to have changed over as short a time-span as five or ten years.

Several further questions naturally arise. ASEAN negotiated a preferential trading arrangement within its membership in 1977, although serious efforts to remove of barriers did not begin until 1987.[15] In early 1992, the members proclaimed plans for an ASEAN Free Trade Area, albeit with exemptions for many sectors. Does this grouping constitute a small bloc nested within the others? We include in our model a dummy variable for common membership in ASEAN. It turns out to have a significant coefficient only if none of the broader Asian blocs are included. The conclusion seems to be that ASEAN is not, in fact, functioning as a trade bloc.[16]

We know that Singapore and Hong Kong are especially open countries, and engage in a large amount of entrepôt trade. A dummy variable for these two countries' trade with other Asian Pacific countries is highly significant when it is included, as shown in the first row of Table 14.5. Its presence reduces slightly the coefficient on the East Asian grouping, but does not otherwise change the results.

TABLE 14.5 Gravity estimates with allowance for Asian openness

GNP	Per capita GNP	Distance	Adjacent	Western Hemisphere	EA	APEC	EC	JapEA	HKSEA	HKS1	EA1	Adj. R²/ SEE	No. of Observations
							1980						
0.78** (0.02)	0.24** (0.02)	−0.64** (0.04)	0.62** (0.18)	0.58** (0.15)	0.51†† (0.34)	1.29** (0.17)	0.18 (0.18)	−0.11 (0.16)		1.33** (0.12)		0.73/1.16	1708
0.73** (0.02)	0.31** (0.02)	−0.66** (0.04)	0.63** (0.18)	0.65** (0.15)	0.31 (0.34)	1.22** (0.17)	0.18 (0.18)	−0.12 (0.49)	1.06** (0.41)		0.52** (0.07)	0.72/1.18	1708
0.78** (0.02)	0.26** (0.02)	−0.67** (0.04)	0.59** (0.18)	0.64** (0.15)	0.53† (0.34)	1.19** (0.17)	0.15 (0.17)	−0.16 (0.48)	0.01 (0.42)	1.16** (0.14)	0.25** (0.08)	0.73/1.16	1708
							1985						
0.78** (0.02)	0.22** (0.02)	−0.74** (0.04)	0.69** (0.18)	0.37** (0.15)	0.36 (0.26)	1.18** (0.17)	0.45** (0.17)	0.09 (0.16)		0.76** (0.12)		0.74/1.16	1647
0.76** (0.02)	0.26** (0.02)	−0.77** (0.04)	0.69** (0.18)	0.42** (0.15)	0.16 (0.34)	1.10** (0.17)	0.44** (0.18)	−0.08 (0.48)	0.80** (0.40)		0.34** (0.07)	0.74/1.16	1647
0.78** (0.02)	0.23** (0.02)	−0.77** (0.04)	0.67** (0.18)	0.41** (0.15)	0.26 (0.34)	1.09** (0.17)	0.44** (0.18)	−0.10 (0.48)	0.28 (0.42)	0.59** (0.14)	0.20* (0.08)	0.74/1.16	1647
							1990						
0.80** (0.02)	0.04** (0.02)	−0.63 (0.04)	0.69** (0.18)	0.97** (0.13)	0.40† (0.23)	1.18** (0.15)	0.49** (0.16)	−0.15 (0.14)		1.23** (0.11)		0.79/1.03	1573
0.75** (0.02)	0.10** (0.02)	−0.66** (0.04)	0.69** (0.18)	1.06** (0.14)	0.14 (0.30)	1.11** (0.15)	0.49** (0.16)	−0.27 (0.43)	1.09** (0.37)		0.50** (0.07)	0.78/1.05	1573
0.79** (0.02)	0.06** (0.02)	−0.67** (0.04)	0.65** (0.18)	1.03** (0.14)	0.34 (0.30)	1.08** (0.15)	0.49** (0.15)	−0.31 (0.42)	0.15 (0.38)	1.06** (0.12)	0.25** (0.07)	0.79/1.02	1573

Notes: †, ††, * and ** denote significance at the 85, 90, 95 and 99 per cent levels respectively. Standard errors appear in parentheses. All regressions have an intercept, which is not reported here. All variables except the dummies are in logs. JapEA = trade between Japan and other East Asian countries; HKSEA = trade between Hong Kong or Singapore and other East Asian countries; HKS1 = trade between Hong Kong or Singapore and any other countries; EA1 = trade involving at least one East Asian country.

We also know that most East Asian countries are open to trade of all sorts. So we added a dummy variable to indicate when *at least* one of the pair of countries is located in East Asia, to supplement the dummy variable that indicates when both are. Its coefficient is significant. It is also positive, which appears to rule out any 'trade-diversion' effects arising from the existence of the East Asian bloc: these countries trade an estimated 22 per cent more with all parts of the world, other things being equal, than do average countries [exp(.20) = 1.22]. The addition of the openness dummy reduces further the level and significance of the East Asian bloc dummy. Indeed, when the APEC bloc dummy and East-Asian-openness dummy are both added at the same time, the East Asian bloc term becomes only marginally significant in 1980 and insignificant in 1985 and 1990. There may be no East Asian bloc effect at all!

We now add a few checks for econometric robustness regarding the sample of countries and their size. There are some missing values in our data set (245 of them in 1985, for example), normally because of levels of trade too small to be recorded. The exclusion of these data points might bias the results. We try running the equation in multiplicative form, instead of log-linear, so as to allow the inclusion of pairs of countries that are reported as undertaking zero trade. (Under our log-linear specification, any pair of countries that shows up with zero trade must necessarily be dropped from the sample.) We find that the inclusion or omission of such countries in the multiplicative specification makes little difference to the results. The results are reported in Tables 14.A2 and 14.A3 in the Appendix on pp. 408 and 409.[17] A correction for heteroscedasticity based on the size of the countries also makes little difference (reported in Table 14.A4 on p. 410).

As another extension, we have tried disaggregating total trade into three categories: manufactured products, agricultural products, and other raw materials.[18] The findings are overall little affected by the disaggregation. Raw materials show the greatest Asian bloc effect if judged by the estimated coefficient. Manufactures shows the greatest effect if judged by *t*-statistics. Perhaps surprisingly, the effect of distance is as high or higher for manufactures as for the other categories. We interpret this finding, and the finding that the distance coefficient does not decline over time, as evidence that the effect of distance is much more than mere physical transportation costs.

We have also tried to capture classic Heckscher–Ohlin effects. First we tried including bilateral absolute differences in GNP/per capita figures. The variable did not have the positive effect that one would expect if countries traded capital-intensive products for unskilled- labour-in-tensive products. Rather, it had a moderately significant *negative* effect, as in the Linder hypothesis that similar countries trade more than dissimilar ones.

Next we tried gravity estimates that include more direct measures of factor endowments: the two countries' differences in capital/labour ratios, educational attainment levels, and land/labour ratios. The data (for a subset of 656 of our 1953 pairs of countries) was generously supplied by Gary Saxonhouse (1989). There is some support for these terms, particularly for capital/labour ratios and educational attainment in 1980. The other coefficients are little affected.[19]

What about bilateral trade between Asian Pacific countries, and Japan in particular? Like intra-regional trade overall, trade with Japan increased rapidly in the second half of the 1980s. Most of this increase merely reversed a decline in the first half of the 1980s, however.[20] More importantly, the recent trend in bilateral trade between Japan and its neighbours can readily be explained as the natural outcome of the growth in Japanese trade overall and the growth in trade levels attained by other Asian countries overall. Lawrence (1991b) has calculated that, out of the 28 per cent increase in the market share of Asian Pacific developing countries in Japanese imports from 1985 to 1988, 11 per cent is attributable to improved competitiveness (as reflected in increased exports from Pacific Asia to world-wide markets), and 18 per cent is attributable to the commodity mix of these countries' exports. There is no residual to be attributed to Japan's development of special trading relations with other countries in its region.[21]

We confirmed this finding (though without as yet decomposing trade by commodity, or including language or factor endowment terms) by adding to our gravity model a separate dummy variable for bilateral Asian trade, with Japan in particular. It was not even remotely statistically significant in any year, and indeed the point estimate was a small negative number, as is shown in Table 14.5 on p. 399. Thus there was no evidence that Japan has established or come to dominate a trading bloc in Asia.

To summarize the most relevant effects: if two countries both lie within the boundaries of APEC, they trade with each other a little over three times as much as they otherwise would. The nested EAEC bloc is less strong (especially if one allows also for the openness of East Asian countries), and has declined a little in magnitude and significance during the course of the 1980s. The Western Hemisphere and EC blocs, by contrast, intensified rapidly during the decade. Indeed, by 1990, the Western Hemisphere bloc was stronger than the EAEC bloc, if one takes into account the existence of the APEC effect. There was never a special Japan effect within Pacific Asia.

In short, beyond the evident facts that countries near each other trade with one another, and that Japan and other East Asian countries are growing rapidly, there is no evidence that Japan is concentrating its trade with other East Asian countries in any special way, nor that they are moving collectively towards a trade bloc in the way that Western Europe and the Western Hemisphere appear to be.

That still leaves the possibility of special Japanese influence in the region through monetary or financial effects, as may be implicit in the phrase 'yen bloc'. We now turn from trade to a brief consideration of finance.

14.2 JAPAN'S INVESTMENT IN THE REGION

In the case of financial flows, proximity is less important than it is for trade flows. For some countries the buying and selling of foreign exchange and highly-rated bonds is characterized by the absence of significant government capital controls, transaction costs or information costs. In such cases, there would be no particular reason to expect greater capital flows between close countries than among distant ones. Rather, each country would be viewed as depositing into the world capital pool, or borrowing from it, whatever quantity of funds it wished at the going world interest rate. Thus even if we could obtain reliable data on bilateral capital flows (which we cannot), and whatever pattern they happened to show, such statistics would not be particularly interesting.

14.2.1 Tōkyō's influence on regional financial markets

Many East Asian countries still have substantial capital controls, and financial markets that are in other respects less than fully developed. Even financial markets in Singapore and Hong Kong, the most open in Asia, retain some minor frictions. Where the links with world capital markets are obstructed by even small barriers, it is an interesting question to ask whether those links are stronger with some major financial centres than with others. This question is explored econometrically elsewhere, by looking at interest rates.[22]

We find that, over the period 1982–92, US interest rates have had a rising influence, at the expense of Japanese interest rates, on some English-speaking countries of the Pacific Rim: Australia and New Zealand. But we also find a shift of influence from the USA to Japan in determining interest rates in some East Asian countries. The trend is highly significant in the case of Indonesia, somewhat less so for Korea, and positive but not significant for Malaysia and Singapore. In the case of Indonesia, there is evidence that the increasing Japanese influence may be coming via an increased link between the rupiah and the yen; for the other countries, it is harder to distinguish such a currency effect.

14.2.2 Foreign direct investment

We now consider briefly direct investment. Many observers of East Asia have concluded that Japan's establishment in neighbouring countries of mines, factories, infrastructure and other facilities is a key attribute of efforts to form an economic bloc. Indeed, there is no question that direct investment frequently goes hand in hand with trade. Proximity clearly matters in the case of direct investment, in a way that we would not expect for securities. This is partly because much of direct investment is linked to trade, and partly because linguistic and cultural proximity matter for direct investment.

Here there is not much point looking at rates of return, because the data are not as available or as reliable as for interest rates, and because there is no realistic null hypothesis entailing perfect arbitrage across countries. Instead, we look at quantities. We look only at aggregate quantities; unquestionably some sectors would show more investment links than the average and some less, just as they would if we disaggregated the trade numbers.

Table 14.6 shows the standard Ministry of Finance figures for Japanese direct investment. The steady stream of direct investment by Japanese firms in East Asia and the Pacific (including Australia) has received much attention. But the table shows that, whether measured in terms of annual flows or accumulated stocks, Japan's direct investment in the region is approximately equal to its investment in Europe, and is much less than its investment in North America.[23]

It has been argued that once one scales the Table 14.6 figures for GNP among the host countries, an East Asian bias to Japanese direct investment might indeed appear.[24] However if one scales the FDI figures by the host region's role in world trade, one finds that Japan's investment in East Asia and Oceania is almost exactly in proportion to their size.

TABLE 14.6 Japan's foreign direct investment by country, millions of dollars

	FY 1991			FY 1992			Cumulative total FY 1951–92		
	Cases	Amount	Percentage distribution	Cases	Amount	Percentage distribution	Cases	Amount	Percentage distribution
USA	1 607	18 026	43.3	1 170	13 819	40.5	25 721	162 373	42.0
Canada	107	797	1.9	88	753	2.2	1 476	7 207	1.9
Sub-total (North America)	1 714	18 823	45.3	1 258	14 572	42.7	27 197	169 580	43.9
Sub-total (Latin America)	290	3 337	8.0	307	2 726	8.0	7 794	46 547	12.0
Sub-total (Middle Near East)	10	90	0.2	16	709	2.1	366	4 231	1.1
Sub-total (Europe)	803	9 371	22.5	617	7 061	20.7	8 845	75 697	19.6
Sub-total (Africa)	76	748	1.8	23	238	0.7	1 557	6 813	1.8
Australia	261	2 550	6.1	174	2 150	6.3	3 195	20 763	5.4
New Zealand	32	236	0.6	24	67	0.2	427	1 228	0.3
North Mariana	31	391	0.9	14	82	0.2	373	929	0.2
Papua New Guinea	6	10	0.0	4	5	0.0	223	241	0.1
Fiji	19	34	0.1	13	32	0.1	129	174	0.0
Polynesia	37	46	0.1	11	19	0.1	90	139	0.0
Vanuatu	1	0	0.0	3	17	0.1	64	125	0.0
Others	7	11	0.0	8	33	0.1	101	182	0.0
Sub-total (Oceania)	394	3 278	7.9	251	2 406	7.0	4 602	23 782	6.2

Indonesia	148	1 193	2.9	122	1 676	4.9	2 143	14 409	3.7
Hong Kong	178	925	2.2	154	735	2.2	4 705	11 510	3.0
Singapore	103	613	1.5	100	670	2.0	2 762	7 837	2.0
Thailand	258	807	1.9	130	657	1.9	2 853	5 887	1.5
Malaysia	136	880	2.1	111	704	2.1	1 756	4 815	1.2
Republic of Korea	48	260	0.6	28	225	0.7	1 923	4 623	1.2
China	246	579	1.4	490	1 070	3.1	1 595	4 472	1.2
Taiwan	87	405	1.0	48	292	0.9	2 535	3 427	0.9
Philippines	42	203	0.5	45	160	0.5	937	1 943	0.5
India	9	14	0.0	15	122	0.4	191	332	0.1
Pakistan	2	14	0.0	2	18	0.1	62	142	0.0
Bangladesh	4	8	0.0	5	60	0.2	40	125	0.0
Sri Lanka	7	4	0.0	7	19	0.1	133	121	0.0
Brunei	1	0	0.0	–	–	–	32	109	0.0
Others	8	31	0.1	12	18	0.1	143	127	0.0
Sub-total	1 277	5 936	14.3	1 269	6 425	18.8	21 180	59 880	15.5
Total	4 564	41 584	100.0	3 741	34 138	100.0	71 541	386 530	100.0

Source: *Financial Statistics of Japan*, 1993, Ministry of Finance, p. 95.

There is no regional bias. Japan's FDI in the USA and Canada, on the other hand, is more than twice what one would expect from their share of world trade, and Japan's investment in Europe is about half the continent's share of trade.

Furthermore, Ramstetter (1991a, pp. 95–6; 1991b, pp. 8–9) has pointed out forcefully that the standard Ministry of Finance figures on Japanese foreign direct investment in fact represent statistics on investment either approved by or reported to the government, and greatly overstate the extent of true Japanese investment in developing countries. The more accurate balance of payments data from the Bank of Japan show a smaller percentage of investment going to East Asia.

In short, Japan's direct investment in East Asia is at most keeping pace with its trade.

14.3   CONCLUSIONS

We may draw six conclusions:

1. The *level* of trade in East Asia, like trade within the European Community and within the Western Hemisphere, is biased towards intraregional trade, to a greater extent than can be explained naturally by distance. By way of contrast to Paul Krugman's 'natural' trade blocs, one might call these three regions 'super-natural' blocs.
2. There is no evidence of a special Japan effect within Asia.
3. Although growth in Japan, the four NICs and other East Asian countries are increasing their weight in world output and trade rapidly, the statistics do not bear out a *trend* toward intraregional bias of trade and direct investment flows.
4. The intraregional trade bias did increase in Europe in the 1980s, in the Western Hemisphere in the late 1980s, and in the grouping that includes the USA and Canada together with the Asian Pacific countries, that is, APEC.
5. The APEC trade grouping appears to be the world's strongest, whether judged by rate of change of intragroup bias or (as of 1990) by level of bias. Far from being shut out of a strong Asian bloc centred on Japan, the USA and Canada are in the enviable position of belonging to *both* of the world's strongest groupings.
6. Japan's direct investment in Pacific Asia has grown, but at most in proportion to its trade in the region.

APPENDIX

TABLE 14.A1   List of countries used in the gravity equation, showing regional groupings, and main cities

Americas (Western Hemisphere (WH), 13)		East Asia (East Asia Economic Caucasus (EAEC), 10)	
Canada	Ottawa	Japan	Tōkyō
USA	Chicago	Indonesia	Jakarta
Argentina	Buenos Aires	Taiwan	Taipei
Brazil	São Paulo	Hong Kong	Hong Kong
Chile	Santiago	S. Korea	Seoul
Colombia	Bogotá	Malaysia	Kuala Lumpur
Ecuador	Quito	Philippines	Manila
Mexico	Mexico City	Singapore	Singapore
Peru	Lima	Thailand	Bangkok
Venezuela	Caracas	China	Shanghai
Bolivia	La Paz		
Paraguay	Asuanción	**Other countries (23)**	
Uruguay	Montevideo	S. Africa	Pretoria
		Turkey	Ankara
European Community (EC, 11)		Yugoslavia	Belgrade
W. Germany	Bonn	Israel	Jerusalem
France	Paris	Algeria	Algiers
Italy	Rome	Libya	Tripoli
UK	London	Nigeria	Lagos
Belgium	Brussels	Egypt	Cairo
Denmark	Copenhagen	Morocco	Casablanca
Netherlands	Amsterdam	Tunisia	Tunis
Greece	Athens	Sudan	Khartoum
Ireland	Dublin	Ghana	Accra
Portugal	Lisbon	Kenya	Nairobi
Spain	Madrid	Ethiopia	Addis Ababa
		Iran	Tehran
European Free Trade Area (EFTA)		Kuwait	Kuwait
Austria	Vienna	Saudi Arabia	Riyadh
Finland	Helsinki	India	New Delhi
Norway	Oslo	Pakistan	Karachi
Sweden	Stockholm	Hungary	Budapest
Switzerland	Geneva	Poland	Warsaw
Iceland	Reykjavik	Australia	Sydney
		New Zealand	Wellington

Notes: APEC (Asia-Pacific Economic Co-operation) consists of East Asia, plus Australia, New Zealand, Canada and the United States.
   The distance between countries was computed as the great circle distance between the relevants pairs of cities.

TABLE 14.A2 Non-linear least square estimation, Including data points for which trade is zero

	GNP	GNP/capita	Distant	Adjacent	WH	EC	EFTA	EAEC	APEC	Adj. R²	SEE^a	Number of observations
1980	.56**	.23**	−.28**	.47**	.29**	.51**		.58**	.82**	.86	1347	1953
	.01	.02	.02	.03	.04	.05		.08	.03			
	.58**	.22**	−.31**	.45**	.26**	.43**	.09	.57**	.81**	.86	1360	1953
	.01	.02	.02	.03	.04	.05	.23	.08	.03			
1985	.65**	.18**	−.44**	.42**	−.21**	.40**		.13*	.95**	.93	1164	1953
	.01	.01	.02	.03	.04	.04		.06	.03			
	.67**	.18**	−.46**	.42**	−.23**	.38**	.23	.16*	.94**	.93	1301	1953
	.01	.01	.02	.03	.04	.04	.22	.06	.03			
1990	.59**	.14**	−.36**	.47**	.10**	.45**		.00	1.03**	.90	2373	1953
	.01	.01	.02	.03	.04	.04		.06	.03			
	.60**	.13**	−.38**	.48**	.08**	.41**	−.00	.01	1.00**	.90	2393	1953
	.01	.01	.02	.03	.04	.04	.22	.06	.03			

Notes: **, *, ## denotes 'significantly different from zero at the 1 per cent, 5 per cent, 15 per cent level respectively'. All the regressions have an intercept whose estimates are not reported here. All variables are in levels.
^a Standard error estimate.

TABLE 14.A3 Non-linear least square estimation, excluding data points for which trade is zero

	GNP	GNP/capita	Distant	Adjacent	WH	EC	EFTA	EAEC	APEC	Adj. R²	SEE[a]	Number of Observations
1980	.56**	.23**	-.28**	.47**	.29**	.51**		.57**	.83**	.86	1439	1708
	.01	.02	.02	.04	.05	.05		.09	.04			
	.58**	.21**	-.31**	.45**	.25**	.43**	.09	.55**	.81**	.86	1453	1708
	.01	.02	.02	.04	.05	.05	.25	.09	.04			
1985	.65**	.18**	-.45**	.42**	-.23**	.38**		.10##	.95**	.93	1262	1647
	.01	.01	.02	.03	.04	.05		.07	.03			
	.65**	.18**	-.46**	.41**	-.24**	.36**	.20	.10##	.95**	.93	1266	1647
	.01	.01	.02	.03	.04	.05	.23	.07	.03			
1990	.59**	.13**	-.37**	.47**	.09*	.44**		-.02	1.04**	.90	2634	1573
	.01	.02	.02	.03	.04	.04		.06	.03			
	.60**	.12**	-.38**	.47**	.06##	.39**	-.02	-.03	1.02**	.90	2669	1573
	.01	.02	.02	.03	.04	.04	.23	.06	.03			

Notes:
**, *, ## denotes 'significantly different from zero at the 1%, 5%, 15% level, respectively.
All the regressions have an intercept whose estimates are not reported here. All variables are in levels.
[a] standard error of estimate.

TABLE 14.A4 Sensitivity of results to overweighting small countries
(weighted least squares, with the log of the product of the GNPs as the weights)

	GNP	GNP/capita	Distant	Adjacent	WH	EC	EFTA	EAEC	APEC	Adj. R^2	SEE[a]	Number of Observations
1980	.75**	.29**	-.56**	.69*	.53**	.24		.89**	1.48**	.72	1.19	1708
	.02	.02	.04	.17	.15	.17		.26	.16			
	.74**	.29**	-.56**	.68**	.53**	.23	.07	.89**	1.48**	.72	1.20	1708
	.02	.02	.04	.18	.15	.17	.32	.26	.16			
1985	.77**	.25**	-.70**	.72**	.31*	.43**		.59**	1.26**	.74	1.16	1647
	.02	.02	.04	.18	.15	.17		.25	.16			
	.76**	.25**	-.70**	.72**	.31*	.44**	-.06	.59*	1.26**	.74	1.16	1647
	.02	.02	.04	.18	.15	.17	.32	.25	.16			
1990	.75**	.09**	-.56**	.76**	.90**	.47**		.69**	1.35**	.78	1.05	1573
	.02	.02	.04	.16	.14	.15		.23	.14			
	.74**	.10**	-.55**	.71**	.86**	.51**	-.04	.68**	1.33**	.79	1.03	1573
	.02	.02	.04	.15	.14	.14	.28	.22	.13			

Notes:
**, *, ## denotes 'significantly different from zero at the 1%, 5% , 15% level, respectively'.
All the regressions have an intercept whose estimates are not reported here. All variables except the dummies are in logarithm.
[a] standard error of estimate.

NOTES

1. Those who fear the blocs do so because they think they will tend to be protectionist. Froot and Yoffie (1993) pursue this logic, and point out some implications of foreign direct investment. Krugman (1991b) argues in favour of the three blocs on the grounds that they are 'natural', in the sense explained below. Lawrence's (1991c) argument in favour of blocs is that they can cement politically pro-liberalization sentiment in individual countries.
2. Reviews of recent developments in regional trading arrangements are offered by Fieleke (1992) and Torre and Kelly (1992).
3. For example, Petri (1992).
4. For one of many examples, see Dornbusch (1989).
5. Similar statistics are presented in more detail in table 1 in Frankel, 1991.
6. Petri (1991) calls this measure the 'double-relative', while Drysdale and Garnaut (1992), and Anderson and Norheim (1993) use similar calculations of 'intensity-of-trade indexes'. All find that, once one holds constant for growth in this simple way, the existing intraregional bias in Asia did not increase in the 1980s.
7. See Deardorff (1984, pp. 503–4) for a survey of the (short) subject of gravity equations. Wang and Winters (1991) and Hamilton and Winters (1992) have recently applied the gravity model to the question of potential Eastern European trade patterns.
8. Krugman (1991b) has made a crude first pass at applying the gravity model to the question of whether Europe and North America are separate trading blocs, but did not get as far as including other countries, or including a variable for distance.
9. The list of countries, and regional groupings, appears in an appendix.
10. Details on the data sources, list of countries, groupings, method for computing distances and so on, are available on request.
11. The specification implies that trade between two equal-sized countries (say, of size 0.5) will be greater than trade between a large and small country (say, of size 0.9 and 0.1). This property of models with imperfect competition is not a property of the classical Heckscher–Ohlin theory of comparative advantage. Helpman (1987), and Helpman and Krugman (1985, section 1.5). Foundations for the gravity model are also offered by Anderson (1979) and other papers surveyed by Deardorff (1984, pp. 503–6).
12. The coefficient on the log of distance was about 0.8 when the adjacency variable was not included.
13. Petri infers, from the data on intraregional trade shares, a decrease in East Asian interdependence up to the middle of the 1980s, followed by a reversal in the second half of the decade.
14. Others have emphasized the high volume of trans-Pacific trade. But it has been difficult to evaluate such statistics when no account is taken of these countries' collective size. A higher percentage of economic activity will consist of intraregional trade in a larger region than in a smaller region, even when there is no intraregional bias, merely because smaller regions tend by their nature to trade across their boundaries more than

do larger ones. At the limit, when the unit is the world, 100 per cent of trade is intra'regional'.

15. Jackson (1991).

16. In tests similar to ours, Wang (1992), Wang and Winters (1991), and Hamilton and Winters (1992) found the ASEAN dummy to reflect one of the most significant trading areas in the world. That they did not include a broader dummy variable for intra-Asian trade may explain the difference in results.

17. The use of the multiplicative form itself changes the results, however. Linnemann (1966) and Wang and Winters (1991) addressed the problem of trade flows so small as to be recorded as zero in another way: by trying the tests with fractions (like 0.5) of the minimum recordable unit substituted for the zeros. Eichengreen and Irwin (1993), examining the inter-war period, use a third approach: they run the dependent variable (trade) in levels rather than logs, and use TOBIT to truncate negative values. They find that exclusion of zero values does make a difference to two parameter estimates: the coefficients on income per capita, and adjacency.

18. Frankel et al. (1993).

19. The estimates with differences in GNP per capita and differences in factor endowments are reported in tables 4 an 5, respectively, of Frankel and Wei (1993b).

20. Petri, 1991.

21. The empirical literature on whether Japan is an outlier in its trading patterns, particularly with respect to imports of manufactures, includes Saxonhouse (1989), Noland (1991) and Lawrence (1991a), among others.

22. The foreign influences on East Asian interest rates are examined in three places, in increasing order of completeness: Frankel (1991), the second half of the NBER paper of which this chapter is the first half, and Chinn and Frankel (1994). These papers also give references to other work on the subject.

23. See also Komiya and Wakasugi (1991).

24. Nigel Holloway, 'Half-full, half empty', *Far Eastern Economic Review*, December 1991, p. 69.

REFERENCES

Anderson, James 1979. 'A Theoretical Foundation for the Gravity Equation', *American Economic Review*, 69, 1 (March), pp. 106–16.

Anderson, Kym and Hege Norheim 1993. 'History, Geography and Regional Economic Integration', GATT Secretariat Conference Geneva, October 1992, in K. Anderson and R. Blackhurst (eds), *Regionalism and the Global Trading System*, London: Harvester Wheatsheaf.

Balassa, Bela and John Williamson 1990. *Adjusting to Success: Balance of Payments Policy in the East Asian NICs*, Policy Analyses in International Economics, 17, Washington, D.C., Institute for International Economics, April.

Bergsten, C. Fred 1991. 'Comment on Krugman', in *Policy Implications of Trade and Currency Zones*, A Symposium Sponsored by the Federal Reserve Bank of Kansas City, Jackson Hole, Wyoming, August, pp. 43–57.

Bhagwati, Jagdish 1990. 'Regional Accords Be-GATT Trouble For Free Trade', *Wall Street Journal*, 5 (December).

Bhagwati, Jagdish 1992. 'Regionalism vs. Multilateralism: An Overview', Conference on New Dimensions in Regional Integration, World Bank, Washington, D.C., 2–3 April.

Chinn, Menzie and Jeffrey A. Frankel 1994. 'Financial Links Around the Pacific Rim: 1982–92', forthcoming as Chapter 2 in Reuven Glick and Michael Hitchison (eds.), *Exchange Rate Policy and Interdependence: Perspectives from the Pacific Basin*, Cambridge University Press.

Deardorff, Alan 1984. 'Testing Trade Theories and Predicting Trade Flows', in R. Jones and P. Kenen (eds), *Handbook of International Economics*, vol. I, Amsterdam: Elsevier Science Publishers, ch. 10, pp. 467–517.

Dornbusch, Rudiger 1989. 'The Dollar in the 1990s: Competitiveness and the Challenges of New Economic Blocs', in *Monetary Policy Issues in the 1990s*, Kansas City, Missouri: Federal Reserve Bank of Kansas City.

Drysdale, Peter and Ross Garnaut 1992. 'The Pacific: An Application of a General Theory of Economic Integration', Twentieth Pacific Trade and Development Conference, Washington, D.C., 10–12 September.

Eichengreen, Barry and Douglas Irwin 1993. 'Trade Blocs, Currency Blocs and the Disintegration of World Trade in the 1930s', U.C. Berkeley, Calif., June.

Fieleke, Norman 1992. 'One Trading World, or Many: The Issue of Regional Trading Blocs', *New England Economic Review*, Federal Reserve Bank of Boston, May/June, pp. 3–20.

Frankel, Jeffrey 1991. 'Is a Yen Bloc Forming in Pacific Asia?', in Richard O'Brien (ed.), *Finance and the International Economy*, The AMEX Bank Review Prize Essays, Oxford University Press.

Frankel, Jeffrey, and Shang-Jin Wei 1992. 'Trade Blocs and Currency Blocs', La Coruña, Spain, 11 December 1992, NBER Working Paper No. 4335; and in *The Monetary Future of Europe*, Centre for Economic Policy Research, London, 1993.

Frankel, Jeffrey and Shang-Jin Wei 1994. 'Yen Bloc or Dollar Bloc? Exchange Rate Policies of the East Asian Economies', in Takatoshi Ito and Anne Krueger (eds), *Third Annual East Asian Seminar on Economics*, University of Chicago Press.

Frankel, Jeffrey and Shang-Jin Wei 1993a. 'Is There A Currency Bloc in the Pacific?', 12–3 July, Kirribilli, Australia, in A. Blundell-Wignall and S. Grenville (eds) *Exchange Rates, International Trade and Monetary Policy*, Sydney: Reserve Bank of Australia.

Frankel, Jeffrey and Shang-Jin Wei 1993b. 'Emerging Currency Blocs', Geneva, 2–4 September. CIDER Discussion Paper, U.C. Berkeley, Calif. Abridged version forthcoming in *The Future of the International Monetary System and its Institutions*, Hans Genberg, (ed.).

Frankel, Jeffrey, Ernesto Stein and Shang-Jin Wei 1993. 'Trading Blocs: The Natural, the Unnatural, and the Super-Natural', NBER, Sixth Inter American Seminar in Economics organized by Sebastian Edwards and Gustavo Marquez, Caracas, Venezuela, 29 May. Abridged version forthcoming, *Journal of Development Economics*.

Froot, Kenneth and David Yoffie 1993. 'Trading Blocs and the Incentives to Protect: Implications for Japan and East Asia', in J. Frankel and M. Kahler (eds), *Regionalism and Rivalry: Japan and the United States in Pacific Asia*, Chicago, University of Chicago Press.

Hamilton, Carl and L. Alan Winters 1992. 'Opening Up International Trade in Eastern Europe', *Economic Policy* (April) pp. 77–116.

Helpman, Elhanan 1987. 'Imperfect Competition and International Trade: Evidence from Fourteen Industrial Countries', *Journal of the Japanese and International Economies*, 1, pp. 62–81.

Helpman, Elhanan and Paul Krugman 1985. *Market Structure and Foreign Trade*, Cambridge, Mass.: MIT Press.

Jackson, Tom 1991. 'A Game Model of ASEAN Trade Liberalization', *Open Economies Review*, 2, 3, pp. 237–54.

Komiya, Ryutaro and Ryuhei Wakasugi 1991. 'Japan's Foreign Direct Investment', *Annals of the American Academy of Political and Social Science*, January.

Krugman, Paul 1991a. 'Is Bilateralism Bad?' in E. Helpman and A. Razin (eds), *International Trade and Trade Policy*, Cambridge, Mass.: MIT Press.

Krugman, Paul 1991b. 'The Move Toward Free Trade Zones', in *Policy Implications of Trade and Currency Zones*, A Symposium Sponsored by the Federal Reserve Bank of Kansas City, Jackson Hole, Wyoming, August, pp. 7–42.

Lawrence, Robert 1991a. 'How Open is Japan?', in Paul Krugman (ed.) *Trade With Japan: Has the Door Opened Wider?*, Chicago: University of Chicago Press, pp. 9–50.

Lawrence, Robert 1991b. 'An Analysis of Japanese Trade with Developing Countries', Brookings Discussion Papers No. 87, April.

Lawrence, Robert 1991c. 'Emerging Regional Arrangements: Building Blocks or Stumbling Blocks?', in R. O'Brien (ed.), *Finance and the International Economy*, The AMEX Bank Review Prize Essays, Oxford University Press, pp. 24–36.

Linneman, Hans 1966. *An Econometric Study of International Trade Flows*, Amsterdam: North-Holland.

Noland, Marcus 1990. *Pacific Basin Developing Countries: Prospects for the Future*, Washington, D.C., Institute for International Economics.

Noland, Marcus 1991. 'Public Policy, Private Preferences, and the Japanese Trade Pattern', Washington, D.C.: Institute for International Economics' (November).

Petri, Peter 1991. 'Market Structure, Comparative Advantage and Japanese Trade Under the Strong Yen', in Paul Krugman (ed.), *Trade With Japan: Has the Door Opened Wider?*, University of Chicago Press, pp. 51–84.

Petri, Peter 1992. 'One Bloc, Two Blocs or None? Political-Economic Factors in Pacific Trade Policy', in Kaoru Okuzumi, Kent Calder and Gerrit Gong (eds) *The U.S.–Japan Economic Relationship in East and Southeast Asia: A Policy Framework for Asia-Pacific Economic Cooperation*, Significant Issues Series, vol. XIV, no. 1. Washington, D.C.: Center for Strategic and International Studies, pp. 39–70.

Ramstetter, Eric 1991a. 'Regional Patterns of Japanese Multinational Activities in Japan and Asia's Developing Countries', *Economic and Political Studies Series* No. 74, Ōsaka: Kansai University.

Ramstetter, Eric 1991b. 'An Overview of Multinational Firms in Asia-Pacific Economies: An Introduction to the Commonplace Ignorance', Faculty of Economics, Ōsaka: Kansai University.

Saxonhouse, Gary 1989. 'Differentiated Products, Economies of Scale, and Access to the Japanese Market', in Robert Feenstra (ed.), *Trade Policies for International Competitiveness*, University of Chicago Press, pp. 145–74.

Schott, Jeffrey 1991. 'Trading Blocs and the World Trading System', *The World Economy*, 14, 1 (March), pp. 1–17.

Torre, Augusto de la and Margaret Kelly 1992. *Regional Trading Arrangements*, Occasional Paper No. 93, Washington, D.C.: International Monetary Fund (March).

Wang, Zhen Kun 1992. 'China's Potential Trade: An Analysis Based on the Gravity Model', Department of Economics, University of Birmingham, UK.

Wang, Zhen Kun and L. Alan Winters 1991. 'The Trading Potential of Eastern Europe', Centre for Economic Policy Research Discussion Paper No. 610, November, London.

15 Recent Balance of Payments Developments in Japan: Is the Current Account Surplus Structural or Temporary?

Mahito Uchida
and Takashi Ui*

15.1 INTRODUCTION

Reflecting the synergistic effects of trade volume adjustment occasioned by the yen's appreciation, domestic demand expansion and structural change in Japan's economy, Japan's current account surplus steadily contracted to $35.8 billion in 1990 after peaking in 1987. However, the surplus has rapidly increased again since 1991 and it reached a new peak of $117.6 billion in 1992 (3.3 per cent in terms of percentage of GNP). Such a recent surge in Japan's current account surplus is provoking a serious problem. For Japan, one solution may be the recovery of domestic demand. Also, the effort to eliminate trade barriers in order to help to draw more imports must and will continue.

'To what extent is it structural surplus?' is the key question in this chapter. In answering this question, many have been arguing from a variety of viewpoints, such as investment-saving imbalance, export and import functions, Japan's international competitiveness, income elasticity of exports and so on. Instead, this chapter analyzes and evaluates recent balance of payments developments in Japan from the viewpoints of both current account components and the investment-saving balance. Section 15.2 reviews the recent developments of sur-

* An earlier version of this chapter was presented as a paper at the First Conference on the Contemporary Japanese Economy on 25–26 March 1993 at Macquarie University, Sydney. Views expressed herein are of the authors and not necessarily those of the Bank of Japan.

plus components and Section 15.3 analyzes the structural change in the surplus from the standpoint that the balance of payments and investment-saving balance are determined simultaneously.

15.2 RECENT EXPANSION OF THE CURRENT ACCOUNT SURPLUS

The recent expansion of the current account surplus is mainly due to the trade surplus, though the contraction of deficits in the services and unrequited transfers accounts have also contributed. In the following, we briefly review the recent development of each account.

15.2.1 Trade balance

The trade surplus contracted in the last half of the 1980s but has been expanding since 1991, and explains the development of the current account surplus to a considerable extent (See Figure 15.1).

Exports have expanded constantly since the second half of the 1980s (see Figure 15.2), mainly due to the increase in prices occasioned by (i) the strong yen;[1] (ii) the high ratio of exports contracted in strong currencies such as the yen or DM; and (iii) the growing proportion of high value-added products.[2]

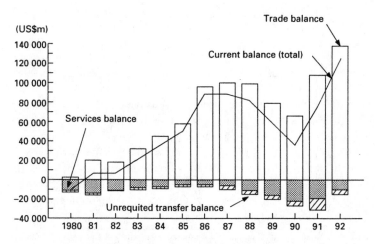

Source: Bank of Japan, *Balance of Payments Monthly*.

FIGURE 15.1 Japan's current balance

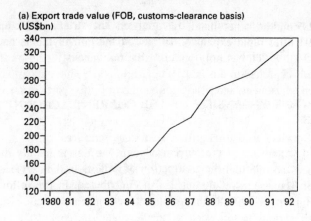

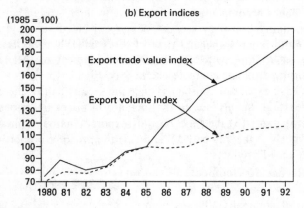

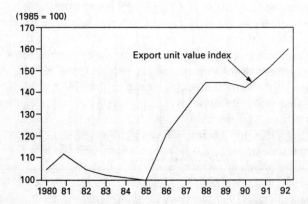

Source: Ministry of Finance, *Summary Report on Trade of Japan.*

FIGURE 15.2 Developments in Japan's exports

Imports, on the other hand, have traced only a sluggish increase since 1991 after rapid expansion in the second half of the 1980s (see Figure 15.3), which has only widened the fluctuation in the trade balance. The background to this is: (i) sluggish import volume under ongoing production adjustment; and (ii) declining import prices, particularly owing to lower raw material prices.[3]

15.2.2 Services and unrequited transfers balances

The services account deficit (see Figure 15.4) contracted in 1991 as the number of Japanese travelling overseas declined because of the Gulf War, and fell further in 1992 as the surplus in investment income expanded because of various factors such as smaller interest payments by foreign exchange banks accompanying the decrease in their foreign liabilities.

The unrequited transfers account deficit expanded substantially in 1991 owing to Japan's financial support of the allied forces during the Gulf War (see Figure 15.1). However, it subsequently returned to the average for the 1980s.

15.3 CURRENT BALANCE AND THE INVESTMENT-SAVING BALANCE

15.3.1 Recent developments in the investment-saving balance

As a ratio of nominal GNP (see Figure 15.5), Japan's excess savings expanded in the first half of the 1980s as a result of the contraction of excess investment by the public sector. Then, since the second half of the 1980s, they have contracted and expanded because of the contraction and expansion of the excess savings of the private sector. Considering expenditure developments in each sector, it can be said that the contraction of the current account surplus in the first half of the 1980s corresponded to the decrease in public expenditure accompanying fiscal reform, and that the contraction and expansion since the second half of the 1980s has corresponded to the increase and decrease in private investment, especially plant and equipment investment.

Plant and equipment investment exhibited double-digit growth from 1988 to 1990 and, as a ratio of nominal GNP, reached 20 per cent in late 1990 and early 1991, comparable with figures in the rapid expansionary period of the late 1960s and early 1970s (see Figure 15.6). Such a rapid increase in plant and equipment investment cannot be explained just by the cyclical movement of capacity utilization, interest

(a) Import trade value (CIF, customs-clearance basis)
(US$bn)

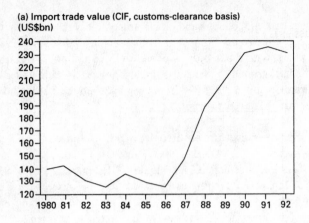

(b) Import indices

(1985 = 100)

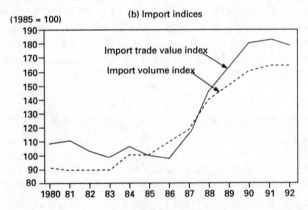

(1985 = 100)

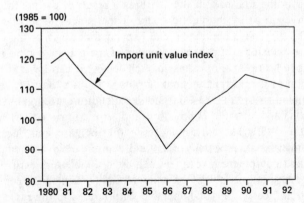

Source: Ministry of Finance, *Summary Report on Trade of Japan.*

FIGURE 15.3 Developments in Japan's imports

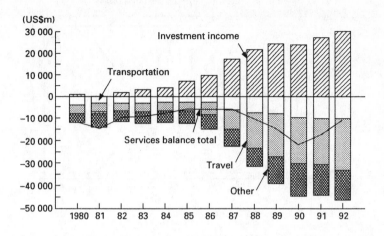

Source: Bank of Japan, *Balance of Payments Monthly.*

FIGURE 15.4   Japan's services balance

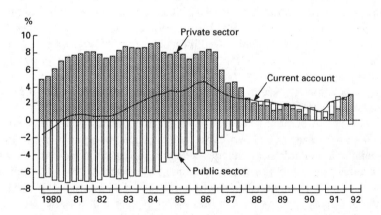

Source: Bank of Japan, *Flow of Funds Accounts.*

FIGURE 15.5   Net financial savings to GNP, seasonally adjusted

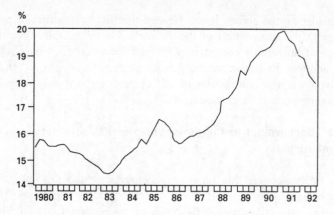

Source: Economic Planning Agency, *National Income Statistics.*

FIGURE 15.6   Nominal plant and equipment investment to GNP, seasonally
adjusted

rates or corporate profits. Thus, it is considered that the following two
factors contributed to a great extent.

First, active fund-raising became much easier than could be explained
by low interest rates, because of the upsurge in asset prices and other
factors. In the second half of the 1980s, financial institutions adopted
an active lending stance aimed at expanding business scale under financial liberalization[4] and, in addition, the rise in stock prices made
equity financing quite active. These factors made it much easier for
each company to employ its own creativity than when indirect financing was dominant, which triggered active corporate investment in plant
and equipment.[5]

Second, corporations had a strong incentive to effect plant and equipment investment other than capacity-expansion investment, reflecting
social and technological changes which occurred in the period. As for
manufacturers, the yen's appreciation, technological progress, and a
labour shortage triggered restructuring, R&D and labour-saving investments, respectively. As for non-manufacturers, the shift toward a service-
orientated economy[6] accelerated plant and equipment investment.

However, since 1991, the fall in asset prices has reduced equity financing and led to bank lending standards becoming stricter. In addition, growing fixed costs accompanying previous aggressive investment
have exerted considerable downward pressure on profit growth. Therefore
the growth rate of plant and equipment investment has fallen, also as
a ratio of nominal GNP.

Considering the above, it can be said that the contraction of excess savings in the second half of the 1980s is due to the rather rapid expansion of absorption compared with past economic expansionary periods, and that the consecutive expansion of excess savings is a reaction. In this sense, the contraction of the current account surplus can be seen as temporary, or extraordinary.

15.3.2 Background to the development of the structural current account surplus

Based on the above, this section analyzes factors of the investment-saving balance using a simple model, which originates in Branson (1985), consisting of a consumption function, an investment function, an export function, an import function, and an exchange rate equation, aiming at exploring the background to development of the structural current account surplus.

The basic model is as follows:

$$Y - C - I - G = EX - IM. \tag{1}$$

where Y: GNP; C: consumption; I: investment;
        G: public expenditure (exogenous);
        EX: exports; IM: imports.

GNP components are assumed to be:

$$C = C(Y), \tag{2}$$
$$I = I(Y, r, \alpha_1), \tag{3}$$
$$EX = EX(Y_f, e, \beta_{EX}), \tag{4}$$
$$IM = IM(Y, e, \beta_{IM}). \tag{5}$$

where Y_f: world real imports (except Japan);
      α_f: shift parameter for investment in the last half of the 1980s (exogenous);
      β_{EX}: shift parameter for export drive (exogenous);
      β_{IM}: shift parameter for inventory adjustment of imported materials (exogenous);
      r: real interest rate;
      e: exchange rate (logarithm of the price of a foreign currency in yen terms).

Accordingly, we can write equation (1) as follows:

$$Y - C\,(Y) - I\,(Y, r, \alpha_I) - G = EX(Y_f, e, \beta_{EX}) - IM\,(Y, e, \beta_{IM}) \quad (1)'$$

Exchange rate is given by:

$$r^* = r - \theta\,(\bar{e} - e) + \rho \qquad\qquad\qquad (6)$$

where $\bar{e}$:   expected long-term equilibrium exchange rate;
      r^*: world real interest rate;
      θ: speed at which the real exchange rate e is expected to con-
          verge to its long-term equilibrium rate $\bar{e}$.
      ρ: risk premium

In the model, the investment-saving balance (1)' indicates the relationship between real interest rate r and exchange rate e under 'goods market equilibrium', where GNP is assumed to be on a full-employment basis. In order to maintain 'goods market equilibrium' (1)', a higher e (i.e. a weaker yen), which corresponds to the larger current account surplus, requires a higher real interest rate r, which corresponds to smaller domestic demand (for example, decrease of plant and equipment investment). Thus, *GG*-curve shows upward slope in Figure 15.7.

Exchange rate equation (6) indicates the relationship between real interest rate r and exchange rate e under financial market equilibrium. As shown in the *FF*-curve in Figure 15.7, in order to maintain financial market equilibrium (6), a higher e, which increases the right side of (6), requires a lower real interest rate r, which decreases the right side of (6).

The real interest rate and exchange rate are determined at point A in Figure 15.7. A current account surplus to GNP is then determined by the exchange rate – at point *B* as shown in Figure 15.7.

Based on the above framework, recent developments in the structural current account surplus can be interpreted as follows. In the second half of the 1980s (see Figure 15.8), the Plaza Agreement changed the expected long-term equilibrium exchange rate $\bar{e}$, which shifted the *FF*-curve to *F'F'*. In addition, the rapid expansion of plant and equipment investments, a temporary or extraordinary factor, as explained before, shifted the *GG*-curve to *G'G'*. These changes caused the yen to appreciate and so the current account surplus contracted considerably.

On the other hand, the unwinding backward shift of the *GG*-curve has caused the recent expansion of the current account surplus (see Figure 15.9). In addition, it is probable that the competitiveness of Japan's exporting industries has increased as a result of the expansion

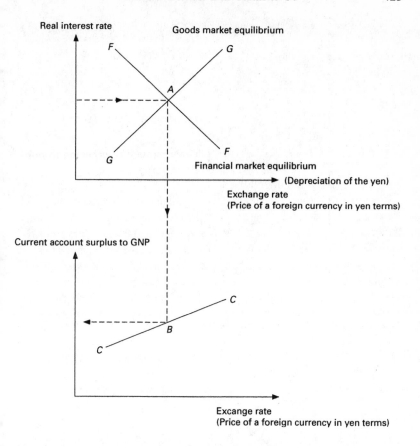

FIGURE 15.7 Basic model connecting external balance and exchange rate to IS-LM model

of plant and equipment investments in the second half of the 1980s, shifting the *CC*-curve upwards somewhat (from *CC* to *C'C'* in Figure 15.9).

15.3.3 Estimation of the structural current account surplus

In the above, we considered the background to development of the structural current account surplus. The rest of this section considers the estimation of the current account surplus in a full-employment output situation, which is obtained by excluding cyclical factors such as income and interest rates.[7]

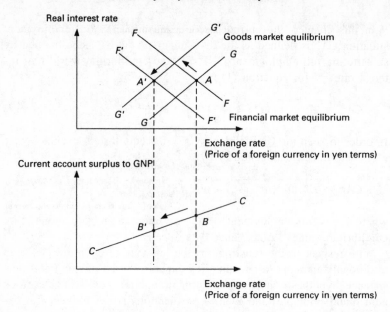

FIGURE 15.8   Current account surplus in the second half of the 1980s

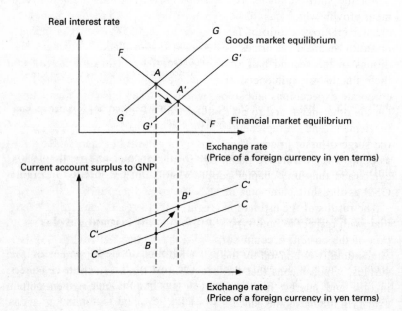

FIGURE 15.9   Current account surplus since 1991

In this chapter, the current account surplus in a full-employment situation CA^* is defined as the investment-saving balance obtained by substituting full-employment GNP Y^{*8} and equilibrium world real interest rate r^{*9} for equation (1)':

$$CA^* \equiv Y^* - C(Y^*) - I(Y^*, r^*, \alpha_I) - G. \tag{7}$$

In order to keep the GNP's identity (7), the equilibrium exchange rate e^* is determined endogenously by:

$$CA^* = EX(Y_f^*, e^*, \beta_{EX}^*) - IM(Y^*, e^*, \beta_{IM}^*), \tag{8}$$

where Y_f^* is full-employment world real imports; and β_{EX}^* and β_{IM}^* are equilibrium values[10] of β_{EX} and β_{IM}, respectively.

With respect to the functions of the left side of equation (1), both traditional functions (a consumption function based on the habit persistence hypothesis, and an investment function based on the stock adjustment principle) and ECM-type functions are employed. For export and import functions, traditional functions, including income and relative prices as explanatory variables, are employed.[11]

For the shift parameter α_I, that explains a portion of rapid investment growth which cannot be explained by cyclical factors alone, this chapter employs a ratio of land prices to nominal GNP. It is inappropriate to regard asset prices as the main factor affecting business conditions in the second half of the 1980s. Nevertheless, it is true that their fluctuation influenced the financial environment, personal and corporate expectations and so on, which widened business fluctuations. On the other hand, and to no small extent, the rapid growth of domestic demand and entrepreneurship during the period were reflected in the surge of asset prices. Therefore, it is natural to regard asset prices as being a representative parameter for factors expanding the business cycle, and thus this chapter adopts a ratio of land prices to nominal GNP as the shift parameter of an investment function.[12]

The results of the estimation (Figures 15.10, 15.11, and 15.12) show that, with respect to both types of function, the expansion and contraction of the current account surplus in the second half of the 1980s is almost totally explained by the full-employment-based current account surplus, which means that the exclusion of the cyclical movement of income and interest rates would not affect the surplus to any great extent. In the meantime, since $CA^* = EX(Y_f^*, e, \beta_{EX}^*) - IM(Y^*, e, \beta_{IM}^*)$, the equilibrium exchange rate e^* is considered to be near the actual exchange rate e.

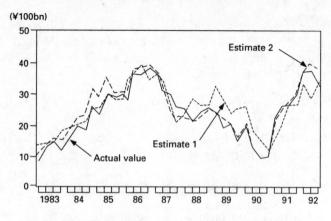

Consumption functions

(Real private consumption) = 1.77×10^4 + 0.466 (Real private
                                     (4.1)   (3.8)   consumption) $_{-1}$
                             + 0.264 × (Real GNP)
                                     (4.3)

Sample period: 1Q83 – 3Q92
                 R^2 = 0.996
                 SE = 1413
                 DW = 1.57

Investment functions

(Real private investment) = 1.10×10^5 + 0.584 (Real GNP)
                                     (3.2)   (9.8)
                             – 0.0957 × (Capital stock) $_{-1}$
                                     (5.3)
                             – 344 × (Real long-term interest rate)
                                     (1.5)
                             + 2.01×10^4 × log (Land price index/
                                     (7.7)   nominal GNP)

Sample period: 1Q83 – 3Q92
                 R^2 = 0.997
                 SE = 1178
                 DW = 1.36

Notes: Estimate 1. Cyclical changes in the income and interest rate factor
                    eliminated from estimated value.
       Estimate 2. Cyclical changes in the income and interest rate factor
                    eliminated from actual value.

FIGURE 15.10   Estimation of the structural current account:
                    traditional functions

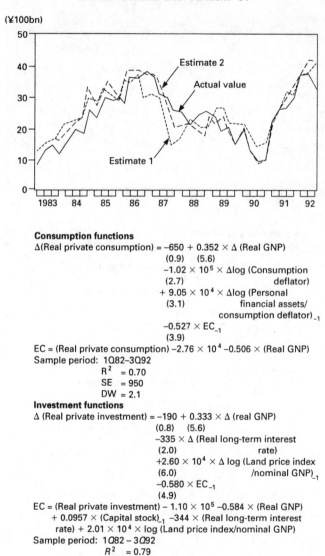

Consumption functions

Δ(Real private consumption) = –650 + 0.352 × Δ (Real GNP)
　　　　　　　　　　　　　　(0.9)　　(5.6)
　　　　　　　　　　　　　　–1.02 × 10^5 × Δlog (Consumption
　　　　　　　　　　　　　　(2.7)　　　　　　　　　　　deflator)
　　　　　　　　　　　　　　+ 9.05 × 10^4 × Δlog (Personal
　　　　　　　　　　　　　　(3.1)　　　　　　　financial assets/
　　　　　　　　　　　　　　　　　　　consumption deflator)$_{-1}$
　　　　　　　　　　　　　　–0.527 × EC$_{-1}$
　　　　　　　　　　　　　　(3.9)

EC = (Real private consumption) –2.76 × 10^4 –0.506 × (Real GNP)

Sample period: 1Q82–3Q92
　　　　　　R^2　= 0.70
　　　　　　SE　= 950
　　　　　　DW = 2.1

Investment functions

Δ (Real private investment) = –190 + 0.333 × Δ (real GNP)
　　　　　　　　　　　　　　　(0.8)　　(5.6)
　　　　　　　　　　　　　　　–335 × Δ (Real long-term interest
　　　　　　　　　　　　　　　(2.0)　　　　　　　　　　　rate)
　　　　　　　　　　　　　　　+2.60 × 10^4 × Δ log (Land price index
　　　　　　　　　　　　　　　(6.0)　　　　　　　/nominal GNP)$_{-1}$
　　　　　　　　　　　　　　　–0.580 × EC$_{-1}$
　　　　　　　　　　　　　　　(4.9)

EC = (Real private investment) – 1.10 × 10^5 –0.584 × (Real GNP)
　+ 0.0957 × (Capital stock)$_{-1}$ –344 × (Real long-term interest
　rate) + 2.01 × 10^4 × log (Land price index/nominal GNP)

Sample period: 1Q82 – 3Q92
　　　　　　R^2　= 0.79
　　　　　　SE　= 831
　　　　　　DW = 1.8

Notes: Estimate 1. Cyclical changes in the income and interest rate factor
　　　　　　　　　eliminated from estimated value.
　　　　Estimate 2. Cyclical changes in the income and interest rate factor
　　　　　　　　　eliminated from actual value.

FIGURE 15.11　Estimation of the structural current account:
　　　　　　　　ECM-type functions

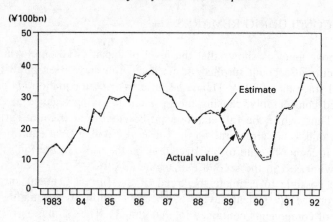

Export functions

log (Export volume) = +1.59 + 0.89 × log (Real world imports (except
  　　　　　　　　　　(6.5)　(16.0)　　　　　　　　　　　　　　　Japan))
  　　　　　　　　　　　　　　　　　　　8
  　　　　　　　　　−0.58 × log(1/9)Σ (Real effective
  　　　　　　　　　　(7.7)　　　　　t=0　　　exchange rate)$_{-t}$
  　　　　　　　　　+0.02 × log (Private inventory)$_{-1}$
  　　　　　　　　　　(3.0)

Sample period: 1Q83 – 1Q92
  　　　　　R^2　= 0.958
  　　　　　SE　= 0.03
  　　　　　DW　= 0.89

Import functions

log (Import volume (except oil)) = −7.77 + 1.24 × log (Domestic
  　　　　　　　　　　　　　　　(7.4)　(20.9)　　　　demand)
  　　　　　　　　　　　　　　　　　　　　　　5
  　　　　　　　　　　　　　−0.25 × log (1/6) Σ (IPI/WPI)$_{-t}$
  　　　　　　　　　　　　　　(8.6)　　　　　t=0
  　　　　　　　　　　　　　　　　　　　　　2
  　　　　　　　　　　　　　−0.71 × log (1/2) Σ (Index of
  　　　　　　　　　　　　　　(7.7)　　　　　t=1　　raw materials
  　　　　　　　　　　　　　　　　　　　　　　　inventory ratio)$_{-t}$

Sample period: 1Q83 – 3Q92
  　　　　　R^2　= 0.995
  　　　　　SE　= 0.02
  　　　　　DW　= 1.80

Note:　Cyclical changes in the income and interest rate factor eliminated from
  　　　actual value.

FIGURE 15.12　Estimation of the structural current account:
  　　　　　　　using import and export functions

15.4 CONCLUDING REMARKS

The above analysis shows that the level of Japan's full-employment-based current account surplus and its fluctuation have been quite substantial since the 1980s.[13] This is because α_l, or G in equation (7) have changed considerably, causing the investment–saving balance to fluctuate. Thus, while the full-employment-based current account surplus can be said to be 'structural' in the sense of the long-term equilibrium value, it cannot be said to be 'structural' in the sense of the long-term trend witnessed in the second half of the 1980s.

It is possible to estimate the trend of the current account surplus based on the investment–saving balance (1) simply by estimating the trends of components contained in equation (1). The estimation results (see Figure 15.13) suggest that the recent current account surplus is probably not far from its trend and, in this sense, is 'structural', which coincides with the result obtained by the 'full-employment' approach.

Based on these results, most of Japan's current account surplus is probably structural in the sense that it is mainly explained by the investment–saving balance under full employment. Thus, in order to reduce Japan's continuing current account surplus, which involves the risk of intensifying trade friction and thereby threatening the free trade system, a change in the investment–saving balance is unavoidable. In the long run, as Horioka (1991) says, demographic factors will reduce

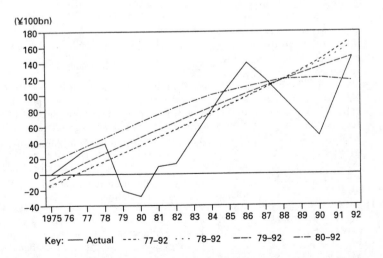

FIGURE 15.13 Trends of current account surplus

the current account surplus. However, in the shorter run, it is not clear whether or not the investment–saving balance can change enough to reduce the current account surplus. Of course, changes in trade patterns or market structure can affect the investment–saving balance somewhat, but to what extent is unknown. In any case, what is very clear is that Japan must not neglect efforts to proceed to deregulation still further for increased domestic investment and to further liberalize its markets. Further investigation on this kind of issue is necessary.

NOTES

1. Many Japanese exporters have raised the prices of their goods in response to the yen's appreciation.
2. Factor analysis of export prices shows that the exchange rate effect and shift to higher value-added products have contributed simultaneously to higher export prices since 1991 (see Figure 15.N2).
3. Imports (IMF base) in 1991 were influenced by some temporary factors such as the change in crude oil prices and a reactionary decrease to the big increase in gold imports (for gold-based funds) in the previous year. In addition, the decrease in the import of luxury goods, which had increased during the previous expansionary phase, also contributed. See Bank of Japan (1991).
4. See Bank of Japan (1992).
5. Under these circumstance, the external monitoring of corporate productivity and return on investment seems to have been relatively impaired. See Bank of Japan (1993).
6. See Bank of Japan (1989).
7. This chapter concentrates on the stationary state of the economy as a long-term trend. In the estimation, dummy variables were not employed for temporary or extraordinary factors which reduced the current account surplus in the last half of the 1980s.
8. This chapter estimates Y^*, r^* and Y_f^* in the same way as in Fukao (1987). Namely, Y^* is regarded as Y's trend which connects the mid-points of expansionary periods and has a constant growth rate between two consecutive mid-points. r^* is a five-period moving average of real long-term interest rates in the USA. Y_f^* is a five-period moving average of Y_f.
9. Equilibrium real world interest rate r^* is employed here since it is assumed that real interest rates are equalized when exchange rates are stable under long-term equilibrium.
10. Average values are employed here.
11. Different types of functions are employed here to check robustness of the results, while the propriety of each function is not necessarily definite.
12. Essentially, asset prices have a close relationship with interest rates, and thus it is not usual to adopt asset prices and interest rates simultaneously as independent variables. However, (i) the fluctuation in asset prices in the second half of the 1980s did not parallel interest-rate developments;

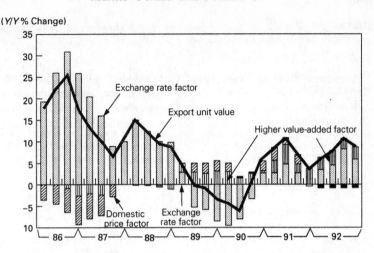

(Y/Y % Change)

Note: Factor analysis of export price increase is computed as follows:

$$\Delta P/P = \Delta(P/E) / (P/E) + \Delta(E/W) / (E/W) + \Delta W/W$$

              Shift to higher   Exchange   Domestic
              value-added   rate factor   price factor
              products factor

where P = export unit value index (customs-clearance basis, $)
        E = Export price index ($)
        W = domestic wholesale price index

Source: Ministry of Finance, *Summary Report on Trade of Japan*.

FIGURE 15.N2   Factor analysis of export unit value increase

and (ii) the alternative model, which contains asset prices endogenously, is too complicated for our analysis.
13. For the first half of the 1980s, Fukao (1987) obtained similar results.

REFERENCE

Bank of Japan 1989. 'Expansion of Japan's Tertiary Sector–Background and Macroeconomic Implications', Special Paper No. 183, December.
Bank of Japan 1991. 'Recent Balance of Payments Developments in Japan', Special Paper No. 208, November.
Bank of Japan 1992. 'Deregulation, Technological Progress, and Efficiency of the Banking Industry in Japan. Special Paper No. 211, January.
Bank of Japan 1993. 'Functions of Stock Markets: Implications for Corporate Financial Activities', Special Paper No. 225, February.

Branson, W. 1985. 'Causes of Appreciation and Volatility of the Dollar, *The U.S. Dollar–Recent Developments, Outlook, and Policy Options*', Kansas City, Missouri: Federal Reserve Bank of Kansas City.

Fukao, K. 1987. 'The Japanese Investment–Savings Balance, the Current Account, and the Exchange Rates', (in Japanese) *Economic Review*, 38, 3.

Horioka, C. Y. 1991. 'Future Trends in Japan's Saving Rate and the Implications thereof for Japan's External Imbalance', *Japan and the World Economy*, 3, pp. 307–30.

Ueda, K. 1986. 'Current Account and Exchange Rate – Investment–Saving Balance Approach', (in Japanese), *Monetary and Economic Studies*, 5, 1.

Ueda, K. 1992. 'Monetary Policy under External Imbalance' (in Japanese), *Toyokeizai Shinposha*.

16 Structural Changes in Japanese Long-term Capital Flows

Shinji Takagi*

16.1 INTRODUCTION

This chapter will review the recent structural changes in Japan's long-term capital flows, and analyze the statistical relationship between current and long-term capital transactions. It will show that long-term capital outflows from Japan expanded rapidly after 1981, mainly as a result of the progressive liberalization of regulations on the acquisition of foreign securities by resident institutional investors. With increased international portfolio diversification, it is believed that the portfolio motive for acquiring foreign securities has abated, and we can no longer expect net long-term capital outflows in the future to correspond with the size of the expected current account surplus. This prediction receives support from the results of causality tests, which suggest that current transactions and long-term capital transactions (securities transactions, in particular) had no causal relationship in the 1980s.

A primary motivation for this study comes from the continued interest of policy-makers and academic economists in the extent to which Japan will remain a net exporter of long-term capital in the coming years. There appears to be a fairly general consensus that Japan's current account surplus will remain sizeable for some time. Recent developments (which will be discussed later in the chapter) have, however, made it clear that this fact alone should not lead automatically to the

* This chapter is a revised and updated version of a paper presented at the 12th MOF–NBER Conference held in Tokyo on 5 March 1993. The original version was published in Japanese in the proceedings of the conference. The author has benefited from the useful comments of Professor Mitsuaki Okabe, participants of the MOF–NBER Conference, and seminar participants at Macquarie University, Sydney. He also gratefully acknowledges the capable research assistance of Yushi Yoshida.

conclusion that Japan will remain a net exporter of correspondingly sizeable long-term capital. It is true that, in the absence of official intervention in the foreign exchange market, a current account surplus is exactly equal to a capital account deficit. However, the current account surplus does not have to be exactly matched by a corresponding deficit in the *long-term* capital account, if the short-term capital account is in a large enough deficit.

Certainly, the conventional distinction between long-term and short-term capital may be losing its economic significance in the Japanese context. According to the widely-used accounting system of the International Monetary Fund (IMF, 1977), upon which Japanese balance of payments accounting is also based, long-term capital is defined as 'capital with an original contractual maturity of more than one year, or with no stated maturity (e.g., corporate equities)'; and short-term capital is 'capital payable on demand or with an original contractual maturity of one year or less and includes currency' (p. 128). At least in Japan, this distinction may have been useful in making a distinction between permanent capital movements and temporary movements which were likely to be reversed, when there were extensive restrictions on capital transactions (as explained later in the chapter). With the recent liberalization of capital transactions, however, there is an increasing awareness that, for example, some so-called 'long-term' capital transactions are, in fact, made for short-term purposes.[1]

While being cognizant of this and other conceptual problems, this chapter will start with the current accounting practice of making a distinction between long-term and short-term capital on the basis of contractual length, and investigate the structural changes in Japanese long-term capital flows as currently defined. This approach stems from three considerations. First, public policy discussions as well as government regulations in Japan are still based on the conventional distinction between long-term and short-term capital. Second, the supply of stable and permanent capital flows from Japan is certainly a component of the currently-defined long-term capital account, although it may not be the only component. Third, looking at the conventional statistics from a medium-term standpoint should yield useful information about the economic forces underlying Japan's cross-border capital transactions.

The paper is organized as follows. Section 16.2 takes a quick overview of the structure of Japan's balance of payments for the rather long period 1951–92. Section 16.3 outlines the history of capital controls in the post-war period (especially after the 1970s) as a background for interpreting the past structural changes in long-term capital flows. Section 16.4 then reviews the qualitative and quantitative developments of major components of the long-term capital account for the more recent period 1975–92. Section 16.5 uses quarterly data to perform causality tests of current transactions and long-term capital transactions. Finally, Section 16.6 presents concluding remarks and an outlook for the future. A brief chronology of principal regulatory measures relating to long-term capital flows is summarized in the Appendix.

16.2 THE OVERVIEW OF JAPAN'S BALANCE OF PAYMENTS, 1951–92

It may be useful to take a longer-run overview of Japan's balance of payments. From Table 16.1, which summarizes major components of Japan's annual balance of payments for the period 1951–92, we note that the current account was generally in balance through the middle of the 1960s, with surplus years and deficit years alternating with each other, and then chronic surpluses in the current account became a prominent feature of Japan's balance of payments in the latter part of the decade. On a calendar year basis, its current account balance has recorded a deficit only during 1973–75 and 1979–80 in the past twenty-five years, both resulting from the sharp increases in crude oil prices. Although the balance on unrequited transfers, a component of the current account, was initially in a surplus, the balance showed a deficit during much of this period, mainly reflecting the outflow of official grants to developing countries (Takagi, 1994).[2]

Although the statistics on net flows conceal the magnitude of gross flows, it is apparent that long-term capital transactions were not very active during the 1950s and early 1960s. It is safe to conclude that short-term capital flows (mainly through commercial banks) and official reserves were more important sources of finance for current transactions, because the sign and magnitude of the basic balance was broadly in line with those of the current account. From the middle of the 1960s, however, there was a noticeable increase in the activity of long-term capital transactions, as evidenced by the increased net size of the long-term capital account. The level of activity in long-term capital transactions seems to have risen even more in the 1980s (more will be said later on this point).

Given the surpluses in the current account during most of this period, Japan's long-term capital account was generally in deficit. In fact, until

TABLE 16.1 Components of Japan's balance of payments, 1951–92, US$m

Year	Goods and services	Unrequited transfers	Current account	Long-term capital	Basic balance	Short-term capital[1]	Change in foreign exchange reserves
1951	158	171	329	22	351	n.a.	n.a.
1952	190	35	225	−61	164	n.a.	n.a.
1953	−226	21	−205	−138	−343	187	−156
1954	−80	29	−51	49	−2	−83	−85
1955	205	22	227	2	229	−198	31
1956	−59	25	−34	74	40	132	172
1957	−590	−30	−620	65	−555	138	−417
1958	460	−195	265	115	380	43	337
1959	384	−23	361	−214	147	314	461
1960	170	−16	154	−71	83	419	502
1961	−941	−41	−982	−11	−993	655	−338
1962	−29	−29	−48	172	124	231	355
1963	−735	−45	−780	467	−313	350	37
1964	−407	−73	−480	107	−373	494	121
1965	1 017	−85	932	−415	517	−409	108
1966	1 389	−135	1 254	−808	446	−479	−33
1967	−12	−178	−190	−812	−1 002	934	−68
1968	1 223	−175	1 048	−239	809	76	885
1969	2 300	−181	2 119	−155	1 964	1 359	605
1970	2 178	−208	1 970	−1 591	379	524	903

1971	6 049	−252	5 797	−1 082	4 715	6 121	10 836
1972	7 088	−414	6 624	−4 487	2 137	993	3 130
1973	178	−314	−136	−9 750	−9 886	3 767	−6 119
1974	−4 406	−287	−4 693	−3 881	−8 574	9 846	1 272
1975	−326	−356	−682	−272	−954	251	−703
1976	4 020	−340	3 680	−984	2 696	1 093	3 789
1977	11 307	−389	10 918	−3 184	7 734	−1 490	6 224
1978	17 209	−675	16 534	−12 389	4 145	6 026	10 171
1979	−7 627	−1 127	−8 754	−12 976	−21 730	9 038	−12 692
1980	−9 218	−1 528	−10 746	2 324	−8 422	13 327	4 905
1981	6 394	−1 624	4 770	−9 672	−4 902	8 073	3 171
1982	8 231	−1 381	6 850	−14 969	−8 119	2 978	−5 141
1983	22 348	−1 549	20 799	−17 700	3 099	−1 865	1 234
1984	36 510	−1 507	35 003	−49 651	−14 648	16 465	1 817
1985	50 821	−1 652	49 169	−64 542	−15 373	15 570	197
1986	87 895	−2 050	85 845	−131 461	−45 616	61 345	15 729
1987	90 684	−3 669	87 015	−136 532	−49 517	88 757	39 240
1988	83 749	−4 118	79 631	−130 930	−51 299	67 482	16 183
1989	61 391	−4 234	57 157	−89 246	−32 089	19 322	−12 767
1990	41 236	−5 475	35 761	−43 586	−7 825	−17	−7 842
1991	85 384	−12 483	72 901	37 057	109 958	−101 885	−8 073
1992	122 236	−4 685	117 551	−28 459	89 092	−89 387	−295

Note: 1. Including errors and omissions.

Sources: Ministry of Finance, *Zaisei Kinyu Tokei Geppo*, various issue; Bank of Japan, *Balance of Payments Monthly*, various issues.

1990, the long-term capital account was in deficit even in those years when the current account was also in deficit, except in 1980. In each year from 1981 to 1990, moreover, the deficit in the long-term capital account exceeded the current account surplus, except in 1983, so that the basic balance was in deficit. The Japanese balance of payments in recent years can thus be characterized by a surplus in the current account (with a small deficit in the balance on unrequited transfers) and a somewhat larger deficit in the long-term capital account.

From this standpoint, it is possible that an important structural change took place in the relationship between the current account and the long-term capital account in 1991. In 1991, the long-term capital account showed a surplus of $37bn, despite the sizeable current account surplus of almost $73bn. In 1992, the long-term capital account did return to a deficit in the second quarter of 1992. However, while the current account surplus increased to almost $118bn, the long-term capital account did show a deficit, but only to the small extent of $28bn. This means that less than a quarter of the current account surplus was *financed* by net long-term capital outflows in 1992. In 1991 and 1992, the basic balance registered a surplus of $110bn and $90bn respectively. In order to provide insight into interpreting the structural changes in long-term capital flows, we will first review the history of capital controls in Japan.

16.3   LIBERALIZATION OF CAPITAL FLOWS IN JAPAN[3]

16.3.1   Early post-war years

From the end of the Second World War to 1964, the Japanese authorities maintained strict controls on the country's external transactions. The Foreign Exchange and Foreign Trade Control Law (abbreviated as the Foreign Exchange Law, hereafter) of December 1949 prohibited in principle all external transactions unless specifically approved. Although there were some official capital flows, such as official loans to developing countries (beginning in 1958) and development loans from the World Bank (beginning in 1953),[4] private capital flows were virtually absent during this period. The absence of significant private capital transactions during this period was reflected in the generally small net value of the long-term capital account, as noted in Section 16.2 with reference to Table 16.1.

In April 1964, Japan accepted the obligations of Article VIII of the Articles of Agreement of the International Monetary Fund (IMF) by abolishing exchange controls on current transactions. As Japan simultaneously became a member of the Organization for Economic Co-operation and Development (OECD), it began the gradual process of liberalizing international capital transactions unrelated to current transactions. Beginning in July 1967, the authorities took measures in several steps to liberalize non-residents' direct investment in Japan (see the Appendix on pp. 455–7 for a chronology of principal measures related to long-term capital flows). Similarly, starting in October 1969, the authorities introduced measures to liberalize residents' direct investment abroad. Along with the liberalization and subsequent expansion of current transactions, moreover, short-term capital transactions became active through leads and lags, that is, by the actions of traders to adjust the length of payment periods.

16.3.2 1970s

Throughout the 1970s, the Japanese authorities often changed the regulatory stance towards capital controls, depending on the direction of pressure on the exchange rate (Komiya and Suda, 1991; Takagi, 1991). In particular, when the yen was under depreciating pressure, they tended to implement measures to encourage capital inflows and to discourage capital outflows; and when the yen was subjected to appreciating pressure they tended to implement measures to discourage capital inflows and to encourage capital outflows. Taking the decade as a whole, however, the stance of the authorities was by and large directed towards the liberalization of external capital transactions.

To highlight some of the major measures implemented in relation to long-term capital flows in the 1970s (see the Appendix on pp. 455–7 for a brief summary), the Japanese authorities began to encourage capital outflows so as to mitigate the appreciating pressure on the yen at the beginning of the decade. In particular, they allowed Japanese residents to purchase foreign securities for the first time, by first granting permission to investment trusts (April 1970), and then to insurance companies (January 1971). In December 1970, the Asian Development Bank became the first issuer of yen-denominated bonds in the Japanese capital market.

After the de-linking of the dollar from gold in August 1971, however, the yen was subjected to a renewed appreciating pressure. During 1972, therefore, the authorities further relaxed controls on capital outflows, including the full liberalization of residents' foreign direct investment abroad, in June 1972. As a result, long-term capital outflows expanded significantly after 1972.

With the first oil shock in October 1973, the yen was placed under depreciating pressure. Thus, from the end of 1973, the authorities began to relax exchange controls on capital inflows and to strengthen controls on capital outflows. They eased controls on non-residents' purchases of Japanese stocks in November 1973, and on bonds in December of that year. In January 1974, the authorities tightened controls on capital outflows; in August 1974, they fully liberalized purchases of Japanese securities by non-residents.

As the yen began to strengthen in 1977, the authorities reversed their stance by relaxing exchange controls on capital outflows and by strengthening controls on capital inflows. For example, they liberalized residents' purchases of unlisted foreign bonds in April 1977 and of short-term foreign securities in 1977. In November 1977, moreover, the authorities increased the margin requirement on yen-denominated bank accounts held by non-residents and placed a virtual ban on non-residents' acquisition of short-term government securities.

As the yen began to weaken again in 1979 (particularly after the second oil shock), however, the stance of the authorities was reversed, with the abolishment of all controls on capital inflows, including the abolition of controls on non-residents' acquisition of Japanese bonds in February 1979 and the liberalization of non-residents' participation in the short-term Gensaki market in May 1979 (Takagi, 1988; Fukao, 1990). Finally, the series of these and other *ad hoc* liberalization measures introduced during the 1970s were codified in a major revision of the Foreign Exchange Law in December 1980, which in principle allowed all external transactions to be conducted freely, unless specifically prohibited (Takagi, 1988).

16.2.3   1980s

Even after the enactment of the new Foreign Exchange Law, some prudential regulations on the foreign securities investment of financial institutions and institutional investors (such as trust banks and insurance companies) remained. During the first half of the 1980s, the authorities actively used these remaining regulations to influence the movement of the yen exchange rate in a desired direction (Fukao, 1990; Takagi, 1991; and Koo, 1993). For the decade of the 1980s taken as a whole, however, the stance of the authorities was again in the direction of full liberalization, just as it was during the 1970s.

The scope of financial institutions authorized to invest in foreign securities expanded in the early 1980s (prior to this time, only investment trusts and insurance companies had been authorized). For example, pension trusts were authorized in January 1981 to invest in foreign securities up to 10 per cent of total assets; and the Postal Life Insurance System was authorized in May 1983 to purchase foreign securities up to 10 per cent of total assets. At the same time, however, the authorities introduced temporary restrictions on foreign securities investment in order to halt the depreciation of the yen during 1981–5. In April 1982, life insurance companies were requested to 'voluntarily' limit the net purchase of foreign bonds to 10 per cent of net increases in assets. Pension trusts, the Postal Life Insurance System and non-life-insurance companies were subject to similar voluntary restrictions.

With the appreciation of the yen following the Plaza Agreement in autumn 1985, however, these flow restrictions began to be relaxed. Over subsequent years, for example, the flow limit on the acquisition of foreign currency assets by life insurance companies and pension trusts was increased gradually. It was eventually raised to 40 per cent of the increase in total assets in April 1986; the limit was then abolished altogether in August 1986, when similar flow restrictions were suspended for other types of institutional investor.

Along with the relaxation of flow restrictions, stock restrictions were also relaxed, beginning in 1986. In March and April 1986, the ceiling on foreign securities investments for insurance companies and trust banks (for pension trust accounts) was raised from 10 per cent to 25 per cent of total assets; the ceiling was further raised to 30 per cent in August 1986. Trust banks were authorized to invest in foreign bonds (for loan trust accounts) up to 1 per cent of total assets (in February 1986); up to 3 per cent (June 1986); and then up to 5 per cent (February 1989). In April 1987, the Trust Fund Bureau of the Ministry of Finance was authorized to invest in foreign securities for the first time, up to 10 per cent of total assets. In June 1987, the ceiling on foreign securities for the Postal Life Insurance System was increased from 10 per cent to 20 per cent of total assets.

16.4 THE STRUCTURE OF LONG-TERM CAPITAL FLOWS, 1975–92

16.4.1 Foreign assets and liabilities

As a result of these and other liberalization measures, the volume of international capital transactions expanded rapidly in the 1980s. In particular, owing to the relaxation of restrictions on the acquisition of foreign securities by institutional investors, the expansion of long-term private capital outflows was indeed phenomenal. These developments can be seen by looking at the annual changes in Japan's long-term assets and liabilities (shown in Table 16.2).[5]

Three features are noteworthy. First, while both assets and liabilities steadily increased, the expansion was considerably more rapid on the asset side. Second, the share of the public sector in total assets and liabilities declined steadily, from over 20 per cent in the late 1970s to a little over 10 per cent in the early 1990s (the percentage figures are not directly reported in the table). Third, the expansion of capital transactions particularly accelerated in the latter part of the 1980s.

Reflecting the expansion of long-term capital transactions on both sides, the balances of Japan's long-term foreign assets and liabilities increased rapidly as a percent of GNP during this period (not directly reported in the table): the balance of foreign assets rose from 6.6 per cent of GNP at the end of 1976 to 36.8 (35.4) per cent at the end of 1991 (1992); the balance of foreign liabilities rose from 3.2 to 19.1 (17.7) per cent during the same period. On a net basis, the net long-term asset position of Japan *vis-à-vis* the rest of the world rose from 3.4 per cent of GNP at the end of 1976 to 21.4 per cent at the end of 1990 (17.7 per cent at the ends of both 1991 and 1992).

16.4.2   Breakdown of the long-term capital account

A more detailed look at the structure of Japan's long-term capital account can be obtained by breaking it down into 'direct investments', 'trade credits', 'loans', 'securities investments', and 'other'. Table 16.3 reports these sub-accounts (except for residual 'other') for the years 1975–92, further decomposing each into changes in assets and liabilities.

Several features are notable. First, and most important, from the early part of the 1980s the volume of securities transactions dominated the volume of other types of long-term capital transaction. Second, even though the net value of foreign securities investment steadily declined after 1986, the net value of foreign direct investment continued to increase. Third, during most of the period under consideration, net outflows of Japanese long-term capital in direct investment, trade credits and loans mainly took the form of increases in foreign assets, while changes in both assets and liabilities were behind the long-term capital flows in securities investment. However, there were a significant amount of loan transaction associated with declines in foreign liabilities during 1989–92.

TABLE 16.2 Japan's long-term foreign assets and liabilities, 1976–92, US$bn unless indicated otherwise

Year	Assets				Liabilities				Net
	Total	Private sector	(Of which: direct investment)	Public sector	Total	Private sector	(Of which: direct investment)	Public sector	Total (percentage of GNP)
1976	37	28	(10)	9	18	15	(2)	3	19 (3.4)
1977	42	31	(12)	11	20	16	(2)	4	22 (3.2)
1978	63	46	(14)	17	29	23	(3)	6	34 (3.5)
1979	84	62	(17)	22	36	28	(3)	8	48 (4.8)
1980	88	67	(20)	21	47	35	(3)	12	41 (4.0)
1981	117	89	(25)	28	70	50	(4)	20	47 (4.2)
1982	139	110	(29)	29	78	53	(4)	25	61 (5.7)
1983	171	138	(32)	33	103	77	(4)	26	68 (5.9)
1984	229	192	(38)	37	113	84	(5)	29	116 (9.2)
1985	301	264	(44)	37	122	92	(5)	30	179 (13.5)
1986	476	425	(58)	51	192	152	(7)	40	284 (14.5)
1987	646	565	(77)	81	236	179	(9)	57	410 (17.2)
1988	833	728	(111)	105	311	268	(10)	43	522 (18.3)
1989	1 019	902	(154)	117	447	405	(9)	42	572 (20.2)
1990	1 096	974	(201)	122	464	408	(10)	56	632 (21.4)
1991	1 248	1 090	(232)	158	647	565	(12)	82	601 (17.7)
1992	1 316	1 132	(248)	183	658	579	(16)	80	658 (17.7)

Source: Bank of Japan, *Balance of Payments Monthly*, various issues.

TABLE 16.3 Components of Japan's long-term capital account, 1975–92, US$m

Year	Long-term capital	Of which: Direct investment			Trade credits		
		Assets	Liabilities	Net	Assets	Liabilities	Net
1975	−272	−1 763	226	−1 537	−29	−29	−58
1976	−984	−1 991	113	−1 878	−571	−5	−576
1977	−3 184	−1 645	21	−1 624	−1 388	−13	−1 401
1978	−12 389	−2 371	8	−2 363	−142	−22	−164
1979	−12 976	−2 898	239	−2 659	1 288	−33	1 255
1980	2 324	−2 385	278	−2 107	−717	−16	−733
1981	−9 672	−4 894	189	−4 705	−2 731	−15	−2 746
1982	−14 969	−4 540	439	−4 101	−3 239	−6	−3 245
1983	−17 700	−3 612	416	−3 196	−2 589	8	−2 581
1984	−49 651	−5 965	−10	−5 975	−4 937	3	−4 934
1985	−64 542	−6 452	642	−5 810	−2 817	29	−2 788
1986	−131 461	−14 480	226	−14 254	−1 836	−40	−1 876
1987	−136 532	−19 519	1 165	−18 354	−535	−1	−536
1988	−130 930	−34 210	−485	−34 695	−6 939	−18	−6 957
1989	−89 246	−44 130	−1 054	−45 184	−4 002	−9	−4 011
1990	−43 586	−48 024	1 753	−46 271	680	−10	670
1991	37 057	−30 726	1 368	−29 358	3 928	−2	3 926
1992	−28 459	−17 222	2 728	−14 494	5 293	−5	5 288

Year	Loans			Securities			Memorandum: Loans and Securities	
	Assets	Liabilities	Net	Assets	Liabilitis	Net	Outflows	Inflows
1975	−1 295	166	−1 129	−24	2 753	2 729	−5 497	7 097
1976	−1 525	326	−1 199	−146	3 104	2 958	−8 076	9 835
1977	−472	−324	−796	−1 718	2 355	637	−11 963	11 804
1978	−6 299	−7	−6 306	−5 300	2 487	−2 813	−30 328	21 209
1979	−8 102	−169	−8 271	−5 865	4 282	−1 583	−38 775	28 921
1980	−2 553	−231	−2 784	−3 753	13 113	9 360	−41 547	48 123
1981	−5 083	−186	−5 269	−8 777	13 220	4 443	−64 573	63 747
1982	−7 902	−181	−8 083	−9 743	11 860	2 117	−75 550	69 584
1983	−8 425	−37	−8 462	−16 024	14 148	−1 876	−108 213	97 875
1984	−11 922	−77	−11 999	−30 795	7 194	−23 601	−187 509	151 909
1985	−10 427	−75	−10 502	−59 773	16 741	−43 032	−466 435	408 377
1986	−9 281	−34	−9 315	−101 977	545	−101 432	−1 702 277	1 591 530
1987	−16 190	−119	−16 309	−87 757	−6 081	−93 838	−1 866 183	1 756 036
1988	−15 211	−82	−15 293	−86 949	20 298	−66 651	−1 949 078	1 867 134
1989	−22 495	17 813	−4 682	−113 178	85 144	−28 034	−2 333 689	2 300 973
1990	−22 182	39 112	16 930	−39 681	34 653	−5 028	−1 844 011	1 855 913
1991	−13 097	38 124	25 027	−74 306	115 284	40 978	−1 617 476	1 683 481
1992	−7 623	15 899	8 276	−34 362	8 171	−26 191	−1 488 197	1 430 282

Sources: Bank of Japan, *Balance of Payments Monthly*, various issues; the author's estimates.

The last column of Table 16.3 reports the estimated values of capital outflows and inflows in the form of loans and securities investments. Here, the outflows are loans and securities transactions which result in increases in assets or decreases in liabilities, including extension of loans by residents to non-residents; repayment of foreign loans by residents; acquisition of foreign securities by residents; disposal of Japanese securities by non-residents; issues of bonds by non-residents in the Japanese capital market; and redemption of external bonds by residents. Conversely, the capital inflows are those transactions which result in decreases in assets or increases in liabilities, including repayment of Japanese loans by non-residents; borrowing of foreign loans by residents; disposal of foreign securities by residents; acquisition of Japanese securities by non-residents; redemption of Japanese external bonds by non-residents; and issues of external bonds by residents. These figures clearly indicate the high degree of two-way flows in long-term capital.

16.4.3 Geographical distribution of long-term capital flows

In terms of geographical distribution, an overwhelming portion (from 60 to 80 per cent) of the deficit in Japan's long-term capital account in the second half of the 1980s was with the industrial countries, notably the USA (see Table 16.4). In fact, the balance with the USA alone constituted about a half of the long-term capital account balance. The share of the developing countries was between 17 and 33 per cent of the total, while the share of the (current and former) socialist countries was negligible. This characterization applies to both the overall long-term capital account and the direct investment account.

In 1990, the overall deficit with the industrial countries sharply increased, while the overall balance with the developing countries turned to a surplus. In 1991, the overall long-term capital account turned to a surplus, although the balance with the USA remained in deficit. The balance with the industrial countries returned to a deficit again in 1992.

16.5 CAUSALITY TESTS OF CURRENT AND LONG-TERM CAPITAL TRANSACTIONS

Undoubtedly the magnitude and direction of long-term capital flows are influenced by many factors, including interest rate differentials, changes in the stock of national wealth, and exchange rate expectations (Ueda and Fujii, 1986). It seems safe to argue, however, that the recent

TABLE 16.4 Geographical distribution of Japan's long-term capital account balance, 1975–92 (as percentage of total)[1]

Year	Industrial countries (USA)[2]	Socialist countries[3]	Developing countries	Direct investment only		
				Industrial countries (USA)[2]	Socialist countries[3]	Developing countries
1975	619 (−14)	−153	−566	−41 (−35)	0	−59
1976	164 (23)	−45	−219	−47 (−27)	0	−53
1977	− (−)	−16	−84	−49 (−26)	0	−51
1978	−31 (−27)	−11	−58	−47 (−36)	0	−53
1979	−40 (−12)	−6	−54	−44 (−28)	−	−56
1980	152 (69)	−22	−30	−56 (−35)	−	−44
1981	−1 (−41)	−24	−75	−66 (−40)	−	−34
1982	−32 (−11)	−10	−58	−58 (−35)	0	−42
1983	−35 (−31)	−6	−59	−58 (−33)	−	−42
1984	−68 (−30)	−2	−30	−68 (−53)	−	−32
1985	−74 (−51)	−1	−25	−66 (−35)	−1	−33
1986	−83 (−50)	−	−17	−78 (−55)	−1	−21
1987	−78 (−45)	−	−22	−77 (−49)	−1	−22
1988	−76 (−45)	−2	−22	−81 (−56)	−1	−18
1989	−62 (−60)	−5	−33	−81 (−50)	−2	−17
1990	−103 (−27)	−4	7	−84 (−54)	−1	−15
1991	42 (−50)	−5	63	−83 (−52)	−1	−16
1992	−132 (−96)	−6	38	−82 (−55)	−4	−14

Notes: [1] A minus sign indicates a deficit; a plus sign, a surplus; − means negligible.
   [2] Includes the OECD countries and, except for 1992, South Africa.
   [3] Includes both current and former socialist countries.

Sources: Bank of Japan, *Balance of Payments Monthly*, various issues; the author's estimates.

expansion of long-term capital transactions was significantly affected
by the liberalization of controls on cross-border capital transactions,
particularly those on the acquisition of foreign securities by resident
institutional investors.

The phenomenal expansion of two-way, long-term capital flows in
recent years also seems to suggest that an autonomous component of
long-term capital transactions has been increasing. For example, in 1975,
the value of exports and service receipts was $68.2bn, while the value
of long-term capital outflows in the form of loans and securities investments was $5.5bn. In 1991, in contrast, the value of exports and
service receipts was $495.1bn, while the value of long-term capital
outflows in the form of loans and securities investments was $1617.5bn.

The hypothesis that long-term capital transactions became largely
autonomous (in the sense that they are made independently of the need
to finance current transactions) in recent years may be examined by
Granger causality tests. As a preliminary investigation, it was decided
to use simple bivariate tests between current transactions and long-
term capital transactions, using quarterly data for the period 1981:Q1–
1992:Q2. The variables are current receipts, loan outflows, securities
outflows, current payments, loan inflows and securities inflows, all
expressed in logarithms.

As an initial step, Dicky–Fuller (DF) and Augmented Dicky–Fuller
(ADF)[6] tests were performed to test whether or not the time-series
were stationary (see Table 16.5). As the results of the tests indicated
the presence of unit roots in all the variables, it was decided to take the
first logarithmic difference of each variable. Causality was then tested
between a credit item (current receipts or capital inflows) and a debit
item (current payments or capital outflows), using 8 lags (i.e., two
years). If capital transactions are not autonomous, we should expect
them to be Granger-caused by current transactions. It must be emphasized,
however, that because causality tests are known to be sensitive to how
they are specified, the test results should be interpreted with care.

The results, obtained for the sample period of 1981:Q1–1992:Q2,
are summarized in Table 16.6. The table reports the results of two
types of specification: one in which the contemporary value of the
explanatory variable is included, and the other in which only the lagged
values are included. In both specifications, there was no evidence of
causality in either direction between current payments and capital inflows (loans and securities). Between current receipts and securities
outflows, there was no evidence of causality running in either direction,
either. There was, however, mixed evidence of causality running from

TABLE 16.5 Unit root tests, from first quarter 1981 to second quarter 1992

Current	DF	−0.010
receipts	ADF (1)	0.408
	ADF (2)	0.201
Current	DF	0.288
payments	ADF (1)	−0.260
	ADF (2)	−0.292
Loan	DF	−1.581
outflows	ADF (1)	−1.263
	ADF (2)	−1.255
Securities	DF	−2.031
outflows	ADF (1)	−1.781
	ADF (2)	−1.733
Loan	DF	−0.359
inflows	ADF (1)	−0.034
	ADF (2)	0.201
Securities	DF	−1.696
inflows	ADF (1)	−1.569
	ADF (2)	−1.551

Note: No statistic is significant either at the 1 or 5 per cent level.

TABLE 16.6 Granger causality tests, from first quarter 1981 to second quarter 1992

		Without contemporaneous feedback: $F(8, 21)$	With contemporaneous feedback: $F(9, 20)$
x:	Current receipts		
	y: Loan outflows		
	$x \rightarrow y$	2.27	2.77*
	$x \leftarrow y$	1.13	1.61
	y: Securities outflows		
	$x \rightarrow y$	0.62	0.81
	$x \leftarrow y$	1.28	1.43
x:	Current payments		
	y: Loan inflows		
	$x \rightarrow y$	1.28	1.29
	$x \leftarrow y$	1.01	1.05
	y: Securities inflows		
	$x \rightarrow y$	0.69	0.62
	$x \leftarrow y$	2.11	1.83

Note: The number of lags is set at 8; * indicates that the statistic is significant at the 5 per cent level.

current receipts to loan outflows, possibly indicating that part of the loan extension was still associated with the sale of goods and services. There was no evidence of causality running from loan outflows to current receipts.

Overall, the weight of the evidence seems to favour the conclusion that the long-term capital transactions were largely exogenous to the current transactions during the sample period, particularly given the fact that the volume of securities transactions far dominated the volume of loan transactions during this period. Clearly, long-term capital flows are sensitive to many factors, including financing needs as well as changes in the economy's net asset position associated with current transactions. Moreover, the causality tests of the type performed here by no means prove anything about the structural determinants of capital flows. However, we may safely state the possibility that, given the apparently autonomous nature of long-term capital flows, the size of the current account surpluses in the coming years may not have much to do with the size of net long-term capital outflows from Japan.

16.6. CONCLUDING REMARKS

Against the background of chronic current account surpluses, there have been major structural changes in Japan's long-term capital flows in recent years. During the 1970s, although exchange restrictions were gradually lifted over time, the volume of long-term capital flows was relatively limited. As a result, the deficit on the long-term capital account was not generally large enough to offset the surplus in the current account: the basic balance was thus in surplus.

From the early 1980s, however, long-term capital transactions (outflows, in particular) expanded rapidly, primarily owing to the lifting of prudential restrictions on the foreign portfolio investment of resident institutional investors. The important feature of Japan's balance of payments during most of the 1980s was that the deficit in the long-term capital account exceeded the surplus in the current account: the basic balance was in deficit. As a parallel development, international capital transactions became increasingly autonomous. Granger causality tests indicate that the long-term capital transactions (securities transactions, in particular) were largely exogenous to the current transactions.

In 1991, an important structural change apparently took place in Japan's long-term capital account. Despite the continuing large current account surplus, the balance on the long-term capital account turned to a surplus (net inflow) for the first time since 1980 (in the aftermath of the second oil crisis when the current account was in deficit). In 1992, while the long-term capital account returned to a deficit (net outflow), the size of the deficit fell far short of the size of the surplus in the current account. In both 1991 and 1992, the basic balance was in a large surplus, amounting to $110bn and $90bn, respectively.

The emergence of a large surplus in the basic balance in 1991 and 1992 may be a reminder that the accumulation of long-term foreign assets cannot continue indefinitely. Japan's current level of long-term foreign assets (21 per cent of GNP in 1990; 18 per cent in 1991) is high in relation to the historical levels of net foreign assets in other major industrial countries (see Table 16.2 on p. 445, and Table 16.7). Even in Germany and the UK, two major European countries with a high degree of openness, the GNP share of net foreign assets was around 20 per cent at its peak.

In this respect, the prediction of Fukao and Okina (1989) that the share of foreign assets in the portfolios of Japanese institutional investors could not be expected to continue, may well have been correct. In fact, after rising sharply in the early 1980s, the share of foreign securities in the portfolios of Japanese institutional investors levelled off in the latter part of the 1980s (see Table 16.8). Moreover, the share has been well below the maximum ceiling allowed by the prudential regulations for the foreign securities investment of institutional investors in recent years (for example, 30 per cent for insurance companies). Thus, although it is possible for the stock of foreign securities to increase over time along with the increase in the stock of total assets, it is difficult to foresee a major increase in the share of foreign securities in the portfolios of Japanese institutional investors in the coming years.

If Japanese institutional investors do continue to make a downward adjustment (either in absolute or relative terms) of their portfolio investment in long-term foreign securities, there are two possible implications of the projected continuation of current account surpluses. First, portfolio balance considerations suggest that the yen may appreciate so as to realize a lower value of long-term foreign assets held by Japanese residents. A higher value of the yen will result in a lower relative value of the outstanding stock of foreign securities held in the yen-denominated portfolios of Japanese investors.[7]

Second, the existence of a surplus in the basic balance means that much of Japanese savings will be invested in short-term assets. In order to predict the flow of Japanese savings to different parts of the world, it would thus be more useful to analyze the financial intermediation

TABLE 16.7 Net foreign assets of major countries in selected years
(as percentage of GNP)

Japan[1]		
	(end of 1990)	11.5
	(end of 1991)	11.3
Germany		
	(end of 1990)	22.0
	(end of 1991)	20.0
UK		
	(end of 1988)	17.3
	(end of 1989)	16.4
USA[2]		
	(end of 1981)	4.6
	(end of 1982)	4.3

Notes: [1] The figures for Japan differ from those in Table 16.2 because of the inclusion of short-term assets and liabilities.
[2] After reaching the peak net creditor position in 1981, the USA became a net debtor country in 1985.

Source: Ministry of Finance, *Zaisei Kinyu Tokei Geppo*, various issues.

TABLE 16.8 Foreign securities investment by Japanese institutional investors, 1980–92, as percentage of total assets

End of year	Trust banks[1]	Life insurance companies	Non-life insurance companies	Investment trusts
1980–85 (average)	2.1	6.4	5.4	3.6
1986	7.5	11.7	11.2	12.5
1987	7.9	13.7	10.4	9.3
1988	7.1	14.2	10.4	9.1
1989	7.5	15.4	11.6	8.2
1990	7.5	13.5	12.2	7.9
1991	9.2	12.4	12.0	12.5
1992	8.4	11.4	13.3	9.8

Note: [1] Including banking and trust accounts.

Sources: Bank of Japan (1992); the author's estimates from Bank of Japan, *Economic Statistics Monthly*.

role of the Euro-currency markets than to analyze the investment behaviour of Japanese investors. Moreover, given the historical concentration of Japanese capital transactions with the industrial countries, it
is even more doubtful that a significant amount of long-term capital
will flow to the developing world. In this respect, the role of official
capital flows, including official development assistance (ODA), will
remain important as the only significant means of recycling Japanese
current account surpluses to the developing countries.

APPENDIX: A SELECTIVE CHRONOLOGY OF PRINCIPAL
MEASURES RELATING TO LONG-TERM CAPITAL FLOWS IN
JAPAN, 1970–PRESENT[8]

Measures relating to loans and securities investments

Outflows

April 1970	Investment trusts authorized to purchase foreign se-curities up to $100m.
January 1971	Insurance companies authorized to purchase listed foreign securities up to $100m.
July 1971	Securities companies authorized to purchase and sell listed foreign securities on behalf of individual in-vestors; ceiling on foreign securities purchases by investment trusts and insurance companies abolished.
February 1972	Trust banks authorized to purchase and sell listed foreign securities.
March 1972	Major foreign exchange banks authorized to pur-chase and sell listed foreign securities.
May 1972	Purchases of unlisted foreign securities by residents liberalized; over-the-counter sales of foreign secu-rities by domestic securities companies authorized.
October 1972	Medium- and long-term loans subject to blanket ap-proval.
January 1974	Foreign-exchange banks, securities companies, in-surance companies and investment trusts requested to refrain voluntarily from increasing the net value of foreign securities investments; medium- and long-term loans no longer subject to blanket approval (now subject to item-by-item approval).
August 1974	Medium- and long-term loans prohibited in principle.
June 1975	The above voluntary restriction on foreign securities investments lifted except for foreign-exchange banks.
June 1976	Purchases of foreign securities by residents subject to automatic approval.
November 1976	Regulation on medium- and long-term loans relaxed.

March 1977	The above voluntary restriction on foreign securities investments lifted for foreign exchange banks.
April 1977	Purchases of unlisted bonds liberalized.
July 1978	Foreign-currency-denominated medium- and long-term loans by major foreign exchange banks subject to blanket approval.
October 1980	Yen-denominated medium- and long-term loans liberalized.
December 1980	Purchases of securities liberalized; medium- and long-term loans subject only to notification (with the exemption of major foreign exchange banks from the notification requirement).
April 1982	Life insurance companies requested to limit voluntarily the net purchase of foreign bonds to about 10 per cent of the net increase in assets.
May 1983	The Postal Life Insurance System authorized to purchase foreign securities up to 10 per cent of total assets.
November 1983	Controls introduced on increases in the foreign currency assets of pension trusts.
April 1984	Yen-denominated foreign loans by banks liberalized.
April 1985	Medium- and long-term Euro-yen lending to non-residents liberalized by overseas branches of Japanese banks.
February 1986	Trust banks authorized to invest in foreign bonds up to 1 per cent of total assets (for loan trust accounts).
March/April 1986	Regulations on foreign securities investments by life and non-life insurance companies and trust banks (for pension trust accounts) relaxed from 10 per cent to 25 per cent of total assets.
April 1986	Acquisition of foreign currency assets by life insurance companies and pension trusts limited to 40 per cent of the increase in total assets (until August 1986).
June 1986	Regulations on investment in foreign bonds for the loan trust accounts of trust banks relaxed from 1 per cent to 3 per cent of total assets.
August 1986	The above voluntary restriction on purchases of foreign bonds relaxed for life insurance companies and pension trusts, from 25 per cent to 30 per cent of total assets.
April 1987	The Trust Fund Bureau authorized to invest in foreign securities up to 10 per cent of total assets.
June 1987	The investment limit on foreign securities for the Postal Life Insurance System increased from 10 per cent to 20 per cent of total assets.
February 1989	The investment limit on foreign bonds for the loan trust accounts of trust banks further relaxed, from 3 per cent to 5 per cent of total assets.

Inflows

November 1973	Regulation on purchases of Japanese stocks by non-residents abolished.
December 1973	Regulation on purchases of Japanese secondary bonds by non-residents abolished (except for unlisted bonds with remaining maturities of less than one year).
August 1974	Purchases of Japanese primary bonds by non-residents liberalized; the above regulation regarding remaining maturity length abolished.
June 1977	Purchases of Japanese stocks and bonds by non-residents subject to automatic approval.
March 1978	Purchases, by foreign investors, of yen-denominated domestic bonds with remaining maturities of less than 5 years and one month prohibited.
January/ February 1979	The above restriction eased and then abolished.
December 1980	Purchases of securities through designated securities companies liberalized.
July 1984	The system of designated securities companies abolished.
May 1989	The voluntary restraint on medium- and long-term Euro-yen loans to residents abolished.

Measures relating to direct investments

September 1970	Regulations on foreign direct investment in Japan further relaxed.
August 1971	Regulation on foreign direct investment in Japan further relaxed.
June 1972	Residents' direct investment abroad fully liberalized in principle.
May 1973	Foreign direct investment in Japan fully liberalized in principle.
December 1980	Foreign direct investment in Japan now subject only to notification.

NOTES

1. In view of this and other conceptual problems with the practice of making a distinction between long-term and short-term capital, some countries, notably the USA and Australia, do not officially report balance-of-payments statistics which are disaggregated into long-term and short-term capital accounts. These problems are likely to be addressed in the new edition of IMF's *Balance of Payments Manual*.
2. The large deficit of over $12bn in 1991 reflected a special factor associated with Japan's financial contribution to the military operations of the USA and its coalition partners in the Persian Gulf region.

3. The history of capital controls in Japan is more extensively reviewed in Fukao (1990), Komiya and Suda (1991) and Koo (1993). A selective summary is provided in the Appendix.
4. Japan obtained its last loan from the World Bank in July 1966.
5. An annual change in the stock of assets or liabilities may not correspond exactly to the annual flow of cross-border investment because of the valuation effect associated with exchange rate changes.
6. In ADF tests, additional lagged terms are included.
7. This will, in turn, have repercussions on the current account.
8. Compiled from various issues of Ministry of Finance, *Annual Report of the International Finance Bureau* and *Zaisei Kinyu Tokei Geppo*; Ueda and Fujii (1986); Fukao (1990); Komiya and Suda (1991); and Koo (1993).

REFERENCES

Bank of Japan, *Balance of Payments Monthly*, various dates.
Bank of Japan 1992. *Developments in Cross-Border Securities Investment in 1991*, Special Paper No. 215, June.
Fukao, Mitsuhiro 1990. 'Liberalization of Japan's Foreign Exchange Controls and Structural Changes in the Balance of Payments', *Bank of Japan Monetary and Economic Studies*, 8, September, pp. 101–65.
Fukao, Mitsuhiro and Kunio Okina 1989. 'Internationalization of Financial Markets and Balance of Payments Imbalances: A Japanese Perspective', *Carnegie–Rochester Conference Series on Public Policy*, 30, pp. 167–220.
IMF (International Monetary Fund) 1977. *Balance of Payments Manual*, 4th edn, Washington, D.C.: IMF.
Komiya, Ryutaro and Miyako Suda 1991. *Japan's Foreign Exchange Policy, 1971–1982*, Sydney: Allen & Unwin.
Koo, Richard C. 1993. 'International Capital Flows and an Open Economy: the Japanese Experience', in Shinji Takagi (ed.), *Japanese Capital Markets: New Developments in Regulations and Institutions*, Oxford: Blackwell, pp. 78–129.
McKenzie, Colin 1985. 'Liberalisation of the Japanese Capital Market and the Determination of the Yen/Dollar Rate', Pacific Economic Papers, No. 130, Australia–Japan Research Centre, Australian National University.
Ministry of Finance, *Annual Report of the International Finance Bureau* (in Japanese), various years.
Ministry of Finance, *Zaisei Kinyu Tokei Geppo* (in Japanese), various issues.
Takagi, Shinji 1988. 'Recent Developments in Japan's Bond and Money Markets', *Journal of the Japanese and International Economies*, 2, March, pp. 63–91.
Takagi, Shinji 1991. 'Foreign Exchange Market Intervention and Domestic Monetary Control in Japan, 1973–89', *Japan and the World Economy*, 3, September, pp. 147–80.
Takagi, Shinji 1994. 'From a Recipient to a Donor: Japan's Official Aid Flows, 1945–90 and Beyond', *Princeton Essays in International Finance* (forthcoming).
Ueda, Kazuo and Mariko Fujii 1986. 'Saikin niokeru Wagakuni no Shihon Ryushutsu nitsuite' (in Japanese), *Finansharu Rebyu*, 3, December, pp. 9–53.

Index

instability of 235–6, 247, 251
determination of 237–8
fundamental influences 259–61
straight bonds 58–60
structural changes (*see also* financial
liberalization; international linkage
of interest rates) 3–5
decline in growth rate 203, 205,
215–16, 226
and monetary policy 323
in financial markets 333
in long-term capital account 440,
452–3
structural current account surplus
425–32
structural features of Japanese
economy 19
Suda, Mikayo 441, 458n3, 458
Sumita, Satoshi 278
Sumitomo Bank 265, 296, 304
Sumitomo *keiretsu* 314–15
Sumitomo *zaibatsu* 291–2, 297, 298–9,
304, 306–7
Summers, Lawrence H. 52, 136, 169,
172, 173, 176, 202, 364, 371, 382
Sunamura, Satoshi 80
Suzuki & Co. 266
Suzuki, Yoshio ix, 350n3, 357, 384
Suzuki, Yoshiro 285
Symons, J. 130

Tabellini, Guido 366, 374, 383
Tachibanaki, Toshiaki xiii, 81–108
Taiwan Bank 266
Takagi, Shinji xiv, 52, 435–58
Takahashi, Kamekichi 264, 286
Takahashi, Wataru xiii, 135–67
Takakashi, Korekiyo 275
Takayama, N. 137, 160, 167
Takeda, Masahiko 287, 322
take-overs 34–5, 37
Taki, Atsuhiro xiv, 81–108
Tanaka, Kakuei 197, 200n10, 268
Tatom, J. A. 356
Taylor, J. B. 353n49, 357
technological progress 204, 216,
217–18, 229–30
Teikoku Bank 296, 318n7
tenure–earnings profiles 109–27
Teranishi, Juro 293, 295, 296, 301,
312, 322
Tesar, L. 182–5, 202
Thakor, Anjan V. 52
Thomas, A. 169, 171, 202

Thomson, A. 120, 130
Tirole, Jean 28, 34, 36, 50
Tobin's *q* ratio 185, 330–1
Todd, Gregory F. W. 366, 383
Toikka, R. S. 95, 108
Tokkin 240, 250
Tokyo Stock Exchange (*see also* stock
market) 265, 286
Tomita, Y. 84, 108
Topel, R. 111, 114, 131
Torre, Augusto de la 411n2, 415
Toyoda, Eiji 312
Toyota Auto company 312
trade friction 334, 431
trade surplus 417–19
trading blocs *see* economic blocs
training 110, 114, 126–7
transition probabilities in labour
market 81–102
transmission channels of monetary
policy 324–31
Tsuchiya, M. 262
Tsuda, Hisashi 314, 315, 322
Tsutsui, Y. 262

Uchida, Kenji 270
Uchida, Mahito xiv, 416–34
Ueda, Kazuo 357, 434, 448, 458
Ui, Takashi xiv, 416–34
UK (United Kingdom)
employment 83, 208
tenure–earnings profiles 109–10,
120–5, 127
New Earnings Survey 119, 128
training 126
manufacturing industry 226–7
foreign assets 453, 454
Umemura, Mataji 208, 231, 321
unemployment 2, 4, 83–94, 270
unrequited transfers 419, 437
USA (United States of America)
short-termism 25, 26, 30, 34, 40
labour market 83, 106, 208
tenure–earnings relationship 109
economic growth 205, 212–14
effect of oil crisis 226
growth of stock index (1980s) 237
Securities and Exchange
Commission 282
fiscal policy 284
role in preventing break-up of
zaibatsu 316
monetary policy 331–2
trade friction with Japan 334, 397